CONSERVATIV

By the same author

  ART AND IMAGINATION
  THE AESTHETICS OF ARCHITECTURE
* THE MEANING OF CONSERVATISM
  A SHORT HISTORY OF MODERN PHILOSOPHY
  KANT
  FORTNIGHT'S ANGER
  THE POLITICS OF CULTURE
* A DICTIONARY OF POLITICAL THOUGHT
  THE AESTHETIC UNDERSTANDING
  THINKERS OF THE NEW LEFT
  SEXUAL DESIRE
  SPINOZA
* UNTIMELY TRACTS
  A LAND HELD HOSTAGE
  THE PHILOSOPHER ON DOVER BEACH
  FRANCESCA

* *Also published by Macmillan*

Conservative Texts

An Anthology

Edited with an introduction by
Roger Scruton

Selection, editorial matter and Chapter 1 © Roger Scruton 1991

For further copyrights please see the Acknowledgements.

All rights reserved. No reproduction, copy or transmission of this publication may be made without written permission.

No paragraph of this publication may be reproduced, copied or transmitted save with written permission or in accordance with the provisions of the Copyright, Designs and Patents Act 1988, or under the terms of any licence permitting limited copying issued by the Copyright Licensing Agency, 33-4 Alfred Place, London WC1E 7DP.

Any person who does any unauthorised act in relation to this publication may be liable to criminal prosecution and civil claims for damages.

First published 1991

Published by
MACMILLAN ACADEMIC AND PROFESSIONAL LTD
Houndmills, Basingstoke, Hampshire RG21 2XS
and London
Companies and representatives
throughout the world

Printed in Hong Kong

British Library Cataloguing in Publication Data
Scruton, Roger
Conservative texts: an anthology.
1. Political ideologies: Conservatism, history
I. Title
320.5209

ISBN 0-333-54172-3 (hardcover)
ISBN 0-333-54816-7 (paperback)

Contents

Preface		vii
A Note on the Texts		viii
Acknowledgements		ix
1	Introduction: What is Conservatism?	1
2	Edmund Burke	29
3	F.H. Bradley	40
4	G.K. Chesterton	59
5	Samuel Taylor Coleridge	63
6	Benjamin Disraeli	71
7	Max Eastman	78
8	T.S. Eliot	85
9	F.A. Hayek	94
10	G.W.F. Hegel	129
11	Russell Kirk	164
12	Joseph de Maistre	170
13	F.W. Maitland	193
14	W.H. Mallock	204
15	J.C. Murray	218

16	Robert Nozick	227
17	Michael Oakeshott	242
18	Vilfredo Pareto	257
19	Roger Scruton	266
20	Sir James Fitzjames Stephen	285
21	Gustave Thibon	297
22	Alexis de Tocqueville	310
23	Eric Voegelin	317
24	Simone Weil	332
Bibliography		341
Index of Names		346
Subject Index		350

Preface

The idea for this digest of Conservative texts was suggested to me by a friend in Czechoslovakia, a place where, officially, there has been no such thing as conservative thinking since 1948. Looking at the existing anthologies, I came to the conclusion that there is nothing available that would enable a citizen of modern Czechoslovakia to understand, through the study of a single volume, the central intellectual and moral concerns of European and American conservatives. Nor is there anything that could be recommended to a Western student of political science, which would present, in a relatively brief format, the major ideas of modern conservatism, as these have taken shape since the French Revolution. This volume is therefore intended as a kind of a textbook: as I explain in the Introduction, it is both selective, and expressive of one particular point of view. Nevertheless, I believe that it accurately represents the central elements of conservatism – an outlook which, like it or not, is increasingly influential in the modern world.

I have arranged the texts according to the alphabetical order of their authors, rather than chronologically or thematically (placing Burke, however, before Bradley, in order to provide a fitting introduction to the volume). Like every method, this one has its disadvantages; but it seems to emphasise, what the reader should never doubt, that the choice of authors was by no means compelled by the subject, and that another editor, proceeding with the task that I set myself, might have gone about it in quite another way.

R. S.
London, 1990

A Note on the Texts

In this collection, I have brought together extracts from some of the major conservative thinkers of the modern period. The texts have been chosen at least partly for their representative quality: not all of them rise to the intellectual level of Hayek or Hegel; not all are written with the subtlety and sensitivity of Burke; not all express the vivacity of engagement that we find in Mallock or Maitland. But the authors of all of them have made leading contributions to the line of argument which I have sketched, and the texts chosen to represent them convey, I hope something of the intellectual, moral and spiritual basis of their thinking. There are other thinkers, not represented here, who have an equal title to be called conservative: Newman, de Bonald, Ruskin, Gierke, Carlyle, Donoso Cortes, Ortego y Gasset, Santayana – and, from more recent times, Röpke, Leo Strauss, Gehlen, Gadamer and Aron. Nevertheless, constraints of space are not the only reasons for my restricted selection. I have been equally concerned with a particular tradition of thought, which I believe to be more centrally represented by the thinkers whom I have included than by those whom I have reluctantly left out. I only regret that the literary executors of F.R. Leavis and Bertrand de Jouvenal did not see fit to allow these two important conservative thinkers to appear in these pages.

Although, as I remarked, the conservative argument is distinctive of the modern (post-Enlightenment) era, it draws on conceptions and ideas which are as old as politics. Most conservatives would therefore count among their number thinkers from every age of recorded thought – for instance, Aristotle, Augustine, Ibn Khaldun, Aquinas, Machiavelli, Grotius, Hobbes, Montesquieu, Hume and Johnson. Even without the inclusion of those thinkers, however, this anthology contains, I hope, sufficient indication of the direction of its argument, as to enable the reader to make the connection with the history of political thinking.

Acknowledgements

In the preparation of this volume I have been greatly assisted by Andrea Christofidou, whose editorial skills were invaluable in preparing the first selection of texts. I have also been helped by research and detective work from Rosalind Barrs and Fiona Ellis. I am grateful to all three.

The editor and the publishers wish to thank the following, who have kindly given permission for the use of copyright material:

Basil Blackwell, for the material from Robert Nozick's *Anarchy, State and Utopia* and from *Vilfredo Pareto's Sociological Writings*, edited by S.E. Finer;
The Bodley Head, on behalf of Hollis & Carter, for the material from Gustave Thibon's *Back to Reality*;
Cambridge University Press, for the material from F.W. Maitland's *Collected Papers* (1911), edited by H.A.L. Fisher;
Devin-Adair, Publishers, for the material from *Reflections on the Failure of Socialism* by Max Eastman, New York, 1955. Copyright by Devin-Adair, Publishers Inc., Old Greenwich, Connecticut 06870;
Alfred A. Knopf Inc., for the material from *Democracy in America* by Alexis de Tocqueville, edited by Phillips Bradley. Copyright 1945 and renewed 1973 by Alfred A. Knopf Inc.;
Methuen & Co., for the material from T.S. Eliot's *The Sacred Wood* and from Michael Oakeshott's *Rationalism in Politics*;
Oxford University Press, for the material from *Hegel's Philosophy of Right*, translated by T.M. Knox (1942);
Regnery Gateway Inc., for the material from *Conservative Mind: From Burke to Eliot* by Russell Kirk. Copyright © 1953 by Regnery Gateway Inc., Washington, DC, all rights reserved, and for the material from *Science, Politics, and Gnosticism* by Eric Voegelin. Copyright © 1968 by Regnery Gateway Inc., Washington, DC, all rights reserved;
Routledge for the material from *Law, Legislation & Liberty* by F.A. Hayek, and from *The Need for Roots* by Simone Weil;
Sheed & Ward for the material from *We Hold These Truths*. Copyright © 1960, 1988 by Sheed & Ward Inc., Kansas City, Missouri, USA.

Every effort has been made to trace all the copyright-holders but, if any have been inadvertently overlooked, the publishers will be pleased to make the necessary arrangements at the earliest opportunity.

Introduction: What is Conservatism?
Roger Scruton

If you ask a conservative for a statement of his political convictions, he may well say that he has none, and that the greatest heresy of modernity is precisely to see politics as a matter of *conviction*: as though one could recuperate, at the level of political purpose, the consoling certainty which once was granted by religious faith. In another sense, however, conservatism does rest in a system of belief, and is opposed as much to the theory as to the practice of socialist and liberal politics.

Many have argued that conservatism is a distinctly *modern* outlook, born of an uprooted consciousness and a disturbed equanimity. To some extent the same could be said of liberalism and socialism. Nevertheless, there are good reasons for thinking that conservatism (as here and now understood) arose out of a reaction, first to the French Revolution, and secondly to the habit engendered by that revolution, of seeking large-scale social transformation as a remedy for the unhappiness of man. This habit is shared, not only by revolutionaries, but also by constitutionally-minded socialists, and even by many who would describe themselves as liberals, and who locate the instrument of social transformation not in violent confrontation, but in law. So long as people seek, through social and political change, for a solution to problems that cannot be solved, just so long, the conservative argues, is the body politic threatened by the malady of agitation. The sentiment of legitimacy is put in question, and individual responsibility eroded; institutions, expectations and values lose their authority, and, deprived of continuity and pattern, we experience a joylessness which serves only to exacerbate the prevailing sentiments of rebellion.

Many modern liberals share the conservative hostility to socialism, and to state bureaucracy. Nevertheless, in the conservative view, liberalism has been careless of the sense of legitimacy, and blind to the sources of social harmony and satisfaction. It has also been committed to an abstract idea of emancipation, thereby threatening the real and concrete freedom which has obedience as its price. Consequently, liberalism has shown itself unable to take a stand against that which it opposes in the socialist programme: all customs, institutions and powers that would defend us from the new socialist state are fatally weakened by the liberal hostility to 'establishment' and 'authority'. It is precisely with the upkeep of establishment that the conservative is most urgently concerned, and he looks for the alternative to socialism, in the concrete realities of an existing social life, rather than in some abstract idea of freedom. From its first articulation, therefore, in the writings of Hume and Burke, modern conservatism has made the defence of custom and prejudice into one of its most important – albeit paradoxical – intellectual endeavours.

In order to understand conservative thinking in the modern world it is necessary first to cultivate a habit of semantic hygiene. The language of politics is everywhere contaminated by rotting theories, and by the feverish ideologies which rise from them, and a writer who does not choose his words with care is apt to find his whole thinking being turned against him and corrupted from its purpose. An important example of this process – and one that has proved decisive in the conduct of modern politics – is the unwitting adoption of the terms 'socialism' and 'capitalism', as descriptive of opposing social and political systems. To speak in this way is to assume that social and political arrangements can be usefully described as systems of interdependent parts; that customs and institutions are dependent upon an economic 'base'; that 'capitalism' – i.e. the deployment by private individuals of investment capital – is the distinctive and decisive feature of the economic system in which it occurs; and that 'socialism' describes a real and feasible alternative, with its own rival social and political system.

All those propositions are false; all come to us burdened by a theory which was already half-dead at the time of its systematic utterance; and all are more or less irrelevant to the world as we now confront it. Social customs, political institutions and economic activities are not necessarily parts of a single system, nor do they develop in accordance with any known causal law. It is not the private disposition of capital that is the decisive feature of modern Western economies, but the existence of free markets, dependent upon a legal disposition of property rights, and upon a public morality of enterprise, responsibility and contractual obligation. To speak of 'socialism' and 'capitalism', as though these terms denoted the single decisive and exhaustive choice lying before mankind, is to surrender history to myth, and critical intelligence to the conjuring of spectres. It is to suffer what Wittgenstein called 'the bewitchment of the intelligence by means of language'.

No one can study the great thinkers of the conservative tradition without noticing the delicacy and control with which so many of them use the written word. Burke, de Tocqueville, Bradley, Eliot, Maitland and Weil are not only elegant writers, but writers with a sense of the gravity of human utterance. If their language is subtle it is because they match it to what they describe – to our social and political condition, which is in itself as intricate and nuanced as the words necessary to describe it. The apparent resistance of such writers to theory stems partly from their respect for truth, and from the corresponding reluctance to embark on theories before the facts are known. They approach the matter of politics as living matter, which cannot be carelessly torn apart in the service of pseudo-scientific categories. It is not surprising, therefore, if those who seek for a comprehensive theory of man's nature, together with an enunciation of his goals, will always be impatient with conservative thinking, and will regard the conservative's scrupulousness as no better than a feeble-minded reluctance to be clear. The conservative vision of politics will always be harder to understand to those who do not instinctively sympathise with it than are the visions of the liberal and the socialist. It lacks the attempt at system, and its careful language will rarely be persuasive to those for whom the only reasonable answers are those which are conveyed in systematic terms. That is another reason for the conservative defence of prejudice – of the instinctive moral sense whereby people come to act with understanding, even though they have no understanding of why they act.

Discussion of the modern forms of conservatism might reasonably begin from a consideration of the concept of a free market – not because this is the fundamental conservative idea, but because it is a standard error to think it so. There is another, and better reason, however, for considering the market first in our list of critical conceptions, namely, that it provides a vivid illustration of just what the demand for semantic hygiene amounts to, and just how important it is to defend the realm of prejudice without prejudice of one's own.

THE MARKET

Some defend the market as the most efficient form of distribution and exchange – the form which, in the long run, maximises the social benefit, and minimises the social cost. Others have defended it as a paradigm of human freedom, whereby people, acting freely in their own interest, secure a beneficial result which, in Adam Smith's famous words, was 'no part of their intention'.

If Hayek is of such importance as a conservative theorist, it is partly because he has extracted from Adam Smith's intuition another, and deeper, observation. Hayek sees in the market a paradigm of 'social epistemology' – of a body of knowledge, indispensable to social relations, which exists only within the social practice that creates it. The argument (which derives from theories expressed in different ways by Böhm-Bawerk and Michael Polanyi) maintains that the price or value of a commodity is fully determined only within the context of free exchange: and only in such circumstances is price an effective measure of what people are prepared to sacrifice in order to obtain anything. In a free market the price of a commodity embodies an extremely complex piece of information, concerning the social behaviour of all those to whom the individual purchaser is economically related. Interference in the market requires the preservation of precisely this information, since it requires the knowledge of the totality of the relevant human wants. But if prices are fixed, work regulated, and rewards controlled by a comprehensive plan, then neither price nor wage nor labour-time can serve as a measure of the crucial information.

The argument involves an extension to the economic sphere of three ideas about the nature of collective rationality. Economic reasoning, it is supposed, depends upon knowledge that is (a) practical, (b) tacit, and (c) social, arising only in conditions of cooperation, and not available outside the social activity that engenders it. This knowledge is both premise and conclusion of a dynamic calculation. There is no necessary paradox in this; indeed, it is a standard assumption of game theory that such reasoning occurs, and that the problems to which it is addressed (problems of coordination) are sometimes soluble. Nevertheless, the application of the idea in the theory of the market is extremely controversial.

There is a core of indisputable truth in Hayek's argument, and this truth is one which even socialists (indeed, especially socialists) have been driven to accept. The paradigm of free social relations is that of willing cooperation, in which several people achieve together that which they lack the knowledge, skill and strength to achieve alone. Such activities must inevitably include forms of reasoning which are simultaneously tacit, practical and collective in the way that Hayek describes. Hayek's contention is simply that, in the case of the open-ended economic cooperation suited to Adam Smith's 'great society', such reasoning will be not only predominant, but also basic. If the conditions under which it can be successfully conducted are impaired, then so is the social order which depends upon it. In such circumstances, the pursuit of self-interest will be at variance with the self-interest of others, and the invisible hand will be the hand of the strangler.

TRADITION

The argument just sketched is applied in the field of economics, to provide a defence of the market economy. However, it should not be thought that conservatives share the libertarian enthusiasm for the market, as the sole and sufficient source of political freedom. On the contrary, the conservative may reject the libertarian theory of the market, as an instance of the very fallacy which vitiates Marxism: the fallacy of supposing that economic structures are prior to institutions, and that political order depends upon economics alone.

In *The Communist Manifesto*, Marx and Engels praised 'capitalism' (by which they meant the market economy) for its power to break down the old order of society, to turn every belief, value and custom upside down, and to void all institutions of their life and content. In this way, they supposed, capitalism more effectively prepares the ground for revolution, by destroying every moral obstacle that opposes it. Socialism was to be the heir to the disenchanted world of capitalism, and socialism, they believed, would neither need nor tolerate the enchantment upon which man, in his 'pre-history', had depended.

Some years before the publication of *The Communist Manifesto* another, profounder and more lasting contribution to our understanding of modern society appeared – de Tocqueville's *Democracy in America*. De Tocqueville saw the market economy as simply one feature of the democratic process – the process whereby social order and institutions emerge from contract, consent or acquiescence among equals. The tendency of such a process is not towards crisis, but towards stability, mediocrity, and ordinariness. At the same time, the equalising movement of American democracy would destroy associations and institutions far less surely and far less rapidly than it would create them. Through its very mobility the American political process was able to recreate the customary order and enduring institutions upon which the old regimes of Europe had been founded.

To the unprejudiced observer it is de Tocqueville and not Marx whose prophecies have been vindicated. The free market has undone many things: but it is one expression of a vaster social force – the force of human agreement – which is as capable of establishing institutions as it is of destroying them. And whatever has changed under the impact of this force, it has proved less destructive of political institutions than the comprehensive plans of the socialist.

In order to understand the conservative attitude to the free market one should first consider a phenomenon which the market is supposed to jeopardise, and which a conservative is committed to defending: tradition. The following propositions seem to emerge, from the discussions of Burke, Eliot, Oakeshott, and others, as defining the conservative idea of traditional order:

(i) Society is more than the sum of the individuals who compose it.
(ii) Social cooperation depends upon a delicate mechanism of mutual adjustment.
(iii) This mechanism emerges in the individual through his steady and growing familiarity with 'the way things are done'.
(iv) As a result of this familiarity, the individual acquires a 'tacit understanding' of social forms.
(v) This tacit understanding mediates between the individual and society, enabling him to 'know what he does' when he engages in social relations. It is what we mean by a 'tradition'.

So understood, of course, tradition is another instance of the phenomenon that is exhibited by a market – the phenomenon of tacit and collective understanding, realised through social intercourse. However, while economic behaviour has individual advantage as its goal, tradition involves a willing submission to what is socially established. It looks backward rather than forward for its justification, and aims not at personal profit but at social acceptance and respect. Nevertheless, the dependence of both tradition and the market upon an evolving and consensual mutuality, suggests that their seeming antagonism must be manageable. It is indeed difficult to envisage the conditions that would encourage the one, without also encouraging the other.

Traditions cannot be imposed by central authority, any more than an economy can be rationally planned. Each exhibits what Hayek, in a happy phrase, calls 'spontaneous order': an order which depends upon spontaneity for its achievement. Hence any attempt to uphold traditions will make room precisely for the tacit understanding which is expressed in a market economy, and any attempt to destroy market relations will undermine the core of social knowledge from which traditions grow. If there is a conflict between tradition and the market it lies in the nature of things – in the tension between the forward-looking energies of business, and the backward-looking attitudes of social repose. To reconcile these opposing currents, to manage the crises which they generate, and to restore the balance upon which both depend, is simply one part of the continuous task of politics. But it is not a task that can be accomplished once and for all, and any attempt to destroy either party to the conflict will infallibly destroy the other.

Here then is a deep reason for discarding the apocalyptic vision of *The Communist Manifesto*: traditional order and a free economy are aspects of a single social process, and the conflict between them *must* be manageable if anything is to survive. And once we throw away the Marxist spectacles we will perceive how very well the conflict has been managed over the many centuries of its existence. If it is the destiny of traditional order to destroy itself through its dependence on exchange – as the spear of Wotan is destroyed through its inner dependence on the ring of Alberich – then this is not because the tensions between the two can be resolved or overcome, but because, as Wagner shows, *Alles was ist, endet* – a proposition which, though impeccable, generates no political programme.

Such a defence of tradition is of course exceedingly abstract, and 'second-order'. For this reason it is hardly likely to appeal to the majority of conservatives, whose sense of the value of tradition emerges precisely from their own immersion in it, rather than from an abstract *theory* of its social use. Nevertheless, the theory offers support to many specific practices. On the above analysis, marriage is a tradition; so too is law, and in particular the common law which has always served as the conservative's paradigm of flexible and authoritative judgement. The detail of conservative theory lies in the attempt to understand such institutions, not from outside but from within, from the standpoint of their own life and purposes.

THE SOCIAL INDIVIDUAL

It is here, however, that the conservative and the liberal part company. At the heart of the liberal view of society is the conception of the autonomous individual, dependent on society for his benefits, but with an identity, and a destiny, that are entirely his own. For such an individual the chief political benefit is freedom – freedom from the constraint and coercion exercised by others. The metaphysical picture of the individual who flourishes in liberty, through self-aggrandisement and self-release, leads liberals to accept the conservative defence of market economy and traditional order. But it also leads them to reject the concept which, for the conservative, takes precedence over all others in understanding the *inner* life and *inner* purposes of institutions: the concept of authority. The conservative defence of authority derives not merely from a rooted antipathy to unbridled freedom, but also from a rival conception of human nature – a conception developed in striking ways by Hegel, Bradley, and other metaphysical idealists.

According to this conception, human freedom and human personality are social artefacts, and the human person emerges already encumbered by obligations to those who have gone before. He has an indefeasible duty to history, and to a culture which he did not choose. Bradley suggests a way of understanding this process. Autonomy, he argues, is achieved only by acquiring the obligations of a social 'station'. These obligations are not undertaken but incurred; they are founded neither in consent nor in contract, but in the accumulated burden of piety and gratitude. The obligations of autonomy are freely undertaken: but we can honour them only if we also honour those other duties, upon the execution of which the whole fragile order of autonomy depends. Take away the sense of duty, and autonomy becomes a husk, with neither intrinsic purpose nor justifying ground. If we adopt autonomy as our social goal, and bend all politics to the task of achieving it, then we deprive ourselves of true community. If we are to value freedom as it should be valued, therefore, we must also value something else, which is not the effect of freedom but its precondition – namely the social order from which duties and values spring, and upon which the human personality depends for its identity.

Conservatism arose in reaction not to absolute power, but to the anarchy which invites it. The longed-for release of the self from all restraint, from customary usage and authoritative guidance, may seem to be the fullest flowering of human freedom. For the conservative, however, this self-release is a self-dissipation: it is not the gain of freedom but the loss of it. Conservative politics does not aim to generate ever wider and more comprehensive liberties, but to 'care for institutions' – to maintain and invigorate what has been established for the common good. Because they impede the boisterous appetite for novelty, institutions are increasingly mistaken for obstacles to the free flowering of the self: it is institutions therefore, and not individuals, which have always been the prime object of conservative concern.

It is from institutions and customs that authority is born, and congenial authority is one of the goals of conservative politics. Even if, at some high philosophical level, the liberal and the conservative may live in harmony, at the level of everyday politics they are seriously opposed. The liberal seeks to emancipate the individual from authority, the conservative seeks to protect authority from individual rebellion. Without authority, the conservative argues, there is not will but appetite, not individuality but a herd-like conformity, not freedom but an aimless pursuit of 'alternatives', none of which has value to the person whose energy is squandered in obtaining it.

ALLEGIANCE

Hegel – the theoretical master of the conservative idea of legitimacy – proposed a threefold division among the ties of social obligation. 'Society' denotes a composite arrangement, held together by interlocking obligations which are of separate provenance. The individual is bound by obligations to the family and to the state, and also by obligations which arise during the course of free and spontaneous dealings with his neighbours: the obligations of 'civil society'. Civil society is the sphere of contract, but not founded on a contract. It depends for its reality upon the family which nurtures it and the state which protects it, and neither the obligations to the family nor those to the state can be understood in contractual terms. Obligations of the hearth belong to piety: they are motives only for those who can recognise the reality of a debt that was not freely undertaken, and who can honour those arrangements through which they entered the world. Only such people can be fully autonomous agents, since only they can understand the value, depth and gravity of human existence. Such people would also recognise that they owe to the state a duty of a different kind from the duties that they incur in the marketplace.

Civil society is the totality of free associations. It depends for its continuation upon institutions which, by defining the obligations of their members, have an inherent tendency to transcend any contractual legitimacy. The principal instance of such an institution is the state, without which there could be no law, and therefore no guarantee of the justice upon which civil society depends for its survival. Our obligation to the state, like our obligation to the family and its members, does not arise through a free undertaking, but rather through a slow process of development, during which we acquire obligations long before we can freely answer to their claim on us.

The conservative rejection of the contractual theory of the state does not involve a repudiation of the liberal idea that government must be founded on consent. But 'consent' means many things, and what it amounts to in the given case cannot be separated from the process whereby it is engendered. The consent of a man to remain in the house that he has inherited is not the same thing as his consent to sell his apples at £100 a ton. Rather than depend upon so vast and vague an idea, therefore, we should re-express the consensual basis of social and political obligations in terms of their distinctive genealogy. The consent that informs legitimate government is the consent which stems from allegiance. The individual is bound by allegiance to society, to institutions, to customs and associations, and also to the state. In no case is this allegiance a matter of choice freely undertaken, and in no case is it separable from the history through which it is acquired, and from which it derives its specific content and motivating power.

PARTNERSHIP

The allegiance that underpins human society was described by Burke as a 'partnership', although a partnership of a peculiar kind, which extends beyond the living to the unborn and the dead. This partnership, according to the conservative, has no single or overriding purpose. Like love and friendship, it is its own goal. 'Civil association' (in Oakeshott's phrase) is not 'for a purpose', in the way that an army or business partnership is 'for a purpose'; and those who belong to it are entitled to no specific benefit besides the benefit of membership itself. Of course, there are *particular* purposes, within the state, within civil society, and within the family, which arise during the course of social existence and which may wholly occupy those whom they impinge upon. And for some of these purposes – defence, the relief of poverty, the provision of law – constant preparation is necessary. But these purposes are not the ends of society so much as its preconditions. A society no more exists *for* the satisfaction of human needs, than a plant exists for its own health. The health of a plant *constitutes* its existence: it is not a purpose towards which the plant is directed. Political association likewise has no goal detachable from itself, and even if men are happier within a political order than outside it, the order itself is no more a *means* to happiness than is love or friendship.

Burke argued that political order is always threatened by enthusiasm, and by the attempt to realise, through the institutions of political power, the aims and ideals of an all-encompassing programme. When politics is subjugated to a moral purpose (to an 'armed doctrine', as Burke described it), then society must be subjected to the state as to a military commander, mobilised about a ruling activity, and directed towards a future goal. The necessary balance between state and civil society is then destroyed, and politics launched on the path towards totalitarian power.

Conservatives find many things wrong with socialism, but perhaps nothing so wrong as this search for a 'common purpose'. However the purpose is conceived – as equality, fraternity, liberty or 'social justice' – it is not so much the conception as the common pursuit of it that we should abhor. Such a common pursuit is inherently destructive of allegiance, through the very fact of imposing on society a purpose besides itself.

AUTHORITY AND PERSONALITY

Authority is distinct from power, although it both generates power and – in favourable circumstances – arises from it. Authority means the right to exercise power; to recognise authority is therefore to concede a right to power. One of the major aims of conservatism has been to formulate, to establish and if possible to justify a system of authority that will be suitable to modern conditions, and acceptable to those who are subject to it.

It is a mistake to suppose that the decline of monarchy has led to the decline of personal authority in matters of government. It is not only human individuals who possess personality, and not only human individuals who can exercise the kind of authority that one person may exercise over another. The state too is (or ought to be) a person – both in the sense known to Roman law, and in the more intricate moral sense familiar from the experience of society. The state should be a source of agency and responsibility, and not an instrument of impersonal administration. The state must do things, be seen to do them, and maintain a stance of answerability for the consequences. Its actions must be those of a rational being, responsive to criticism, capable of remorse, shame, pride, honour, self-affirmation and regret.

The idea of the corporate person is therefore fundamental to conservative thinking. Under the influence of Marxist thinking, the instruments of social change are frequently described as 'classes'. Classes, however, are not agents, but the by-products of an economic process which originates outside political choice. It is not suprising, therefore, if the Marxist way of seeing the political process confers upon it an air of impersonality. The conservative would object, indeed, that the resulting vision is a *mis*perception of the political realm. Precisely what is most real and intelligible – the pattern of collective agency – begins to seem least real; and precisely what is most resistant to political understanding – the 'deep' structure of the economic 'base' – becomes the focus of an attention that is profoundly oppositional in tone. This habit of thought presages the actual destruction of civil society by the Marxist state. The remedy, for the conservative, is to restore the political centrality of the idea of rational agency. The world should be seen as it really is – in terms of reason, choice, emotion, responsibility, right, duty and personality. Without the concept of corporate personality the social world is voided of those crucial features. Authority can then be located nowhere within the world, but remains a shadow, a fleeting memory to which we can assign no name.

A conservative believes in the 'priority of appearance'. The objects of our allegiance, the sources of authority, and the foci of our political concern are corporate agents: institutions, the law, parliaments, churches and schools. It is from our personal relation with these things that our sense of legitimacy is derived, and to uphold that sense is to support and maintain the institutions which create it. If Maitland and his mentor, Gierke, are important as conservative thinkers, it is in large part because they helped to place the concept of corporate personality at the centre of legal and political thinking.

THE STATE

To provide a timeless prescription for the state is no part of the conservative ambition; all that is possible, and all that is desirable, is that we should understand and assess the existing order, and mark out the possibilities for change. The following ideas have proved important in conservative political theory:

(a) The institutions of the state are part of a political *process*, through which those needs of civil society which cannot be satisfied at the level of free association find expression. Among such needs are those which can be satisfied only by a unified and authoritative 'chain of command', such as is established within a personal state. Law, defence, and the provision of basic welfare are instances of these 'public goods' – although the status of the last of them is doubted by libertarian economists.

(b) The resolution of social conflict is one of the most important tasks of government. The state must therefore possess the power needed to disarm any association that sets itself up in opposition to it, and the authority required for its judgements to be accepted. In other words, it must have *sovereignty* over all citizens and all associations.

(c) Conflict can be effectively resolved only if the interests of citizens are *represented* before the sovereign power. In other words, the political process must be permeable to representation, through parliamentary institutions, administrative courts, and rights of appeal. Since representative institutions are always more easily destroyed than created, and depend upon constant vigilance if they are to be maintained, their defence has become a major conservative policy.

Democratic election is neither necessary nor sufficient for representation. Indeed, constant democratisation of the instruments of authority will inevitably have the effect of transferring power to those who can evade answerability for its exercise. Such democratisation will therefore defeat the purpose which it was intended to achieve – namely, that of guaranteeing the representation, in the highest forum of command, of those interests which stand to be commanded. It is this thought which is at the root of conservative hesitation concerning the ideals of democracy: hesitation variously expressed in these pages by Thibon and Mallock.

Representation is a property of institutions, and requires a background of stable authority if it is to achieve its political purpose. At an election or referendum some matter of importance is put in question. The larger the electorate, the less able will it be to understand the question; and when everything is questioned, nothing makes sense, not even the question. Hence even the democratic process must depend upon a kind of continuity that it cannot generate: a continuity of institutions and authorities against which to assess the present demands. To put it shortly, democracy requires a constitution, and a constitution must be set beyond the reach of democratic change.

(d) De Maistre, reflecting on the French Revolution, argued that constitutions cannot be made but only acquired. De Maistre (like his fellow Ultramontanists, de Bonald and de Lammenais) believed that a constitution must be given by God. It would be more in keeping with his arguments, however, to suggest that a constitution must *emerge* from the political process, and can be neither exhaustively embodied, nor effectively introduced, in a written document. (Here is another instance of the 'invisible hand' of tradition, whose benefits are conferred precisely because we do not aim at them.) For the conservative the American Constitution is not a refutation but a confirmation of de Maistre's thesis: for it is a document which makes explicit and canonical the common-law assumptions by which Americans were already governed.

Moreover, a constitution cannot be identified with a single document, nor with the institutions specified therein. A constitution is, in Spinoza's words, the soul of the state, its animating principle, manifest not only in written laws and clauses, but in conventions, assumptions, tacit understanding, mutual trust and shared expectations. That which is explicitly written is merely the articulate voice of an organism whose life is manifested in a hundred different ways. The countless pieces of paper described by the United Nations as 'constitutions', and lodged under that title in the libraries of the world, are for the most part no such thing. They do not, as a rule, describe the animating principles of a body politic, but the mask that is adopted by tyrannical power.

(e) *Limited government* One of the beneficial effects of a constitution is that it limits the power of government, in definite and predictable ways. Or if it does not do so – if, for example, it has only 'conditional' force, and may be overriden by 'necessities' (as defined by the sovereign, the supreme command, the junta or the vanguard party) – then it is not a genuine constitution, but only a sham. The major intellectual question has always been *how* to limit power, while retaining that inner unity of power which seems to be required by sovereignty.

One important device, recommended by Locke and Montesquieu from their study of the English constitution, and explicitly embodied in the US constitution, is that of the division or separation of powers. The theory of this division, both as it is and as it ought to be, is intricate and full of pitfalls. Nevertheless, one vital principle has emerged from two centuries of discussion as stating the *sine qua non*, without which limited government will never be better than a fiction – the principle of judicial independence. Unless the judiciary is independent of the executive arm of government, the judgements of the courts cannot serve as a reliable barrier between sovereign and subject. If the judges are independent, however, they can use the full force of the law on behalf of the citizen against the state. Only in such conditions (which do not generally prevail in the modern world) is the state's power genuinely limited by a constitution, while being at the same time an expression of a unified sovereignty. For only then is the state's power predictably and accessibly limited by itself.

Judicial independence is a delicate constitutional artefact, involving not merely explicit rules, but also tacit conventions, an established tradition, a confidence and mutuality between the various parties – and most of all a certain public spirit or *Rechtsgefühl*. Liberals commonly defend judicial independence as a prerequisite of individual rights. But they do not usually tell us how judicial independence is to be achieved or maintained. Like so much that makes liberal politics possible, judicial independence is the outcome of a profoundly un-liberal history. It is sustained by conventions, traditions and offices in which much tacit understanding, and much accumulated authority, have been cooperatively engendered. Here as elsewhere liberal politics is parasitic on conservative institutions, and seriously to uphold the liberal principles, one must, in practice, be a conservative. (This is in effect what we find, in Hayek's suprising and brilliant defence of common law against statutory legislation, here reprinted – a defence that was anticipated by Sir William Blackstone, in Volume I of his *Commentaries on the Laws of England*.)

(f) *The rule of law* The dealings between sovereign and subject (or state and citizen) must be mediated by law, and the conflicts between individuals must be resolved, wherever possible, through adjudication, or at least through some practice of impartial judgement which shares the characteristic features of law. Anything less than this is a derogation from the conservative idea of sovereignty. A rule of law involves many things, and is again difficult to separate from its historical circumstances. Judicial independence is a necessary condition; so too is the system of appeal, whereby irregularities and partialities can be corrected. So too is the freedom from arbitrary arrest or imprisonment without trial – the freedom guaranteed under the traditional English writ of *habeas corpus*. Without that freedom, law and its 'due process' can always be by-passed by those in power. Nobody doubts that there are states of emergency when such niceties must be set aside. But nobody doubts too that a state of emergency is an abnormality, and that a state of emergency which endures from year to year (as in one part of the world it has endured since 1917), is tantamount to an absence of legality.

(g) *Human rights* In the modern world, where tyranny is constantly extending and enhancing its power, the demand for the 'rights of man' seems ever more urgent, and ever more likely to be disregarded. For the conservative, the demand for human rights owes its power and precision not to the idea expressed in it, but to the circumstances in which it is made. It is not to be interpreted as an appeal for abstract justice, but as a demand for a restoration of legitimacy and the rule of law. If there are any natural rights, there is at least this one: the right to adjudication. Until the affairs of men are governed by law, in the full sense of that term, you can specify rights until you are blue (or red) in the face, but you will make no difference to the world. Until people are ruled by law, the pieces of paper which specify their rights are no more than exercises in amateur metaphysics. Moreover, it has been a common observation among conservatives since Burke and de Maistre, that the absorption of our political energies in the pursuit of ever more and ever more ambitious 'rights of man', while neglecting the delicate apparatus of law and authority that enable us to make those rights into a reality, is one of the greatest causes of tyranny.

Leo Strauss (a political scientist who is widely credited as a conservative) has considered that the search for natural law, and the endeavour to build institutions that conform to it, are the prime tasks of political theory and practice. However, it is more characteristic of conservatism to distance itself from an idea which can be justified, if at all, only on the basis of abstruse metaphysical argument. Of greater interest is the real confrontation – increasingly desperate in the modern world – between the human individual, and the impersonal bureaucratic state. What the individual needs, in this conflict, is not a metaphysical doctrine of his natural rights, but an effective legal process that will stand between him and those in power.

A political right is a kind of veto, placed in the hands of the citizen, that enables him to shield himself from threat. The creation of rights, and especially of rights against the state, is indispensable to limited government. But the language of rights may also generate the very threat against which we hope for protection. For sometimes it may be used, not to guarantee liberties, but to make new and far-reaching *claims*. Consider the 'right to work'. On one interpretation this means the right to engage in work unimpeded by others. A law guaranteeing such a right will be designed to prevent people from obstructing the individual who wishes to go about his business. Under the pressure of socialist thinking, however, the 'right to work' has come to mean not a liberty but a massive claim against the state, and, through the state, against all those who must bear the burden of its expenditure. On this interpretation, a right to work is a right to have work provided – irrespective of whether one has done anything to deserve such a gift. This right can be satisfied, if at all, only by a vast extension of state control over the economy, and by measures which, whether or not coercive, are certainly calculated to curtail the liberties that may be enjoyed in a free economy.

A 'claim right' of this kind can be satisfied, therefore, only by simultaneously increasing the powers of the state and turning them in a socialist direction. The language which seemed to justify the limitation of the state, now justifies its expansion. Moreover, the whole movement for the affirmation of human rights has been turned, in recent years, in a direction repugnant to conservatives.

The cry for rights means, now, a constant increase in the claims made by the individual and by the groups which seek to usurp the state's sovereignty over him, without any increase in the individual's duties. Rights without duties are morally and legally repugnant. In the political sphere, where they are used to justify every unwarranted claim and every act of rebellion, they have posed a serious threat, both to the freedom of the individual citizen, and to the habit of obedience upon which the state is founded.

PERSONAL GOVERNMENT

As I have suggested, conservatism is sceptical towards ideals, and concerned rather to maintain the body politic in its natural equilibrium than to direct it to some ulterior purpose which is not its own. Nevertheless, there is a definite picture of political and civic virtue which emerges from conservative thinking, and it is one of great immediate appeal to anyone who has reflected seriously on the catastrophes of modern history.

The picture is of the developed personal state. This state is not only a corporate person, in the sense outlined above, but one also endowed with the distinctive virtues of a person. It stands in a personal relation to its subjects and (wherever possible) to other personal states. Unlike the impersonal tyrannies which have grown from revolutionary sentiments, the conservative state is everywhere informed by principles of answerability. In such a state, collective actions no more escape the net of law than the actions of individuals – nor are they threatened or undermined by the law, which is protective of free association, and rich in the ideas that are needed for the building of institutions.

The apparatus of personal government possesses an authority that is willingly conceded by those subject to it, and yet which neither aims to put itself above the law nor succeeds in doing so. At the same time the interests of those subject to the law are diversely represented – through parliament, law courts, and rights of appeal – before the sovereign power, so that sovereign and subject are joined through a constant process of mutual accommodation. Such a state tends towards perfection through the development of good habits, virtuous dispositions, and a love of good deeds. But it is no more likely to be perfect than is any other person, and its imperfections, where they cannot be corrected, must be tolerated. Nevertheless, within the historical circumstances which bind such a state, and which determine its field of action, it is capable of reform, and will reform itself, just so long as its subjects are public-spirited, and just so long as they are able to influence those in power.

The personal state cannot exist without legal opposition, properly protected by law. When opposition is eliminated, as it is eliminated by every revolutionary government, the first component of rational decision-making, which is the free discussion of alternatives, is destroyed, and with it the possibility of correcting error. From this one fault a thousand others flow: a state without opposition is not rational; nor is it personal, since nothing now compels it to accept responsibility for its errors and crimes; nor is it easily bound by law, since it may distort and amend the law every time that the law offers its protection to the opposing voice; nor can it be set upon the path of virtue, since it has neither the reason to desire such an aim, nor the pressure of habit that is necessary to accomplish it. Even if, by some miracle, such a state may be, for a while, under the control of virtuous people, nothing can guarantee that their virtue will remain, or that the pressure for constant change will not replace them with people more vicious than themselves.

Like other persons, the personal state is not a means to an end but an end in itself, with aims and attitudes that must be respected even when they should be changed. Its identity is historically determined, and it can be wrenched from its circumstances only by doing violence to all that has formed its will and personality, and by destroying the allegiance upon which its life depends. The personal state deals with the citizen as an equal before the law whose dignity and authority it upholds. It is not surprising if many conservatives, attempting to give concrete form to this personal relation between citizen and state, have looked back to the archetype from which it has developed – the relation between sovereign and subject – and have argued for constitutional monarchy as a paradigm of personal government. Such a position will seem anachronistic only to those who have yet to appreciate the full force of the doctrine of English common law, that the crown is a 'corporation sole'.

PROPERTY AND JUSTICE

The above sketch of a conservative political theory does not address itself to the principal socialist question – the question of the distribution of property, power and 'life chances'. Nevertheless, it has certain non-socialist, and perhaps even anti-socialist, implications, concerning which it is necessary to be clear.

There are at least two attitudes which go by the name of socialism. The first – typified by Leninism – is millenarian, apocalyptic, wishing to sweep away the old order of things and to replace it with a new and righteous order, in which justice and equality will be finally achieved. Animated by religious zeal, and impatient with the moderating influences of politics – in particular with laws and institutions, and with the habits of compromise which they engender – such a socialism is repudiated by all who recognise in law and compromise the foundations of political existence. At the same time, conservative thinkers have devoted considerable energy to describing and criticising the spiritual condition of millenarian socialism. For it was precisely in opposition to this attempt to transfer religious enthusiasm to the secular world that modern conservatism arose, forced by the revolutionary sickness into a consciousness of itself that it would have been happier not to acquire.

The second type of socialism differs from the first, not only in disclaiming the 'revolutionary road', and adopting in place of it the path of constitutional government and piecemeal reform, but also in adopting a more realistic and less intransigent goal. It believes less in an order of perfect justice, than in the need for political action in order to correct the injustices of a 'spontaneous' market economy. A believer in this kind of socialism will usually support constitutional government and the rule of law, and endeavour to reconcile his inherently 'purposeful' politics with the continuing operation of devices which for him are to be esteemed more for their corrective than for their authoritative character. He does not advocate the 'withering away' of the state, but proposes rather to use the state, as presently established, for a purpose that the state alone can satisfy – that of alleviating widespread suffering.

Conservatives have often expressed a certain qualified sympathy for this second kind of socialism. For if the state really is a person, standing to the citizen in a relation of mutual regard and answerability, then it can scarcely look with indifference on avoidable suffering. Indeed, the first legislative measures that originated the growth of the welfare state were the work of nineteenth-century conservatives.

Conservatives are increasingly hostile, however, to the welfare state, arguing against its extension in broadly three ways. First, the idea of 'social justice' on which the welfare state is founded – where social justice is supposed to be something other than charity, a 'right' of the recipient rather than a virtue of the one who gives – seems to sponsor and condone a corruption of the moral sense. Secondly, the welfare state that is built upon this conception seems to move precisely away from the conservative conception of authoritative and personal government, towards a labyrinthine, privilege-sodden structure of anonymous power, nurturing a citizenship that is increasingly reluctant to answer for itself, increasingly void of personal responsibility, and increasingly parasitic on the dispensations of a bureaucracy towards which it can feel no gratitude.

The third argument – more familiar, perhaps, but of less central ideological concern – is that the welfare state promises more than it can provide, grows like a cancer in the economic order, and finally threatens the process of wealth-creation itself. If the lot of the poor is changed by the welfare state, it is because something else changes also – namely, the productive capacity upon which the welfare state depends, and which it also threatens to extinguish.

Socialist self-confidence has been shaken by many recent events, and by the increasing scepticism of Western electorates towards its promises. But it has been far more deeply afflicted by arguments which strike at its intellectual heart. Consider the critique of socialist conceptions of 'social justice', given in various forms by von Mises and Hayek, and most recently by Robert Nozick. The socialist sees justice as a property of *distributions*, and concerns himself principally with the distribution of the 'social product' – i.e. the sum total of property, privilege and power which exists only because men live and work together in society. This total, the socialist supposes, comes into existence without any absolute rights of ownership, and is then distributed by 'society' (a ghostly entity which is somehow incarnate in the state). The product, which ought to be distributed on grounds of fairness – say, to those who did most to produce it, or to those who are most in need

– is in fact distributed most unfairly, according to legal entitlements which are the expression of entrenched and unjustifiable privileges.

In other words, the socialist constructs a vision of society from which 'rights of ownership' have been abolished. He then supposes that these rights come into being by an act of distribution exercised by 'society'. Each member of society has no other qualification for receiving a share than his membership, and the work that he has contributed. It would therefore seem to be a violation of the first principles of justice, that those who work least gain the most from their social membership. Hence 'society' must take the matter into its own hands, and out of the hands of individuals, so as to ensure that the distribution of the social product is truly just.

There are many objections to such a theory of 'social justice'. Why is it assumed, for instance, that products and advantages come into the world unowned? Surely, the transactions whereby these things are created *already* establish rights of ownership in them – the granting of rights being the normal price of economic cooperation? Such rights cannot be cancelled without injustice to the parties: and yet they must be cancelled if the product is to be distributed according to some socialist plan. Moreover, there is no such agent as 'society', and no such task as the distribution of the 'social product'. The only *agent* capable of fulfilling such a task – the state – comes into existence already bound by contracts, treaties and engagements with its citizens, and fatally obliged by law and constitution to uphold rights to which it is not itself a party. And if we think that the 'task' exists, then surely this is because we have misperceived the relations of ownership and citizenship, neither of which can be derived, as the socialist seeks to derive them, from some simpler, de-legalised idea of social 'membership'.

The true application of the idea of justice is not in some overarching calculation concerning the distribution of goods and benefits, but in the transactions between particular agents, and between agents and the world. To uphold a freely-undertaken agreement is, *prima facie*, just; to break it unilaterally is unjust. To compel another to work and to seize the product without his consent is unjust. And so on. By virtue of these individual transactions – in which the state too may participate, as one person among others – rights of ownership and advantage are distributed naturally. Justice is done so long as rights are upheld; but the very process of creating and acquiring rights, ensures their unequal distribution.

Rights soon cease to be respected, however, when the fiction of 'social justice' dominates our thinking. The result of this conception is to remove the sense of personal liability and obligation from the sphere of social interaction, and to destroy the coherence of our cooperative endeavours. If nothing is truly mine until redistributed by 'society', then nothing is rightly given or rightly received. If no privilege is deserved until the god 'society' has appended its approving signature, having first erased all natural entitlements, then I can neither share my advantage with you, nor proudly take possession of it, as a mark of the good fortune that is mine. In these, and countless other ways, we experience the corrupting influence of the socialist abstraction. In sweeping the world clean of every historical entitlement, socialism jeopardises the fundamental law of personality: the law that relations are to be mediated by the rights and the responsibilities which they themselves engender. Under socialism the state subsumes all rights, all privileges and every power, and the aim of social 'equality' becomes equivalent to a total subjugation of the human individual to an all-powerful entity – the 'society' of socialist thinking. And this all-powerful 'society' transforms itself by an expected magic into the bureaucratic and tyrannical state.

The conservative sees property as an institution which, while guaranteed by the state, has its moral and practical origin in civil society, and in the spontaneous dispositions to appropriate that which is near to hand, to cooperate with others, and to transform the realm of matter into an expression of individuality and will. This pre-political disposition is taken up by politics, but cannot be annihilated by it. It is precisely the attempt to annihilate it, indeed, which has led to the cruellest forms of modern government. If no philosophical argument sufficed to persuade us of the intrinsic value of private property, then the sheer barbarity of the methods standardly used to destroy that institution, into which so much human spontaneity has been distilled, would serve to educate our perceptions. Once conceded, moreover, the right of property has a 'natural history' of its own. It is this natural history, rather than the operation of some underlying system of 'production relations', which has produced the existing web of industry and commerce. And only a narrow view of history – one focused on the crises induced by technological discovery – will close our eyes to the fact that 'capitalism' is a permanent feature of human society. The system of private property and market exchange is neither historically transitory nor destructible – it can be driven underground by socialism; but when this happens socialism itself begins to depend upon it, and is forced to tolerate the 'second economy' of natural human intercourse if it is to survive.

FAMILY AND HIERARCHY

There is a natural human disposition to confer benefits on friends. This disposition is an essential part both of friendship and of love, each of which involves the selective and systematic granting of favours. Family and friendship define the unchosen obligations from which our obligation to the state is formed. Hence there is no conservative outlook on the state which does not involve, at some point, the acceptance of social differentiation, of the kind that follows automatically from the ties of affection, kinship and love. To prevent this result would require so great an interference in the spontaneous practices of gift and cooperation, as to threaten the very fabric of society.

'Equality' is a mysterious and irrational ambition. It is possible to defend equality in this or that *respect*: but, elevated to an absolute value, the idea of equality is empty and unappealing. The conservative will usually defend 'equality before the law'; and he may also subscribe to a general principle of justice, according to which each person is to receive his due, and in that sense be treated 'equally'. But 'equality' in this (Aristotelian) sense (the sense known as 'equity' in law), is compatible with, and indeed even *requires*, considerable inequalities in wealth and advantage. Any more radical form of equality is incoherent as a goal, and undesirable as an outcome. People are unequal in intelligence, strength, looks, talent, health, and original social position – in other words, in every respect relevant to our disposition to join ourselves to them in friendship and in love. Hence natural inequalities nourish social inequalities: to think otherwise is to fail to notice that intelligence, strength and beauty are actually more *attractive* than stupidity, weakness and ugliness. Hierarchy and advantage are therefore unavoidable. Our task is not to oppose them, but to strive to prevent their pathological forms, and to sustain those forms which are most readily accepted by those with least to gain.

This issue – illustrated in the quiet ruminations of Gustave Thibon, in Pareto's severely scientific defence of élites, and in Mallock's elaborate criticisms of egalitarianism – is increasingly difficult to discuss openly. Although it is universally admitted that social 'equality' is unattainable, the peculiar thought persists that it is nevertheless, in some obscure way, desirable. Whoever is prepared to set aside the idea of equality stands out from the crowd, and, unless he adopts the defiant and paradoxical posture of a Nietzsche, he will at once be regarded as an enemy of the people. Nevertheless, it is hard to retain a conservative attitude towards order, authority and institutions, without seeing stratification in general, and hereditary stratification in particular, as natural parts of a stable political organism. The problem here is that the truth cannot be loudly uttered, and conservative politics must proceed by means of convenient subterfuges.

This does not mean that conservative politics is the politics of 'class rule', or even that the upkeep of social stratification is in any clear sense a political *goal* for conservatives. On the contrary, stratification, like property, arises by an invisible hand from actions which have no such intention. To *aim* at this effect is precisely to jeopardise its achievement. It is to *put in question* that which is valuable only so long as it is not questioned – only so long, that is, as it forms the stable background to our social choices and concerns.

CLASS AND INSTITUTION

Here opens one of the greatest of all conflicts between conservative and socialist thinking. For the conservative, classes play, and ought to play, no part in politics; for the socialist it is precisely classes that define the political agenda and use it in pursuit of their goals. Classes do indeed exist, and we should not school ourselves to ignore them, however sceptical we may be of the theories of class developed by Marx and Weber. The objection to the socialist position stems, however, from the idea of personal government.

Classes are not agents and have no corporate personality. The division of society into classes serves an explanatory rather than a moral purpose, and even if we believe that the explanation so provided is important and true, it does not establish the possibility of a genuine 'class politics'. Moreover, there are dangerous consequences of the thought that it is classes, rather than corporations, which compete for political power. Classes are acknowledged on all sides not to be moral agents – to be strictly beyond praise, blame, and rectification. Those who enter politics as the self-conscious representatives of a class can therefore appropriate the primordial blamelessness of their constituency. Whatever they – the 'vanguard' – might do, it is not that 'they' are 'doing' it, but rather that the favoured class is blamelessly causing it. Here is sown the seed of impersonal government. The 'vanguard party' expressly removes itself from liability, and can be held publicly to account for nothing that it does. Agency, divorced from liability, becomes impersonal: and when government itself is conducted by such an agency, then political order comes to an end, and law and legitimacy stand on the verge of extinction.

It is corporations, rather than classes, that determine the character of the social order. By corporations I mean not only firms and partnerships, but also churches, teams, clubs, schools, universities, orchestras, theatres, dining circles, dances and discussion groups. These institutions, which grow less from work than from leisure, encapsulate our concrete experience of peaceful cooperation, and attain to the state of purposelessness in which our satisfaction resides. As Maitland has shown, it is one of the tasks of law to protect and uphold autonomous institutions, to determine their rights and duties, and to endow them with legal and moral personality.

Here we encounter, not only the main source of conservative disapproval towards 'class politics', but also one of the principal objects of conservative affection. Though state and civil society are not the same, neither can flourish in isolation. The perversion of the state by totalitarian control brings with it the perversion of society – a subjugation of all institutions to a ruling purpose, and the loss of the autonomy upon which corporations depend. The ensuing 'militarisation' of society – its regimentation around a common goal – is a feature which I have already referred to. But the significance of this transformation for conservative thinking is not always fully appreciated. The conservative state must protect a conservative society. In particular, it must provide whatever guarantees are necessary for the personality of institutions to emerge and establish itself as a social force. The transition from association to personal institution is integral to the formation of the individual. It is by his involvement in subordinate institutions – in what Burke referred to as the 'little platoons' – that the individual acquires the experience of membership, and learns not only to extend his activity into the realm of peaceful and purposeless cooperation, but also to extend, along with it, his sense of liability towards the surrounding world. It is through this process that the root conceptions of authority are acquired, and the individual learns to judge himself by requirements that are not his own.

This returns us to the root conservative attitude: the 'care of institutions'. In protecting autonomous institutions the state shores up its own authority. And in destroying autonomous institutions it leaves itself with no court of appeal wherein its own claim to obedience might be defended. By destroying institutions, the state destroys its own personality, transforming itself from an authoritative person to a naked and alienating power. The forbidding of autonomous institutions by the French revolutionaries, and by modern totalitarian governments, has therefore been the decisive move towards the modern impersonal state, and towards the popular resentment of revolutionary politics.

RELIGION AND MORALITY

Liberals have always argued, with J.S. Mill, for the maximum of toleration in matters of religion and morality, while conservatives have argued, with Sir James Fitzjames Stephen, that the separation of law from moral and religious feeling is neither possible nor desirable, being tantamount, in the end, to the alienation of the people from the rule of law.

This issue has become increasingly important in recent times, partly because of the undeniable loosening of traditional religious and moral ties, and partly because of the inevitable recrudescence of religious passion in strange, and sometimes dangerous forms – of which totalitarian socialism is by no means the least important. Conservatism has seen religion as a necessary bulwark to morality, and morality as a *sine qua non* of social order. Religion, however, when it breaks free from institutions, and elects the individual conscience as its sovereign, is as much a danger to the social order as a support to it. It can never be a matter of indifference when the institutions of religion decline, or impetuously discard their inheritance. The conservative vision of a stable establishment has therefore always made room for churches, and sought to protect them with the legal privileges suited to their spiritual task. Since religion and morality are both forms of intolerance, it is impossible to secure them within the legal order while also liberalising every institution in which they take root. Whatever the state of religious belief, therefore, the conservative view of law will always lean in the direction of traditional dogma.

Moreover, recognising that values are more easily destroyed than engendered, the conservative will naturally sympathise with the religious worldview. It is through the language, symbols and folk-morality of a religion that a people is rendered competent to confront its greatest fears and sufferings, and to work for its own continuity, so as to establish a 'partnership' of the living, the unborn and the dead. Without this great social force – by which selfish passions are overcome, individual energies collected, and charity, sacrifice and chastity made honourable – social fragmentation must inevitably occur. This fragmentation, which the liberal promises as the release of the individual from the chains of centuries, may seem like the gain of freedom. In fact, as I have suggested, it is the loss of freedom; for it necessitates the loss of the social order in which freedom flourishes.

The interface of politics and religion (the interface where Voegelin has pitched his own highly personal discourse) presents the greatest difficulties for every political theory. If conservatism deserves our attention for nothing else, it is at least for having recognised these difficulties, and for having refused to consign to the private realm (the realm of 'consenting adults') a phenomenon that is manifestly public both in its content and in its effects. For the conservative, as for the socialist, the public and the private are far more intricately intertwined than the liberal tends to acknowledge. The virtuous state depends on the public spirit of its citizens. In the absence of a common morality, of an accepted habit of piety, and of a willing disposition to obey, no public spirit can emerge completely or endure for long. The public spirit which upholds the law is private morality writ large. It is therefore absurd to suppose that the law may be severed from our deepest moral sentiments, and still attract the support and the sacrifice of those whose virtue is needed to uphold it.

2

Edmund Burke

Edmund Burke (1729–97) was the second son of an Irish Protestant attorney and his Roman Catholic wife. Burke was educated at Trinity College, Dublin, and entered the Middle Temple, London in 1750. More interested in literature than law, he joined Dr Johnson's club as a founding member. Burke married in 1756, in which year he published his Vindication of Natural Society, to be followed a year later by the profoundly influential Philosophical Enquiry into the Sublime and the Beautiful. Burke became private assistant in 1758 to W.G. Hamilton MP, transferring his services in 1765 to the Marquis of Rockingham, and being elected that year as MP for Wendover. In 1774 he became MP for Bristol, but lost his seat in 1780 on account of his championship of free trade with Ireland and Catholic emancipation. Burke became paymaster of forces in 1782, and delivered his famous speeches on the East India Bill in 1783 and 1785. He supported Wilberforce's campaign to abolish the slave trade in 1788, and retired in 1794. His most important works from the point of view of conservative thought are: Reflections on the Revolution in France (1790) – from which the following extracts are taken – An Appeal from the New to the Old Whigs (1791), and Letters on a Regicide Peace (1795–7). In all his later political works, Burke was concerned to awaken his contemporaries not only to the dangers of revolutionary thinking, but also to the virtue and wisdom inherent in the customs which the French Revolution had held up to scorn. His subtle and intricate defence of traditional order, as expressing a partnership between the living, the unborn and the dead, set a context for conservative thinking which it has retained until the present day.

Burke mounted one of the first sustained critiques of the Enlightenment view of man, as a creature whose rights and duties stem from his pre-political nature as a rational agent. He believed that the individual finds fulfilment only in society, and only in norms, customs and institutions which reflect back to him a sense of his unity with his fellows. Nevertheless he was a warm defender of the liberal economic theories that we associate with Adam Smith, and was the first serious thinker to attempt a reconciliation between the ideas of economic freedom and traditional order.

In the famous law of the 3rd of Charles I, called the *Petition of Right*, the parliament says to the king, 'Your subjects have *inherited* this freedom,' claiming their franchises, not on abstract principles as the 'rights of men,' but as the rights of Englishmen, and as a patrimony derived from their forefathers. Selden, and the other profoundly learned men, who drew this petition of right, were as well acquainted, at least, with all the general theories concerning the 'rights of men,' as any of the discoursers in our pulpits, or on your tribune; full as well as Dr. Price, or as the Abbé Sieyès. But, for reasons worthy of that practical wisdom which superseded their theoretic science, they preferred this positive, recorded, *hereditary* title to all which can be dear to the man and the citizen, to that vague speculative right, which exposed their sure inheritance to be scrambled for and torn to pieces by every wild litigious spirit.

The same policy pervades all the laws which have since been made for the preservation of our liberties. In the 1st of William and Mary, in the famous statute, called the Declaration of Right, the two houses utter not a syllable of 'a right to frame a government for themselves.' You will see, that their whole care was to secure the religion, laws, and liberties, that had been long possessed, and had been lately endangered. 'Taking into their most serious consideration the *best* means for making such an establishment, that their religion, laws, and liberties might not be in danger of being again subverted,' they auspicate all their proceedings, by stating as some of those *best* means, 'in the *first place*' to do 'as their *ancestors in like cases have usually* done for vindicating their *antient* rights and liberties to *declare;*' – and then they pray the king and queen, 'that it may be *declared* and enacted, that *all and singular* the rights and liberties *asserted and declared* are the true *antient* and indubitable rights and liberties of the people of this kingdom.'

You will observe, that from Magna Charta to the Declaration of Right, it has been the uniform policy of our constitution to claim and assert our liberties, as an *entailed inheritance* derived to us from our forefathers, and to be transmitted to our posterity; as an estate specially belonging to the people of this kingdom without any reference whatever to any other more general or prior right. By this means our constitution preserves an unity in so great a diversity of its parts. We have an inheritable crown; an inheritable peerage; and an house of commons and a people inheriting privileges, franchises, and liberties, from a long line of ancestors.

This policy appears to me to be the result of profound reflection;

or rather the happy effect of following nature, which is wisdom without reflection, and above it. A spirit of innovation is generally the result of a selfish temper and confined views. People will not look forward to posterity, who never look backward to their ancestors. Besides, the people of England well know, that the idea of inheritance furnishes a sure principle of conservation, and a sure principle of transmission; without at all excluding a principle of improvement. It leaves acquisition free; but it secures what it acquires. Whatever advantages are obtained by a state proceeding on these maxims, are locked fast as in a sort of family settlement; grasped as in a kind of mortmain for ever. By a constitutional policy, working after the pattern of nature, we receive, we hold, we transmit our government and our privileges, in the same manner in which we enjoy and transmit our property and our lives. The institutions of policy, the goods of fortune, the gifts of Providence, are handed down, to us and from us, in the same course and order. Our political system is placed in a just correspondence and symmetry with the order of the world, and with the mode of existence decreed to a permanent body composed of transitory parts; wherein, by the disposition of a stupenduous wisdom, moulding together the great mysterious incorporation of the human race, the whole, at one time, is never old, or middle-aged, or young, but in a condition of unchangeable constancy, moves on through the varied tenour of perpetual decay, fall, renovation, and progression. Thus, by preserving the method of nature in the conduct of the state, in what we improve, we are never wholly new; in what we retain we are never wholly obsolete. By adhering in this manner and on those principles to our forefathers, we are guided not by the superstition of antiquarians, but by the spirit of philosophic analogy. In this choice of inheritance we have given to our frame of polity the image of a relation in blood; binding up the constitution of our country with our dearest domestic ties; adopting our fundamental laws into the bosom of our family affections; keeping inseparable, and cherishing with the warmth of all their combined and mutually reflected charities, our state, our hearths, our sepulchres, and our altars.

Through the same plan of a conformity to nature in our artificial institutions, and by calling in the aid of her unerring and powerful instincts, to fortify the fallible and feeble contrivances of our reason, we have derived several other, and those no small benefits, from considering our liberties in the light of an inheritance.

Always acting as if in the presence of canonized forefathers, the spirit of freedom, leading in itself to misrule and excess, is tempered with an awful gravity. This idea of a liberal descent inspires us with a sense of habitual native dignity, which prevents that upstart insolence almost inevitably adhering to and disgracing those who are the first acquirers of any distinction. By this means our liberty becomes a noble freedom. It carries an imposing and majestic aspect. It has a pedigree and illustrating ancestors. It has its bearings and its ensigns armorial. It has its gallery of portraits; its monumental inscriptions; its records, evidences, and titles. We procure reverence to our civil institutions on the principle upon which nature teaches us to revere individual men; on account of their age; and on account of those from whom they are descended. All your sophisters cannot produce any thing better adapted to preserve a rational and manly freedom than the course that we have pursued, who have chosen our nature rather than our speculations, our breasts rather than our inventions, for the great conservatories and magazines of our rights and privileges. . . .

Nothing is a due and adequate representation of a state, that does not represent its ability, as well as its property. But as ability is a vigorous and active principle, and as property is sluggish, inert, and timid, it never can be safe from the invasions of ability, unless it be, out of all proportion, predominant in the representation. It must be represented too in great masses of accumulation, or it is not rightly protected. The characteristic essence of property, formed out of the combined principles of its acquisition and conservation, is to be *unequal*. The great masses therefore which excite envy, and tempt rapacity, must be put out of the possibility of danger. Then they form a natural rampart about the lesser properties in all their gradations. The same quantity of property, which is by the natural course of things divided among many, has not the same operation. Its defensive power is weakened as it is diffused. In this diffusion each man's portion is less than what, in the eagerness of his desires, he may flatter himself to obtain by dissipating the accumulations of others. The plunder of the few would indeed give but a share inconceivably small in the distribution to the many. But the many are not capable of making this calculation; and those who lead them to rapine, never intend this distribution.

The power of perpetuating our property in our families is one of the most valuable and interesting circumstances belonging to it, and that which tends the most to the perpetuation of society itself.

It makes our weakness subservient to our virtue; it grafts benevolence even upon avarice. The possessors of family wealth, and of the distinction which attends hereditary possession (as most concerned in it) are the natural securities for this transmission. With us, the house of peers is formed upon this principle. It is wholly composed of hereditary property and hereditary distinction; and made therefore the third of the legislature; and in the last event, the sole judge of all property in all its subdivisions. The house of commons too, though not necessarily, yet in fact, is always so composed in the far greater part. Let those large proprietors be what they will, and they have their chance of being amongst the best, they are at the very worst, the ballast in the vessel of the commonwealth. For though hereditary wealth, and the rank which goes with it, are too much idolized by creeping sycophants, and the blind abject admirers of power, they are too rashly slighted in shallow speculations of the petulant, assuming, short-sighted coxcombs of philosophy. Some decent regulated pre-eminence, some preference (not exclusive appropriation) given to birth, is neither unnatural, nor unjust, nor impolitic. . . .

Far am I from denying in theory; full as far is my heart from withholding in practice, (if I were of power to give or to withhold,) the *real* rights of men. In denying their false claims of right, I do not mean to injure those which are real, and are such as their pretended rights would totally destroy. If civil society be made for the advantage of man, all the advantages for which it is made become his right. It is an institution of beneficence; and law itself is only beneficence acting by a rule. Men have a right to live by that rule; they have a right to justice; as between their fellows, whether their fellows are in politic function or in ordinary occupation. They have a right to the fruits of their industry; and to the means of making their industry fruitful. They have a right to the acquisitions of their parents; to the nourishment and improvement of their offspring; to instruction in life, and to consolation in death. Whatever each man can separately do, without trespassing upon others, he has a right to do for himself; and he has a right to a fair portion of all which society, with all its combinations of skill and force, can do in his favour. In this partnership all men have equal rights; but not to equal things. He that has but five shillings in the partnership, has as good a right to it, as he that has five hundred pound has to his larger proportion. But he has not a right to an equal dividend in the product of the joint stock; and as to the share of power, authority, and direction which each individual ought to have in the management of the state, that I must deny to be amongst the direct original rights of man in civil society; for I have in my contemplation the civil social man, and no other. It is a thing to be settled by convention.

If civil society be the offspring of convention, that convention must be its law. That convention must limit and modify all the descriptions of constitution which are formed under it. Every sort of legislative, judicial, or executory power are its creatures. They can have no being in any other state of things; and how can any man claim, under the conventions of civil society, rights which do not so much as suppose its existence? Rights which are absolutely repugnant to it? One of the first motives to civil society, and which becomes one of its fundamental rules, is, *that no man should be judge in his own cause*. By this each person has at once divested himself of the first fundamental right of uncovenanted man, that is, to judge for himself, and to assert his own cause. He abdicates all right to be his own governor. He inclusively, in a great measure, abandons the right of self-defence, the first law of nature. Men cannot enjoy the rights of an uncivil and of a civil state together. That he may obtain justice he gives up his right of determining what it is in points the most essential to him. That he may secure some liberty, he makes a surrender in trust of the whole of it.

Government is not made in virtue of natural rights, which may and do exist in total independence of it; and exist in much greater clearness, and in a much greater degree of abstract perfection: but their abstract perfection is their practical defect. By having a right to every thing they want every thing. Government is a contrivance of human wisdom to provide for human *wants*. Men have a right that these wants should be provided for by this wisdom. Among these wants is to be reckoned the want, out of civil society, of a sufficient restraint upon their passions. Society requires not only that the passions of individuals should be subjected, but that even in the mass and body as well as in the individuals, the inclinations of men should frequently be thwarted, their will controlled, and their passions brought into subjection. This can only be done *by a power out of themselves*; and not, in the exercise of its function, subject to that will and to those passions which it is its office to bridle and subdue. In this sense the restraints on men, as well as their liberties, are to be reckoned among their rights. But as the liberties and the restrictions vary with times and circumstances, and admit of infinite modifications, they cannot be settled upon any abstract rule; and nothing is so foolish as to discuss them upon that principle.

The moment you abate any thing from the full rights of men, each to govern himself, and suffer any artificial positive limitation upon those rights, from that moment the whole organization of government becomes a consideration of convenience. This it is which makes the constitution of a state, and the due distribution of its powers, a matter of the most delicate and complicated skill. It requires a deep knowledge of human nature and human necessities, and of the things which facilitate or obstruct the various ends which are to be pursued by the mechanism of civil institutions. The state is to have recruits to its strength, and remedies to its distempers. What is the use of discussing a man's abstract right to food or to medicine? The question is upon the method of procuring and administering them. In that deliberation I shall always advise to call in the aid of the farmer and the physician, rather than the professor of metaphysics.

The science of constructing a commonwealth, or renovating it, or reforming it, is, like every other experimental science, not to be taught *a priori*. Nor is it a short experience that can instruct us in that practical science: because the real effects of moral causes are not always immediate; but that which in the first instance is prejudicial may be excellent in its remoter operation; and its excellence may arise even from the ill effects it produces in the beginning. The reverse also happens; and very plausible schemes, with very pleasing commencements, have often shameful and lamentable conclusions. In states there are often some obscure and almost latent causes, things which appear at first view of little moment, on which a very great part of its prosperity or adversity may most essentially depend. The science of government being therefore so practical in itself, and intended for such practical purposes, a matter which requires experience, and even more experience than any person can gain in his whole life, however sagacious and observing he may be, it is with infinite caution that any man ought to venture upon pulling down an edifice which has answered in any tolerable degree for ages the common purposes of society, or on building it up again, without having models and patterns of approved utility before his eyes.

These metaphysic rights entering into common life, like rays of light which pierce into a dense medium, are, by the laws of nature, refracted from their straight line. Indeed in the gross and complicated mass of human passions and concerns, the primitive rights of men undergo such a variety of refractions and reflections, that it becomes absurd to talk of them as if they continued in the simplicity of their original direction. The nature of man is intricate; the objects of society are of the greatest possible complexity; and therefore no simple disposition or direction of power can be suitable either to man's nature, or to the quality of his affairs. When I hear the simplicity of contrivance aimed at and boasted of in any new political constitutions, I am at no loss to decide that the artificers are grossly ignorant of their trade, or totally negligent of their duty. The simple governments are fundamentally defective, to say no worse of them. If you were to contemplate society in but one point of view, all these simple modes of polity are infinitely captivating. In effect each would answer its single end much more perfectly than the more complex is able to attain all its complex purposes. But it is better that the whole should be imperfectly and anomalously answered, than that, while some parts are provided for with great exactness, others might be totally neglected, or perhaps materially injured, by the over-care of a favourite member.

The pretended rights of these theorists are all extremes; and in proportion as they are metaphysically true, they are morally and politically false. The rights of men are in a sort of *middle*, incapable of definition, but not impossible to be discerned. The rights of men in governments are their advantages; and these are often in balances between differences of good; in compromises sometimes between good and evil, and sometimes, between evil and evil. Political reason is a computing principle; adding, subtracting, multiplying, and dividing, morally and not metaphysically or mathematically, true moral denominations.

By these theorists the right of the people is almost always sophistically confounded with their power. The body of the community, whenever it can come to act, can meet with no effectual resistance; but till power and right are the same, the whole body of them has no right inconsistent with virtue, and the first of all virtues, prudence. Men have no right to what is not reasonable, and to what is not for their benefit; for though a pleasant writer said, *Liceat perire poetis*, when one of them, in cold blood, is said to have leaped into the flames of a volcanic revolution, *Ardentem frigidus Ætnam insiluit*, I consider such a frolic rather as an unjustifiable poetic licence, than as one of the franchises of Parnassus; and whether he were poet, or divine, or politician, that chose to exercise this kind of right, I think that more wise, because more charitable thoughts would urge me rather to save the man, than to preserve his brazen slippers as the monuments of his folly.

. . . We are not the converts of Rousseau; we are not the disciples of Voltaire; Helvetius has made no progress amongst us. Atheists are not our preachers; madmen are not our lawgivers. We know that we have made no discoveries; and we think that no discoveries are to be made, in morality; nor many in the great principles of government, nor in the ideas of liberty, which were understood long before we were born, altogether as well as they will be after the grave has heaped its mould upon our presumption, and the silent tomb shall have imposed its law on our pert loquacity. In England we have not yet been completely embowelled of our natural entrails: we still feel within us, and we cherish and cultivate, those inbred sentiments which are the faithful guardians, the active monitors of our duty, the true supporters of all liberal and manly morals. We have not been drawn and trussed, in order that we may be filled, like stuffed birds in a museum, with chaff and rags and paltry blurred shreds of paper about the rights of man. We preserve the whole of our feelings still native and entire, unsophisticated by pedantry and infidelity. We have real hearts of flesh and blood beating in our bosoms. We fear God; we look up with awe to kings; with affection to parliaments; with duty to magistrates; with reverence to priests; and with respect to nobility. Why? Because when such ideas are brought before our minds, it is *natural* to be so affected; because all other feelings are false and spurious, and tend to corrupt our minds, to vitiate our primary morals, to render us unfit for rational liberty; and by teaching us a servile, licentious, and abandoned insolence, to be our low sport for a few holidays, to make us perfectly fit for, and justly deserving of, slavery, through the whole course of our lives.

You see, sir, that in this enlightened age I am bold enough to confess, that we are generally men of untaught feelings; that, instead of casting away all our old prejudices, we cherish them to a very considerable degree, and, to take more shame to ourselves, we cherish them because they are prejudices; and the longer they have lasted and the more generally they have prevailed, the more we cherish them. We are afraid to put men to live and trade each on his own private stock of reason; because we suspect that the stock in each man is small, and that the individuals would do better to avail themselves of the general bank and capital of nations and of ages. Many of our men of speculation, instead of exploding general prejudices, employ their sagacity to discover the latent wisdom which prevails in them. If they find what they seek, and they seldom fail, they think it more wise to continue the prejudice, with the reason involved, than to cast away the coat of prejudice, and to leave nothing but the naked reason; because prejudice, with its reason, has a motive to give action to that reason, and an affection which will give it permanence. Prejudice is of ready application in the emergency; it previously engages the mind in a steady course of wisdom and virtue, and does not leave the man hesitating in the moment of decision, sceptical, puzzled, and unresolved. Prejudice renders a man's virtue his habit; and not a series of unconnected acts. Through just prejudice, his duty becomes a part of his nature.

Your literary men, and your politicians, and so do the whole clan of the enlightened among us, essentially differ in these points. They have no respect for the wisdom of others; but they pay it off by a very full measure of confidence in their own. With them it is a sufficient motive to destroy an old scheme of things, because it is an old one. As to the new, they are in no sort of fear with regard to the duration of a building run up in haste; because duration is no object to those who think little or nothing has been done before their time, and who place all their hopes in discovery. They conceive, very systematically, that all things which give perpetuity are mischievous, and therefore they are at inexpiable war with all establishments. They think that government may vary like modes of dress, and with as little ill effect. That there needs no principle of attachment, except a sense of present conveniency, to any constitution of the state. They always speak as if they were of opinion that there is a singular species of compact between them and their magistrates, which binds the magistrate, but which has nothing reciprocal in it, but that the majesty of the people has a right to dissolve it without any reason, but its will. Their attachment to their country itself, is only so far as it agrees with some of their fleeting projects; it begins and ends with that scheme of polity which falls in with their momentary opinion. . . .

Society is indeed a contract. Subordinate contracts, for objects of mere occasional interest, may be dissolved at pleasure; but the state ought not to be considered as nothing better than a partnership agreement in a trade of pepper and coffee, callico or tobacco, or some other such low concern, to be taken up for a little temporary interest, and to be dissolved by the fancy of the parties. It is to be looked on with other reverence; because it is not a partnership in things subservient only to the gross animal existence of a temporary and perishable nature. It is a partnership in all science; a partnership in all art; a partnership in every virtue, and in all perfection. As the ends of such a partnership cannot be obtained in many generations, it becomes a partnership not only between those who are living, but between those who are living, those who are dead, and those who are to be born. Each contract of each particular state is but a clause in the great primæval contract of eternal society, linking the lower with the higher natures, connecting the visible and invisible world, according to a fixed compact sanctioned by the inviolable oath which holds all physical and all moral natures, each in their appointed place. This law is not subject to the will of those, who by an obligation above them, and infinitely superior, are bound to submit their will to that law. The municipal corporations of that universal kingdom are not morally at liberty at their pleasure, and on their speculations of a contingent improvement, wholly to separate and tear assunder the bands of their subordinate community, and to dissolve it into an unsocial, uncivil, unconnected chaos of elementary principles. It is the first and supreme necessity only, a necessity that is not chosen but chooses, a necessity paramount to deliberation, that admits no discussion, and demands no evidence, which alone can justify a resort to anarchy. This necessity is no exception to the rule; because this necessity itself is a part too of that moral and physical disposition of things to which man must be obedient by consent or force. But if that which is only submission to necessity should be made the object of choice, the law is broken; nature is disobeyed; and the rebellious are outlawed, cast forth, and exiled, from this world of reason, and order, and peace, and virtue, and fruitful penitence, into the antagonist world of madness, discord, vice, confusion, and unavailing sorrow.

3
F.H. Bradley

Francis Herbert Bradley (1846–1924), brother of the literary critic A.C. Bradley, is the most important representative of British philosophical idealism as this flourished in the late nineteenth and early twentieth centuries. Bradley had an uneventful life as Fellow of Merton College Oxford, although he enjoyed the friendship of Elinor Glyn and expressed, in his philosophical prose, an attitude to life that was far from donnish. (T.S. Eliot singled out Bradley's writings as a model of English prose style.)

Only one work of Bradley's is of major significance for the student of conservative thought – the Ethical Studies, *published in 1876. Heavily influenced by Hegel and German idealism, this work endeavoured to provide a metaphysical refutation of the prevailing individualist and utilitarian philosophies of morals, and to reaffirm the importance, in the make-up of the human person, of institutions and the forms of social life.*

The following extracts are from the famous chapter of Ethical Studies *entitled 'My Station and its Duties'.*

The 'individual' man, the man into whose essence his community with others does not enter, who does not include relation to others in his very being, is, we say, a fiction, and in the light of facts we have to examine him. Let us take him in the shape of an English child as soon as he is born; for I suppose we ought not to go further back. Let us take him as soon as he is separated from his mother, and occupies a space clear and exclusive of all other human beings. At this time, education and custom will, I imagine, be allowed to have not as yet operated on him or lessened his 'individuality'. But is he now a mere 'individual', in the sense of not implying in his being identity with others? We can not say that, if we hold to the teaching of modern physiology. Physiology would tell us, in one language or another, that even now the child's mind is no passive 'tabula rasa'; he has an inner, a yet undeveloped nature, which must largely determine his future individuality. What is this inner nature? Is it particular to himself? Certainly not all of it, will have to be the answer. The child is not fallen from heaven. He is born of certain parents who come of certain families, and he has in him the qualities of his parents, and, as breeders would say, of the strains from both sides. Much of it we can see, and more we believe to be latent, and, given certain (possible or impossible) conditions, ready to come to light. On the descent of mental qualities, modern investigation and popular experience, as expressed in uneducated vulgar opinion, altogether, I believe, support one another, and we need not linger here. But if the intellectual and active qualities do descend from ancestors, is it not, I would ask, quite clear that a man may have in him the same that his father and mother had, the same that his brothers and sisters have? And if any one objects to the word 'same', I would put this to him. If, concerning two dogs allied in blood, I were to ask a man, 'Is that of the same strain or stock as this?' and were answered, 'No, not the same, but similar', should I not think one of these things, that the man either meant to deceive me, or was a 'thinker', or a fool?

But the child is not merely the member of a family; he is born into other spheres, and (passing over the subordinate wholes, which nevertheless do in many cases qualify him) he is born a member of the English nation. It is, I believe, a matter of fact that at birth the child of one race is not the same as the child of another; that in the children of the one race there is a certain identity, a developed or undeveloped national type, which may be hard to recognize, or which at present may even be unrecognizable, but which nevertheless in some form will appear. If that be the fact, then again we must say that one English child is in some points, though perhaps it does not as yet show itself, the same as another. His being is so far common to him with others; he is not a mere 'individual'.

We see the child has been born at a certain time of parents of a certain race, and that means also of a certain degree of culture. It is the opinion of those best qualified to speak on the subject, that civilization is to some not inconsiderable extent hereditary; that aptitudes are developed, and are latent in the child at birth; and that it is a very different thing, even apart from education, to be born of civilized and of uncivilized ancestors. These 'civilized tendencies', if we may use the phrase, are part of the essence of the child: he would only partly (if at all) be himself without them; he owes them to his ancestors, and his ancestors owe them to society. The ancestors were made what they were by the society they lived in. If in answer it be replied, 'Yes, but individual ancestors were prior to their society', then that, to say the least of it, is a hazardous and unproved assertion, since man, so far as history can trace him back, is social; and if Mr. Darwin's conjecture as to the development of man from a social animal be received, we must say that man has never been anything but social, and society never was made by individual men. Nor, if the (baseless) assertion of the priority of individual men were allowed, would that destroy our case; for certainly our more immediate ancestors were social; and, whether society was manufactured previously by individuals or not, yet in their case it certainly was not so. They at all events have been so qualified by the common possessions of social mankind that, as members in the organism, they have become relative to the whole. If we suppose then that the results of the social life of the race are present in a latent and potential form in the child, can we deny that they are common property? Can we assert that they are not an element of sameness in all? Can we say that the individual is this individual, because he is exclusive, when, if we deduct from him what he includes, he loses characteristics which make him himself, and when again he does include what the others include, and therefore does (how can we escape the consequence?) include in some sense the others also, just as they include him? By himself, then, what are we to call him? I confess I do not know, unless we name him a theoretical attempt to isolate what can not be isolated; and that, I suppose, has, out of our heads, no existence. But what he is really, and not in mere theory, can be described only as the specification or particularization of that which is common, which is the same amid diversity, and without which the 'individual' would be so other than he is that we could not call him the same.

Thus the child is at birth; and he is born not into a desert, but into a living world, a whole which has a true individuality of its own, and into a system and order which it is difficult to look at as anything else than an organism, and which, even in England, we are now beginning to call by that name. And I fear that the 'individuality' (the particularness) which the child brought into the light with him, now stands but a poor chance, and that there is no help for him until he is old enough to become a 'philosopher'. We have seen that already he has in him inherited habits, or what will of themselves appear as such; but, in addition to this, he is not for one moment left alone, but continually tampered with; and the habituation which is applied from the outside is the more insidious that it answers to this inborn disposition. Who can resist it? Nay, who but a 'thinker' could wish to have resisted it? And yet the tender care that receives and guides him is impressing on him habits, habits, alas, not particular to himself, and the 'icy chains' of universal custom are hardening themselves round his cradled life. As the poet tells us, he has not yet thought of himself; his earliest notions come mixed to him of things and persons, not distinct from one another, nor divided from the feeling of his own existence. The need that he can not understand moves him to foolish, but not futile, cries for what only another can give him; and the breast of his mother, and the soft warmth and touches and tones of his nurse, are made one with the feeling of his own pleasure and pain; nor is he yet a moralist to beware of such illusion, and to see in them mere means to an end without them in his separate self. For he does not even think of his separate self; he grows with his world, his mind fills and orders itself; and when he can separate himself from that world, and know himself apart from it, then by that time his self, the object of his self-consciousness, is penetrated, infected, characterized by the existence of others. Its content implies in every fibre relations of community. He learns, or already perhaps has learnt, to speak, and here he appropriates the common heritage of his race, the tongue that he makes his own is his country's language, it is (or it should be) the same that others speak, and it carries into his mind the ideas and sentiments of the race (over this I need not stay), and stamps them in indelibly. He grows up in an atmosphere of example and general custom, his life widens out from one little world to other and higher worlds, and he apprehends through successive stations the whole in which he lives, and in which he has lived. Is he now to try and develop his 'individuality', his self which is not the same as other selves? Where is it? What is it? Where can he find it? The soul within him is saturated, is filled, is qualified by, it has assimilated, has got its substance, has built itself up from, it *is* one and the same life with the universal life, and if he turns against this he turns against himself; if he thrusts it from him, he tears his own vitals; if he attacks it, he sets his weapon against his own heart. He has found his life in the life of the whole, he lives that in himself, 'he is a pulse-beat of the whole system, and himself the whole system'. . . .

. . . So far, I think, without aid from metaphysics, we have seen that the 'individual' apart from the community is an abstraction. It is not anything real, and hence not anything that we can realize, however much we may wish to do so. We have seen that I am myself by sharing with others, by including in my essence relations to them, the relations of the social state. If I wish to realize my true being, I must therefore realize something beyond my being as a mere this or that; for my true being has in it a life which is not the life of any mere particular, and so must be called a universal life.

What is it then that I am to realize? We have said it in 'my station and its duties'. To know what a man is (as we have seen) you must not take him in isolation. He is one of a people, he was born in a family, he lives in a certain society, in a certain state. What he has to do depends on what his place is, what his function is, and that all comes from his station in the organism. Are there then such organisms in which he lives, and if so, what is their nature? Here we come to questions which must be answered in full by any complete system of Ethics, but which we can not enter on. We must content ourselves by pointing out that there are such facts as the family, then in a middle position a man's own profession and society, and, over all, the larger community of the state. Leaving out of sight the question of a society wider than the state, we must say that a man's life with its moral duties is in the main filled up by his station in that system of wholes which the state is, and that this, partly by its laws and institutions, and still more by its spirit, gives him the life which he does live and ought to live. That objective institutions exist is of course an obvious fact; and it is a fact which every day is becoming plainer that these institutions are organic, and further, that they are moral. The assertion that communities have been manufactured by the addition of exclusive units is, as we have seen, a mere fable; and if, within the state, we take that which seems wholly to depend on individual caprice, e.g. marriage,[1] yet even here we find that a man does give up his self so far as it excludes others; he does bring himself under a unity which is superior to the particular person and the impulses that belong to his single existence, and which makes him fully as much as he makes it. In short, man is a social being; he is real only because he is social, and can realize himself only because it is as social that he realizes himself. The mere individual is a delusion of theory; and the attempt to realize it in practice is the starvation and mutilation of human nature, with total sterility or the production of monstrosities.

Let us now in detail compare the advantages of our present view with the defects of 'duty for duty's sake'. The objections we found fatal to that view may be stated as follows: (1) The universal was abstract. There was no content which belonged to it and was one with it; and the consequence was, that either nothing could be willed, or what was willed was willed not because of the universal, but capriciously. (2) The universal was 'subjective'. It certainly gave itself out as 'objective', in the sense of being independent of this or that person, but still it was not real in the world. It did not come to us as what *was* in fact, it came as what in itself merely was to be, an inner notion in moral persons, which, at least perhaps, had not power to carry itself out and transform the world. And self-realization, if it means will, does mean that we, in fact, do put ourselves forth and see ourselves actual in outer existence. Hence, by identifying ourselves with that which has not necessarily this existence, which is not master of the outer world, we can not secure our self-realization; since, when we have identified ourselves with the end, the end may still remain a mere inner end which does not accomplish itself, and so does not satisfy us.(3) The universal left a part of ourselves outside it. However much we tried to be good, however determined we were to make our will one with the good will, yet we never succeeded. There was always something left in us which was in contradiction with the good. And this we saw was even necessary, because morality meant and implied this contradiction, unless we accepted that form of conscientiousness which consists in the simple identification of one's conscience with one's own self (unless, i.e., the consciousness of the relation of my private self to myself as the good self be degraded into my self-consciousness of my mere private self as the good self); and this can not be, if we are in earnest with morality. There thus remains a perpetual contradiction in myself, no less than in the world, between the 'is to be' and the 'is', a contradiction that can not be got rid of without getting rid of morality; for, as we saw, it is inherent in morality. The man can not realize himself in himself as moral, because the conforming of his sensuous nature to the universal would be the radical suppression of it, and hence not only of himself, but also of the morality which is constituted by the relation of himself to the universal law. The man then can not find self-realization in the morality of pure duty; because (1) he can not look on his subjective self as the realized moral law; (2) he can not look on the objective world as the realization of the moral law;

(3) he can not realize the moral law at all, because it is defined as that which has no particular content, and therefore no reality; or, if he gives it a content, then it is not the law he realizes, since the content is got not from the law, but from elsewhere. In short, duty for duty's sake is an unsolved contradiction, the standing 'is to be', which, therefore, because it is to be, is *not*; and in which, therefore, since it is *not*, he can not find himself realized nor satisfy himself.

These are serious defects: let us see how they are mended by 'my station and its duties'. In that (1) the universal is concrete; (2) it is objective; (3) it leaves nothing of us outside it.

(1) It is concrete, and yet not given by caprice. Let us take the latter first. It is not given by caprice; for, although within certain limits I may choose my station according to my own liking, yet I and every one else must have some station with duties pertaining to it, and those duties do not depend on our opinion or liking. Certain circumstances, a certain position, call for a certain course. How I in particular know what my right course is, is a question we shall recur to hereafter – but at present we may take it as an obvious fact that in my station my particular duties are prescribed to me, and I have them whether I wish to or not. And secondly, it is concrete. The universal to be realized is no abstraction, but an organic whole; a system where many spheres are subordinated to one sphere, and particular actions to spheres. This system is real in the detail of its functions, not out of them, and lives in its vital processes, not away from them. The organs are always at work for the whole, the whole is at work in the organs. And I am one of the organs. The universal then which I am to realize is the system which penetrates and subordinates to itself the particulars of all lives, and here and now in my life has this and that function in this and that case, in exercising which through my will it realizes itself as a whole, and me in it.

(2) It is 'objective'; and this means that it does not stand over against the outer world as mere 'subject' confronted by mere 'object'. In that sense of the words it is neither merely 'objective' nor merely 'subjective'; but it is that real identity of subject and object, which, as we have seen, is the only thing that satisfies our desires. The inner side does exist, but it is no more than the inside; it is one factor in the whole, and must not be separated from the other factor; and the mistake which is made by the morality which confines itself to the individual man, is just this attempt at the separation of what can not be separated. The inner side certainly is

a fact, and it can be distinguished from the rest of the whole; but it really is one element of the whole, depends on the whole for its being, and can not be divided from it. Let us explain. The moral world, as we said, is a whole, and has two sides. There is an outer side, systems and institutions, from the family to the nation; this we may call the body of the moral world. And there must also be a soul, or else the body goes to pieces; every one knows that institutions without the spirit of them are dead. In the moral organism this spirit is in the will of the organs, as the will of the whole which, in and by the organs, carries out the organism and makes it alive, and which also (and this is the point to which attention is requested) is, and must be felt or known, in each organ as his own inward and personal will. It is quite clear that a nation is not strong without public spirit, and is not public-spirited unless the members of it are public-spirited, i.e. feel the good of the public as a personal matter, or have it at their hearts. The point here is that you can not have the moral world unless it is willed; that to be willed it must be willed by persons; and that these persons not only have the moral world as the content of their wills, but also must in some way be aware of themselves as willing this content. This being inwardly aware of oneself as willing the good will falls in the inside of the moral whole; we may call it the soul; and it is the sphere of personal morality, or morality in the narrower sense of the consciousness of the relation of my private self to the inwardly presented universal will, my being aware of and willing myself as one with that or contrary to that, as dutiful or bad. We must never let this out of our sight, that, where the moral world exists, you have and you must have these two sides; neither will stand apart from the other; moral institutions are carcasses without personal morality, and personal morality apart from moral institutions is an unreality, a soul without a body.

Now this inward, this 'subjective', this personal side, this knowing in himself by the subject of the relation in which the will of him as this or that man stands to the will of the whole within him, or (as was rightly seen by 'duty for duty's sake') this consciousness in the one subject of himself as two selves, is, as we said, necessary for all morality. But the form in which it is present may vary very much, and, beginning with the stage of mere feeling, goes on to that of explicit reflection. The reader who considers the matter will perceive that (whether in the life of mankind or of this or that man) we do not begin with a consciousness of good and evil, right and wrong, as such, or in the strict sense. The child is taught to will a content which is universal and good, and he learns to identify his will with it, so that he feels pleasure when he feels himself in accord with it, uneasiness or pain when his will is contrary thereto, and he feels that it is contrary. This is the beginning of personal morality, and from this we may pass to consider the end. . . . It consists in the explicit consciousness in myself of two elements which, even though they exist in disunion, are felt to be really one; these are myself as the will of this or that self, and again the universal will as the will for good; and this latter I feel to be my true self, and desire my other self to be subordinated to and so identified with it; in which case I feel the satisfaction of an inward realization. That, so far as form goes, is correct. But the important point on which 'duty for duty's sake' utterly failed us was as to the content of the universal will. We have seen that for action this must have a content, and now we see where the content comes from. The universal side in personal morality is, in short, the reflection of the objective moral world into ourselves (or into itself). The outer universal which I have been taught to will as my will, and which I have grown to find myself in, is now presented by me inwardly to myself as the universal which is my true being, and which by my will I must realize, if need be, against my will as this or that man. So this inner universal has the same content as the outer universal, for it *is* the outer universal in another sphere; it is the inside *of* the outside. *There* was the whole system as an objective will, including my station, and realizing itself here and now in my function. *Here* is the same system presented as a will in me, standing above my will, which wills a certain act to be done by me as a will which is one with the universal will. This universal will is not a blank, but it is filled by the consideration of my station in the whole with reference to habitual and special acts. The ideal self appealed to by the moral man is an ideally presented will, in his position and circumstances, which rightly particularizes the general laws which answer to the general functions and system of spheres of the moral organism. That is the content, and therefore, as we saw, it is concrete and filled. And therefore also (which is equally important) it is not merely 'subjective'.

If, on the inner side of the moral whole, the universal factor were (as in would-be morality it is) filled with a content which is not the detail of the objective will particularizing itself in such and such functions, then there would be no true identity of subject and object, no need why that which is moral should be that which is real, and we should never escape from a practical postulate, which, as we saw, is a practical standing contradiction. But if, as we have seen, the universal on the inside is the universal on the outside reflected in us, or (since we can not separate it and ourselves) into itself in us; if the objective will of the moral organism is real only in the will of its organs, and if, in willing morally, we will ourselves as that will, and that will wills itself in us – then we must hold that this universal on the inner side is the will of the whole, which is self-conscious in us, and wills itself in us against the actual or possible opposition of the false private self. This being so, when we will morally, the will of the objective world wills itself in us, and carries both us and itself out into the world of the moral will, which is its own realm. We see thus that, when morals are looked at as a whole, the will of the inside, so far as it is moral, *is* the will of the outside, and the two are one and can not be torn apart without *ipso facto* destroying the unity in which morality consists. To be moral, I must will my station and its duties; that is, I will to particularize the moral system truly in a given case; and the other side to this act is, that the moral system wills to particularize itself in a given station and functions, i.e. in my actions and by my will. In other words, my moral self is not simply mine, it is not an inner which belongs simply to me; and further, it is not a mere inner at all, but it is the soul which animates the body and lives in it, and would not be the soul if it had not a body and *its* body. The objective organism, the systematized moral world, is the reality of the moral will; my duties on the inside answer to due functions on the outside. There is no need here for a pre-established or a postulated harmony, for the moral whole is the identity of both sides; my private choice, so far as I am moral, is the mere form of bestowing myself on, and identifying myself with, the will of the moral organism, which realizes in its process both itself and myself. Hence we see that what I have to do I have not to force on a recalcitrant world; I have to fill my place – the place that waits for me to fill it; to make my private self the means, my life the sphere and the function of the soul of the whole, which thus, personal in me, externalizes both itself and me into a solid reality, which is both mine and its.

(3) What we come to now is the third superiority of 'my station

and its duties'. The universal which is the end, and which we have seen is concrete and does realize itself, does also more. It gets rid of the contradiction between duty and the 'empirical' self; it does not in its realization leave me for ever outside and unrealized.

In 'duty for duty's sake' we were always unsatisfied, no nearer our goal at the end than at the beginning. There we had the fixed antithesis of the sensuous self on one side and a non-sensuous moral ideal on the other – a standing contradiction which brought with it a perpetual self-deceit, or the depressing perpetual confession that I am not what I ought to be in my inner heart, and that I never can be so. Duty, we thus saw, was an infinite process, an unending 'not-yet'; a continual 'not' with an everlasting 'to be', or an abiding 'to be' with a ceaseless 'not'.

From this last peevish enemy we are again delivered by 'my station and its duties'. There I realize myself morally, so that not only what ought to be in the world is, but I am what I ought to be, and find so my contentment and satisfaction. If this were not the case, when we consider that the ordinary moral man is self-contented and happy, we should be forced to accuse him of immorality, and we do not do this; we say he most likely might be better, but we do not say that he is bad, or need consider himself so. Why is this? It is because 'my station and its duties' teaches us to identify others and ourselves with the station we fill; to consider that as good, and by virtue of that to consider others and ourselves good too. It teaches us that a man who does his work in the world is good, notwithstanding his faults, if his faults do not prevent him from fulfilling his station. It tells us that the heart is an idle abstraction; we are not to think of it, nor must we look at our insides, but at our work and our life, and say to ourselves, Am I fulfilling my appointed function or not? Fulfil it we can, if we will: what we have to do is not so much better than the world that we can not do it; the world is there waiting for it; my duties are my rights. On the one hand, I am not likely to be much better than the world asks me to be; on the other hand, if I can take my place in the world I ought not to be discontented. Here we must not be misunderstood; we do not say that the false self, the habits and desires opposed to the good will, are extinguished. Though negated, they never are all of them entirely suppressed, and can not be. Hence we must not say that any man really does fill his station to the full height of his capacity; nor must we say of any man that he can not perform his function better than he does, for we all can do so, and should try to do so. We do not wish to deny what are plain moral facts, nor in any way to slur them over.

How then does the contradiction disappear? It disappears by my identifying myself with the good will that I realize in the world, by my refusing to identify myself with the bad will of my private self. So far as I am one with the good will, living as a member in the moral organism, I am to consider myself real, and I am not to consider the false self real. That can not be attributed to me in my character of member in the organism. Even in me the false existence of it has been partly suppressed by that organism; and, so far as the organism is concerned, it is wholly suppressed, because contradicted in its results, and allowed no reality. Hence, not existing for the organism, it does not exist for me as a member thereof; and only as a member thereof do I hold myself to be real. And yet this is not justification by faith, for we not only trust, but see, that despite our faults the moral world stands fast, and we in and by it. It is like faith, however, in this, that not merely by thinking ourselves, but by willing ourselves as such, can we look on ourselves as organs in a good whole, and so ourselves good. And further, the knowledge that as members of the system we are real, and not otherwise, encourages us more and more to identify ourselves with that system; to make ourselves better, and so more real, since we see that the good is real, and that nothing else is.

Or, to repeat it, in education my self by habituation has been growing into one with the good self around me, and by my free acceptance of my lot hereafter I consciously make myself one with the good, so that, though bad habits cling to and even arise in me, yet I can not but be aware of myself as the reality of the good will. That is my essential side; my imperfections are not, and practically they do not matter. The good will in the world realizes itself by and in imperfect instruments, and in spite of them. The work is done, and so long as I will my part of the work and do it (as I do), I feel that, if I perform the function, I *am* the organ, and that my faults, if they do not matter to my station, do not matter to me. My heart I am not to think of, except to tell by my work whether it is in my work, and one with the moral whole; and if that is so, I have the consciousness of absolute reality in the good because of and by myself, and in myself because of and through the good; and with that I am satisfied, and have no right to be dissatisfied.

The individual's consciousness of himself is inseparable from the knowing himself as an organ of the whole; and the residuum falls more and more into the background, so that he thinks of it, if at all, not as himself, but as an idle appendage. For his nature now is not distinct from his 'artificial self'. He is related to the living moral system not as to a foreign body; his relation to it is 'too inward even for faith', since faith implies a certain separation. It is no other-world that he can not see but must trust to: he feels himself in it, and it in him; in a word, the self-consciousness of himself *is* the self-consciousness of the whole in him, and his will is the will which sees in him its accomplishment by him; it is the free will which knows itself as the free will, and, as this, beholds its realization and is more than content.

The non-theoretical person, if he be not immoral, is at peace with reality; and the man who in any degree has made this point of view his own, becomes more and more reconciled to the world and to life, and the theories of 'advanced thinkers' come to him more and more as the thinnest and most miserable abstractions. He sees evils which can not discourage him, since they point to the strength of the life which can endure such parasites and flourish in spite of them. If the popularizing of superficial views inclines him to bitterness, he comforts himself when he sees that they live in the head, and but little, if at all, in the heart and life; that still at the push the doctrinaire and the quacksalver go to the wall, and that even that too is as it ought to be. He sees the true account of the state (which holds it to be neither mere force nor convention, but the moral organism, the real identity of might and right) unknown or 'refuted', laughed at and despised, but he sees the state every day in its practice refute every other doctrine, and do with the moral approval of all what the explicit theory of scarcely one will morally justify. He sees instincts are better and stronger than so-called 'principles'. He sees in the hour of need what are called 'rights' laughed at, 'freedom', the liberty to do what one pleases, trampled on, the claims of the individual trodden under foot, and theories burst like cobwebs. And he sees, as of old, the heart of a nation rise high and beat in the breast of each one of her citizens, till her safety and her honour are dearer to each than life, till to those who live her shame and sorrow, if such is allotted, outweigh their loss, and death seems a little thing to those who go for her to their common and nameless grave. And he knows that what is stronger than death is hate or love, hate here for love's sake, and that love does not fear death, because already it is the death into life of what our philosophers tell us is the only life and reality.

Yes, the state is not put together, but it lives; it is not a heap nor a machine; it is no mere extravagance when a poet talks of a nation's soul. It is the objective mind which is subjective and self-conscious in its citizens: it feels and knows itself in the heart of each. It speaks the word of command and gives the field of accomplishment, and in the activity of obedience it has and bestows individual life and satisfaction and happiness.

First in the community is the individual realized. He is here the embodiment of beauty, goodness, and truth: of truth, because he corresponds to his universal conception; of beauty, because he realizes it in a single form to the senses or imagination; of goodness, because his will expresses and is the will of the universal. . . .

Once let us take the point of view which regards the community as the real moral organism, which in its members knows and wills itself, and sees the individual to be real just so far as the universal self is in his self, as he in it, and we get the solution of most, if not all, of our previous difficulties. There is here no need to ask and by some scientific process find out what is moral, for morality exists all round us, and faces us, if need be, with a categorical imperative, while it surrounds us on the other side with an atmosphere of love.

The belief in this real moral organism is the one solution of ethical problems. It breaks down the antithesis of despotism and individualism; it denies them, while it preserves the truth of both. The truth of individualism is saved, because, unless we have intense life and self-consciousness in the members of the state, the whole state is ossified. The truth of despotism is saved, because, unless the member realizes the whole by and in himself, he fails to reach his own individuality. Considered in the main, the best communities are those which have the best men for their members, and the best men are the members of the best communities. Circle as this is, it is not a vicious circle. The two problems of the best man and best state are two sides, two distinguishable aspects of the one problem, how to realize in human nature the perfect unity of homogeneity and specification; and when we see that each of these without the other is unreal, then we see that (speaking in general) the welfare of the state and the welfare of its individuals are questions which it is mistaken and ruinous to separate. Personal morality and political and social institutions can not exist apart, and (in general) the better the one the better the other. The community is moral, because it realizes personal morality; personal morality is moral, because and in so far as it realizes the moral whole.

It is here we find a *partial* answer to the complaint of our day on the dwindling of human nature. The higher the organism (we are told), the more are its functions specified, and hence narrowed. The man becomes a machine, or the piece of a machine; and, though the world grows, 'the individual withers'. On this we may first remark that, if what is meant is that, the more centralized the system, the more narrow and monotonous is the life of the member, that is a very questionable assertion. If it be meant that the individual's life can be narrowed to 'file-packing', or the like, without detriment to the intensity of the life of the whole, that is even more questionable. If again it be meant that in many cases we have a one-sided specification, which, despite the immediate stimulus of particular function, implies ultimate loss of life to the body, that, I think, probably is so, but it is doubtful if we are compelled to think it always must be so. But the root of the whole complaint is a false view of things. . . . The moral organism is not a mere animal organism. In the latter (it is no novel remark) the member is not aware of itself as such, while in the former it knows itself, and therefore knows the whole in itself. The narrow external function of the man is not the whole man. He has a life which we can not see with our eyes; and there is no duty so mean that it is not the realization of this, and knowable as such. What counts is not the visible outer work so much as the spirit in which it is done. The breadth of my life is not measured by the multitude of my pursuits, nor the space I take up amongst other men; but by the fullness of the whole life which I know as mine. It is true that less now depends on each of us, as this or that man; it is not true that our individuality is therefore lessened, that therefore we have less in us. . . .

If a man is to know what is right, he should have imbibed by precept, and still more by example, the spirit of his community, its general and special beliefs as to right and wrong, and, with this whole embodied in his mind, should particularize it in any new case, not by a reflective deduction, but by an intuitive subsumption, which does not know that it is a subsumption; by a carrying out of the self into a new case, wherein what is before the mind is the case and not the self to be carried out, and where it is indeed the whole that feels and sees, but all that is seen is seen in the form of *this* case, *this* point, *this* instance. Precept is good, but example is better; for by a series of particulars (as such forgotten) we get the general spirit, we identify ourselves on the sides both of will and judgement with the basis, which basis (be it remembered) has not got to be explicit.

There are a number of questions which invite consideration here, but we can not stop. We wished to point out briefly the character of our common moral judgements. This (on the intellectual side) is the way in which they are ordinarily made; and, in the main, there is not much practical difficulty. What is moral *in any particular given case* is seldom doubtful. Society pronounces beforehand; or, after some one course has been taken, it can say whether it was right or not; though society can not generalize much, and, if asked to reflect, is helpless and becomes incoherent. But I do not say there are no cases where the morally-minded man has to doubt; most certainly such do arise, though not so many as some people think, far fewer than some would be glad to think. A very large number arise from reflection, which wants to act from an explicit principle, and so begins to abstract and divide, and, thus becoming one-sided, makes the relative absolute. Apart from this, however, collisions must take place; and here there is no guide whatever but the intuitive judgement of oneself or others.

This intuition must not be confounded with what is sometimes mis-called 'conscience'. It is not mere individual opinion or caprice. It presupposes the morality of the community as its basis, and is subject to the approval thereof. Here, if anywhere, the idea of universal and impersonal morality is realized. For the final arbiters are the φρόνιμοι, persons with a will to do right, and not full of reflections and theories. If they fail you, you must judge for yourself, but practically they seldom do fail you. Their private peculiarities neutralize each other, and the result is an intuition which does not belong merely to this or that man or collection of men. 'Conscience' is the antipodes of this. It wants you to have no law but yourself, and to be better than the world. But this intuition tells you that, if you could be as good as your world, you would be better than most likely you are, and that to wish to be better than the world is to be already on the threshold of immorality.

This perhaps 'is a hard saying', but it is least hard to those who know life best; it is intolerable to those mainly who, from inexperience or preconceived theories, can not see the world as it is. Explained it may be by saying that enthusiasm for good dies away – the ideal fades –

> Dem Herrlichsten, was auch der Geist empfangen,
> Drängt immer fremd und fremder Stoff sich an;

but better perhaps if we say that those who have seen most of the world (not one side of it) – old people of no one-sided profession nor of immoral life – know most also how much good there is in it. They are tolerant of new theories and youthful opinions that everything would be better upside down, because they know that this also is as it should be, and that the world gets good even from these. They are intolerant only of those who are old enough, and should be wise enough, to know better than that they know better than the world; for in such people they can not help seeing the self-conceit which is pardonable only in youth.

Let us be clear. What is that wish to be better, and to make the world better, which is on the threshold of immorality? What is the 'world' in this sense? It is the morality already existing ready to hand in laws, institutions, social usages, moral opinions and feelings. This is the element in which the young are brought up. It has given moral content to themselves, and it is the only source of such content. It is not wrong, it is a duty, to take the best that there is, and to live up to the best. It is not wrong, it is a duty, standing on the basis of the existing, and in harmony with its general spirit, to try and make not only oneself but also the world better, or rather, and in preference, one's own world better. But it is another thing, starting from oneself, from ideals in one's head, to set oneself and them against the moral world. The moral world with its social institutions, &c., is a fact; it is real; our 'ideals' are not real. 'But we will make them real.' We should consider what we are, and what the world is. We should learn to see the great moral fact in the world, and to reflect on the likelihood of our private 'ideal' being anything more than an abstraction, which, because an abstraction, is all the better fitted for our heads, and all the worse fitted for actual existence.

We should consider whether the encouraging oneself in having opinions of one's own, in the sense of thinking differently from the world on moral subjects, be not, in any person other than a heaven-born prophet, sheer self-conceit. And though the disease may spend itself in the harmless and even entertaining sillinesses by which we are advised to assert our social 'individuality', yet still the having theories of one's own in the face of the world is not far from having practice in the same direction; and if the latter is (as it often must be) immorality, the former has certainly but stopped at the threshold.

But the moral organism is strong against both. The person anxious to throw off the yoke of custom and develop his 'individuality' in startling directions, passes as a rule into the common Philistine, and learns that Philistinism is after all a good thing. And the licentious young man, anxious for pleasure at any price, who, without troubling himself about 'principles', does put into practice the principles of the former person, finds after all that the self within him can be satisfied only with that from whence it came. And some fine morning the dream is gone, the enchanted bower is a hideous phantasm, and the despised and common reality has become the ideal.

We have thus seen the community to be the real moral idea, to be stronger than the theories and the practice of its members against it, and to give us self-realization. And this is indeed limitation; it bids us say farewell to visions of superhuman morality, to ideal societies, and to practical 'ideals' generally. But perhaps the unlimited is not the perfect, nor the true ideal. And, leaving 'ideals' out of sight, it is quite clear that if anybody wants to realize himself as a perfect man without trying to be a perfect member of his country and all his smaller communities, he makes what all sane persons would admit to be a great mistake. There is no more fatal enemy than theories which are not also facts; and when people inveigh against the vulgar antithesis of the two, they themselves should accept their own doctrine, and give up the harbouring of theories of what should be and is not. Until they do that, the vulgar are in the right; for a theory of that which (only) is to be, is a theory of that which in fact is not, and that I suppose is only a theory.

There is nothing better than my station and its duties, nor anything higher or more truly beautiful. It holds and will hold its own against the worship of the 'individual', whatever form that may take. It is strong against frantic theories and vehement passions, and in the end it triumphs over the fact, and can smile at the literature, even of sentimentalism, however fulsome in its impulsive setting out, or sour in its disappointed end. It laughs at its frenzied apotheosis of the yet unsatisfied passion it calls love; and at that embitterment too which has lost its illusions, and yet can not let them go – with its kindness for the genius too clever in general to do anything in particular, and its adoration of stargazing virgins with souls above their spheres, whose wish to be something in the world takes the form of wanting to do something with it, and who in the end do badly what they might have done in the beginning well; and, worse than all, its cynical contempt for what deserves only pity, sacrifice of a life for work to the best of one's lights, a sacrifice despised not simply because it has failed, but because it is stupid, and uninteresting, and altogether unsentimental.

And all these books (ah! how many) it puts into the one scale, and with them the writers of them; and into the other scale it puts three such lines as these:

> One place performs like any other place
> The proper service every place on earth
> Was framed to furnish man with. . . .

Notes

1. Marriage is a contract, a contract to pass out of the sphere of contract; and this is possible only because the contracting parties are already beyond and above the sphere of mere contract.

4
G.K. Chesterton

Gilbert Keith Chesterton (1874–1936) is chiefly known as a novelist, poet and literary critic. His essays on social and political themes are written with great vivacity and distinction, and contain striking and original formulations of his distinctive viewpoint. Some hold that they lack philosophical depth; others commend them for their strange combination of foolery and seriousness.

Chesterton was a powerful expositor of the old values of Christendom, which he delivered to the modern world with wit and conviction. He was also an ardent critic of socialism, and especially of the snobbish, self-intoxicated socialism, as he saw it, of the Fabians. He was sceptical of 'capitalism', which he believed to be a social and spiritual disease – socialism being merely the substitution of another disease, equally disastrous. He described himself as believing in Liberalism, adding, however, that 'there was a rosy time when I believed in Liberals'. It would be more reasonable, in retrospect, to describe Chesterton as a conservative, for it is among conservatives that his influence has been most pronounced.

Chesterton married, becoming notoriously fat and famously eccentric. His success as a writer matched that of his rival, G.B. Shaw, with whom he shared many stylistic mannerisms – including an opinionated tone, an affectation of common sense, and an effrontery which lent zest to his love of paradox. Chesterton was received into the Roman Catholic Church in 1922, so completing a spiritual journey begun in 1908, with Orthodoxy *– described by Chesterton as 'a sort of slovenly autobiography' – from which the following extract is taken.*

. . . the principle of democracy, as I mean it, can be stated in two propositions. The first is this: that the things common to all men are more important than the things peculiar to any men. Ordinary things are more valuable than extraordinary things; nay, they are more extraordinary. Man is something more awful than men; something more strange. The sense of the miracle of humanity itself should be always more vivid to us than any marvels of power, intellect, art, or civilization. The mere man on two legs, as such, should be felt as something more heartbreaking than any music and more startling than any caricature. Death is more tragic even than death by starvation. Having a nose is more comic even than having a Norman nose.

This is the first principle of democracy: that the essential things in men are the things they hold in common, not the things they hold separately. And the second principle is merely this: that the political instinct or desire is one of these things which they hold in common. Falling in love is more poetical than dropping into poetry. The democratic contention is that government (helping to rule the tribe) is a thing like falling in love, and not a thing like dropping into poetry. It is not something analogous to playing the church organ, painting on vellum, discovering the North Pole (that insidious habit), looping the loop, being Astronomer Royal, and so on. For these things we do not wish a man to do at all unless he does them well. It is, on the contrary, a thing analogous to writing one's own love-letters or blowing one's own nose. These things we want a man to do for himself, even if he does them badly. I am not here arguing the truth of any of these conceptions; I know that some moderns are asking to have their wives chosen by scientists, and they may soon be asking, for all I know, to have their noses blown by nurses. I merely say that mankind does recognize these universal human functions, and that democracy classes government among them. In short, the democratic faith is this: that the most terribly important things must be left to ordinary men themselves – the mating of the sexes, the rearing of the young, the laws of the state. This is democracy; and in this I have always believed.

But there is one thing that I have never from my youth up been able to understand. I have never been able to understand where people got the idea that democracy was in some way opposed to tradition. It is obvious that tradition is only democracy extended through time. It is trusting to a consensus of common human voices rather than to some isolated or arbitrary record. The man who quotes some German historian against the tradition of the Catholic Church, for instance, is strictly appealing to aristocracy. He is appealing to the superiority of one expert against the awful authority of a mob. It is quite easy to see why a legend is treated, and ought to be treated, more respectfully than a book of history. The legend is generally made by the majority of people in the village, who are sane. The book is generally written by the one man in the village who is mad. Those who urge against tradition that men in the past were ignorant may go and urge it at the Carlton Club, along with the statement that voters in the slums are ignorant. It will not do for us. If we attach great importance to the opinion of ordinary men in great unanimity when we are dealing with daily matters, there is no reason why we should disregard it when we are dealing with history or fable. Tradition may be defined as an extension of the franchise. Tradition means giving votes to the most obscure of all classes, our ancestors. It is the democracy of the dead. Tradition refuses to submit to the small and arrogant oligarchy of those who merely happen to be walking about. All democrats object to men being disqualified by the accident of birth; tradition objects to their being disqualified by the accident of death. Democracy tells us not to neglect a good man's opinion, even if he is our groom; tradition asks us not to neglect a good man's opinion, even if he is our father. I, at any rate, cannot separate the two ideas of democracy and tradition; it seems evident to me that they are the same idea. We will have the dead at our councils. The ancient Greeks voted by stones; these shall vote by tombstones. It is all quite regular and official, for most tombstones, like most ballot papers, are marked with a cross.

I have first to say, therefore, that if I have had a bias, it was always a bias in favour of democracy, and therefore of tradition. Before we come to any theoretic or logical beginnings I am content to allow for that personal equation; I have always been more inclined to believe the ruck of hard-working people than to believe that special and troublesome literary class to which I belong. I prefer even the fancies and prejudices of the people who see life from the inside to the clearest demonstrations of the people who see life from the outside. I would always trust the old wives' fables against the old maids' facts. As long as wit is mother wit it can be as wild as it pleases.

Now, I have to put together a general position, and I pretend to no training in such things. I propose to do it, therefore, by writing down one after another the three or four fundamental ideas which I have found for myself, pretty much in the way that I found them. Then I shall roughly synthesise them, summing up my personal philosophy or natural religion; then I shall describe my startling discovery that the whole thing had been discovered before. It had been discovered by Christianity. But of these profound persuasions which I have to recount in order, the earliest was concerned with this element of popular tradition. And without the foregoing explanation touching tradition and democracy I could hardly make my mental experience clear. As it is, I do not know whether I can make it clear, but I now propose to try. . . .

5
Samuel Taylor Coleridge

Samuel Taylor Coleridge (1772–1834), the son of a country vicar, was educated at Christ's Hospital, and at Jesus College, Cambridge. His career at Cambridge was interrupted by a short and unexplained spell in the 15th Dragoons, in which he enlisted, but from which he was discharged after a few months. Together with Robert Southey he dreamed up the utopian principles of 'Pantisocracy' – an extreme egalitarianism, from the lure of which Coleridge subsequently retrieved himself. He married in 1795, and in the same year met Wordsworth, together with whom he published Lyrical Ballads (1798), containing Coleridge's 'Rime of the Ancient Mariner'.

Coleridge visited Germany in 1798–9, was an enthusiast for Kant and Schelling, and endeavoured in his later writings to introduce German philosophy to the English public. Under the combined influence of that philosophy and the writings of Burke, Coleridge became a spokesman for constitutional, anti-Revolutionary politics, and endeavoured to combine his attack on individualism with an articulate defence of English institutions and the Anglican heritage. Coleridge introduced conservatism as an attitude to culture, and was the first in the long line of 'cultural conservatives', among whom should be numbered John Ruskin, Matthew Arnold, T.S. Eliot, F.R. Leavis and Russell Kirk. His most important political thinking is contained in On the Constitution of Church and State (1830), from the 1852 edition of which the following extracts are taken.

Every reader of Rousseau, or of Hume's Essays, will understand me when I refer to the original social contract assumed by Rousseau, and by other and wiser men before him, as the basis of all legitimate government. Now, if this be taken as the assertion of an historical fact, or as the application of a conception, generalised from ordinary compacts between man and man, or nation and nation, to an alleged actual occurrence in the first ages of the world; namely, the formation of a first contract, in which men should have covenanted with each other to associate, or in which a multitude should have entered into a compact with a few, the one to be governed and the other to govern under certain declared conditions; I shall run little hazard at this time of day in declaring the pretended fact a pure fiction, and the conception of such a fact an idle fancy. It is at once false and foolish.[1] For what if an original contract had actually been entered into and formally recorded? Still I cannot see what addition of moral force would be gained by the fact. The same sense of moral obligation which binds us to keep it, must have pre-existed in the same force and in relation to the same duties, impelling our ancestors to make it. For what could it do more than bind the contracting parties to act for the general good, according to their best lights and opportunities? It is evident that no specific scheme or constitution can derive any other claim to our reverence, than that which the presumption of its necessity or fitness for the general good shall give it; and which claim of course ceases, or rather is reversed, as soon as this general presumption of its utility has given place to as general a conviction of the contrary. It is true, indeed, that from duties anterior to the formation of the contract, because they arise out of the very constitution of our humanity, which supposes the social state – it is true, that in order to a rightful removal of the institution or law thus agreed on, it is required that the conviction of its inexpediency shall be as general as the presumption of its fitness was at the time of its establishment. This, the first of the two great paramount interests of the social state, that of permanence, demands; but to attribute more than this to any fundamental articles, passed into law by any assemblage of individuals, is an injustice to their successors, and a high offence against the other great interest of the social state, namely, its progressive improvement. The conception, therefore, of an original contract, is, I repeat, incapable of historic proof as a fact, and it is senseless as a theory.

But if instead of the conception or theory of an original social contract, we say the idea of an ever-originating social contract, this is so certain and so indispensable, that it constitutes the whole ground of the difference between subject and serf, between a commonwealth and a slave plantation. And this, again, is evolved out of the yet higher idea of person in contra-distinction to thing; all social law and justice being grounded on the principle that a person can never, but by his own fault, become a thing, or, without grievous wrong, be treated as such; and the distinction consisting in this, that a thing may be used altogether and merely as the means to an end; but the person must always be included in the end; his interest must form a part of the object, a means to which he by consent, that is, by his own act, makes himself. We plant a tree and we fell it; we breed the sheep and we shear or we kill it; in both cases wholly as means to our ends; for trees and animals are things. The wood-cutter and the hind are likewise employed as means, but on agreement, and that too an agreement of reciprocal advantage, which includes them as well as their employer in the end; for they are persons. And the government, under which the contrary takes place, is not worthy to be called a state, if, as in the kingdom of Dahomey, it be unprogressive; or only by anticipation, where, as in Russia, it is in advance to a better and more man-worthy order of things. Now, notwithstanding the late wonderful spread of learning through the community, and though the schoolmaster and the lecturer are abroad, the hind and the woodman may, very conceivably, pass from cradle to coffin without having once contemplated this idea, so as to be conscious of the same. And there would be even an improbability in the supposition that they possessed the power of presenting this idea to the minds of others, or even to their own thoughts, verbally as a distinct proposition. But no man, who has ever listened to labourers of this rank, in any alehouse, over the Saturday night's jug of beer, discussing the injustice of the present rate of wages, and the iniquity of their being paid in part out of the parish poor-rates, will doubt for a moment that they are fully possessed by the idea.

In close, though not perhaps obvious, connection with this is the idea of moral freedom, as the ground of our proper responsibility. Speak to a young Liberal, fresh from Edinburgh or Hackney or the hospitals, of free-will as implied in free-agency, he will perhaps confess with a smile that he is a necessitarian, – proceed to assure his hearer that the liberty of the will is an impossible conception, a contradiction in terms,[2] and finish by recommending a perusal of the works of Jonathan Edwards or Dr. Crombie; or as it may happen he may declare the will itself a mere delusion, a nonentity, and advise the study of Mr. Lawrence's Lectures. Converse on the same subject with a plain, single-minded, yet reflecting, neighbour, and he may probably say, (as St. Augustine had said long before him, in reply to the question, What is time?) 'I know it well enough when you do not ask me.' But alike with both the supposed parties, the self-complacent student, just as certainly as with our less positive neighbour; if we attend to their actions, their feelings, and even to their words, we shall be in ill luck, if ten minutes pass without having full and satisfactory proof that the idea of man's moral freedom possesses and modifies their whole practical being, in all they say, in all they feel, in all they do and are done to; even as the spirit of life, which is contained in no vessel, because it permeates all.

Just so is it with the Constitution.[3] Ask any of our politicians what is meant by the Constitution, and it is ten to one that he will give a false explanation; as for example, that it is the body of our laws, or that it is the Bill of Rights; or perhaps, if he have read Thomas Paine, he may say that we do not yet possess one; and yet not an hour may have elapsed, since we heard the same individual denouncing, and possibly with good reason, this or that code of laws, the excise and revenue laws, or those for including peasants, or those for excluding Roman Catholics, as altogether unconstitutional; and such and such acts of Parliament as gross outrages on the Constitution. Mr. Peel, who is rather remarkable for groundless and unlucky concessions, owned that the late Act broke in on the Constitution of 1688: whilst in 1689 a very imposing minority of the then House of Lords, with a decisive majority in the Lower House of Convocation, denounced this very Constitution of 1688, as breaking in on the English Constitution.

But a Constitution is an idea arising out of the idea of a State; and because our whole history from Alfred onwards demonstrates the continued influence of such an idea, or ultimate aim, on the minds of our forefathers, in their characters and functions as public men, alike in what they resisted and in what they claimed; in the institutions and forms of polity, which they established, and with regard to those against which they more or less successfully contended; and because the result has been a progressive, though not always a direct or equable, advance in the gradual realisation of the idea; and because it is actually, though even because it is an idea not adequately, represented in a correspondent scheme of means really existing; we speak, and have a right to speak, of the idea itself, as actually existing, that is, as a principle existing in the only way in which a principle can exist, – in the minds and consciences of the persons whose duties it prescribes, and whose rights it determines. In the same sense that the sciences of arithmetic and of geometry, that mind, that life itself, have reality; the Constitution has real existence, and does not the less exist in reality, because it both is, and exists as, an idea. . . .

Now, in every country of civilised men, acknowledging the rights of property, and by means of determined boundaries and common laws united into one people or nation, the two antagonist powers or opposite interests of the State, under which all other state interests are comprised, are those of permanence and of progression.

It will not be necessary to enumerate the several causes that combine to connect the permanence of a state with the land and the landed property. To found a family, and to convert his wealth into land, are twin thoughts, births of the same moment, in the mind of the opulent merchant, when he thinks of reposing from his labours. From the class of the *novi homines* he redeems himself by becoming the staple ring of the chain, by which the present will become connected with the past, and the test and evidence of permanency be afforded. To the same principle appertain primogeniture and hereditary titles, and the influence which these exert in accumulating large masses of property, and in counteracting the antagonist and dispersive forces, which the follies, the vices, and misfortunes of individuals can scarely fail to supply. To this, likewise, tends the proverbial obduracy of prejudices characteristic of the humbler tillers of the soil, and their aversion even to benefits that are offered in the form of innovations. But why need I attempt to explain a fact which no thinking man will deny, and where the admission of the fact is all that my argument requires?

On the other hand, with as little chance of contradiction, I may assert that the progression of a State in the arts and comforts of life, in the diffusion of the information and knowledge, useful or necessary for all; in short, all advances in civilisation, and the rights and privileges of citizens, are especially connected with, and derived from, the four classes, the mercantile, the manufacturing, the distributive, and the professional. . . .

THE ROLE OF THE STATE

The chief object for which men, who from the beginning existed as a social band, first formed themselves into a state, and on the social super-induced the political relation, was not the protection of their lives but of their property. The natural man is too proud an animal to admit that he needs any other protection for his life than what his own courage and that of his clan can bestow. Where the nature of the soil and climate has precluded all property but personal, and admitted that only in its simplest forms, as in Greenland for instance, – there men remain in the domestic state and form neighbourhoods, not governments. And in North America the chiefs appear to exercise government in those tribes only which possess individual landed property. Among the rest the chief is the general, a leader in war; not a magistrate. To property and to its necessary inequalities must be referred all human laws, that would not be laws without and independent of any conventional enactment; that is, all State-legislation.

Next comes the King, as the head of the National Church or Clerisy, and the protector and supreme trustee of the Nationality: the power of the same in relation to its proper objects being exercised by the King and the Houses of Convocation, of which, as before of the State, the King is the head and arm. . . .

And if superior talents, and the mere possession of knowledges, such as can be learned at Mechanics' Institutions, were regularly accompanied with a will in harmony with the reason, and a consequent subordination of the appetites and passions to the ultimate ends of our being; – if intellectual gifts and attainments were infallible signs of wisdom and goodness in the same proportion, and the knowing and clever were always rational; – if the mere facts of science conferred or superseded the softening humanising influences of the moral world, that habitual presence of the beautiful or the seemly, and that exemption from all familiarity with the gross, the mean, and the disorderly, whether in look or language, or in the surrounding objects, in which the main efficacy of a liberal education consists; – and if, lastly, these requirements and powers of the understanding could be shared equally by the whole class, and did not, as by a necessity of nature they ever must do, fall to the lot of two or three in each several group, club, or neighbourhood; – then, indeed, by an enlargement of the Chinese system, political power might not unwisely be conferred as the *honorarium* or privilege on having passed through all the forms in the national schools, without the security of political ties, without those fastenings and radical fibres of a collective and registrable property, by which the citizens inheres in and belongs to the commonwealth, as a constituent part either of the Proprietage, or of the Nationality; either of the State or of the National Church. But as the contrary of all these suppositions may be more safely assumed, the practical conclusion will be – not that the requisite means of intellectual development and growth should be withholden from any native of the soil, which it was at all times wicked to wish, and which it would be now silly to attempt; but that the gifts of the understanding, whether the boon of a genial nature, or the reward of more persistent application, should be allowed fair play in the acquiring of that proprietorship, to which a certain portion of political power belongs as its proper function. For in this way there is at least a strong probability that intellectual power will be armed with political power, only where it has previously been combined with and guarded by the moral qualities of prudence, industry, and self-control. . . .

THE ROLE OF THE CHURCH

I respect the talents of many, and the motives and character of some, among you too sincerely to court the scorn which I anticipate. But neither shall the fear of it prevent me from declaring aloud, and as a truth which I hold it the disgrace and calamity of a professed statesman not to know and acknowledge, that a permanent, nationalised, learned order, a national clerisy or Church is an essential element of a rightly constituted nation, without which it wants the best security alike for its permanence and its progression; and for which neither tract societies nor conventicles, nor Lancasterian schools, nor mechanics' institutions, nor lecture bazaars under the absurd name of universities, nor all these collectively, can be a substitute. For they are all marked with the same asterisk of spuriousness, show the same distemper-spot on the front, that they are empirical specifics for morbid symptoms that help to feed and continue the disease.

But you wish for general illumination: you would spur-arm the toes of society: you would enlighten the higher ranks *per ascensum ab imis*? You begin, therefore, with the attempt to popularise science: but you will only effect its plebification. It is folly to think of making all, or the many, philosophers, or even men of science and systematic knowledge. But it is duty and wisdom to aim at making as many as possible soberly and steadily religious; inasmuch as the morality which the State requires in its citizens for its own well-being and ideal immortality, and without reference to their spiritual interest as individuals, can only exist for the people in the form of religion. But the existence of a true philosophy, or the power and habit of contemplating particulars in the unity and fontal mirror of the idea, – this in the rulers and teachers of a nation is indispensable to a sound state of religion in all classes. In fine, religion, true or false, is and ever has been the centre of gravity in a realm, to which all other things must and will accommodate themselves.

Notes

1. I am not indeed certain that some operational farce, under the name of a social contract or compact, may not have been acted by the Illuminati and constitution-manufacturers at the close of the eighteenth century; a period which how far it deserved the name, so complacently affixed to it by contemporaries, of 'this enlightened age,' may be doubted. That it was an age of enlighteners no man will deny.
2. In fact, this is one of the distinguishing characters of ideas, and marks at once the difference between an idea (a truth-power of the reason) and a conception of the understanding; namely, that the former, as expressed in words, is always, and necessarily, a contradiction in terms.
3. I do not say, with the idea: for the Constitution itself is an idea. This will sound like a paradox or a sneer to those with whom an idea is but another word for a fancy, a something unreal; but not to those who in the ideas contemplate the most real of all realities, and of all operative powers the most actual.

6

Benjamin Disraeli

Benjamin Disraeli (1804–81) was the eldest son of Isaac D'Israeli, the man of letters, who, although of Jewish extraction, had caused the young Benjamin to be baptised into the Anglican Church. Disraeli is best known as the foremost Tory statesman of his day, friend of Queen Victoria (who created him Earl of Beaconsfield), and a novelist of considerable talent, who published his first novel, Vivian Gray, *at the age of 22.*

Much of Disraeli's social and political thinking in fact occurs in the course of his fictional works – notably in Coningsby *(1844) and* Sybil *(1845), in the latter of which Disraeli expounds his celebrated vision of industrial Britain, as sundered into 'Two Nations'. Disraeli also wrote a* Vindication of the English Constitution *(1835), and – in a series of addresses and speeches, from which the following extracts are taken – endeavoured to recast the conservative principles of Edmund Burke as a philosophy for a democratic age. Although not a thinker of the first rank, Disraeli is unique among conservative intellectuals, in having occupied the summit of politics in the world's most powerful state, at a time when the battle between conservatism and socialism was just beginning to acquire its modern contours. The extracts are from 'Speech on Conservative and Liberal Principles' of June 1872, published in* Selected Speeches *of the Earl of Beaconsfield, Vol. II, ed. by T.E. Kebbel (London: Longmans Green, 1882).*

. . . I have always been of opinion that the Tory party has three great objects. The first is to maintain the institutions of the country – not from any sentiment of political superstition, but because we believe that they embody the principles upon which a community like England can alone safely rest. The principles of liberty, of order, of law, and of religion ought not to be entrusted to individual opinion or to the caprice and passion of multitudes, but should be embodied in a form of permanence and power. We associate with the Monarchy the ideas which it represents – the majesty of law, the administration of justice, the fountain of mercy and of honour. We know that in the Estates of the Realm and the privileges they enjoy, is the best security for public liberty and good government. We believe that a national profession of faith can only be maintained by an Established Church, and that no society is safe unless there is a public recognition of the Providential government of the world, and of the future responsibility of man. Well, it is a curious circumstance that during all these same forty years of triumphant Liberalism, every one of these institutions has been attacked and assailed – I say, continuously attacked and assailed. And what, gentlemen, has been the result? For the last forty years the most depreciating comparisons have been instituted between the Sovereignty of England and the Sovereignty of a great Republic. We have been called upon in every way, in Parliament, in the Press, by articles in newspapers, by pamphlets, by every means which can influence opinion, to contrast the simplicity and economy of the Sovereignty of the United States with the cumbrous cost of the Sovereignty of England.

Gentlemen, I need not in this company enter into any vindication of the Sovereignty of England on that head. I have recently enjoyed the opportunity, before a great assemblage of my countrymen, of speaking upon that subject. I have made statements with respect to it which have not been answered either on this side of the Atlantic or the other. Only six months ago the advanced guard of Liberalism, acting in entire unison with that spirit of assault upon the Monarchy which the literature and the political confederacies of Liberalism have for forty years encouraged, flatly announced itself as Republican, and appealed to the people of England on that distinct issue. Gentlemen, what was the answer? I need not dwell upon it. It is fresh in your memories and hearts. The people of England have expressed, in a manner which cannot be mistaken, that they will uphold the ancient Monarchy of England, the Constitutional Monarchy of England, limited by the co-ordinate authority of the Estates of the Realm, but limited by nothing else. Now, if you consider the state of public opinion with regard to those Estates of the Realm, what do you find? Take the case of the House of Lords. The House of Lords has been assailed during this reign of Liberalism in every manner and unceasingly. Its constitution has been denounced as anomalous, its influence declared pernicious; but what has been the result of this assault and criticism of forty years? Why, the people of England, in my opinion, have discovered that the existence of a second Chamber is necessary to Constitutional Government; and, while necessary to Constitutional Government, is, at the same time, of all political inventions the most difficult. Therefore, the people of this country have congratulated themselves that, by the aid of an ancient and famous history, there has been developed in this country an Assembly which possesses all the virtues which a Senate should possess – independence, great local influence, eloquence, all the accomplishments of political life, and a public training which no theory could supply.

The assault of Liberalism upon the House of Lords has been mainly occasioned by the prejudice of Liberalism against the land laws of this country. But in my opinion, and in the opinion of wiser men than myself, and of men in other countries beside this, the liberty of England depends much upon the landed tenure of England – upon the fact that there is a class which can alike defy despots and mobs, around which the people may always rally, and which must be patriotic from its intimate connection with the soil. Well, gentlemen, so far as these institutions of the country – the Monarchy and the Lords Spiritual and Temporal – are concerned, I think we may fairly say, without exaggeration, that public opinion is in favour of those institutions, the maintenance of which is one of the principal tenets of the Tory party, and the existence of which has been unceasingly criticised for forty years by the Liberal party. Now, let me say a word about the other Estate of the Realm, which was first attacked by Liberalism.

One of the most distinguishing features of the great change effected in 1832 was that those who brought it about at once abolished all the franchises of the working classes. They were franchises as ancient as those of the Baronage of England: and, while they abolished them, they proposed no substitute. The discontent upon the subject of the representation which has from that time more or less pervaded our society dates from that period, and that discontent, all will admit, has now ceased. It was terminated by the Act of Parliamentary Reform of 1867–8. That Act was founded on a confidence that the great body of the people of this country were 'Conservative.' When I say 'Conservative,' I use the word in its purest and loftiest sense. I mean that the people of England, and especially the working classes of England, are proud of belonging to a great country, and wish to maintain its greatness – that they are proud of belonging to an Imperial country, and are resolved to maintain, if they can, their empire – that they believe, on the whole, that the greatness and the empire of England are to be attributed to the ancient institutions of the land. . . .

I say with confidence that the great body of the working class of England utterly repudiate such sentiments. They have no sympathy with them. They are English to the core. They repudiate cosmopolitan principles. They adhere to national principles. They are for maintaining the greatness of the kingdom and the empire, and they are proud of being subjects of our Sovereign and members of such an Empire. Well, then, as regards the political institutions of this country, the maintenance of which is one of the chief tenets of the Tory party, so far as I can read public opinion, the feeling of the nation is in accordance with the Tory party. It was not always so. There was a time when the institutions of this country were decried. They have passed through a scathing criticism of forty years: they have passed through that criticism when their political upholders have, generally speaking, been always in opposition. They have been upheld by us when we were unable to exercise any of the lures of power to attract force to us, and the people of this country have arrived at these conclusions from their own thought and their own experience.

Let me say one word upon another institution, the position of which is most interesting at this time. No institution of England, since the advent of Liberalism, has been so systematically, so continuously assailed as the Established Church. Gentlemen, we were first told that the Church was asleep, and it is very possible, as everybody, civil and spiritual, was asleep forty years ago, that that might have been the case. Now we are told that the Church is too active, and that it will be destroyed by its internal restlessness and energy. I see in all these efforts of the Church to represent every mood of the spiritual mind of man, no evidence that it will fall, no proof that any fatal disruption is at hand. I see in the Church, as I believe I see in England, an immense effort to rise to national feelings and recur to national principles. The Church of England, like all our institutions, feels it must be national, and it knows that, to be national, it must be comprehensive. Gentlemen, I have referred to what I look upon as the first object of the Tory party – namely, to maintain the institutions of the country, and reviewing what has occurred, and referring to the present temper of the times upon these subjects, I think that the Tory party, or, as I will venture to call it, the National party, has everything to encourage it. I think that the nation, tested by many and severe trials, has arrived at the conclusion which we have always maintained, that it is the first duty of England to maintain its institutions, because to them we principally ascribe the power and prosperity of the country.

Gentlemen, there is another and second great object of the Tory party. If the first is to maintain the institutions of the country, the second is, in my opinion, to uphold the Empire of England. If you look to the history of this country since the advent of Liberalism – forty years ago – you will find that there has been no effort so continuous, so subtle, supported by so much energy, and carried on with so much ability and acumen, as the attempts of Liberalism to effect the disintegration of the Empire of England. . . .

Gentlemen, another great object of the Tory party, and one not inferior to the maintenance of the Empire, or the upholding of our institutions, is the elevation of the condition of the people. Let us see in this great struggle between Toryism and Liberalism that has prevailed in this country during the last forty years what are the salient features. It must be obvious to all who consider the condition of the multitude with a desire to improve and elevate it, that no important step can be gained unless you can effect some reduction of their hours of labour and humanise their toil. The great problem is to be able to achieve such results without violating those principles of economic truth upon which the prosperity of all States depends. You recollect well that many years ago the Tory party believed that these two results might be obtained – that you might elevate the condition of the people by the reduction of their toil and the mitigation of their labour, and at the same time inflict no injury on the wealth of the nation. You know how that effort was encountered – how these views and principles were met by the triumphant statesmen of Liberalism. They told you that the inevitable consequence of your policy was to diminish capital, that this, again, would lead to the lowering of wages, to a great diminution of the employment of the people, and ultimately to the impoverishment of the kingdom.

These were not merely the opinions of Ministers of State, but those of the most blatant and loud-mouthed leaders of the Liberal party. And what has been the result? Those measures were carried, but carried, as I can bear witness, with great difficulty and after much labour and a long struggle. Yet they were carried; and what do we now find? That capital was never accumulated so quickly, that wages were never higher, that the employment of the people was never greater, and the country never wealthier. I ventured to say a short time ago, speaking in one of the great cities of this country, that the health of the people was the most important question for a statesman. It is, gentlemen, a large subject. It has many branches. It involves the state of the dwellings of the people, the moral consequences of which are not less considerable than the physical. It involves their enjoyment of some of the chief elements of nature – air, light, and water. It involves the regulation of their industry, the inspection of their toil. It involves the purity of their provisions, and it touches upon all the means by which you may wean them from habits of excess and of brutality. Now, what is the feeling upon these subjects of the Liberal party – that Liberal party who opposed the Tory party when, even in their weakness, they advocated a diminution of the toil of the people, and introduced and supported those Factory Laws, the principles of which they extended, in the brief period when they possessed power, to every other trade in the country? What is the opinion of the great Liberal party – the party that seeks to substitute cosmopolitan for national principles in the government of this country – on this subject? Why, the views which I expressed in the great capital of the country of Lancaster have been held up to derision by the Liberal Press. A leading member – a very rising member, at least, among the new Liberal members – denounced them the other day as the 'policy of sewage.'

Well, it may be the 'policy of sewage' to a Liberal member of Parliament. But to one of the labouring multitude of England, who has found fever always to be one of the inmates of his household – who has, year after year, seen stricken down the children of his loins, on whose sympathy and material support he has looked with hope and confidence, it is not a 'policy of sewage,' but a question of life and death. And I can tell you this, gentlemen, from personal conversation with some of the most intelligent of the labouring class – and I think there are many of them in this room who can bear witness to what I say – that the policy of the Tory party – the hereditary, the traditionary policy of the Tory party, that would improve the condition of the people – is more appreciated by the people than the ineffable mysteries and all the pains and penalties of the Ballot Bill. Gentlemen, is that wonderful? Consider the condition of the great body of the working classes of this country. They are in possession of personal privileges – of personal rights and liberties – which are not enjoyed by the aristocracies of other countries. Recently they have obtained – and wisely obtained – a great extension of political rights; and when the people of England see that under the constitution of this country, by means of the constitutional cause which my right honourable friend the Lord Mayor has proposed, they possess every personal right of freedom, and, according to the conviction of the whole country, also an adequate concession of political rights, is it at all wonderful that they should wish to elevate and improve their condition, and is it unreasonable that they should ask the Legislature to assist them in that behest as far as it is consistent with the general welfare of the realm?

Why, the people of England would be greater idiots than the Jacobinical leaders of London even suppose, if, with their experience and acuteness, they should not long have seen that the time had arrived when social, and not political improvement is the object which they ought to pursue. I have touched, gentlemen, on the three great objects of the Tory party. I told you I would try to ascertain what was the position of the Tory party with reference to the country now. I have told you also with frankness what I believe the position of the Liberal party to be. Notwithstanding their proud position, I believe they are viewed by the country with mistrust and repugnance. But on all the three great objects which are sought by Toryism – the maintenence of our institutions, the preservation of our Empire, and the improvement of the condition of the people – I find a rising opinion in the country sympathising with our tenets, and prepared, I believe, if the opportunity offers, to uphold them until they prevail. . . .

7
Max Eastman

Max Eastman (1883–1969), American poet, critic and social thinker, began his literary career as an ardent radical of the left. His journal, Masses, *was closed down under the US Sedition Act for its opposition to the First World War, while its successor* The Liberator *(which he edited in conjunction with his sister, Crystal) preached the cause of revolution with as great a fervour as the American constitution permitted. During two years in the Soviet Union, from 1922 to 1924, he became friendly with Trotsky, whom he later defended against Stalin, for which error, and for his publication of Lenin's testament warning against Stalin, he was boycotted by the New York intelligentsia. Gradually becoming disillusioned, not only with Stalinism, but with the whole revolutionary experiment, he began to marshal the arguments against socialism in three trenchantly argued books:* Stalin's Russia and the Crisis in Socialism *(1939),* Marxism, Is It a Science? *(1940) and* Reflections on the Failure of Socialism *(1955), from which the following extracts are taken. By the time of the publication of this last work, Eastman was describing himself as a 'conservative'; and although his arguments are far from original – being contained, for the most part, in L. von Mises's* Socialism *(1921) – they are expounded with a freshness and synoptic power that have caused them to have considerable influence. I include them, partly because they provide a useful summary of thoughts which are more diffusely expressed in the writings of the Austrian economists; partly because they give a fair illustration of the current of ideas which retrieved the American intelligentsia in the forties and fifties from the grip of socialist ideology.*

It is the bureaucratic socializers – if I may devise that label for the champions of a lawyer-manager-politician-intellectual revolution – who constitute a real and subtle threat to America's democracy. It is their dream that is moving into focus as that of Lenin grows dim.

The assumption common to these two dreams is that society can be made more free and equal, and incidentally more orderly and prosperous, by a state apparatus which takes charge of the economy, and runs it according to a plan. And this assumption, through alluringly plausible, does not happen to be true. A state apparatus which plans and runs the business of a country must have the authority of a business executive. And that is the authority to tell all those active in the business where to go and what to do, and if they are insubordinate put them out. It must be an authoritarian state apparatus. It may not want to be, but the economy will go haywire if it is not. . . .

A false and undeliberated conception of what man is lies at the bottom, I think, of the whole bubble-castle of socialist theory. Although few seem to realize it, Marxism rests on the romantic notion of Rousseau that nature endows men with the qualities necessary to a free, equal, fraternal, family-like living together, and our sole problem is to fix up the external conditions. All Marx did about this with his dialectic philosophy was to change the tenses in the romance: Nature *will* endow men with these qualities *as soon as* the conditions are fixed up. Because of his stress upon economic conditions, Marx is commonly credited with the cynical opinion that economic self-interest is dominant in human nature. Marx was far from a cynic about human nature. He believed that human nature is a function of the economic conditions, completely variable and capable of operating, once these conditions are 'ripe,' on the divinely rational and benign principle: 'From each according to his abilities, to each according to his needs.' It was to protect this optimistic dogma about human nature that the Stalin government felt obliged to stamp out the true science of genetics. According to that science, traits acquired during the lifetime of an organism are not appreciably transmitted in heredity. Only by selective breeding, whether artificial or natural, can profound changes be made in the nature of any species. While men's acquired characters may, and undoubtedly do, change with changing economic (and other) conditions, the underlying traits of human nature remain the same. There is little doubt that the Marxian bigots in the Kremlin were moved by this consideration in liquidating the world-famous geneticist, Avilov, and supporting the charlatan, Lysenko, in popularizing a belief in the wholesale heredity of acquired characteristics. Without such belief, the whole Marxian myth that economic evolution will bring us to the millennium falls to the ground.

Once we have abandoned this myth, we can give heed to the real contribution of Karl Marx: his sense of the great part played by economic relations in determining political and cultural ways of life. His own sagacity will conduct us, then, to a genuinely scientific study of the economic foundations of political freedom. This study has been made by various economists of the 'neo-liberal' school – Wilhelm Roepke, F. A. Hayek, Ludwig von Mises and others. Taking human nature as it functions in average life, they have shown that the competitive market and the price system are the basis of whatever real political freedom exists, or can be imagined to exist, where there is an elaborate division of labour.

I am not an economist, but I have watched with some care the destinies of these men's earnest writings. There has been no answer, and I don't see how there can be an answer, to their assertion that mankind is confronted with a choice between two and only two business systems – a choice which involves the fate of democratic civilization. We can choose a system in which the amount and kind of goods produced is determined by the *impersonal* mechanism of the market, issuing its decrees in the form of fluctuating prices. Or we can choose a system in which this is determined by commands issuing from a *personal* authority backed by armed force. You cannot dodge this issue by talking about a 'mixed economy.' The economy is inevitably mixed; nobody in his right mind proposes a total abandonment of government enterprise. You can not dodge it by insisting the state must *regulate* the market or *intervene* in its operations. If carefully defined, that statement is obvious. The question is whether the economy is mixed to the point of destroying the essential directing function of the market, whether the regulations are a substitute for the market or a framework within which it shall operate, whether intervention is compatible or incompatible with the general control of the economy by the whole people as consumers of goods. That is the difference between collectivism and the market economy. That is the alternative with which mankind is confronted. You can not dodge it, or pray it away, or hide it from yourself with smokescreens of ideas. It is a fact, not an idea. We have to choose. And the choice is between freedom and tyranny.

There is no conflict between freedom so conditioned and a humane regard on the part of the state for people who fail utterly in the competitive struggle. No one need starve, no one need to be destitute, in order to preserve the sovereignty of the market. The principle of collective responsibility for those actually in want can be maintained without violating the principle of competition. But we need no longer deceive ourselves that liberty in a human world is compatible with economic equality. Liberty means absence of external restraint. To democrats, it meant absence of arbitrary governmental restraint, and was to a degree synonymous with equality before the law. But to the Socialists it meant absence of all governmental restraint, and also of those more subtle restraints imposed by a minority who own the land and the wealth-producing machinery. Who, in the absence of these restraints, is going to impose equality? What is to bring it about that men, once granted leave to behave as they please, will behave as though the whole human race were a loving family? We have to make up our minds, if we are going to defend this free world against an on-creeping totalitarian state control, whether, in fact, our primary interest is in freedom from state control, or in an attempt at economic equality enforced by a controlling state. We have to accept such inequalities as are presumed by, and result from, economic competition.

Equality apart, however, there is something vitally democratic, as well as impersonal, in the control exercised by the market. When a man buys something on a free market, he is casting his vote as a citizen of the national economy. He is making a choice which, by influencing prices, will enter into the decision as to how, and toward what ends, the economy shall be conducted. His choice may be outweighed by others who buy more; that is inevitably true. But in placing the major economic decisions in the hands of the whole people as consumers, recording these decisions automatically through the mechanism of price, the market makes freedom possible in a complex industrial society. It is the only thing that makes it possible.

Strangely enough Marx himself as a historian was the first to perceive this. Looking backward, he observed that all our freedoms had evolved together with, and in dependence upon, private capitalism with its free competitive market. Had he been a man of science instead of a mystic believer in the inevitability of a millennium, he might have guessed at what is so clearly obvious now: that this dependence of other freedoms upon the free market extends into the future also. It is a brief step indeed from Marxism – once the Hegelian wishful thinking is weeded out of it – to such a passage as this from Wilhelm Roepke:

It is hardly forgivable naiveté to believe that a state can be all-powerful in the economic sphere without also being autocratic in the political and intellectual domain and vice versa. . . . It therefore makes no sense to reject collectivism politically, if one does not at the same time propose a decidedly non-socialist solution of the problems of economic and social reform. If we are not in earnest with this relentless logic, we have vainly gone through a unique and costly historical object-lesson.

The failure of the Social Democrats, and still more in America of the 'left' liberals, to learn this lesson is now a major threat to freedom in the western world. I am not sure it is always a failure to learn. I think a good number of these Fabians and crypto-socialists – a new breed to which political expediency under the New Deal gave rise – have a suspicion that freedom will go down the drain. Travers Clement, one of the old-timers, has explicitly proposed hauling down the watchwords: 'Liberty, Equality, Fraternity,' and running up: 'Cradle-to-grave Security. Full Employment and Sixty Million Jobs.'[2] It was no accident of old age that both Sidney and Beatrice Webb and their brilliant colleague and co-evangelist in Fabian socialism, Bernard Shaw, ended their careers as loyal defenders of the most complete and ruthless tyranny mankind has known.

However, our American creepers toward socialism are most of them less bold and forthright than that. Often they don't even know where they are creeping. They see with the tail of an eye that political liberty is incompatible with economic subjection, but they refuse to look straight in the face of this fact. They refuse to learn the lesson that the history of these last thirty years has been spread out on the table, it almost seems, to teach them. They remain indecisive, equivocal – lured by the idea of security, orderly production, and universal welfare under a planning state, yet not quite ready to renounce in behalf of it those rights and liberties of the individual which stand or fall with the free market economy.

An ironical truth is that these socializers will not achieve security, orderly production, or the prosperity that makes universal welfare possible, by sacrificing freedom. They will be duped and defeated on all fronts. For me that also is proven by the history of the last three decades. But that is not the theme of this chapter.

Its theme is that our progress in democracy is endangered by democratic enthusiasts who imagine that they can preserve freedom politically while hacking away at its economic foundations. More even than the fellow travelers with their vicarious flair for violent revolution, or the Communists with their courageous belief in it, these piously aspiring reformers are undermining our hopes. Yearning to do good and obsessed by the power of the state to do it, relieved by this power of their age-old feeling of futility, they are destroying in the name of social welfare the foundations of freedom.

Arthur Koestler warned us some years ago against the 'men of good will with strong frustrations and feeble brains, the wishful thinkers and idealistic moral cowards, the fellow-travelers of the death train.' We have accepted his warning. At least we have learned the meaning of the word fellow traveler, and are no longer falling in droves for these unlovely accomplices of the tyrant. We must arm our minds now against the less obvious, the more strong and plausible and patriotic enemies of freedom, the advocates of a state-planned economy. They are not on the train and have no thought of getting on, but they are laying the tracks along which another death train will travel. . . .

There occurred no change in my feeling on this subject when I abandoned the idea of proletarian revolution. I still think the worst enemy of human hope is not brute facts, but men of brains who will not face them. For that reason I had no high expectations of the liberal intelligentsia when it came to acknowledging that the 'revolution of our times,' as so far conceived and conducted, is, has been, and will be, a failure. I never dreamed, however, that they could sink to the depths of maudlin self-deception and perfectly abject treason to truth, freedom, justice, and mercy that many of them have reached in regard to the Russian debacle. That has indeed profoundly, and more than any other shock, whether emotional or intellectual, disabused me of the dream of liberty under a socialist state. If these supposedly elevated and detached minds, free of any dread, of any pressure, of any compulsion to choose except between truth and their own mental comfort, can not recognize absolute horror, the absolute degradation of man, the end of science, art, law, human aspiration, and civilized morals, when these arrive in a far country, what will they be worth when the pressure is put upon them at home? They will be worth nothing except to those dark powers which will most certainly undertake to convert state-owned property into an instrument of exploitation beside which the reign of private capital will seem to have been, in truth, a golden age of freedom and equality for all.

Notes

1. I pointed out this vital conflict between Marxism and modern science in my early book *Marx and Lenin, the Science of Revolution* in 1925, anticipating by twenty years – although far indeed from expecting – the physical liquidation of the scientists. The passage will be found unchanged in *Marxism Is It Science* (pp. 267–269).

    The question of Marxism and the present conception of man is more fully discussed in my last chapter: 'Socialism and Human Nature.'
2. In the *New Leader* for August 4, 1945, answering my argument that democratic socialism is impossible.

8
T.S. Eliot

Thomas Stearns Eliot (1888–1965) was born in America, but became a British subject. It is no exaggeration to say that his poetry changed the course of English literature. It is equally true that his criticism (and especially the early collection The Sacred Wood *(1920)), changed the way in which English literature was perceived. And, in a series of remarkable essays on social and political themes, Eliot (who was an admirer of Bradley, the subject of his doctoral thesis in philosophy), endeavoured to apply the vision expressed in his poetry and criticism to the social disorders of his day. Tradition was a key concept for Eliot: without this concept, he believed, neither social life nor culture could be understood. Eliot combined artistic modernism with social conservatism, and defended modernism precisely as an attempt to revitalise, and to belong again to, a threatened tradition. The most brilliant of the 'cultural conservatives', he was drawn, like Coleridge, to the Anglican Church, his growing attachment to which he expressed in his later poetry. Eliot's political vision was never clearly expressed, and only in* The Idea of a Christian Society *(1938) and* Notes Towards The Definition of Culture *(1945), did he attempt to give a synoptic view of the social philosophy underlying his poetic and critical writings. Nevertheless, scattered among his writings we find one of the most sustained and serious defences in the literature, of the view that individual freedom and traditional order are inseparably conjoined.*

The following extract comes from 'Tradition and the Individual Talent', which was published in The Sacred Wood.

I

In English writing we seldom speak of tradition, though we occasionally apply its name in deploring its absence. We cannot refer to 'the tradition' or to 'a tradition'; at most, we employ the adjective in saying that the poetry of So-and-so is 'traditional' or even 'too traditional.' Seldom, perhaps, does the word appear except in a phrase of censure. If otherwise, it is vaguely approbative, with the implication, as to the work approved, of some pleasing archæological reconstruction. You can hardly make the word agreeable to English ears without this comfortable reference to the reassuring science of archæology.

Certainly the word is not likely to appear in our appreciations of living or dead writers. Every nation, every race, has not only its own creative, but its own critical turn of mind; and is even more oblivious of the shortcomings and limitations of its critical habits than of those of its creative genius. We know, or think we know, from the enormous mass of critical writing that has appeared in the French language the critical method or habit of the French; we only conclude (we are such unconscious people) that the French are 'more critical' then we, and sometimes even plume ourselves a little with the fact, as if the French were the less spontaneous. Perhaps they are; but we might remind ourselves that criticism is as inevitable as breathing, and that we should be none the worse for articulating what passes in our minds when we read a book and feel an emotion about it, for criticizing our own minds in their work of criticism. One of the facts that might come to light in this process is our tendency to insist, when we praise a poet, upon those aspects of his work in which he least resembles anyone else. In these aspects or parts of his work we pretend to find what is individual, what is the peculiar essence of the man. We dwell with satisfaction upon the poet's difference from his predecessors, especially his immediate predecessors; we endeavour to find something that can be isolated in order to be enjoyed. Whereas if we approach a poet without his prejudice we shall often find that not only the best, but the most individual parts of his work may be those in which the dead poets, his ancestors, assert their immortality most vigorously. And I do not mean the impressionable period of adolescence, but the period of full maturity.

Yet if the only form of tradition, of handling down, consisted in following the ways of the immediate generation before us in a blind or timid adherence to its successes, 'tradition' should positively be discouraged. We have seen many such simple currents soon lost in the sand; and novelty is better than repetition. Tradition is a matter of much wider significance. It cannot be inherited, and if you want it you must obtain it by great labour. It involves, in the first place, the historical sense, which we may call nearly indispensable to anyone who would continue to be a poet beyond his twenty-fifth year; and the historical sense involves a perception, not only of the pastness of the past, but of its presence; the historical sense compels a man to write not merely with his own generation in his bones, but with a feeling that the whole of the literature of Europe from Homer and within it the whole of the literature of his own country has a simultaneous existence and composes a simultaneous order. This historical sense, which is a sense of the timeless as well as of the temporal and of the timeless and of the temporal together, is what makes a writer traditional. And it is at the same time what makes a writer most acutely conscious of his place in time, of his contemporaneity.

No poet, no artist of any art, has his complete meaning alone. His significance, his appreciation is the appreciation of his relation to the dead poets and artists. You cannot value him alone; you must set him, for contrast and comparison, among the dead. I mean this as a principle of æsthetic, not merely historical, criticism. The necessity that he shall conform, that he shall cohere, is not one-sided; what happens when a new work of art is created is something that happens simultaneously to all the works of art which preceded it. The existing monuments form an ideal order among themselves, which is modified by the introduction of the new (the really new) work of art among them. The existing order is complete before the new work arrives; for order to persist after the supervention of novelty, the *whole* existing order must be, if ever so slightly, altered; and so the relations, proportions, values of each work of art toward the whole are readjusted; and this is conformity between the old and the new. Whoever has approved this idea of order, of the form of European, of English literature, will not find it preposterous that the past should be altered by the present as much as the present is directed by the past. And the poet who is aware of this will be aware of great difficulties and responsibilities.

In a peculiar sense he will be aware also that he must inevitably be judged by the standards of the past. I say judged, not amputated, by them; not judged to be as good as, or worse or better than, the dead; and certainly not judged by the canons of dead critics. It is a judgment, a comparison, in which two things are measured by each other. To conform merely would be for the new work not really to conform at all; it would not be new, and would therefore not be a work of art. And we do not quite say that the new is more valuable because it fits in; but its fitting in is a test of its value – a test, it is true, which can only be slowly and cautiously applied, for we are none of us infallible judges of conformity. We say: it appears to conform, and is perhaps individual, or it appears individual, and may conform; but we are hardly likely to find that it is one and not the other.

To proceed to a more intelligible exposition of the relation of the poet to the past: he can neither take the past as a lump, an indiscriminate bolus, nor can he form himself wholly on one or two private admirations, nor can he form himself wholly upon one preferred period. The first course is inadmissible, the second is an important experience of youth, and the third is a pleasant and highly desirable supplement. The poet must be very conscious of the main current, which does not at all flow invariably through the most distinguished reputations. He must be quite aware of the obvious fact that art never improves, but that the material of art is never quite the same. He must be aware that the mind of Europe – the mind of his own country – a mind which he learns in time to be much more important than his own private mind – is a mind which changes, and that this change is a development which abandons nothing *en route*, which does not superannuate either Shakespeare, or Homer, or the rock drawing of the Magdalenian draughtsmen. That this development, refinement perhaps, complication certainly, is not, from the point of view of the artist, any improvement. Perhaps not even an improvement from the point of view of the psychologist or not to the extent which we imagine; perhaps only in the end based upon a complication in economics and machinery. But the difference between the present and the past is that the conscious present is an awareness of the past in a way and to an extent which the past's awareness of itself cannot show.

Some one said: 'The dead writers are remote from us because we *know* so much more than they did.' Precisely, and they are that which we know.

I am alive to a usual objection to what is clearly part of my programme for the *métier* of poetry. The objection is that the doctrine requires a ridiculous amount of erudition (pedantry), a claim which can be rejected by appeal to the lives of poets in any pantheon. It will even be affirmed that much learning deadens or perverts poetic sensibility. While, however, we persist in believing that a poet ought to know as much as will not encroach upon his necessary receptivity and necessary laziness, it is not desirable to confine knowledge to whatever can be put into a useful shape for examinations, drawing-rooms, or the still more pretentious modes of publicity. Some can absorb knowledge, the more tardy must sweat for it. Shakespeare acquired more essential history from Plutarch than most men could from the whole British Museum. What is to be insisted upon is that the poet must develop or procure the consciousness of the past and that he should continue to develop this consciousness throughout his career.

What happens is a continual surrender of himself as he is at the moment to something which is more valuable. The progress of an artist is a continual self-sacrifice, a continual extinction of personality.

There remains to define this process of depersonalization and its relation to the sense of tradition. It is in this depersonalization that art may be said to approach the condition of science. I shall, therefore, invite you to consider, as a suggestive analogy, the action which takes place when a bit of finely filiated platinum is introduced into a chamber containing oxygen and sulphur dioxide.

II

Honest criticism and sensitive appreciation is directed not upon the poet but upon the poetry. If we attend to the confused cries of the newspaper critics and the susurrus of popular repetition that follows, we shall hear the names of poets in great numbers; if we seek not Blue-book knowledge but the enjoyment of poetry, and ask for a poem, we shall seldom find it. In the last article I tried to point out the importance of the relation of the poem to other poems by other authors, and suggested the conception of poetry as a living whole of all the poetry that has ever been written. The other aspect of this Impersonal theory of poetry is the relation of the poem to its author. And I hinted, by an analogy, that the mind of the mature poet differs from that of the immature one not precisely in any valuation of 'personality,' not being necessarily more interesting, or having 'more to say,' but rather by being a more finely perfected medium in which special, or very varied, feelings are at liberty to enter into new combinations.

The analogy was that of the catalyst. When the two gases previously mentioned are mixed in the presence of a filament of platinum, they form sulphurous acid. This combination takes place only if the platinum is present; nevertheless the newly formed acid contains no trace of platinum, and the platinum itself is apparently unaffected; has remained inert, neutral, and unchanged. The mind of the poet is the shred of platinum. It may partly or exclusively operate upon the experience of the man himself; but, the more perfect the artist, the more completely separate in him will be the man who suffers and the mind which creates; the more perfectly will the mind digest and transmute the passions which are its material.

The experience, you will notice, the elements which enter the presence of the transforming catalyst, are of two kinds: emotions and feelings. The effect of a work of art upon the person who enjoys it is an experience different in kind from any experience not of art. It may be formed out of one emotion, or may be a combination of several; and various feelings, inhering for the writer in particular words or phrases or images, may be added to compose the final result. Or great poetry may be made without the direct use of any emotion whatever: composed out of feelings solely. Canto XV of the *Inferno* (Brunetto Latini) is a working up of the emotion evident in the situation; but the effect, though single as that of any work of art, is obtained by considerable complexity of detail. The last quatrain gives an image, a feeling attaching to an image, which 'came,' which did not develop simply out of what precedes, but which was probably in suspension in the poet's mind until the proper combination arrived for it to add itself to. The poet's mind is in fact a receptacle for seizing and storing up numberless feelings, phrases, images, which remain there until all the particles which can unite to form a new compound are present together.

If you compare several representative passages of the greatest poetry you see how great is the variety of types of combination, and also how completely any semi-ethical criterion of 'sublimity' misses the mark. For it is not the 'greatness,' the intensity, of the emotions, the components, but the intensity of the artistic process, the pressure, so to speak, under which the fusion takes place, that counts. The episode of Paolo and Francesca employs a definite emotion, but the intensity of the poetry is something quite different from whatever intensity in the supposed experience it may give the impression of. It is no more intense, furthermore, than Canto XXVI, the voyage of Ulysses, which has not the direct dependence upon an emotion. Great variety is possible in the process of transmutation of emotion: the murder of Agamemnon, or the agony of Othello, gives an artistic effect apparently closer to a possible original than the scenes from Dante. In the *Agamemnon*, the artistic emotion approximates to the emotion of an actual spectator; in *Othello* to the emotion of the protagonist himself. But the difference between art and the event is always absolute; the combination which is the murder of Agamemnon is probably as complex as that which is the voyage of Ulysses. In either case there has been a fusion of elements. The ode of Keats contains a number of feelings which have nothing particular to do with the nightingale, but which the nightingale, partly, perhaps, because of its attractive name, and partly because of its reputation, served to bring together.

The point of view which I am struggling to attack is perhaps related to the metaphysical theory of the substantial unity of the soul: for my meaning is, that the poet has, not a 'personality' to express, but a particular medium, which is only a medium and not a personality, in which impressions and experiences combine in peculiar and unexpected ways. Impressions and experiences which are important for the man may take no place in the poetry, and those which become important in the poetry may play quite a negligible part in the man, the personality.

I will quote a passage which is unfamiliar enough to be regarded with fresh attention in the light – or darkness – of these observations:

> And now methinks I could e'en chide myself
> For doating on her beauty, though her death
> Shall be revenged after no common action.
> Does the silkworm expend her yellow labours
> For thee? For thee does she undo herself?
> Are lordships sold to maintain ladyships
> For the poor benefit of a bewildering minute?
> Why does yon fellow falsify highways,
> And put his life between the judge's lips,
> To refine such a thing – keeps horse and men
> To beat their valours for her? . . .

In this passage (as is evident if it is taken in its context) there is a combination of positive and negative emotions: an intensely strong attraction toward beauty and an equally intense fascination by the ugliness which is contrasted with it and which destroys it. This balance of contrasted emotion is in the dramatic situation to which the speech is pertinent, but that situation alone is inadequate to it. This is, so to speak, the structural emotion, provided by the drama. But the whole effect, the dominant tone, is due to the fact that a number of floating feelings, having an affinity to this emotion by no means superficially evident, have combined with it to give us a new art emotion.

It is not in his personal emotions, the emotions provoked by particular events in his life, that the poet is in any way remarkable or interesting. His particular emotions may be simple, or crude, or flat. The emotion in his poetry will be a very complex thing, but not with the complexity of the emotions of people who have very complex or unusual emotions in life. One error, in fact, of eccentricity in poetry is to seek for new human emotions to express; and in this search for novelty in the wrong place it discovers the perverse. The business of the poet is not to find new emotions, but to use the ordinary ones and, in working them up into poetry, to express feelings which are not in actual emotions at all. And emotions which he has never experienced will serve his turn as well as those familiar to him. Consequently, we must believe that 'emotion recollected in tranquillity' is an inexact formula. For it is neither emotion, nor recollection, nor, without distortion of meaning, tranquillity. It is a concentration, and a new thing resulting from the concentration, of a very great number of experiences which to the practical and active person would not seem to be experiences at all; it is a concentration which does not happen consciously or of deliberation. These experiences are not 'recollected,' and they finally unite in an atmosphere which is 'tranquil' only in that it is a passive attending upon the event. Of course this is not quite the whole story. There is a great deal, in the writing of poetry, which must be conscious and deliberate. In fact, the bad poet is usually unconscious where he ought to be conscious, and conscious where he ought to be unconscious. Both errors tend to make him 'personal.' Poetry is not a turning loose of emotion, but an escape from emotion; it is not the expression of personality, but an escape from personality. But, of course, only those who have personality and emotions know what it means to want to escape from these things.

III

ὁ δὲ νοῦς ἴσως θειότερόν τι καὶ ἀπαθές ἐστιν*

This essay proposes to qalt at the frontier of metaphysics or mysticism, and confine itself to such practical conclusions as can be applied by the responsible person interested in poetry. To divert interest from the poet to the poetry is a laudable aim: for it would conduce to a juster estimation of actual poetry, good and bad. There are many people who appreciate the expression of sincere emotion in verse, and there is a smaller number of people who can appreciate technical excellence. But very few know when there is expression of *significant* emotion, emotion which has its life in the poem and not in the history of the poet. The emotion of art is impersonal. And the poet cannot reach this impersonality without surrendering himself wholly to the work to be done. And he is not likely to know what is to be done unless he lives in what is not merely the present, but the present moment of the past, unless he is conscious, not of what is dead, but of what is already living.

---

* 'Perhaps then the intellect is a thing more divine and untouched by the passions.' Aristotle, *De Anima*, 408b (Ed.)

9
F.A. Hayek

F.A. von Hayek (b. 1899), is a political philosopher, and an economist of the Austrian School founded by Böhm-Bawerk. His denunciation, in The Road to Serfdom *(1945), of the totalitarian systems of government imposed upon Europe by Hitler and Stalin did much to create the postwar consciousness of liberty at bay. Hayek made his name as a political philosopher largely through his defence of liberal constitutionalism. In a postscript to* The Constitution of Liberty *(1961), entitled 'Why I am not a Conservative', he distances himself from those whose main concern in the political sphere is to conserve existing things, and to safeguard traditional values. Nevertheless, Hayek's thought has turned increasingly in a conservative direction, as he has recognised the far-reaching social implications of his theories. His core idea is that society is founded upon dispersed knowledge, which is both practical and tacit. Such knowledge cannot be contained in a single person's mind, and exists actively only in the circumstance of free association. This idea can be applied not only in the economic sphere (where it leads to a revised version of Adam Smith's 'invisible hand' theory of the market); but also in every sphere where rational beings are in potential conflict and in need of coordination. Hayek's works have therefore covered many topics: psychology, sociology, law, politics and economics, for the last of which he was awarded the Nobel Prize.*

Hayek's opposition to socialism is, in the last analysis, epistemological: planning and large-scale social engineering destroy the fund of social knowledge, and therefore remove their own rational foundations. The socialist planner literally does not know what he is doing. His certainty is at best a self-deception, at worst an imposture. Hayek's defence of common law, tradition, custom and the free market arise not so much from a distrust of human rationality, as from a conception of rationality as a social achievement, never so far from being realised as when consciously striven for. In a series of essays – Law, Legislation and Liberty *(1982) – from which the following extracts are taken, Hayek has given a subtle exposition of this thought; while in his latest work –* The Fatal Conceit *(first volume, 1989) – he has begun to summarise his reasons for distrust-*

ing the modern forms of popular government, among which socialism remains, for him, the principal instance of folly.

From 'Cosmos and Taxis' in *Law, Legislation and Liberty*

> The man of system . . . seems to imagine that he can arrange the different members of a great society with as much ease as the hand arranges the different pieces upon a chessboard. He does not consider that the pieces upon the chessboard have no other principle of motion besides that which the hand impresses upon them; but that, in the great chessboard of human society, every single piece has a principle of motion of its own, altogether different from that which the legislature might choose to impress upon it. If those two principles coincide and act in the same direction, the game of human society will go on easily and harmoniously, and is very likely to be happy and successful. If they are opposite or different, the game will go on miserably and the society must be at all times in the highest degree of disorder.
>
> Adam Smith

THE CONCEPT OF ORDER

The central concept around which the discussion of this book will turn is that of order, and particularly the distinction between two kinds of order which we will provisionally call 'made' and 'grown' orders. Order is an indispensable concept for the discussion of all complex phenomena, in which it must largely play the role the concept of law plays in the analysis of simpler phenomena. There is no adequate term other than 'order' by which we can describe it, although 'system', 'structure' or 'pattern' may occasionally serve instead. The term 'order' has, of course, a long history in the social sciences, but in recent times it has generally been avoided, largely because of the ambiguity of its meaning and its frequent association with authoritarian views. We cannot do without it, however, and shall have to guard against misinterpretation by sharply defining the general sense in which we shall employ it and then clearly distinguishing between the two different ways in which such order can originate.

By 'order' we shall throughout describe *a state of affairs in which a multiplicity of elements of various kinds are so related to each other that we may learn from our acquaintance with some spatial or temporal part of the whole to form correct expectations concerning the rest, or at least expectations which have a good chance of proving correct.* It is clear that every society must in this sense possess an order and that such an order will often exist without having been deliberately created. As has been said by a distinguished social anthropologist, 'that there is some order, consistency and constancy in social life, is obvious. If there were not, none of us would be able to go about our affairs or satisfy our most elementary needs.'

Living as members of society and dependent for the satisfaction of most of our needs on various forms of co-operation with others, we depend for the effective pursuit of our aims clearly on the correspondence of the expectations concerning the actions of others on which our plans are based with what they will really do. This matching of the intentions and expectations that determine the actions of different individuals is the form in which order manifests itself in social life; and it will be the question of how such an order does come about that will be our immediate concern. The first answer to which our anthropomorphic habits of thought almost inevitably lead us is that it must be due to the design of some thinking mind. And because order has been generally interpreted as such a deliberate *arrangement* by somebody, the concept has become unpopular among most friends of liberty and has been favoured mainly by authoritarians. According to this interpretation order in society must rest on a relation of command and obedience, or a hierarchical structure of the whole of society in which the will of superiors, and ultimately of some single supreme authority, determines what each individual must do.

This authoritarian connotation of the concept of order derives, however, entirely from the belief that order can be created only by forces outside the system (or 'exogenously'). It does not apply to an equilibrium set up from within (or 'endogenously') such as that which the general theory of the market endeavours to explain. A spontaneous order of this kind has in many respects properties different from those of a made order.

THE TWO SOURCES OF ORDER

The study of spontaneous orders has long been the peculiar task of economic theory, although, of course, biology has from its beginning been concerned with that special kind of spontaneous order which we call an organism. Only recently has there arisen within the physical sciences under the name of cybernetics a special discipline which is also concerned with what are called self-organizing or self-generating systems.

The distinction of this kind of order from one which has been made by somebody putting the elements of a set in their places or directing their movements is indispensable for any understanding of the processes of society as well as for all social policy. There are several terms available for describing each kind of order. The made order which we have already referred to as an exogenous order or an arrangement may again be described as a construction, an artificial order or, especially where we have to deal with a directed social order, as an *organization*. The grown order, on the other hand, which we have referred to as a self-generating or endogenous order, is in English most conveniently described as a *spontaneous order*. Classical Greek was more fortunate in possessing distinct single words for the two kinds of order, namely *taxis* for a made order, such as, for example, an order of battle, and *kosmos* for a grown order, meaning originally 'a right order in a state or a community'. We shall occasionally avail ourselves of these Greek words as technical terms to describe the two kinds of order.

It would be no exaggeration to say that social theory begins with – and has an object only because of – the discovery that there exist orderly structures which are the product of the action of many men but are not the result of human design. In some fields this is now universally accepted. Although there was a time when men believed that even language and morals had been 'invented' by some genius of the past, everybody recognizes now that they are the outcome of a process of evolution whose results nobody foresaw or designed. But in other fields many people still treat with suspicion the claim that the patterns of interaction of many men can show an order that is of nobody's deliberate making; in the economic sphere, in particular, critics still pour uncomprehending ridicule on Adam Smith's expression of the 'invisible hand' by which, in the language of his time, he described how man is led 'to promote an end which was no part of his intentions'. If indignant reformers still complain of the chaos of economic affairs, insinuating a complete absence of order, this is partly because they cannot conceive of an order which is not deliberately made, and partly because to them an order means something aiming at concrete purposes which is, as we shall see, what a spontaneous order cannot do. . . .

THE DISTINGUISHING PROPERTIES OF SPONTANEOUS ORDERS

One effect of our habitually identifying order with a made order or *taxis* is indeed that we tend to ascribe to all order certain properties which deliberate arrangements regularly, and with respect to some of these properties necessarily, possess. Such orders are relatively *simple* or at least necessarily confined to such moderate degrees of complexity as the maker can still survey; they are usually *concrete* in the sense . . . that their existence can be intuitively perceived by inspection; and, finally, having been made deliberately, they invariably do (or at one time did) *serve a purpose* of the maker. None of these characteristics necessarily belong to a spontaneous order or *kosmos*. Its degree of complexity is not limited to what a human mind can master. Its existence need not manifest itself to our senses but may be based on purely *abstract* relations which we can only mentally reconstruct. And not having been made it *cannot* legitimately be said to *have a particular purpose*, although our awareness of its existence may be extremely important for our successful pursuit of a great variety of different purposes.

Spontaneous orders are not necessarily complex, but unlike deliberate human arrangements, they may achieve any degree of complexity. One of our main contentions will be that very complex orders, comprising more particular facts than any brain could ascertain or manipulate, can be brought about only through forces inducing the formation of spontaneous orders.

Spontaneous orders need not be what we have called abstract, but they will often consist of a system of abstract relations between elements which are also defined only by abstract properties, and for this reason will not be intuitively perceivable and not recognizable except on the basis of a theory accounting for their character. The significance of the abstract character of such orders rests on the fact that they may persist while all the particular elements they comprise, and even the number of such elements, change. All that is necessary to preserve such an abstract order is that a certain structure of relationships be maintained, or that elements of a certain kind (but variable in number) continue to be related in a certain manner.

Most important, however, is the relation of a spontaneous order to the conception of purpose. Since such an order has not been created by an outside agency, the order as such also can have no purpose, although its existence may be very serviceable to the individuals which move within such order. But in a different sense it may well be said that the order rests on purposive action of its elements, when 'purpose' would, of course, mean nothing more than that their actions tend to secure the preservation or restoration of that order. The use of 'purposive' in this sense as a sort of 'teleological shorthand', as it has been called by biologists, is unobjectionable so long as we do not imply an awareness of purpose of the part of the elements, but mean merely that the elements have acquired regularities of conduct conducive to the maintenance of the order – presumably because those who did act in certain ways had within the resulting order a better chance of survival than those who did not. In general, however, it is preferable to avoid in this connection the term 'purpose' and to speak instead of 'function'. . . .

IN SOCIETY, RELIANCE ON SPONTANEOUS ORDER BOTH EXTENDS AND LIMITS OUR POWERS OF CONTROL

Since a spontaneous order results from the individual elements adapting themselves to circumstances which directly affect only some of them, and which in their totality need not be known to anyone, it may extend to circumstances so complex that no mind can comprehend them all. Consequently, the concept becomes particularly important when we turn from mechanical to such 'more highly organized' or essentially complex phenomena as we encounter in the realms of life, mind and society. Here we have to deal with 'grown' structures with a degree of complexity which they have assumed and could assume only because they were produced by spontaneous ordering forces. They in consequence present us with peculiar difficulties in our effort to explain them as well as in any attempt to influence their character. Since we can know at most the rules observed by the elements of various kinds of which the structures are made up, but not all the individual elements and never all the particular circumstances in which each of them is placed, our knowledge will be restricted to the general character of the order which will form itself. And even where, as is true of a society of human beings, we may be in a position to alter at least some of the rules of conduct which the elements obey, we shall thereby be able to influence only the general character and not the detail of the resulting order.

This means that, though the use of spontaneous ordering forces enables us to induce the formation of an order of such a degree of complexity (namely comprising elements of such numbers, diversity and variety of conditions) as we could never master intellectually, or deliberately arrange, we will have less power over the details of such an order than we would of one which we produce by arrangement. In the case of spontaneous orders we may, by determining some of the factors which shape them, determine their abstract features, but we will have to leave the particulars to circumstances which we do not know. Thus, by relying on the spontaneously ordering forces, we can extend the scope or range of the order which we may induce to form, precisely because its particular manifestation will depend on many more circumstances than can be known to us – and in the case of a social order, because such an order will utilize the separate knowledge of all its several members, without this knowledge ever being concentrated in a single mind, or being subject to those processes of deliberate coordination and adaptation which a mind performs.

In consequence, the degree of power of control over the extended and more complex order will be much smaller than that which we could exercise over a made order or *taxis*. There will be many aspects of it over which we will possess no control at all, or which at least we shall not be able to alter without interfering with – and to that extent impeding – the forces producing the spontaneous order. Any desire we may have concerning the particular position of individual elements, or the relation between particular individuals or groups, could not be satisfied without upsetting the overall order. The kind of power which in this respect we would possess over a concrete arrangement or *taxis* we would not have over a spontaneous order where we would know, and be able to influence, only the abstract aspects.

It is important to note here that there are two different respects in which order may be a matter of degree. How well ordered a set of objects or events is depends on how many of the attributes of (or the relations between) the elements we can learn to predict. Different orders may in this respect differ from each other in either or both of two ways: the orderliness may concern only very few relations between the elements, or a great many; and, second, the regularity thus defined may be great in the sense that it will be confirmed by all or nearly all instances, or it may be found to prevail only in a majority of the instances and thus allow us to predict its occurrence only with a certain degree of probability. In the first instance we may predict only a few of the features of the resulting structure, but do so with great confidence; such an order would be limited but may still be perfect. In the second instance we shall be able to predict much more, but with only a fair degree of certainty. The knowledge of the existence of an order will however still be useful even if this order is restricted in either or both these respects; and the reliance on spontaneously ordering forces may be preferable or even indispensable, although the order towards which a system tends will in fact be only more or less imperfectly approached. The market order in particular will regularly secure only a certain probability that the expected relations will prevail, but it is, nevertheless, the only way in which so many activities depending on dispersed knowledge can be effectively integrated into a single order.

SPONTANEOUS ORDERS RESULT FROM THEIR ELEMENTS OBEYING CERTAIN RULES OF CONDUCT

We have already indicated that the formation of spontaneous orders is the result of their elements following certain rules in their responses to their immediate environment. The nature of these rules still needs fuller examination, partly because the word 'rule' is apt to suggest some erroneous ideas, and partly because the rules which determine a spontaneous order differ in important respects from another kind of rules which are needed in regulating an organization or *taxis*.

On the first point, the instances of spontaneous orders which we have given from physics are instructive because they clearly show that the rules which govern the actions of the elements of such spontaneous orders need not be rules which are 'known' to these elements; it is sufficient that the elements actually behave in a manner which can be described by such rules. The concept of rules as we use it in this context therefore does not imply that such rules exist in articulated ('verbalized') forms, but only that it is possible to discover rules which the actions of the individuals in fact follow. To emphasize this we have occasionally spoken of 'regularity' rather than of rules, but regularity, of course, means simply that the elements behave according to rules.

That rules in this sense exist and operate without being explicitly known to those who obey them applies also to many of the rules which govern the actions of men and thereby determine a spontaneous social order. Man certainly does not know all the rules which guide his actions in the sense that he is able to state them in words. At least in primitive human society, scarcely less than in animal societies, the structure of social life is determined by rules of conduct which manifest themselves only by being in fact observed. Only when individual intellects begin to differ to a significant degree will it become necessary to express these rules in a form in which they can be communicated and explicitly taught, deviant behaviour corrected, and differences of opinion about appropriate behaviour decided. Although man never existed without laws that he obeyed, he did, of course, exist for hundreds of thousands of years without laws he 'knew' in the sense that he was able to articulate them.

What is of still greater importance in this connection, however, is that not every regularity in the behaviour of the elements does secure an overall order. Some rules governing individual behaviour might clearly make altogether impossible the formation of an overall order. Our problem is what kind of rules of conduct will produce an order of society and what kind of order particular rules will produce.

The classical instance of rules of the behaviour of the elements which will not produce order comes from the physical sciences: it is the second law of thermodynamics or the law of enthropy, according to which the tendency of the molecules of a gas to move at constant speeds in straight lines produces a state for which the term 'perfect disorder' has been coined. Similarly, it is evident that in society some perfectly regular behaviour of the individuals could produce only disorder; if the rule were that any individual should try to kill any other he encountered, or flee as soon as he saw another, the result would clearly be the complete impossibility of an order in which the activities of the individuals were based on collaboration with others.

Society can thus exist only if by a process of selection rules have evolved which lead individuals to behave in a manner which makes social life possible. It should be remembered that for this purpose selection will operate as between societies of different types, that is, be guided by the properties of their respective orders, but that the properties supporting this order will be properties of the individuals, namely their propensity to obey certain rules of conduct on which the order of action of the group as a whole rests.

To put this differently: in a social order the particular circumstances to which each individual will react will be those known to him. But the individual responses to particular circumstances will result in an overall order only if the individuals obey such rules as will produce an order. Even a very limited similarity in their behaviour may be sufficient if the rules which they all obey are such as to produce an order. Such an order will always constitute an adaptation to the multitude of circumstances which are known to all the members of that society taken together but which are not known as a whole to any one person. This need not mean that the different persons will in similar circumstances do precisely the same thing; but merely that for the formation of such an overall order it is necessary that in some respects all individuals follow definite rules, or that their actions are limited to a certain range. In other words, the responses of the individuals to the events in their environment need be similar only in certain abstract aspects to ensure that a determinate overall order will result.

The question which is of central importance as much for social theory as for social policy is thus what properties the rules must possess so that the separate actions of the individuals will produce an overall order. Some such rules all individuals of a society will obey because of the similar manner in which their environment represents itself to their minds. Others they will follow spontaneously because they will be part of their common cultural tradition. But there will be still others which they may have to be made to obey, since, although it would be in the interest of each to disregard them, the overall order on which the success of their actions depends will arise only if these rules are generally followed.

In a modern society based on exchange, one of the chief regularities in individual behaviour will result from the similarity of situations in which most individuals find themselves in working to earn an income; which means that they will normally prefer a larger return from their efforts to a smaller one, and often that they will increase their efforts in a particular direction if the prospects of return improve. This is a rule that will be followed at least with sufficient frequency to impress upon such a society an order of a certain kind. But the fact that most people will follow this rule will still leave the character of the resulting order very indeterminate, and by itself certainly would not be sufficient to give it a beneficial character. For the resulting order to be beneficial people must also observe some conventional rules, that is, rules which do not simply follow from their desires and their insight into relations of cause and effect, but which are normative and tell them what they ought to or ought not to do.

We shall later have to consider more fully the precise relation between the various kinds of rules which the people in fact obey and the resulting order of actions. Our main interest will then be those rules which, because we can deliberately alter them, become the chief instrument whereby we can affect the resulting order, namely the rules of law. At the moment our concern must be to make clear that while the rules on which a spontaneous order rests, may also be of spontaneous origin, this need not always be the case. Although undoubtedly an order originally formed itself spontaneously because the individuals followed rules which had not been deliberately made but had arisen spontaneously, people gradually learned to improve those rules; and it is at least conceivable that the formation of a spontaneous order relies entirely on rules that were deliberately made. The spontaneous character of the resulting order must therefore be distinguished from the spontaneous origin of the rules on which it rests, and it is possible that an order which would still have to be described as spontaneous rests on rules which are entirely the result of deliberate design. In the kind of society with which we are familiar, of course, only some of the rules which people in fact observe, namely some of the rules of law (but never all, even of these) will be the product of deliberate design, while most of the rules of morals and custom will be spontaneous growths.

That even an order which rests on made rules may be spontaneous in character is shown by the fact that its particular manifestation will always depend on many circumstances which the designer of these rules did not and could not know. The particular content of the order will depend on the concrete circumstances known only to the individuals who obey the rules and apply them to facts known only to them. It will be through the knowledge of these individuals both of the rules and of the particular facts that both will determine the resulting order.

THE SPONTANEOUS ORDER OF SOCIETY IS MADE UP OF INDIVIDUALS AND ORGANIZATIONS

In any group of men of more than the smallest size, collaboration will always rest both on spontaneous order as well as on deliberate organization. There is no doubt that for many limited tasks organization is the most powerful method of effective co-ordination because it enables us to adapt the resulting order much more fully to our wishes, while where, because of the complexity of the circumstances to be taken into account, we must rely on the forces making for a spontaneous order, our power over the particular contents of this order is necessarily restricted.

That the two kinds of order will regularly coexist in every society of any degree of complexity does not mean, however, that we can combine them in any manner we like. What in fact we find in all free societies is that, although groups of men will join in organizations for the achievement of some particular ends, the co-ordination of the activities of all these separate organizations, as well as of the separate individuals, is brought about by the forces making for a spontaneous order. The family, the farm, the plant, the firm, the corporation and the various associations, and all the public institutions including government, are organizations which in turn are integrated into a more comprehensive spontaneous order. It is advisable to reserve the term 'society' for this spontaneous overall order so that we may distinguish it from all the organized smaller groups which will exist within it, as well as from such smaller and more or less isolated groups as the horde, the tribe, or the clan, whose members will at least in some respects act under a central direction for common purposes. In some instances it will be the same group which at times, as when engaged in most of its daily routine, will operate as a spontaneous order maintained by the observation of conventional rules without the necessity of commands, while at other times, as when hunting, migrating, or fighting, it will be acting as an organization under the directing will of a chief.

The spontaneous order which we call a society also need not have such sharp boundaries as an organization will usually possess. There will often be a nucleus, or several nuclei, of more closely related individuals occupying a central position in a more loosely connected but more extensive order. Such particular societies within the Great Society may arise as the result of spatial proximity, or of some other special circumstances which produce closer relations among their members. And different partial societies of this sort will often overlap and every individual may, in addition to being a member of the Great Society, be a member of numerous other spontaneous sub-orders or partial societies of this sort as well as of various organizations existing within the comprehensive Great Society.

Of the organizations existing within the Great Society one which regularly occupies a very special position will be that which we call government. Although it is conceivable that the spontaneous order which we call society may exist without government, if the minimum of rules required for the formation of such an order is observed without an organized apparatus for their enforcement, in most circumstances the organization which we call government becomes indispensable in order to assure that those rules are obeyed.

This particular function of government is somewhat like that of a maintenance squad of a factory, its object being not to produce any particular services or products to be consumed by the citizens, but rather to see that the mechanism which regulates the production of those goods and services is kept in working order. The purposes for which this machinery is currently being used will be determined by those who operate its parts and in the last resort by those who buy its products.

The same organization that is charged with keeping in order an operating structure which the individuals will use for their own purposes, will, however, in addition to the task of enforcing the rules on which that order rests, usually be expected also to render other services which the spontaneous order cannot produce adequately. These two distinct functions of government are usually not clearly separated; yet, as we shall see, the distinction between the coercive functions in which government enforces rules of conduct, and its service functions in which it need merely administer resources placed at its disposal, is of fundamental importance. In the second it is one organization among many and like the others part of a spontaneous overall order, while in the first it provides an essential condition for the preservation of that overall order.

In English it is possible, and has long been usual, to discuss these two types of order in terms of the distinction between 'society' and 'government'. There is no need in the discussion of these problems, so long as only one country is concerned, to bring in the metaphysically charged term 'state'. It is largely under the influence of continental and particularly Hegelian thought that in the course of the last hundred years the practice of speaking of the 'state' (preferably with a capital 'S'), where 'government' is more appropriate and precise, has come to be widely adopted. That which acts, or pursues a policy, is however always the organization of government; and it does not make for clarity to drag in the term 'state' where 'government' is quite sufficient. It becomes particularly misleading when 'the state' rather than 'government' is contrasted with 'society' to indicate that the first is an organization and the second a spontaneous order.

THE RULES OF SPONTANEOUS ORDERS AND THE RULES OF ORGANIZATION

One of our chief contentions will be that, though spontaneous order and organization will always coexist, it is still not possible to mix these two principles of order in any manner we like. If this is not more generally understood it is due to the fact that for the determination of both kinds of order we have to rely on rules, and that the important differences between the kinds of rules which the two different kinds of order require are generally not recognized.

To some extent every organization must rely also on rules and not only on specific commands. The reason here is the same as that which makes it necessary for a spontaneous order to rely solely on rules: namely that by guiding the actions of individuals by rules rather than specific commands it is possible to make use of knowledge which nobody possesses as a whole. Every organization in which the members are not mere tools of the organizer will determine by commands only the function to be performed by each member, the purposes to be achieved, and certain general aspects of the methods to be employed, and will leave the detail to be decided by the individuals on the basis of their respective knowledge and skills.

Organization encounters here the problem which any attempt to bring order into complex human activities meets: the organizer must wish the individuals who are to co-operate to make use of knowledge that he himself does not possess. In none but the most simple kind of organization is it conceivable that all the details of all activities are governed by a single mind. Certainly nobody has yet succeeded in deliberately arranging all the activities that go on in a complex society. If anyone did ever succeed in fully organizing such a society, it would no longer make use of many minds but would be altogether dependent on one mind; it would certainly not be very complex but extremely primitive – and so would soon be the mind whose knowledge and will determined everything. The facts which could enter into the design of such an order could be only those which were known and digested by this mind; and as only he could decide on action and thus gain experience, there would be none of that interplay of many minds in which alone mind can grow.

What distinguishes the rules which will govern action within an organization is that they must be rules for the performance of assigned tasks. They presuppose that the place of each individual in a fixed structure is determined by command and that the rules each individual must obey depend on the place which he has been assigned and on the particular ends which have been indicated for him by the commanding authority. The rules will thus regulate merely the detail of the action of appointed functionaries or agencies of government.

Rules of organization are thus necessarily subsidiary to commands, filling in the gaps left by the commands. Such rules will be different for the different members of the organization according to the different roles which have been assigned to them, and they will have to be interpreted in the light of the purposes determined by the commands. Without the assignment of a function and the determination of the ends to be pursued by particular commands, the bare abstract rule would not be sufficient to tell each individual what he must do.

By contrast, the rules governing a spontaneous order must be independent of purpose and be the same, if not necessarily for all members, at least for whole classes of members not individually designated by name. They must, as we shall see, be rules applicable to an unknown and indeterminable number of persons and instances. They will have to be applied by the individuals in the light of their respective knowledge and purposes; and their application will be independent of any common purpose, which the individual need not even know.

In the terms we have adopted this means that the general rules of law that a spontaneous order rests on aim at an abstract order, the particular or concrete content of which is not known or foreseen by anyone; while the commands as well as the rules which govern an organization serve particular results aimed at by those who are in command of the organization. The more complex the order aimed at, the greater will be that part of the separate actions which will have to be determined by circumstances not known to those who direct the whole, and the more dependent control will be on rules rather than on specific commands. In the most complex types of organizations, indeed, little more than the assignment of particular functions and the general aim will be determined by command of the supreme authority, while the performance of these functions will be regulated only by rules – yet by rules which at least to some degree are specific to the functions assigned to particular persons. Only when we pass from the biggest kind of organization, government, which as organization must still be dedicated to a circumscribed and determined set of specific purposes, to the overall order of the whole of society, do we find an order which relies solely on rules and is entirely spontaneous in character.

It is because it was not dependent on organization but grew up as a spontaneous order that the structure of modern society has attained that degree of complexity which it possesses and which far exceeds any that could have been achieved by deliberate organization. In fact, of course, the rules which made the growth of this complex order possible were initially not designed in expectation of that result; but those people who happened to adopt suitable rules developed a complex civilization which then often spread to others. To maintain that we must deliberately plan modern society because it has become so complex is therefore paradoxical, and the result of a complete misunderstanding of these circumstances. The fact is, rather, that we can preserve an order of such complexity not by the method of directing the members, but only indirectly by enforcing and improving the rules conducive to the formation of a spontaneous order.

We shall see that it is impossible, not only to replace the spontaneous order by organization and at the same time to utilize as much of the dispersed knowledge of all its members as possible, but also to improve or correct this order by interfering in it by direct commands. Such a combination of spontaneous order and organization it can never be rational to adopt. While it is sensible to supplement the commands determining an organization by subsidiary rules, and to use organizations as elements of a spontaneous order, it can never be advantageous to supplement the rules governing a spontaneous order by isolated and subsidiary commands concerning those activities where the actions are guided by the general rules of conduct. This is the gist of the argument against 'interference' or 'intervention' in the market order. The reason why such isolated commands requiring specific actions by members of the spontaneous order can never improve but must disrupt that order is that they will refer to a part of a system of interdependent actions determined by information and guided by purposes known only to the several acting persons but not to the directing authority. The spontaneous order arises from each element balancing all the various factors operating on it and by adjusting all its various actions to each other, a balance which will be destroyed if some of the actions are determined by another agency on the basis of different knowledge and in the service of different ends.

What the general argument against 'interference' thus amounts to is that, although we can endeavour to improve a spontaneous order by revising the general rules on which it rests, and can supplement its results by the efforts of various organizations, we cannot improve the results by specific commands that deprive its members of the possibility of using their knowledge for their purposes. . . .

The following extract is from 'The Changing Concept of Law' in *Law, Legislation and Liberty*.

LAW IS OLDER THAN LEGISLATION

Legislation, the deliberate making of law, has justly been described as among all inventions of man the one fraught with the gravest consequences, more far-reaching in its effects even than fire and gun-powder. Unlike law itself, which has never been 'invented' in the same sense, the invention of legislation came relatively late in the history of mankind. It gave into the hands of men an instrument of great power which they needed to achieve some good, but which they have not yet learned so to control that it may not produce great evil. It opened to man wholly new possibilities and gave him a new sense of power over his fate. The discussion about who should possess this power has, however, unduly overshadowed the much more fundamental question of how far this power should extend. It will certainly remain an exceedingly dangerous power so long as we believe that it will do harm only if wielded by bad men.

Law in the sense of enforced rules of conduct is undoubtedly coeval with society; only the observance of common rules makes the peaceful existence of individuals in society possible. Long before man had developed language to the point where it enabled him to issue general commands, an individual would be accepted as a member of a group only so long as he conformed to its rules. Such rules might in a sense not be known and still have to be discovered, because from 'knowing how' to act, or from being able to recognize that the acts of another did or did not conform to accepted practices, it is still a long way to being able to state such rules in words. But while it might be generally recognized that the discovery and statement of what the accepted rules were (or the articulation of rules that would be approved when acted upon) was a task requiring special wisdom, nobody yet conceived of law as something which men could make at will.

It is no accident that we still use the same word 'law' for the invariable rules which govern nature and for the rules which govern men's conduct. They were both conceived at first as something existing independently of human will. Though the anthropomorphic tendencies of all primitive thinking made men often ascribe both kinds of law to the creation of some supernatural being, they were regarded as eternal truths that man could try to discover but which he could not alter.

To modern man, on the other hand, the belief that all law

governing human action is the product of legislation appears so obvious that the contention that law is older than law-making has almost the character of a paradox. Yet there can be no doubt that law existed for ages before it occurred to man that he could make or alter it. The belief that he could do so appeared hardly earlier than in classical Greece and even then only to be submerged again and to reappear and gradually gain wider acceptance in the later Middle Ages. In the form in which it is now widely held, however, namely that all law is, can be, and ought to be, the product of the free invention of a legislator, it is factually false, an erroneous product of that constructivist rationalism which we described earlier. . . .

THE PROCESS OF ARTICULATION OF PRACTICES

Even the earliest deliberate efforts of headmen or chiefs of a tribe to maintain order must . . . be seen as taking place inside a given framework of rules, although they were rules which existed only as a 'knowledge how' to act and not as a 'knowledge that' they could be expressed in such and such terms. Language would certainly have been used early to teach them, but only as a means of indicating the particular actions that were required or prohibited in particular situations. As in the acquisition of language itself, the individual would have to learn to act in accordance with rules by imitating particular actions corresponding to them. So long as language is not sufficiently developed to express general rules there is no other way in which rules can be taught. But although at this stage they do not exist in articulated form, they nevertheless do exist in the sense that they govern action. And those who first attempted to express them in words did not invent new rules but were endeavouring to express what they were already acquainted with.

Although still an unfamiliar conception, the fact that language is often insufficient to express what the mind is fully capable of taking into account in determining action, or that we will often not be able to communicate in words what we well know how to practise, has been clearly established in many fields. It is closely connected with the fact that the rules that govern action will often be much more general and abstract than anything language can yet express. Such abstract rules are learnt by imitating particular actions, from which the individual acquires 'by analogy' the capacity to act in other cases on the same principles which, however, he could never state as principles. . . .

THE CLASSICAL AND THE MEDIEVAL TRADITION

Although the conception that law was the product of a deliberate human will was first fully developed in ancient Greece, its influence over the actual practice of politics remained limited. Of classical Athens at the height of its democracy we are told that 'at no time was it legal to alter the law by a simple decree of the assembly. The mover of such a decree was liable to the famous "indictment for illegal proceedings" which, if upheld by the courts, quashed the decree, and also, brought within the year, exposed the mover to heavy penalties.' A change in the basic rules of just conduct, the *nomoi*, could be brought about only through a complicated procedure in which a specially elected body, the *nomothetae*, was involved. Nevertheless, we find in the Athenian democracy already the first clashes between the unfettered will of the 'sovereign' people and the tradition of the rule of law; and it was chiefly because the assembly often refused to be bound by the law that Aristotle turned against this form of democracy, to which he even denied the right to be called a constitution. It is in the discussions of this period that we find the first persistent efforts to draw a clear distinction between the law and the particular will of the ruler.

The law of Rome, which has influenced all Western law so profoundly, was even less the product of deliberate law-making. As all other early law it was formed at a time when 'law and the institutions of social life were considered to have always existed and nobody asked for their origin. The idea that law might be created by men is alien to the thinking of early people.' It was only 'the naïve belief of later more advanced ages that all law must rest on legislation.' In fact, the classical Roman civil law, on which the final compilation of Justinian was based, is almost entirely the product of law-finding by jurists and only to a very small extent the product of legislation. By a process very similar to that by which later the English common law developed, and differing from it mainly in that the decisive role was played by the opinions of legal scholars (the *jurisconsults*) rather than the decisions of judges, a body of law grew up through the gradual articulation of prevailing conceptions of justice rather than by legislation. It was only at the end of this development, at Byzantium rather than at Rome and under the influence of Hellenistic thinking, that the results of this process were codified under the Emperor Justinian, whose work was later falsely regarded as the model of a law created by a ruler and expressing his 'will'.

Until the rediscovery of Aristotle's *Politics* in the thirteenth century and the reception of Justinian's code in the fifteenth, however, Western Europe passed through another epoch of nearly a thousand years when law was again regarded as something given independently of human will, something to be discovered, not made, and when the conception that law could be deliberately made or altered seemed almost sacrilegious. This attitude, noticed by many earlier scholars, has been given a classical description by Fritz Kern, and we can do no better than quote his main conclusions:

> When a case arises for which no valid law can be adduced, then the lawful men or doomsmen will make new law in the belief that what they are making is good old law, not indeed expressly handed-down, but tacitly existent. They do not, therefore, create the law: they 'discover' it. Any particular judgement in court, which we regard as a particular inference from a general established legal rule, was to the medieval mind in no way distinguishable from the legislative activity of the community; in both cases a law hidden but already existing is discovered, not created. There is, in the Middle Ages, no such thing as the 'first application of a legal rule'. Law is old; new law is a contradiction in terms; for either new law is derived explicitly or implicitly from the old, or it conflicts with the old, in which case it is not lawful. The fundamental idea remains the same; the old law is the true law, and the true law is the old law. According to medieval ideas, therefore, the enactment of new law is not possible at all; and all legislation and legal reform is conceived of as the restoration of the good old law which has been violated.

The history of the intellectual development by which, from the thirteenth century onwards, and mainly on the European continent, law-making slowly and gradually came to be regarded as an act of the deliberate and unfettered will of the ruler, is too long and complex to be described here. From the detailed studies of this process it appears to be closely connected with the rise of absolute monarchy when the conceptions which later governed the aspirations of democracy were formed. This development was accompanied by a progressive absorption of this new power of laying down new rules of just conduct into the much older power which rulers had always exercised, their power of organizing and directing the apparatus of government, until both powers became inextricably mixed up in what came to be regarded as the single power of 'legislation'.

The main resistance to this development came from the tradition of the 'law of nature'. As we have seen, the late Spanish schoolmen used the term 'natural' as a technical term to describe what had never been 'invented' or deliberately designed but had evolved in response to the necessity of the situation. But even this tradition lost its power when in the seventeenth century 'natural law' came to be understood as the design of 'natural reason'.

The only country that succeeded in preserving the tradition of the Middle Ages and built on the medieval 'liberties' the modern conception of liberty under the law was England. This was partly due to the fact that England escaped a wholesale reception of the late Roman law and with it the conception of law as the creation of some ruler; but it was probably due more to the circumstance that the common law jurists there had developed conceptions somewhat similar to those of the natural law tradition but not couched in the misleading terminology of that school. Nevertheless, 'in the sixteenth and early seventeenth century the political structure of England was not yet fundamentally different from that of the continental countries and it might still have seemed uncertain whether she would develop a highly centralized absolute monarchy as did the countries of the continent.' What prevented such development was the deeply entrenched tradition of a common law that was not conceived as the product of anyone's will but rather as a barrier to all power, including that of the king – a tradition which Edward Coke was to defend against King James I and Francis Bacon, and which Matthew Hale at the end of the seventeenth century masterly restated in opposition to Thomas Hobbes.

The freedom of the British which in the eighteenth century the rest of Europe came so much to admire was thus not, as the British themselves were among the first to believe and as Montesquieu later taught the world, originally a product of the separation of powers between legislature and executive, but rather a result of the fact that the law that governed the decisions of the courts was the common law, a law existing independently of anyone's will and at the same time binding upon and developed by the independent courts; a law with which parliament only rarely interfered and, when it did, mainly only to clear up doubtful points within a given body of law. One might even say that a sort of separation of powers had grown up in England, not because the 'legislature' alone made law, but because it did *not*: because the law was determined by courts independent of the power which organized and directed government, the power namely of what was misleadingly called the 'legislature'. . . .

The contention that a law based on precedent is more rather than less abstract than one expressed in verbal rules is so contrary to a view widely held, perhaps more among continental than among Anglo-Saxon lawyers, that it needs fuller justification. The central point can probably not be better expressed than in a famous statement by the great eighteenth-century judge Lord Mansfield, who stressed that the common law 'does not consist of particular cases, but of general principles, which are illustrated and explained by those cases'. What this means is that it is part of the technique of the common law judge that from the precedents which guide him he must be able to derive rules of universal significance which can be applied to new cases.

The chief concern of a common law judge must be the expectations which the parties in a transaction would have reasonably formed on the basis of the general practices that the ongoing order of actions rests on. In deciding what expectations were reasonable in this sense he can take account only of such practices (customs or rules) as in fact could determine the expectations of the parties and such facts as may be presumed to have been known to them. And these parties would have been able to form common expectations, in a situation which in some respects must have been unique, only because they interpreted the situation in terms of what was thought to be appropriate conduct and which need not have been known to them in the form of an articulated rule.

Such rules, presumed to have guided expectations in many similar situations in the past, must be abstract in the sense of referring to a limited number of relevant circumstances and of being applicable irrespective of the particular consequences now appearing to follow from their application. By the time the judge is called upon to decide a case, the parties in the dispute will already have acted in the pursuit of their own ends and mostly in particular circumstances unknown to any authority; and the expectations which have guided their actions and in which one of them has been disappointed will have been based on what they regarded as established practices. The task of the judge will be to tell them what ought to have guided their expectations, not because anyone had told them before that this was the rule, but because this was the established custom which they ought to have known. The question for the judge here can never be whether the action in fact taken was expedient from some higher point of view, or served a particular result desired by authority, but only whether the conduct under dispute conformed to recognized rules. The only public good with which he can be concerned is the observance of those rules that the individuals could reasonably count on. He is not concerned with any ulterior purpose which somebody may have intended the rules to serve and of which he must be largely ignorant; and he will have to apply the rules even if in the particular instance the known consequences will appear to him wholly undesirable. In this task he must pay no attention, as has often been emphasized by common law judges, to any wishes of a ruler or any 'reasons of state'. What must guide his decision is not any knowledge of what the whole of society requires at the particular moment, but solely what is demanded by general principles on which the going order of society is based.

It seems that the constant necessity of articulating rules in order to distinguish between the relevant and the accidental in the precedents which guide him, produces in the common law judge a capacity for discovering general principles rarely acquired by a judge who operates with a supposedly complete catalogue of applicable rules before him. When the generalizations are not supplied ready made, a capacity for formulating abstractions is apparently kept alive, which the mechanical use of verbal formulae tends to kill. The common law judge is bound to be very much aware that words are always but an imperfect expression of what his predecessors struggled to articulate.

If today the commands of a legislator often take the form of those abstract rules which have emerged from the judicial process, it is because they have been shaped after that model. But it is highly unlikely that any ruler aiming at organizing the activities of his subjects for the achievement of definite foreseeable results could ever have achieved his purpose by laying down universal rules intended to govern equally the actions of everybody. To restrain himself, as the judge does, so as to enforce only such rules, would require a degree of self-denial not to be expected from one used to issuing specific commands and to being guided in his decisions by the needs of the moment. Abstract rules are not likely to be invented by somebody concerned with obtaining particular results. It was the need to preserve an order of action which nobody had created but which was disturbed by certain kinds of behaviour that made it necessary to define those kinds of behaviour which had to be repressed.

WHY GROWN LAW REQUIRES CORRECTION BY LEGISLATION

The fact that all law arising out of the endeavour to articulate rules of conduct will of necessity possess some desirable properties not necessarily possessed by the commands of a legislator does not mean that in other respects such law may not develop in very undesirable directions, and that when this happens correction by deliberate legislation may not be the only practicable way out. For a variety of reasons the spontaneous process of growth may lead into an impasse from which it cannot extricate itself by its own forces or which it will at least not correct quickly enough. The development of case-law is in some respects a sort of one-way street: when it has already moved a considerable distance in one direction, it often cannot retrace its steps when some implications of earlier decisions are seen to be clearly undesirable. The fact that law that has evolved in this way has certain desirable properties does not prove that it will always be good law or even that some of its rules may not be very bad. It therefore does not mean that we can altogether dispense with legislation.

There are several other reasons for this. One is that the process of judicial development of law is of necessity gradual and may prove too slow to bring about the desirable rapid adaptation of the law to wholly new circumstances. Perhaps the most important, however, is that it is not only difficult but also undesirable for judicial decisions to reverse a development, which has already taken place and is then seen to have undesirable consequences or to be downright wrong. The judge is not performing his function if he disappoints reasonable expectations created by earlier decisions. Although the judge can develop the law by deciding issues which are genuinely doubtful, he cannot really alter it, or can do so at most only very gradually where a rule has become firmly established; although he may clearly recognize that another rule would be better, or more just, it would evidently be unjust to apply it to transactions which had taken place when a different rule was regarded as valid. In such situations it is desirable that the new rule should become known before it is enforced; and this can be effected only by promulgating a new rule which is to be applied only in the future. Where a real change in the law is required, the new law can properly fulfil the proper function of all law, namely that of guiding expectations, only if it becomes known before it is applied.

The necessity of such radical changes of particular rules may be due to various causes. It may be due simply to the recognition that some past development was based on error or that it produced consequences later recognized as unjust. But the most frequent cause is probably that the development of the law has lain in the hands of members of a particular class whose traditional views made them regard as just what could not meet the more general requirements of justice. There can be no doubt that in such fields as the law on the relations between master and servant, landlord and tenant, creditor and debtor, and in modern times between organized business and its customers, the rules have been shaped largely by the views of one of the parties and their particular interests – especially where, as used to be true in the first two of the instances given, it was one of the groups concerned which almost exclusively supplied the judges. This, as we shall see, does not mean that, as has been asserted, 'justice is an irrational ideal' and that 'from the point of rational cognition there are only interests of human beings and hence conflicts of interests', at least when by interests we do not mean only particular aims but long-term chances which different rules offer to the different members of society. It is even less true that, as would follow from those assertions, a recognized bias of some rule in favour of a particular group can be corrected only by biasing it instead in favour of another. But such occasions when it is recognized that some hereto accepted rules are unjust in the light of more general principles of justice may well require the revision not only of single rules but of whole sections of the established system of case law. This is more than can be accomplished by decisions of particular cases in the light of existing precedents.

THE ORIGIN OF LEGISLATIVE BODIES

There is no determinable point in history when the power of deliberately changing the law in the sense in which we have been considering it was explicitly conferred on any authority. But there always existed of necessity an authority which had power to make law of a different kind, namely the rules of the organization of government, and it was to these existing makers of public law that there gradually accrued the power of changing also the rules of just conduct as the necessity of such changes became recognized. Since those rules of conduct had to be enforced by the organization of government, it seemed natural that those who determined that organization should also determine the rules it was to enforce.

A legislative power in the sense of a power of determining the rules of government existed, therefore, long before the need for a power to change the universal rules of just conduct was even recognized. Rulers faced with the task of enforcing a given law and of organizing defence and various services, had long experienced the necessity of laying down rules for their officers or subordinates, and they would have made no distinction as to whether these rules were of a purely administrative character or subsidiary to the task of enforcing justice. Yet a ruler would find it to his advantage to claim for the organizational rules the same dignity as was generally conceded to the universal rules of just conduct.

But if the laying down of such rules for the organization of government was long regarded as the 'prerogative' of its head, the need for an approval of, or a consent to, his measure by representative or constituted bodies would often arise precisely because the ruler was himself supposed to be bound by the established law. And when, as in levying contributions in money or services for the purposes of government, he had to use coercion in a form not clearly prescribed by the established rules, he would have to assure himself of the support at least of his more powerful subjects. It would then often be difficult to decide whether they were merely called in to testify that this or that was established law or to approve of a particular imposition or measure thought necessary for a particular end.

It is thus misleading to conceive of early representative bodies as 'legislatures' in the sense in which the term was later employed by theorists. They were not primarily concerned with the rules of just conduct or the *nomos*. As F. W. Maitland explains:

> The further back we trace our history the more impossible it is for us to draw strict lines of demarcation between the various functions of the state: the same institution is a legislative assembly, a governmental council, and a court of law. . . . For a long time past political theorists have insisted on the distinction between legislation and the other functions of government, and of course the distinction is important though it is not always easy to draw the line with perfect accuracy. But it seems necessary to notice that the power of a statute is by no means confined to what a jurist or political philosopher would consider the domain of legislation. A vast number of statutes he would class rather as *privilegia* than as *leges*; the statute lays down no general rules but deals only with a particular case.

It was in connection with rules of the organization of government that the deliberate making of 'laws' became a familiar and everyday procedure; every new undertaking of a government or every change in the structure of government required some new rules for its organization. The laying down of such new rules thus became an accepted procedure long before anyone contemplated using it for altering the established rules of just conduct. But when the wish to do so arose it was almost inevitable that the task was entrusted to the body which had always made laws in another sense and often had also been asked to testify as to what the established rules of just conduct were.

ALLEGIANCE AND SOVEREIGNTY

From the conception that legislation is the sole source of law derive two ideas which in modern times have come to be accepted as almost self-evident and have exercised great influence on political developments, although they are wholly derived from that erroneous constructivism in which earlier anthropomorphic fallacies survive. The first of these is the belief that there must be a supreme legislator whose power cannot be limited, because this would require a still higher legislator, and so on in an infinite regress. The other is that anything laid down by that supreme legislator is law and only that which expresses his will is law.

The conception of the necessarily unlimited will of a supreme legislator, which since Bacon, Hobbes and Austin has served as the supposedly irrefutable justification of absolute power, first of monarchs and later of democratic assemblies, appears self-evident only if the term law is restricted to the rules guiding the deliberate and concerted actions of an organization. Thus interpreted, law, which in the earlier sense of *nomos* was meant to be a barrier to all power, becomes instead an instrument for the use of power.

The negative answer which legal positivism gives to the question of whether there can be effective limits to the power of the supreme legislature would be convincing only if it were true that all law is always the product of the deliberate 'will' of a legislator, and that nothing could effectively limit that power except another 'will' of the same sort. The authority of a legislator always rests, however, on something which must be clearly distinguished from an act of will on a particular matter in hand, and can therefore also be limited by the source from which it derives its authority. This source is a prevailing opinion that the legislator is authorized only to prescribe what is right, where this opinion refers not to the particular content of the rule but to the general attributes which any rule of just conduct must possess. The power of the legislator thus rests on a common opinion about certain attributes which the laws he produces ought to possess, and his will can obtain the support of opinion only if its expression possesses those attributes. We shall later have to consider more fully this distinction between will and opinion. Here it must suffice to say that we shall use the term 'opinion', as distinct from an act of will on a particular matter, to describe a common tendency to approve of some particular acts of will and to disapprove of others, according to whether they do or do not possess certain attributes which those who hold a given opinion usually will not be able to specify. So long as the legislator satisfies the expectation that what he resolves will possess those attributes, he will be free so far as the particular contents of its resolutions are concerned, and will in this sense be 'sovereign'. But the allegiance on which this sovereignty rests depends on the sovereign's satisfying certain expectations concerning the general character of those rules, and will vanish when this expectation is disappointed. In this sense all power rests on, and is limited by, opinion, as was most clearly seen by David Hume.

That all power rests on opinion in this sense is no less true of the powers of an absolute dictator than of those of any other authority. As dictators themselves have known best at all times, even the most powerful dictatorship crumbles if the support of opinion is withdrawn. This is the reason why dictators are so concerned to manipulate opinion through that control of information which is in their power.

The effective limitation of the powers of a legislature does therefore not require another organized authority capable of concerted action above it; it may be produced by a state of opinion which brings it about that only certain kinds of commands which the legislature issues are accepted as laws. Such opinion will be concerned not with the particular content of the decisions of the legislature but only with the general attributes of the kind of rules which the legislator is meant to proclaim and to which alone the people are willing to give support. This power of opinion does not rest on the capacity of the holders to take any course of concerted action, but is merely a negative power of withholding that support on which the power of the legislator ultimately rests.

From 'Nomos': The Law of Liberty, in *Law, Legislation and Liberty*:

THE ARTICULATION OF THE LAW AND THE PREDICTABILITY OF JUDICIAL DECISIONS

The order that the judge is expected to maintain is thus not a particular state of things but the regularity of a process which rests on some of the expectations of the acting persons being protected from interference by others. He will be expected to decide in a manner which in general will correspond to what the people regard as just, but he may sometimes have to decide that what *prima facie* appears to be just may not be so because it disappoints legitimate expectations. Here he will have to draw his conclusions not exclusively from articulated premises but from a sort of 'situational logic', based on the requirements of an existing order of actions which is at the same time the undesigned result and the rationale of all those rules which he must take for granted. While the judge's starting point will be the expectations based on already established rules, he will often have to decide which of conflicting expectations held in equally good faith and equally sanctioned by recognized rules is to be regarded as legitimate. Experience will often prove that in new situations rules which have come to be accepted lead to conflicting expectations. Yet although in such situations there will be no known rule to guide him, the judge will still not be free to decide in any manner he likes. If the decision cannot be logically deduced from recognized rules, it still must be consistent with the existing body of such rules in the sense that it serves the same order of actions as these rules. If the judge finds that a rule counted on by a litigant in forming his expectations is false even though it may be widely accepted and might even be universally approved if stated, this will be because he discovers that in some circumstances it clashes with expectations based on other rules. 'We all thought this to be a just rule, but now it proves to be unjust' is a meaningful statement, describing an experience in which it becomes apparent that our conception of the justice or injustice of a particular rule is not simply a matter of 'opinion' or 'feeling', but depends on the requirements of an existing order to which we are committed – an order which in new situations can be maintained only if one of the old rules is modified or a new rule is added. The reason why in such a situation either or even both of the rules counted on by the litigants will have to be modified will not be that their application in the particular case would cause hardship, or that any other consequence in the particular instance would be undesirable, but that the rules have proved insufficient to prevent conflicts.

If the judge here were confined to decisions which could be logically deduced from the body of already articulated rules, he would often not be able to decide a case in a manner appropriate to the function which the whole system of rules serves. This throws important light on a much discussed issue, the supposed greater certainty of the law under a system in which all rules of law have been laid down in written or codified form, and in which the judge is restricted to applying such rules as have become written law. The whole movement for codification has been guided by the belief that it increases the predictability of judicial decisions. In my own case even the experience of thirty odd years in the common law world was not enough to correct this deeply rooted prejudice, and only my return to a civil law atmosphere has led me seriously to question it. Although legislation can certainly increase the certainty of the law on particular points, I am now persuaded that this advantage is more than offset if its recognition leads to the requirement that *only* what has thus been expressed in statutes should have the force of law. It seems to me that judicial decisions may in fact be more predictable if the judge is also bound by generally held views of what is just, even when they are not supported by the letter of the law, than when he is restricted to deriving his decisions only from those among accepted beliefs which have found expression in the written law.

That the judge can, or ought to, arrive at his decisions exclusively by a process of logical inference from explicit premises always has been and must be a fiction. For in fact the judge never proceeds in this way. As has been truly said, 'the trained intuition of the judge continuously leads him to right results for which he is puzzled to give unimpeachable legal reasons'. The other view is a characteristic product of the constructivist rationalism which regards all rules as deliberately made and therefore capable of exhaustive statement. It appears, significantly, only in the eighteenth century and in connection with criminal law where the legitimate desire to restrict the power of the judge to the application of what was unquestionably stated as law was dominant. But even the formula *nulla poena sine lege*, in which C. Beccaria expressed this idea, is not necessarily part of the rule of law if by 'law' is meant only written rules promulgated by the legislator, and not any rules whose binding character would at once be generally recognized if they were expressed in words. Characteristically English common law has never recognized the principle in the first sense, even though it always accepted it in the second. Here the old conviction that a rule may exist which everybody is assumed to be capable of observing, although it has never been articulated as a verbal statement, has persisted to the present day as part of the law.

Whatever one may feel, however, about the desirability of tying the judge to the application of the written law in criminal matters, where the aim is essentially to protect the accused and let the guilty escape rather than punish the innocent, there is little case for it where the judge must aim at equal justice between litigants. Here the requirement that he must derive his decision exclusively from the written law and at most fill in obvious gaps by resort to unwritten principles would seem to make the certainty of the law rather less than greater. It seems to me that in most instances in which judicial decisions have shocked public opinion and have run counter to general expectations, this was because the judge felt that he had to stick to the letter of the written law and dared not depart from the result of the syllogism in which only explicit statements of that law could serve as premises. Logical deduction from a limited number of articulated premises always means following the 'letter' rather than the 'spirit' of the law. But the belief that everyone must be able to foresee the consequences that will follow in an unforeseen factual situation from an application of those statements of the already articulated basic principles is clearly an illusion. It is now probably universally admitted that no code of law can be without gaps. The conclusion to be derived from this would seem to be not merely that the judge must fill in such gaps by appeal to yet unarticulated principles, but also that, even when those rules which have been articulated seem to give an unambiguous answer, if they are in conflict with the general sense of justice he should be free to modify his conclusions when he can find some unwritten rule which justifies such modification and which, when articulated, is likely to receive general assent.

In this connection even John Locke's contention that in a free society all law must be 'promulgated' or 'announced' beforehand would seem to be a product of the constructivist idea of all law as being deliberately made. It is erroneous in the implication that by confining the judge to the application of already articulated rules we will increase the predictability of his decisions. What has been promulgated or announced beforehand will often be only a very imperfect formulation of principles which people can better honour in action than express in words. Only if one believes that all law is an expression of the will of a legislator and has been invented by him, rather than an expression of the principles required by the exigencies of a going order, does it seem that previous announcement is an indispensable condition of knowledge of the law. Indeed it is likely that few endeavours by judges to improve the law have come to be accepted by others unless they found expressed in them what in a sense they 'knew' already.

THE FUNCTION OF A JUDGE IS CONFINED TO A SPONTANEOUS ORDER

The contention that the judges by their decisions of particular cases gradually approach a system of rules of conduct which is most conducive to producing an efficient order of actions becomes more plausible when it is realized that this is in fact merely the same kind of process as that by which all intellectual evolution proceeds. As in all other fields advance is here achieved by our moving within an existing system of thought and endeavouring by a process of piecemeal tinkering, or 'immanent criticism', to make the whole more consistent both internally as well as with the facts to which the rules are applied. Such 'immanent criticism' is the main instrument of the evolution of thought, and an understanding of this process the characteristic aim of an evolutionary (or critical) as distinguished from the constructivist (or naïve) rationalism.

The judge, in other words, serves, or tries to maintain and improve, a going order which nobody has designed, an order that has formed itself without the knowledge and often against the will of authority, that extends beyond the range of deliberate organization on the part of anybody, and that is not based on the individuals doing anybody's will, but on their expectations becoming mutually adjusted. The reason why the judge will be asked to intervene will be that the rules which secure such a matching of expectations are not always observed, or clear enough, or adequate to prevent conflicts even if observed. Since new situations in which the established rules are not adequate will constantly arise, the task of preventing conflict and enhancing the compatibility of actions by appropriately delimiting the range of permitted actions is of necessity a never-ending one, requiring not only the application of already established rules but also the formulation of new rules necessary for the preservation of the order of actions. In their endeavour to cope with new problems by the application of 'principles' which they have to distil from the *ratio decidendi* of earlier decisions, and so to develop these inchoate rules (which is what 'principles' are) that they will produce the desired effect in new situations, neither the judges nor the parties involved need to know anything about the nature of the resulting overall order, or about any 'interest of society' which they serve, beyond the fact that the rules are meant to assist the individuals in successfully forming expectations in a wide range of circumstances.

The efforts of the judge are thus part of that process of adaptation of society to circumstances by which the spontaneous order grows. He assists in the process of selection by upholding those rules which, like those which have worked well in the past, make it more likely that expectations will match and not conflict. He thus becomes an organ of that order. But even when in the performance of this function he creates new rules, he is not a creator of a new order but a servant endeavouring to maintain and improve the functioning of an existing order. And the outcome of his efforts will be a characteristic instance of those 'products of human action but not of human design' in which the experience gained by the experimentation of generations embodies more knowledge than was possessed by anyone. . . .

10
G.W.F. Hegel

Georg Wilhelm Friedrich Hegel (1770–1831), born in Stuttgart, studied at Tübingen, then worked as a private tutor in Berne and Frankfurt. He became Privatdozent *at the University of Jena in 1801, then editor of a pro-French newspaper in Bamberg in 1807, and headmaster of a Gymnasium in Munich in 1808. In 1816 he was appointed professor of philosophy in Heidelberg and in 1818 succeeded Fichte as professor of philosophy in Berlin.*

Hegel's imaginative and all-comprehending metaphysical vision exerted such a profound intellectual influence over his successors that it is very hard now to consider his system objectively, or to separate what is true and useful in it from what is wild, dangerous, or absurd. The fact that Marxism grew out of Hegelian metaphysics – in reaction to its conservative implications, but nevertheless borrowing many of its central arguments and themes – has led many conservatives to be suspicious of Hegel, and to view him as the father of modern ideologies. Moreover the sheer intellectual difficulty of his writing, its abstruse remoteness from the language of action, and its wilful self-reference, have led many to pass over his arguments as of merely scholarly interest. In fact, however, Hegel was probably the greatest of all conservative philosophers, and all the greater for the fact that his political thinking had deep metaphysical roots.

The following extracts are taken from The Philosophy of Right, *in which Hegel tries to derive from the principles of the Dialectic a description of man's moral and political existence. According to the Dialectic, all knowledge is a self-discovery, and the world, in becoming known, 'realises' its spiritual potential. The movement of the mind in gaining knowledge of the world, and the process whereby concepts express themselves in reality, are one and the same. Hence we discover the nature of reality by laying bare the structure of thought. In particular, we understand political reality as the outcome of a dialectical process, whereby the concept of* Recht *(meaning both right and law) attains full reality in an objective order. As against liberalism, Hegel maintains that our rights are only partially defined when considered abstractly, and become clear and secure through the building of 'ethical life'* (Sittlichkeit). *Like every aspect of the human world, ethical life conforms to the structure of the dialectic: it contains* three 'moments', or principles: *that of immediacy, in which the concept and its object are not distinct from each other; that of mediacy or separation, in which the object of knowledge sunders itself so as to become known; and that of 'transcendence'* (Aufhebung) *in which the conflict between the other moments is overcome in a new and reconciled mode of spiritual existence. These three 'moments' exist in political life as separate spheres within the body politic: the spheres of Family, Civil Society and State. Whether or not we accept the dialectical method and all that is implied in it, Hegel's distinction between the three spheres of political life, and his account of the rights and duties which arise within them, carries great conviction.*

The Philosophy of Right *exists as lecture notes, with additional paragraphs added at various dates. In preparing this selection, from the translation by T.M. Knox, I have arranged the paragraphs to form as readable a sequence as possible, retaining Hegel's numbering of sections so that the reader may refer back to the original whenever necessary. In addition to this work, Hegel's* Phenomenology of Spirit *contains important arguments against the individualist account of human nature, and a proper study of Hegel's politics should take both works together.*

1. ON CRIME AND PUNISHMENT

96. It is only the will existent in an object that can suffer injury. In becoming existent in something, however, the will enters the sphere of quantitative extension and qualitative characteristics, and hence varies accordingly. For this reason, it makes a difference to the objective aspect of crime whether the will so objectified and its specific quality is injured throughout its entire extent, and so in the infinity which is equivalent to its concept (as in murder, slavery, enforced religious observance, &c.), or whether it is injured only in a single part or in one of its qualitative characteristics, and if so, in which of these.

The Stoic view that there is only one virtue and one vice, the laws of Draco which prescribe death as a punishment for every offence, the crude formal code of Honour which takes any insult as an offence against the infinity of personality, all have this in common, that they go no further than the abstract thought of the free will and personality and fail to apprehend it in the concrete and determinate existence which it must possess as Idea.

The distinction between robbery and theft is qualitative; when I am robbed, personal violence is done to me and I am injured in my character as consciousness existing here and now and so as *this* infinite subject.

Many qualitative characteristics of crime, e.g. its danger to public safety, have their basis in more concrete circumstances, although in the first instance they also are often fastened on by the indirect route as consequences instead of from the concept of the thing. For instance, the crime which taken by itself is the more dangerous in its immediate character is an injury of a more serious type in its range of its quality.

The subjective, moral, quality of crime rests on the higher distinction implied in the question of how far an event or fact pure and simple is an action, and concerns the subjective character of the action itself, on which see below.

How any given crime is to be punished cannot be settled by mere thinking; positive laws are necessary. But with the advance of education, opinions about crime become less harsh, and today a criminal is not so severely punished as he was a hundred years ago. It is not exactly crimes or punishments which change but the relation between them.

97. The infringement of right as right is something that happens and has positive existence in the external world, though inherently it is nothing at all. The manifestation of its nullity is the appearance, also in the external world, of the annihilation of the infringement. This is the right actualized, the necessity of the right mediating itself with itself by annulling what has infringed it.

A crime alters something in some way, and the thing has its existence in this alteration. Yet this existence is a self-contradiction and to that extent is inherently a nullity. The nullity is that the crime has set aside right as such. That is to say, right as something absolute cannot be set aside, and so committing a crime is in principle a nullity: and this nullity is the essence of what a crime effects. A nullity, however, must reveal itself to be such, i.e. manifest itself as vulnerable. A crime, as an act, is not something positive, not a first thing, on which punishment would supervene as a negation. It is something negative, so that its punishment is only a negation of the negation. Right in its actuality, then, annuls what infringes it and therein displays its validity and proves itself to be a necessary, mediated, reality.

98. In so far as the infringement of the right is only an injury to a possession or to something which exists externally, it is a *malum* or damage to some kind of property or asset. The annulling of the infringement, so far as the infringement is productive of damage, is the satisfaction given in a civil suit, i.e. compensation for the wrong done, so far as any such compensation can be found.

Apropos of such satisfaction, the universal character of the damage, i.e. its 'value', must here again take the place of its specific qualitative character in cases where the damage done amounts to destruction and is quite irreparable.

99. But the injury which has befallen the *implicit* will (and this means the implicit will of the *injuring* party as well as that of the injured and everyone else) has as little positive existence in this implicit will as such as it has in the mere state of affairs which it produces. In itself this implicit will (i.e. the right or law implicit) is rather that which has no external existence and which for that reason cannot be injured. Consequently, the injury from the point of view of the particular will of the injured party and of onlookers is only something negative. The sole positive existence which the injury possesses is that it is the particular will of the criminal. Hence to injure [or penalize] this particular will as a will determinately existent is to annul the crime, which otherwise would have been held valid, and to restore the right.

The theory of punishment is one of the topics which have come off worst in the recent study of the positive science of law, because in this theory the Understanding is insufficient; the essence of the matter depends on the concept.

If crime and its annulment (which later will acquire the specific character of punishment) are treated as if they were unqualified evils, it must, of course, seem quite unreasonable to will an evil merely because 'another evil is there already'.[1] To give punishment this superficial character of an evil is, amongst the various theories of punishment, the fundamental presupposition of those which regard it as a preventive, a deterrent, a threat, as reformative, &c.,

and what on these theories is supposed to result from punishment is characterized equally superficially as a good. But it is not merely a question of an evil or of this, that, or the other good; the precise point at issue is wrong and the righting of it. If you adopt that superficial attitude to punishment, you brush aside the objective treatment of the righting of wrong, which is the primary and fundamental attitude in considering crime; and the natural consequence is that you take as essential the moral attitude, i.e. the subjective aspect of crime, intermingled with trivial psychological ideas of stimuli, impulses too strong for reason, and psychological factors coercing and working on our ideas (as if freedom were not equally capable of thrusting an idea aside and reducing it to something fortuitous!). The various considerations which are relevant to punishment as a phenomenon and to the bearing it has on the particular consciousness, and which concern its effects (deterrent, reformative, &c.) on the imagination, are an essential topic for examination in their place, especially in connexion with modes of punishment, but all these considerations presuppose as their foundation the fact that punishment is inherently and actually just. In discussing this matter the only important things are, first, that crime is to be annulled, not because it is the producing of an evil, but because it is an infringement of the right as right, and secondly, the question of what that positive existence is which crime possesses and which must be annulled; it is this existence which is the real evil to be removed, and the essential point is the question of where it lies. So long as the concepts here at issue are not clearly apprehended, confusion must continue to reign in the theory of punishment.

Feuerbach[2] bases his theory of punishment on threat and thinks that if anyone commits a crime despite the threat, punishment must follow because the criminal was aware of it beforehand. But what about the justification of the threat? A threat presupposes that a man is not free, and its aim is to coerce him by the idea of an evil. But right and justice must have their seat in freedom and the will, not in the lack of freedom on which a threat turns. To base a justification of punishment on threat is to liken it to the act of a man who lifts his stick to a dog. It is to treat a man like a dog instead of with the freedom and respect due to him as a man. But a threat, which after all may rouse a man to demonstrate his freedom in spite of it, discards justice altogether.—Coercion by psychological factors can concern only differences of quantity and quality in crime, not the nature of crime itself, and therefore any legal codes that may be products of the doctrine that crime is due to such coercion lack their proper foundation.

100. The injury [the penalty] which falls on the criminal is not merely *implicitly* just – as just, it is *eo ipso* his implicit will, an embodiment of his freedom, his right; on the contrary, it is also a right *established* within the criminal himself, i.e. in his objectively embodied will, in his action. The reason for this is that his action is the action of a rational being and this implies that it is something universal and that by doing it the criminal has laid down a law which he has explicitly recognized in his action and under which in consequence he should be brought as under his right.

As is well known, Beccaria denied to the state the right of inflicting capital punishment. His reason was that it could not be presumed that the readiness of individuals to allow themselves to be executed was included in the social contract, and that in fact the contrary would have to be assumed. But the state is not a contract at all (see [Remark to] Paragraph 75) nor is its fundamental essence the unconditional protection and guarantee of the life and property of members of the public as individuals. On the contrary, it is that higher entity which even lays claim to this very life and property and demands its sacrifice. Further, what is involved in the action of the criminal is not only the concept of crime, the rational aspect present in crime as such whether the individual wills it or not, the aspect which the state has to vindicate, but also the abstract rationality of the individual's *volition*. Since that is so, punishment is regarded as containing the criminal's right and hence by being punished he is honoured as a rational being. He does not receive this due of honour unless the concept and measure of his punishment are derived from his own act. Still less does he receive it if he is treated either as a harmful animal who has to be made harmless, or with a view to deterring and reforming him.

Moreover, apart from these considerations, the form in which the righting of wrong exists in the state, namely punishment, is not its only form, nor is the state a pre-condition of the principle of righting wrong.

Beccaria's requirement that men should give their consent to being punished is right enough, but the criminal gives his consent already by his very act. The nature of the crime, no less than the private will of the criminal, requires that the injury initiated by the criminal should be annulled. However that may be, Beccaria's endeavour to have capital punishment abolished has had beneficial effects. Even if neither Joseph II nor the French ever succeeded in entirely abolishing it, still we have begun to see which crimes deserve the death penalty and which do not. Capital punishment has in consequence become rarer, as in fact should be the case with this most extreme punishment.

101. The annulment of the crime is retribution in so far as (*a*) retribution in *conception* is an 'injury of the injury', and (*b*) since as existent a crime is something determinate in its scope both qualitatively and quantitatively, its negation as *existent* is similarly determinate. This identity rests on the concept, but it is not an equality between the specific character of the crime and that of its negation; on the contrary, the two injuries are equal only in respect of their implicit character, i.e. in respect of their 'value'.

Empirical science requires that the definition of a class concept (punishment in this case) shall be drawn from ideas universally present to conscious psychological experience. This method would prove that the universal feeling of nations and individuals about crime is and has been that it deserves punishment, that as the criminal has done, so should it be done to him. (There is no understanding how these sciences, which find the source of their class concepts in ideas universally shared, come on other occasions to take for granted propositions contradictory of like 'facts of consciousness' also styled 'universal'.)

But a point of great difficulty has been introduced into the idea of retribution by the category of equality, though it is still true that the justice of specific types or amounts of punishment is a further matter, subsequent to the substance of the thing itself. Even if to determine the later question of specific punishments we had to look round for principles other than those determining the universal character of punishment, still the latter remains what it is. The only thing is that the concept itself must in general contain the *fundamental* principle for determining the particular too. But the determinate character given by the concept to punishment is just that necessary connexion between crime and punishment already mentioned; crime, as the will which is implicitly null, *eo ipso* contains its negation in itself and this negation is manifested as punishment. It is this inner identity whose reflection in the external world appears to the Understanding as 'equality'. The qualitative and quantitative characteristics of crime and its annulment fall, then, into the sphere of externality. In any case, no absolute determinacy is possible in this sphere (compare Paragraph 49); in the field of the finite, absolute determinacy remains only a demand, a demand which the Understanding has to meet by continually increasing delimitation – a fact of the greatest importance – but which continues *ad infinitum* and which allows only of perennially approximate satisfaction.

If we overlook this nature of the finite and then into the bargain refuse to go beyond abstract and specific equality, we are faced with the insuperable difficulty of fixing punishments (especially if psychology adduces in addition the strength of sensual impulses and consequentially either the greater strength of the evil will or the greater weakness, or the restricted freedom, of the will as such – we may choose which we please). Furthermore, it is easy enough from this point of view to exhibit the retributive character of punishment as an absurdity (theft for theft, robbery for robbery, an eye for an eye, a tooth for a tooth – and then you can go on to suppose that the criminal has only one eye or no teeth). But the concept has nothing to do with this absurdity, for which indeed the introduction of this specific equality is solely to blame. Value, as the inner equality of things which in their outward existence are specifically different from one another in every way, is a category which has appeared already in connexion with contracts (see Paragraph 77), and also in connexion with injuries that are the subject of civil suits (see Remark to Paragraph 98); and by means of it our idea of a thing is raised above its immediate character to its universality. In crime, as that which is characterized at bottom by the infinite aspect of the deed, the purely external specific character vanishes all the more obviously, and equality remains the fundamental regulator of the essential thing, to wit the deserts of the criminal, though not for the specific external form which the payment of those deserts may take. It is only in respect of that form that there is a plain inequality between theft and robbery on the one hand, and fines, imprisonment, &c., on the other. In respect of their 'value', however, i.e. in respect of their universal property of being injuries, they are comparable. Thus, as was said above, it is a matter for the Understanding to look for something approximately equal to their 'value' in this sense. If the implicit interconnexion of crime and its negation, and if also the thought of value and the comparability of crime and punishment in respect of their value are not apprehended, then it may become possible to see in a punishment proper only an 'arbitrary'[3] connexion of an evil with an unlawful action.

Retribution is the inner connexion and the identity of two conceptions which are different in appearance and which also exist in the world as two distinct and opposed events. Retribution is inflicted on the criminal and so it has the look of an alien destiny, not intrinsically his own. Nevertheless punishment, as we have seen, is only crime made manifest, i.e. is the second half which necessarily presupposes the first. Prima facie, the objection to retribution is that it looks like something immoral, i.e. like revenge, and that thus it may pass for something personal. Yet it is not something personal, but the concept itself, which carries out retribution. 'Vengeance is mine, saith the Lord', as the Bible says.[4] And if something in the word '*re*pay' calls up the idea of a particular caprice of the subjective will, it must be pointed out that what is meant is only that the form which crime takes is turned round against itself. The Eumenides sleep, but crime awakens them, and hence it is the very act of crime itself which vindicates itself.—Now although requital cannot simply be made specifically equal to the crime, the case is otherwise with murder, which is of necessity liable to the death penalty; the reason is that since life is the full compass of a man's existence, the punishment here cannot simply consist in a 'value', for none is great enough, but can consist only in taking away a second life.

102. The annulling of crime in this sphere where right is immediate is principally revenge, which is just in its content in so far as it is retributive. But in its form it is an act of a subjective will which can place its infinity in every act of transgression and whose justification, therefore, is in all cases contingent, while to the other party too it appears as only particular. Hence revenge, because it is a positive action of a particular will, becomes a new transgression; as thus contradictory in character, it falls into an infinite progression and descends from one generation to another *ad infinitum*.

In cases where crimes are prosecuted and punished not as *crimina publica* but as *crimina privata* (e.g. in Jewish law and Roman law, theft and robbery; in English law to this day, certain crimes,

&c.) punishment is in principle, at least to some extent, revenge. There is a difference between private revenge and the revenge of heroes, knights-errant, &c., which is part of the founding of states.

In that condition of society when there are neither magistrates nor laws, punishment always takes the form of revenge; revenge remains defective inasmuch as it is the act of a subjective will and therefore does not correspond with its content. Those who administer justice are persons, but their will is the universal will of the law and they intend to import into the punishment nothing except what is implied in the nature of the thing. The person wronged, however, views the wrong not as something qualitatively and quantitatively limited but only as wrong pure and simple, and in requiting the injury he may go too far, and this would lead to a new wrong. Amongst uncivilized peoples, revenge is deathless; amongst the Arabs, for instance, it can be checked only by superior force or by the impossibility of its satisfaction. A residue of revenge still lingers in comparatively modern legislation in those cases where it is left to the option of individuals whether to prosecute or not.

103. The demand that this contradiction, which is present here in the manner in which wrong is annulled, be resolved like contradictions in the case of other types of wrong (see Paragraphs 86, 89), is the demand for a justice freed from subjective interest and a subjective form and no longer contingent on might, i.e. it is the demand for justice not as revenge but as punishment. Fundamentally, this implies the demand for a will which, though particular and subjective, yet wills the universal as such. But this concept of *Morality* is not simply something demanded; it has emerged in the course of this movement itself.

2. THE SPHERES OF ETHICAL LIFE

156. The ethical substance, as containing independent self-consciousness united with its concept, is the actual mind of a family and a nation.

157. The concept of this Idea has being only as mind, as something knowing itself and actual, because it is the objectification of itself, the movement running through the form of its moments. It is therefore

(A) ethical mind in its natural or immediate phase – the *Family*. This substantiality loses its unity, passes over into division, and into the phase of relation, i.e. into
(B) *Civil Society* – an association of members as self-subsistent individuals in a universality which, because of their self-subsistence, is only abstract. Their association is brought about by their needs, by the legal system – the means to security of person and property – and by an external organization for attaining their particular and common interests. This external state
(C) is brought back to and welded into unity in the *Constitution of the State* which is the end and actuality of both the substantial universal order and the public life devoted thereto.

The Family

158. The family, as the immediate substantiality of mind, is specifically characterized by love, which is mind's feeling of its own unity. Hence in a family, one's frame of mind is to have self-consciousness of one's individuality within this unity as the absolute essence of oneself, with the result that one is in it not as an independent person but as a member.

159. The right which the individual enjoys on the strength of the family unity and which is in the first place simply the individual's life within this unity, takes on the *form* of right (as the abstract moment of determinate individuality) only when the family begins to dissolve. At that point those who should be family-members both in their inclination and in actuality begin to be self-subsistent persons, and whereas they formerly constituted one specific moment within the whole, they now receive their share separately and so only in an external fashion by way of money, food, educational expenses, and the like.

160. The family is completed in these three phases:
(a) *Marriage*, the form assumed by the concept of the family in its immediate phase;
(b) *Family Property and Capital* (the external embodiment of the concept) and attention to these;
(c) *The Education of Children and The Dissolution of the Family*.

Marriage

161. Marriage, as the immediate type of ethical relationship, contains first, the moment of physical life; and since marriage is a *substantial* tie, the life involved in it is life in its totality, i.e. as the actuality of the race and its life-process.[5] But, secondly, in self-consciousness the natural sexual union – a union purely inward or implicit and for that very reason *existent* as purely external – is changed into a union on the level of mind, into self-conscious love.

162. On the subjective side, marriage may have a more obvious source in the particular inclination of the two persons who are entering upon the marriage tie, or in the foresight and contrivance of the parents, and so forth. But its objective source lies in the free consent of the persons, especially in their consent to make themselves one person, to renounce their natural and individual personality to this unity of one with the other. From this point of view, their union is a self-restriction, but in fact it is their liberation, because in it they attain their substantive self-consciousness.

Our objectively appointed end and so our ethical duty is to enter the married state. The external origin of any *particular* marriage is in the nature of the case contingent, and it depends principally on the extent to which reflective thought has been developed. At one extreme, the first step is that the marriage is arranged by the contrivance of benevolent parents; the appointed end of the parties is a union of mutual love, and their inclination to marry arises from the fact that each grows acquainted with the other from the first as a destined partner. At the other extreme, it is the inclination of the parties which comes first, appearing in them as *these* two infinitely particularized individuals. The more ethical way to matrimony may be taken to be the former extreme or any way at all whereby the decision to marry comes first and the inclination to do so follows, so that in the actual wedding both decision and inclination coalesce. In the latter extreme, it is the uniqueness of the infinitely particularized which makes good its claims in accordance with the subjective principle of the modern world (see Remark to Paragraph 124).

But those works of modern art, dramatic and other, in which the love of the sexes is the main interest, are pervaded by a chill despite the heat of passion they portray, for they associate the passion with accident throughout and represent the entire dramatic interest as if it rested solely on the characters as *these individuals*; what rests on them may indeed be of infinite importance to *them*, but is of none whatever in itself.

163. The ethical aspect of marriage consists in the parties' consciousness of this unity as their substantive aim, and so in their love, trust, and common sharing of their entire existence as individuals. When the parties are in this frame of mind and their union is actual, their physical passion sinks to the level of a physical moment, destined to vanish in its very satisfaction. On the other hand, the spiritual bond of union secures its rights as the substance of marriage and thus rises, inherently indissoluble, to a plane above the contingency of passion and the transience of particular caprice.

It was noted above (in Paragraph 75) that marriage, so far as its essential basis is concerned, is not a contractual relation. On the contrary, though marriage begins in contract, it is precisely a contract to transcend the standpoint of contract, the standpoint from which persons are regarded in their individuality as self-subsistent units. The identification of personalities, whereby the family becomes one person and its members become its accidents (though substance is in essence the relation of accidents to itself[6]), is the ethical mind. Taken by itself and stripped of the manifold externals of which it is possessed owing to its embodiment in *these* individuals and the interests of the phenomenal realm, interests limited in time and numerous other ways, this mind emerges in a shape for representative thinking and has been revered as *Penates*, &c.; and in general it is in this mind that the religious character of marriage and the family, or *pietas*, is grounded. It is a further abstraction still to separate the divine, or the substantive, from its body, and then to stamp it, together with the feeling and consciousness of mental unity, as what is falsely called 'Platonic' love. This separation is in keeping with the monastic doctrine which characterizes the moment of physical life as purely negative and which, precisely by thus separating the physical from the mental, endows the former by itself with infinite importance.

164. Mere agreement to the stipulated terms of a contract in itself involves the genuine transfer of the property in question (see

Paragraph 79). Similarly, the solemn declaration by the parties of their consent to enter the ethical bond of marriage, and its corresponding recognition and confirmation by their family and community,[7] constitutes the formal completion and actuality of marriage. The knot is tied and made ethical only after this ceremony, whereby through the use of signs, i.e. of language (the most mental embodiment of mind – see Paragraph 78), the substantial thing in the marriage is brought completely into being. As a result, the sensuous moment, the one proper to physical life, is put into its ethical place as something only consequential and accidental, belonging to the external embodiment of the ethical bond, which indeed can subsist exclusively in reciprocal love and support.

If with a view to framing or criticizing legal enactments, the question is asked: what should be regarded as the chief end of marriage?, the question may be taken to mean: which single facet of marriage in its actuality is to be regarded as the most essential one? No one facet by itself, however, makes up the whole range of its implicit and explicit content, i.e. of its ethical character, and one or other of its facets may be lacking in an existing marriage without detriment to the essence of marriage itself.

It is in the actual conclusion of a marriage, i.e. in the wedding, that the essence of the tie is expressed and established beyond dispute as something ethical, raised above the contingency of feeling and private inclination. If this ceremony is taken as an external formality, a mere so-called 'civil requirement', it is thereby stripped of all significance except perhaps that of serving the purpose of edification and attesting the civil relation of the parties. It is reduced indeed to a mere *fiat* of a civil or ecclesiastical authority. As such it appears as something not merely indifferent to the true nature of marriage, but actually alien to it. The heart is constrained by the law to attach a value to the formal ceremony and the latter is looked upon merely as a condition which must precede the complete mutual surrender of the parties to one another. As such it appears to bring disunion into their loving disposition and, like an alien intruder, to thwart the inwardness of their union. Such a doctrine pretentiously claims to afford the highest conception of the freedom, inwardness, and perfection of love; but in fact it is a travesty of the ethical aspect of love, the higher aspect which restrains purely sensual impulse and puts it in the background. Such restraint is already present at the instinctive level in shame, and it rises to chastity and modesty as consciousness becomes more specifically intelligent. In particular, the view just criticized casts aside marriage's specifically ethical character, which consists in this, that the consciousness of the parties is crystallized out of its physical and subjective mode and lifted to the thought of what is substantive; instead of continually reserving to itself the contingency and caprice of bodily desire, it removes the marriage bond from the province of this caprice, surrenders to the substantive, and swears allegiance to the *Penates*; the physical moment it subordinates until it becomes something wholly conditioned by the true and ethical character of the marriage relation and by the recognition of the bond as an ethical one. It is effrontery and its buttress, the Understanding, which cannot apprehend the speculative character of the substantial tie; nevertheless, with this speculative character there correspond both ethical purity of heart and the legislation of Christian peoples.

165. The difference in the physical characteristics of the two sexes has a rational basis and consequently acquires an intellectual and ethical significance. This significance is determined by the difference into which the ethical substantiality, as the concept, internally sunders itself in order that its vitality may become a concrete unity consequent upon this difference.

166. Thus one sex is mind in its self-diremption into explicit personal self-subsistence and the knowledge and volition of free universality, i.e. the self-consciousness of conceptual thought and the volition of the objective final end. The other sex is mind maintaining itself in unity as knowledge and volition of the substantive, but knowledge and volition in the form of concrete individuality and feeling. In relation to externality, the former is powerful and active, the latter passive and subjective. It follows that man has his actual substantive life in the state, in learning, and so forth, as well as in labour and struggle with the external world and with himself so that it is only out of his diremption that he fights his way to self-subsistent unity with himself. In the family he has a tranquil intuition of this unity, and there he lives a subjective ethical life on the plane of feeling. Woman, on the other hand, has her substantive destiny in the family, and to be imbued with family piety is her ethical frame of mind.

For this reason, family piety is expounded in Sophocles' *Antigone* – one of the most sublime presentations of this virtue – as principally the law of woman, and as the law of a substantiality at once subjective and on the plane of feeling, the law of the inward life, a life which has not yet attained its full actualization; as the law of the ancient gods, 'the gods of the underworld'; as 'an everlasting law, and no man knows at what time it was first put forth'. This law is there displayed as a law opposed to public law, to the law of the land. This is the supreme opposition in ethics and therefore in tragedy; and it is individualized in the same play in the opposing natures of man and woman.[8]

167. In essence marriage is monogamy because it is personality – immediate exclusive individuality – which enters into this tie and surrenders itself to it; and hence the tie's truth and inwardness (i.e. the subjective form of its substantiality) proceeds only from the mutual, whole-hearted, surrender of this personality. Personality attains its right of being conscious of itself in another only in so far as the other is in this identical relationship as a person, i.e. as an atomic individual.

Marriage, and especially monogamy, is one of the absolute principles on which the ethical life of a community depends. Hence marriage comes to be recorded as one of the moments in the founding of states by gods or heroes.

Civil Society

255. As the family was the first, so the Corporation is the second ethical root of the state, the one planted in civil society. The former contains the moments of subjective particularity and objective universality in a substantial unity. But these moments are sundered in civil society to begin with; on the one side there is the particularity of need and satisfaction, reflected into itself, and on the other side the universality of abstract rights. In the Corporation these moments are united in an inward fashion, so that in this union particular welfare is present as a right and is actualized.

The sanctity of marriage and the dignity of Corporation membership are the two fixed points round which the unorganized atoms of civil society revolve.

256. The end of the Corporation is restricted and finite, while the public authority was an external organization involving a separation and a merely relative identity of controller and controlled. The end of the former and the externality and relative identity of the latter find their truth in the absolutely universal end and its absolute actuality. Hence the sphere of civil society passes over into the state.

The town is the seat of the civil life of business. There reflection arises, turns in upon itself, and pursues its atomizing task; each man maintains himself in and through his relation to others who, like himself, are persons possessed of rights. The country, on the other hand, is the seat of an ethical life resting on nature and the family. Town and country thus constitute the two moments, still ideal moments, whose true ground is the state, although it is from them that the state springs.

The philosophic proof of the concept of the state is this development of ethical life from its immediate phase through civil society, the phase of division, to the state, which then reveals itself as the true ground of these phases. A proof in philosophic science can only be a development of this kind.

Since the state appears as a result in the advance of the philosophic concept through displaying itself as the true ground [of the earlier phases], that show of mediation is now cancelled and the state has become directly present before us. Actually, therefore, the state as such is not so much the result as the beginning. It is within the state that the family is first developed into civil society, and it is the Idea of the state itself which disrupts itself into these two moments. Through the development of civil society, the substance of ethical life acquires its infinite form, which contains in itself these two moments: (1) infinite differentiation down to the inward experience of independent self-consciousness, and (2) the form of universality involved in education, the form of thought whereby mind is objective and actual to itself as an organic totality in laws and institutions which are its will in terms of thought.

The State

257. The state is the actuality of the ethical Idea. It is ethical mind *qua* the substantial will manifest and revealed to itself, knowing and thinking itself, accomplishing what it knows and in so far as it knows it. The state exists immediately in custom, mediately in individual self-consciousness, knowledge, and activity, while self-consciousness in virtue of its sentiment towards the state finds in the state, as its essence and the end and product of its activity, its substantive freedom.

The *Penates* are inward gods, gods of the underworld; the mind of a nation (Athene for instance) is the divine, knowing and willing itself. Family piety is feeling, ethical behaviour directed by feeling; political virtue is the willing of the absolute end in terms of thought.

258. The state is absolutely rational inasmuch as it is the actuality of the substantial will which it possesses in the particular self-consciousness once that consciousness has been raised to consciousness of its universality. This substantial unity is an absolute unmoved end in itself, in which freedom comes into its supreme right. On the other hand this final end has supreme right against the individual, whose supreme duty is to be a member of the state.

If the state is confused with civil society, and if its specific end is laid down as the security and protection of property and personal freedom, then the interest of the individuals as such becomes the ultimate end of their association, and it follows that membership of the state is something optional. But the state's relation to the individual is quite different from this. Since the state is mind objectified, it is only as one of its members that the individual himself has objectivity, genuine individuality, and an ethical life. Unification pure and simple is the true content and aim of the individual, and the individual's destiny is the living of a universal life. His further particular satisfaction, activity, and mode of conduct have this substantive and universally valid life as their starting point and their result.

Rationality, taken generally and in the abstract, consists in the thorough-going unity of the universal and the single. Rationality, concrete in the state, consists (*a*) so far as its content is concerned, in the unity of objective freedom (i.e. freedom of the universal or substantial will) and subjective freedom (i.e. freedom of everyone in his knowing and in his volition of particular ends); and consequently, (*b*) so far as its form is concerned, in self-determining action on laws and principles which are thoughts and so universal.

This Idea is the absolutely eternal and necessary being of mind.[2]

But if we ask what is or has been the historical origin of the state in general, still more if we ask about the origin of any particular state, of its rights and institutions, or again if we inquire whether the state originally arose out of patriarchal conditions or out of fear or trust, or out of Corporations, &c., or finally if we ask in what light the basis of the state's rights has been conceived and consciously established, whether this basis has been supposed to be positive divine right, or contract, custom, &c. – all these questions are no concern of the Idea of the state. We are here dealing exclusively with the philosophic science of the state, and from that point of view all these things are mere appearance and therefore matters for history. So far as the authority of any existing state has anything to do with reasons, these reasons are culled from the forms of the law authoritative within it.

The philosophical treatment of these topics is concerned only with their inward side, with the thought of their concept. The merit of Rousseau's contribution to the search for this concept is that, by adducing the will as the principle of the state, he is adducing a principle which has thought both for its form and its content, a principle indeed which is thinking itself, not a principle, like gregarious instinct, for instance, or divine authority, which has thought as its form only. Unfortunately, however, as Fichte did later, he takes the will only in a determinate form as the individual will, and he regards the universal will not as the absolutely rational element in the will, but only as a 'general' will which proceeds out of this individual will as out of a conscious will. The result is that he reduces the union of individuals in the state to a contract and therefore to something based on their arbitrary wills, their opinion, and their capriciously given express consent; and abstract reasoning proceeds to draw the logical inferences which destroy the absolutely divine principle of the state, together with its majesty and absolute authority. For this reason, when these abstract conclusions came into power, they afforded for the first time in human history the prodigious spectacle of the overthrow of the constitution of a great actual state and its complete reconstruction *ab initio* on the basis of pure thought alone, after the destruction of all existing and given material. The will of its re-founders was to give it what they alleged was a purely rational basis, but it was only abstractions that were being used; the Idea was lacking;

and the experiment ended in the maximum of frightfulness and terror.

259. The Idea of the state
(a) has immediate actuality and is the individual state as a self-dependent organism – the *Constitution* or *Constitutional Law*;
(b) passes over into the relation of one state to other states – *International Law*;
(c) is the universal Idea as a genus and as an absolute power over individual states – the mind which gives itself its actuality in the process of *World-History*.

Constitutional Law

260. The state is the actuality of concrete freedom. But concrete freedom consists in this, that personal individuality and its particular interests not only achieve their complete development and gain explicit recognition for their right (as they do in the sphere of the family and civil society) but, for one thing, they also pass over of their own accord into the interest of the universal, and, for another thing, they know and will the universal; they even recognize it as their own substantive mind; they take it as their end and aim and are active in its pursuit. The result is that the universal does not prevail or achieve completion except along with particular interests and through the co-operation of particular knowing and willing; and individuals likewise do not live as private persons for their own ends alone, but in the very act of willing these they will the universal in the light of the universal, and their activity is consciously aimed at none but the universal end. The principle of modern states has prodigious strength and depth because it allows the principle of subjectivity to progress to its culmination in the extreme of self-subsistent personal particularity, and yet at the same time brings it back to the substantive unity and so maintains this unity in the principle of subjectivity itself.

261. In contrast with the spheres of private rights and private welfare (the family and civil society), the state is from one point of view an external necessity and their higher authority; its nature is such that their laws and interests are subordinate to it and dependent on it. On the other hand, however, it is the end immanent within them, and its strength lies in the unity of its own universal end and aim with the particular interest of individuals, in the fact that individuals have duties to the state in proportion as they have rights against it (see Paragraph 155).

In the Remark to Paragraph 3 above, reference was made to the fact that it was Montesquieu above all who, in his famous work *L'Esprit des Lois*, kept in sight and tried to work out in detail both the thought of the dependence of laws – in particular, laws concerning the rights of persons – on the specific character of the state, and also the philosophic notion of always treating the part in its relation to the whole.

Duty is primarily a relation to something which from my point of view is substantive, absolutely universal. A right, on the other hand, is simply the embodiment of this substance and thus is the particular aspect of it and enshrines my particular freedom. Hence at abstract levels, right and duty appear parcelled out on different sides or in different persons. In the state, as something ethical, as the inter-penetration of the substantive and the particular, my obligation to what is substantive is at the same time the embodiment of my particular freedom. This means that in the state duty and right are united in one and the same relation. But further, since none the less the distinct moments acquire in the state the shape and reality peculiar to each, and since therefore the distinction between right and duty enters here once again, it follows that while implicitly, i.e. in form, identical, they at the same time differ in content. In the spheres of personal rights and morality, the necessary bearing of right and duty on one another falls short of actualization; and hence there is at that point only an abstract similarity of content between them, i.e. in those abstract spheres, what is one man's right ought also to be another's, and what is one man's duty ought also to be another's. The absolute identity of right and duty in the state is present in these spheres not as a genuine identity but only as a similarity of content, because in them this content is determined as quite general and is simply the fundamental principle of both right and duty, i.e. the principle that men, as persons, are free. Slaves, therefore, have no duties because they have no rights, and vice versa. (Religious duties are not here in point.)

In the course of the inward development of the concrete Idea, however, its moments become distinguished and their specific determinacy becomes at the same time a difference of content. In the family, the content of a son's duties to his father differs from the content of his rights against him; the content of the rights of a member of civil society is not the same as the content of his duties to his prince and government.

This concept of the union of duty and right is a point of vital importance and in it the inner strength of states is contained.

Duty on its abstract side goes no farther than the persistent neglect and proscription of a man's particular interest, on the ground that it is the inessential, even the discreditable, moment in his life. Duty, taken concretely as Idea, reveals the moment of particularity as itself essential and so regards its satisfaction as indisputably necessary. In whatever way an individual may fulfil his duty, he must at the same time find his account therein and attain his personal interest and satisfaction. Out of his position in the state, a right must accrue to him whereby public affairs shall be his own particular affair. Particular interests should in fact not be set aside or completely suppressed; instead, they should be put in correspondence with the universal, and thereby both they and the universal are upheld. The *isolated* individual, so far as his duties are concerned, is in subjection; but as a member of *civil society* he finds in fulfilling his duties to it protection of his person and property, regard for his private welfare, the satisfaction of the depths of his being, the consciousness and feeling of himself as a member of the whole; and, in so far as he completely fulfils his duties by performing tasks and services for the *state*, he is upheld and preserved. Take duty abstractly, and the universal's interest would consist simply in the completion as duties of the tasks and services which it exacts.

3. PATRIOTISM

268. The political sentiment, patriotism pure and simple, is assured conviction with truth as its basis – mere subjective assurance is not the outcome of truth but is only opinion – and a volition which has become habitual. In this sense it is simply a product of the institutions subsisting in the state, since rationality is *actually* present in the state, while action in conformity with these institutions gives rationality its practical proof. This sentiment is, in general, trust (which may pass over into a greater or lesser degree of educated insight), or the consciousness that my interest, both substantive and particular, is contained and preserved in another's (i.e. in the state's) interest and end, i.e. in the other's relation to me as an individual. In this way, this very other is immediately not an other in my eyes, and in being conscious of this fact, I am free.

Patriotism is often understood to mean only a readiness for exceptional sacrifices and actions. Essentially, however, it is the sentiment which, in the relationships of our daily life and under ordinary conditions, habitually recognizes that the community is one's substantive groundwork and end. It is out of this consciousness, which during life's daily round stands the test in all circumstances, that there subsequently also arises the readiness for extraordinary exertions. But since men would often rather be magnanimous than law-abiding, they readily persuade themselves that they possess this exceptional patriotism in order to be sparing in the expression of a genuine patriotic sentiment or to excuse their lack of it. If again this genuine patriotism is looked upon as that which may begin of itself and arise from subjective ideas and thoughts, it is being confused with opinion, because so regarded patriotism is deprived of its true ground, objective reality.

269. The patriotic sentiment acquires its specifically determined content from the various members of the organism of the state. This organism is the development of the Idea to its differences and their objective actuality. Hence these different members are the various powers of the state with their functions and spheres of action, by means of which the universal continually engenders itself, and engenders itself in a necessary way because their specific character is fixed by the nature of the concept. Throughout this process the universal maintains its identity, since it is itself the presupposition of its own production. This organism is the constitution of the state.

4. CHURCH AND STATE

270. (1) The abstract actuality or the substantiality of the state consists in the fact that its end is the universal interest as such and the conservation therein of particular interests since the universal interest is the substance of these. (2) But this substantiality of the state is also its *necessity*, since its substantiality is divided into the distinct spheres of its activity which correspond to the moments of its concept, and these spheres, owing to this substantiality, are thus actually fixed determinate characteristics of the state, i.e. its *powers*. (3) But this very substantiality of the state is mind knowing and willing itself after passing through the forming process of education. The state, therefore, knows what it wills and knows it in its universality, i.e. as something thought. Hence it works and acts by reference to consciously adopted ends, known principles, and laws which are not merely implicit but are actually present to consciousness; and further, it acts with precise knowledge of existing conditions and circumstances, inasmuch as its actions have a bearing on these.

This is the place to allude to the relation of the state to religion, because it is often reiterated nowadays that religion is the basis of the state, and because those who make this assertion even have the impertinence to suggest that, once it is made, political science has said its last word. No doctrine is more fitted to produce so much confusion, more fitted indeed to exalt confusion itself to be the constitution of the state and the proper form of knowledge.

In the first place, it may seem suspicious that religion is principally sought and recommended for times of public calamity, disorder, and oppression, and that people are referred to it as a solace in face of wrong or as a hope in compensation for loss. Then further, while the state is mind on earth (*der Geist der in der Welt steht*), religion may sometimes be looked upon as commanding downright indifference to earthly interests, the march of events, and current affairs, and so to turn men's attention to religion does not seem to be the way to exalt the interest and business of the state into the fundamental and serious aim of life. On the contrary, this suggestion seems to assert that politics is wholly a matter of caprice and indifference, either because this way of talking merely amounts to saying that it is only the aims of passion and lawless force &c., which bear sway in the state, or because this recommendation of religion is supposed to be of self-sufficient validity, and religion is to claim to decide the law and administer it. While it might seem a bitter jest to stifle all animus against tyranny by asserting that the oppressed find their consolation in religion, it still must not be forgotten that religion may take a form leading to the harshest bondage in the fetters of superstition and man's degraded subservience to animals. (The Egyptians and the Hindus, for instance, revere animals as beings higher than themselves.) This phenomenon may at least make it evident that we ought not to speak of religion at all in general terms and that we really need a power to protect us from it in some of its forms and to espouse against them the rights of reason and self-consciousness.

The essence of the relation between religion and the state can be determined, however, only if we recall the concept of religion. The content of religion is absolute truth, and consequently the religious is the most sublime of all dispositions. As intuition, feeling, representative knowledge, its task is concentrated upon God as the unrestricted principle and cause on which everything hangs. It thus involves the demand that everything else shall be seen in this light and depend on it for corroboration, justification, and verification. It is in being thus related to religion that state, laws, and duties all alike acquire for consciousness their supreme confirmation and their supreme obligatoriness, because even the state, laws, and duties are in their actuality something determinate which passes over into a higher sphere and so into that on which it is grounded.[9] It is for this reason that in religion there lies the place where man is always assured of finding a consciousness of the unchangeable, of the highest freedom and satisfaction, even within all the mutability of the world and despite the frustration of his aims and the loss of his interests and possessions.[10] Now if religion is in this way the groundwork which includes the ethical realm in general, and the state's fundamental nature – the divine will – in particular, it is at the same time only a groundwork; and it is at this point that state and religion begin to diverge. The state is the divine will, in the sense that it is mind present on earth, unfolding itself to be the actual shape and organization of a world. Those who insist on stopping at the form of *religion*, as opposed to the state, are acting like those logicians who think they are right if they continually stop at the essence and refuse to advance beyond that abstraction to existence, or like those moralists (see Remark to Paragraph 140) who will only good in the abstract and leave it to caprice to decide what is good. Religion is a relation to the Absolute, a relation which takes the form of feeling, representative thinking, faith; and, brought within its all-embracing circumference, everything becomes only accidental and transient. Now if, in relation to the state, we cling to this form of experience and make it the authority for the state and its essential determinant, the state must become a prey to weakness, insecurity, and disorder, because it is an organism in which firmly fixed distinct powers, laws, and institutions have been developed. In contrast with the form of religion, a form which draws a veil over everything determinate, and so comes to be purely subjective, the objective and universal element in the state, i.e. the laws, acquires a negative instead of a stable and authoritative character, and the result is the production of maxims of conduct like the following: 'To the righteous man no law is given; only be pious, and for the rest, practise what thou wilt; yield to thine own caprice and passion, and if thereby others suffer wrong, commend them to the consolations and hopes of religion, or better still, call them irreligious and condemn them to perdition.' This negative attitude, however, may not confine itself to an inner disposition and attitude of mind; it may turn instead to the outside world and assert its authority there, and then there is an outbreak of the religious fanaticism which, like fanaticism in politics, discards all government and legal order as barriers cramping the inner life of the heart and incompatible with its infinity, and at the same time proscribes private property, marriage, the ties and work involved in civil society, &c., &c., as degrading to love and the freedom of feeling. But since even then decisions must somehow be made for everyday life and practice, the same doctrine which we had before (see Remark to Paragraph 140, where we dealt generally with the subjectivity of the will which knows itself to be absolute) turns up again here, namely that subjective ideas, i.e. opinion and capricious inclination, are to do the deciding.

In contrast with the truth thus veiled behind subjective ideas and feelings, the genuine truth is the prodigious transfer of the inner into the outer, the building of reason into the real world, and this has been the task of the world during the whole course of its history. It is by working at this task that civilized man has actually given reason an embodiment in law and government and achieved consciousness of the fact. Those who 'seek guidance from the Lord' and are assured that the whole truth is directly present in their unschooled opinions, fail to apply themselves to the task of exalting their subjectivity to consciousness of the truth and to knowledge of duty and objective right. The only possible fruits of their attitude are folly, abomination, and the demolition of the whole ethical order, and these fruits must inevitably be reaped if the religious disposition holds firmly and exclusively to its intuitive form and so turns against the real world and the truth present in it in the form of the universal, i.e. of the laws. Still, there is no necessity for this disposition to turn outward and actualize itself in this way. With its negative standpoint, it is of course also open to it to remain something inward, to accommodate itself to government and law, and to acquiesce in these with sneers and idle longings, or with a sigh of resignation. It is not strength but weakness which has turned religious feeling nowadays into piety of a polemical kind, whether the polemic be connected with some genuine need or simply with unsatisfied vanity. Instead of subduing one's opinions by the labour of study, and subjecting one's will to discipline and so elevating it to free obedience, the line of least resistance is to renounce knowledge of objective truth. Along this line we may preserve a feeling of abject humility and so also of self-conceit, and claim to have ready to hand in godliness everything requisite for seeing into the heart of law and government, for passing sentence on them, and laying down what their character should and must be; and of course if we take this line, the source of our claims is a pious heart, and they are therefore infallible and unimpeachable, and the upshot is that since we make religion the basis of our intentions and assertions, they cannot be criticized on the score of their shallowness or their immorality.

But if religion be religion of a genuine kind, it does not run counter to the state in a negative or polemical way like the kind just described. It rather recognizes the state and upholds it, and furthermore it has a position and an external organization of its own. The practice of its worship consists in ritual and doctrinal instruction, and for this purpose possessions and property are required, as well as individuals dedicated to the service of the flock. There thus arises a relation between the state and the church. To determine this relation is a simple matter. In the nature of the case, the state discharges a duty by affording every assistance and protection to the church in the furtherance of its religious ends; and, in addition, since religion is an integrating factor in the state, implanting a sense of unity in the depths of men's minds, the state should even require all its citizens to belong to a church – *a* church is all that can be said, because since the content of a man's faith depends on his private ideas, the state cannot interfere with it. A state which is strong because its organization is mature may be all the more liberal in this matter; it may entirely overlook details of religious practice which affect it, and may even tolerate a sect (though, of course, all depends on its numbers) which on religious grounds declines to recognize even its direct duties to the state. The reason for the state's liberal attitude here is that it makes over the members of such sects to civil society and its laws, and is content if they fulfil their direct duties to the state passively, for instance by such means as commutation or the performance of a different service.

But since the church owns property and carries on besides the practice of worship, and since therefore it must have people in its service, it forsakes the inner for the worldly life and therefore enters the domain of the state, and *eo ipso* comes under its laws. The oath and ethical ties generally, like the marriage bond, entail that inner permeation and elevation of *sentiment* which acquires its deepest confirmation through religion. But since ethical ties are in essence ties within the actual *rational* order, the first thing is to affirm within that order the rights which it involves. Confirmation of these rights by the church is secondary and is only the inward, comparatively abstract, side of the matter. . . .

5. CONSTITUTION

271. The constitution of the state is, in the first place, the organization of the state and the self-related process of its organic life, a process whereby it differentiates its moments within itself and develops them to self-subsistence. Secondly, the state is an individual, unique and exclusive, and therefore related to others. Thus it turns its differentiating activity outward and accordingly establishes within itself the ideality of its subsisting inward differentiations.

1. The Constitution (on its internal side only)

272. The constitution is rational in so far as the state inwardly differentiates and determines its activity in accordance with the nature of the concept. The result of this is that each of these powers is in itself the totality of the constitution, because each contains the other moments and has them effective in itself, and because the moments, being expressions of the differentiation of the concept, simply abide in their ideality and constitute nothing but a single individual whole.

... Amongst current ideas, mention may be made (in connexion with Paragraph 269) of the necessity for a division of powers within the state. This point is of the highest importance and, if taken in its true sense, may rightly be regarded as the guarantee of public freedom. It is an idea, however, with which the very people who pretend to talk out of their inspiration and love neither have, nor desire to have, any acquaintance, since it is precisely there that the moment of rational determinacy lies. That is to say, the principle of the division of powers contains the essential moment of difference, of rationality *realized*. But when the abstract Understanding handles it, it reads into it the false doctrine of the absolute self-subsistence of each of the powers against the others, and then one-sidedly interprets their relation to each other as negative, as a mutual restriction. This view implies that the attitude adopted by each power to the others is hostile and apprehensive, as if the others were evils, and that their function is to oppose one another and as a result of this counterpoise to effect an equilibrium on the whole, but never a living unity. It is only the inner self-determination of the concept, not any other consideration, whether of purpose or advantage, that is the absolute source of the division of powers, and in virtue of this alone is the organization of the state something inherently rational and the image of eternal reason.

How the concept and then, more concretely, how the Idea, determine themselves inwardly and so posit their moments – universality, particularity, and individuality – in abstraction from one another, is discoverable from my logic, though not of course from the logic current elsewhere. To take the merely negative as a starting-point and to exalt to the first place the volition of evil and the mistrust of this volition, and then on the basis of this presupposition slyly to construct dikes whose efficiency simply necessitates corresponding dikes over against them, is characteristic in thought of the negative Understanding and in sentiment of the outlook of the rabble (see Paragraph 244).

If the powers (e.g. what are called the 'Executive' and the 'Legislature') become self-subsistent, then as we have recently seen on a grand scale, the destruction of the state is forthwith a *fait accompli*. Alternatively, if the state is maintained in essentials, it is strife which through the subjection by one power of the others, produces unity at least, however defective, and so secures the bare essential, the maintenance of the state.

273. The state as a political entity is thus cleft into three substantive divisions:
  (a) the power to determine and establish the universal – the Legislature;
  (b) the power to subsume single cases and the spheres of particularity under the universal – the Executive;
  (c) the power of subjectivity, as the will with the power of ultimate decision – the Crown. In the crown, the different powers are bound into an individual unity which is thus at once the apex and basis of the whole, i.e. of constitutional monarchy.

The development of the state to constitutional monarchy is the achievement of the modern world, a world in which the substantial Idea has won the infinite form [of subjectivity – see Paragraph 144]. The history of this inner deepening of the world mind – or in other words this free maturation in course of which the Idea, realizing rationality in the external, releases its moments (and they are only its moments) from itself as totalities, and just for that reason still retains them in the ideal unity of the concept – the history of this genuine formation of ethical life is the content of the whole course of world-history.

274. Mind is actual only as that which it knows itself to be, and the state, as the mind of a nation, is both the law permeating all relationships within the state and also at the same time the manners and consciousness of its citizens. It follows, therefore, that the constitution of any given nation depends in general on the character and development of its self-consciousness. In its self-consciousness its subjective freedom is rooted and so, therefore, is the actuality of its constitution.

The proposal to give a constitution – even one more or less rational in content – to a nation *a priori* would be a happy thought overlooking precisely that factor in a constitution which makes it more than an *ens rationis*. Hence every nation has the constitution appropriate to it and suitable for it.

7. MONARCHY

279. . . . Further, however, personality, like subjectivity in general, as infinitely self-related, has its truth (to be precise, its most elementary, immediate, truth) only in a person, in a subject existing 'for' himself, and what exists 'for' itself is just simply a unit. It is only as a person, the monarch, that the personality of the state is actual. Personality expresses the concept as such; but the person enshrines the actuality of the concept, and only when the concept is determined as person is it the Idea or truth. A so-called 'artificial person', be it a society, a community, or a family, however inherently concrete it may be, contains personality only abstractly, as one moment of itself. In an 'artificial person', personality has not achieved its true mode of existence. The state, however, is precisely this totality in which the moments of the concept have attained the actuality correspondent to their degree of truth. All these categories, both in themselves and in their external formations, have been discussed in the whole course of this treatise. They are repeated here, however, because while their existence in their particular external formations is readily granted, it does not follow at all that they are recognized and apprehended again when they appear in their true place, not isolated, but in their truth as moments of the Idea.

The conception of the monarch is therefore of all conceptions the hardest for ratiocination, i.e. for the method of reflection employed by the Understanding. This method refuses to move beyond isolated categories and hence here again knows only *raisonnement*, finite points of view, and deductive argumentation. Consequently it exhibits the dignity of the monarch as something deduced, not only in its form, but in its essence. The truth is, however, that to be something not deduced but purely self-originating is precisely the conception of monarchy. Akin, then, to this reasoning is the idea of treating the monarch's right as grounded in the authority of God, since it is in its divinity that its unconditional character is contained. We are familiar, however, with the misunderstandings connected with this idea, and it is precisely this 'divine' element which it is the task of a philosophic treatment to comprehend.

We may speak of the 'sovereignty of the people' in the sense that any people whatever is self-subsistent *vis-à-vis* other peoples, and constitutes a state of its own, like the British people for instance. But the peoples of England, Scotland, or Ireland, or the peoples of Venice, Genoa, Ceylon, &c., are not sovereign peoples at all now that they have ceased to have rulers or supreme governments of their own.

We may also speak of sovereignty in home affairs residing in the people, provided that we are speaking generally about the whole state and meaning only what was shown above (see Paragraphs 277, 278), namely that it is to the state that sovereignty belongs.

The usual sense, however, in which men have recently begun to speak of the 'sovereignty of the people' is that it is something opposed to the sovereignty existent in the monarch. So opposed to the sovereignty of the monarch, the sovereignty of the people is one of the confused notions based on the wild idea of the 'people'. Taken without its monarch and the articulation of the whole which is the indispensable and direct concomitant of monarchy, the people is a formless mass and no longer a state. It lacks every one of those determinate characteristics – sovereignty, government, judges, magistrates, class-divisions, &c., – which are to be found only in a whole which is inwardly organized. By the very emergence into a people's life of moments of this kind which have a bearing on an organization, on political life, a people ceases to be that indeterminate abstraction which, when represented in a quite general way, is called the 'people'.

280. . . . This ultimate self in which the will of the state is concentrated is, when thus taken in abstraction, a single self and therefore is *immediate* individuality. Hence its 'natural' character is implied in its very conception. The monarch, therefore, is essentially characterized as *this* individual, in abstraction from all his other characteristics, and *this* individual is raised to the dignity of monarchy in an immediate, natural, fashion, i.e. through his birth in the course of nature.

It is often alleged against monarchy that it makes the welfare of the state dependent on chance, for, it is urged, the monarch may be ill-educated, he may perhaps be unworthy of the highest position in the state, and it is senseless that such a state of affairs should exist because it is supposed to be rational. But all this rests on a presupposition which is nugatory, namely that everything depends on the monarch's *particular* character. In a completely organized state, it is only a question of the culminating point of formal decision (and a natural bulwark against passion. It is wrong therefore to demand objective qualities in a monarch);[11] he has only to say 'yes' and dot the 'i', because the throne should be such that the significant thing in its holder is not his particular make-up. (Monarchy in this sense is rational because it corresponds with the concept, but since this is hard to grasp, we often fail to notice the rationality of monarchy.) Monarchy must be inherently stable and whatever else the monarch may have in addition to this power of final decision is part and parcel of his private character and should be of no consequence. Of course there may be circumstances in which it is this private character alone which has prominence, but in that event the state is either not fully developed, or else is badly constructed. In a well-organized monarchy, the objective aspect belongs to law alone, and the monarch's part is merely to set to the law the subjective 'I will'.

281. Both moments in their undivided unity – (*a*) the will's ultimate ungrounded self, and (*b*) therefore its similarly ungrounded objective existence (existence being the category which is at home in nature) – constitute the Idea of something against which caprice is powerless, the 'majesty' of the monarch. In this unity lies the actual unity of the state, and it is only through this, its inward and outward immediacy, that the unity of the state is saved from the risk of being drawn down into the sphere of particularity and its caprices, ends, and opinions, and saved too from the war of factions round the throne and from the enfeeblement and overthrow of the power of the state.

The rights of birth and inheritance constitute the basis of legitimacy, the basis of a right not purely positive but contained in the Idea.

If succession to the throne is rigidly determined, i.e. if it is hereditary, then faction is obviated at a demise of the crown; this is one aspect of hereditary succession and it has long been rightly stressed as a point in its favour. This aspect, however, is only consequential, and to make it the reason for hereditary succession is to drag down the majesty of the throne into the sphere of argumentation, to ignore its true character as ungrounded immediacy and ultimate inwardness, and to base it not on the Idea of the state immanent within it, but on something external to itself, on some extraneous notion such as the 'welfare of the state' or the 'welfare of the people'.

8. THE EXECUTIVE

287. There is a distinction between the monarch's decisions and their execution and application, or in general between his decisions and the continued execution or maintenance of past decisions, existing laws, regulations, organizations for the securing of common ends, and and so forth. This task of merely subsuming the particular under the universal is comprised in the executive power, which also includes the powers of the judiciary and the police. The latter have a more immediate bearing on the particular concerns of civil society and they make the universal interest authoritative over its particular aims.

288. Particular interests which are common to everyone fall within civil society and lie outside the absolutely universal interest of the state proper (see Paragraph 256). The administration of these is in the hands of Corporations (see Paragraph 251), commercial and professional as well as municipal, and their officials, directors, managers, and the like. It is the business of these officials to manage the private property and interests of these particular spheres and, from that point of view, their authority rests on the confidence of their commonalties and professional equals. On the other hand, however, these circles of particular interests must be subordinated to the higher interests of the state, and hence the filling of positions of responsibility in Corporations, &c., will generally be effected by a mixture of popular election by those interested with appointment and ratification by higher authority.

289. The maintenance of the state's universal interest, and of legality, in this sphere of particular rights, and the work of bringing these rights back to the universal, require to be superintended by holders of the executive power, by (*a*) the executive civil servants, and (*b*) the higher advisory officials (who are organized into committees). These converge in their supreme heads who are in direct contact with the monarch.

Just as civil society is the battlefield where everyone's individual private interest meets everyone else's, so here we have the struggle (*a*) of private interests against particular matters of common concern and (*b*) of both of these together against the organization of the state and its higher outlook. At the same time the corporation mind, engendered when the particular spheres gain their title to rights, is now inwardly converted into the mind of the state, since it finds in the state the means of maintaining its particular ends. This is the secret of the patriotism of the citizens in the sense that they know the state as their substance, because it is the state that maintains their particular spheres of interest together with the title, authority, and welfare of these. In the corporation mind the rooting of the particular in the universal is directly entailed, and for this reason it is in that mind that the depth and strength which the state possesses in sentiment is seated.

Notes

1. [E. F.] Klein: *Grundsätze des peinlichen Rechts* [Halle, 1796], §§ 9 ff.
2. P. J. A. Feuerbach (1775–1833). See his *Lehrbuch des gemeinen peinlichen Rechts* (1801). (Messineo.)
3. Klein: op. cit., § 9.
4. Romans xii. 19.
5. Cf. *Enc.* [1st edn.], §§ 167 ff. and §§ 288 ff. [3rd edn. §§ 220 ff. and §§ 366 ff.].
6. See *Enc.* [1st edn.], § 98 [3rd edn. § 150].
7. The fact that the church comes in in this connexion is a further point, but not one for discussion here.
8. Cf. *Phenomenology* [1st edn.], pp. 383 ff., 417 ff. [Eng. tr. pp. 466 ff., 495 ff.].
9. See *Enc.* [1st edn.], § 453 [3rd edn. § 553].
10. Religion, knowledge, and science have as their principle a form peculiar to each and different from that of the state. They therefore enter the state partly as *means* – means to education and [a higher] mentality – partly in so far as they are in essence *ends* in themselves, for the reason that they are embodied in existent institutions. In both these respects the principles of the state have, in their application, a bearing on them. A comprehensive, concrete treatise on the state would also have to deal with those spheres of life as well as with art and such things as mere geographical matters, and to consider their place in the state and their bearing on it. In this book, however, it is the principle of the state in its own special sphere which is being fully expounded in accordance with the Idea, and it is only in passing that reference can be made to the principles of religion, &c., and to the application of the right of the state to them.
11. [The bracketed passages are translated from Gans's third edition; they did not appear in the first.]

11

Russell Kirk

Russell Kirk (b. 1918) is perhaps the most distinguished living conservative in America, and the one who has done most to present conservatism as an outlook that is both intellectually respectable and relevant to the modern age. A friend and disciple of T.S. Eliot, Kirk has devoted his extensive literary labours to expressing and justifying the vision of order which he believes to underlie all true conservative politics, and to reinforcing the belief in the 'permanent things', without which human society must, he argues, fall asunder.

The following extracts from The Conservative Mind *(7th edition 1986) provide a useful summary of the conflict between conservatives and their opponents, as this has been experienced in modern America. The book may not be argued at the deepest level; however, it contains an impressive and comprehensive historical survey of conservative thinking which renders it indispensable to a student of the subject.*

Conscious conservatism, in the modern sense, did not manifest itself until 1790, with the publication of *Reflections on the Revolution in France*. In that year the prophetic powers of Burke fixed in the public consciousness, for the first time, the opposing poles of conservation and innovation. The Carmagnole announced the opening of our era, and the smoky energy of coal and steam in the north of England was the signal for another revolution. If one attempts to trace conservative ideas back to an earlier time in Britain, soon he is enmeshed in Whiggery, Toryism, and intellectual antiquarianism; for the modern issues, though earlier taking substance, were not yet distinct. Nor does the American struggle between conservatives and radicals become intense until Citizen Genêt and Tom Paine transport across the Atlantic enthusiasm for French liberty: the American Revolution, substantially, had been a conservative reaction, in the English political tradition, against royal innovation. If one really must find a preceptor for conservatism who is older than Burke, he cannot rest satisfied with Bolingbroke, whose skepticism in religion disqualifies him, or with the Machiavellian Hobbes, or that old-fangled absolutist Filmer. Falkland, indeed, and Clarendon and Halifax and Strafford, deserve study; still more, in Richard Hooker one discovers profound conservative observations which Burke inherited with his Anglicanism and which Hooker drew in part from the Schoolmen and their authorities; but already one is back in the sixteenth century, and then in the thirteenth, and this book is concerned with modern problems. In any practical sense, Burke is the founder of our conservatism.

Canning and Coleridge and Scott and Southey and Wordsworth owed their political principles to the imagination of Burke; Hamilton and John Adams read Burke in America, and Randolph promulgated Burke's ideas in the Southern states. Burke's French disciples adopted the word 'conservative,' which Croker, Canning and Peel clapped to the great party that no longer was Tory or Whig, once the followers of Pitt and Portland had joined forces. Tocqueville applied the wisdom of Burke to his own liberal ends; Macaulay copied the reforming talents of his model. And these men passed on the tradition of Burke to succeeding generations. With such a roster of pupils, Burke's claim to speak for the real conservative genius should be difficult to deny. Yet scholars of some eminence have endeavored to establish Hegel as a kind of coadjutor to Burke. 'Sir,' said Samuel Johnson concerning Hume, 'the fellow is a Tory by chance.' Hegel's conservatism is similarly accidental, as Tocqueville remarks: 'Hegel exacted submission to the ancient established powers of his own time; which he held to be legitimate, not only from existence, but from their origin. His scholars wished to establish powers of another kind. . . From this Pandora's box have escaped all sorts of moral disease from which the people are still suffering. But I have remarked that a general reaction is taking place against this sensual and socialist philosophy.' Schlegel, Görres, and Stolberg – and Taine's school, in France – were admirers of both Hegel and Burke, which perhaps explains the confounding of their superficial resemblance with their fundamental inimicality. Hegel's metaphysics would have been as abhorrent to Burke as his style; Hegel himself does not seem to have read Burke; and people who think that these two men represent different facets of the same system are in danger of confusing authoritarianism (in the political sense) with conservatism. Marx could draw upon Hegel's magazine; he could find nothing to suit him in Burke.

But such distinctions are more appropriate in a concluding chapter than in a preface. Just now, a preliminary definition of the conservative idea is required.

Any informed conservative is reluctant to condense profound and intricate intellectual systems to a few pretentious phrases; he prefers to leave that technique to the enthusiasm of radicals. Conservatism is not a fixed and immutable body of dogmata; conservatives inherit from Burke a talent for re-expressing their convictions to fit the time. As a working premise, nevertheless, one can observe here that the essence of social conservatism is preservation of the ancient moral traditions of humanity. Conservatives respect the wisdom of their ancestors (this phrase was Strafford's, and Hooker's, before Burke illuminated it); they are dubious of wholesale alteration. They think society is a spiritual reality, possessing an eternal life but a delicate constitution: it cannot be scrapped and recast as if it were a machine. 'What is conservatism?' Abraham Lincoln inquired once. 'Is it not adherence to the old and tried, against the new and untried?' It is that, but it is more. F.J.C. Hearnshaw, in his *Conservatism in England*, lists a dozen principles of conservatives, but possibly these may be comprehended in a briefer catalogue. I think that there are six canons of conservative thought –

(1) Belief in a transcendent order, or body of natural law, which rules society as well as conscience. Political problems, at bottom, are religious and moral problems. A narrow rationality, what Coleridge called the Understanding, cannot of itself satisfy human needs. 'Every Tory is a realist,' says Keith Feiling: 'he knows that there are great forces in heaven and earth that man's philosophy cannot plumb or fathom.' True politics is the art of apprehending and applying the Justice which ought to prevail in a community of souls.

(2) Affection for the proliferating variety and mystery of human existence, as opposed to the narrowing uniformity, egalitarianism, and utilitarian aims of most radical systems; conservatives resist what Robert Graves calls 'Logicalism' in society. This prejudice has been called 'the conservatism of enjoyment' – a sense that life is worth living, according to Walter Bagehot 'the proper source of an animated Conservatism.'

(3) Conviction that civilized society requires orders and classes, as against the notion of a 'classless society.' With reason, conservatives often have been called 'the party of order.' If natural distinctions are effaced among men, oligarchs fill the vacuum. Ultimate equality in the judgment of God, and equality before courts of law, are recognized by conservatives; but equality of condition, they think, means equality in servitude and boredom.

(4) Persuasion that freedom and property are closely linked: separate property from private possession, and Leviathan becomes master of all. Economic levelling, they maintain, is not economic progress.

(5) Faith in prescription and distrust of 'sophisters, calculators, and economists' who would reconstruct society upon abstract designs. Custom, convention, and old prescription are checks both upon man's anarchic impulse and upon the innovator's lust for power.

(6) Recognition that change may not be salutary reform: hasty innovation may be a devouring conflagration, rather than a torch of progress. Society must alter, for prudent change is the means of social preservation; but a statesman must take Providence into his calculations, and a statesman's chief virtue, according to Plato and Burke, is prudence.

Various deviations from this body of opinion have occurred, and there are numerous appendages to it; but in general conservatives have adhered to these convictions or sentiments with some consistency, for two centuries. To catalogue the principles of their opponents is more difficult. At least five major schools of radical thought have competed for public favor since Burke entered politics: the rationalism of the *philosophes*, the romantic emancipation of Rousseau and his allies, the utilitarianism of the Benthamites, the positivism of Comte's school, and the collectivistic materialism of Marx and other socialists. This list leaves out of account those scientific doctrines, Darwinism chief among them, which have done so much to undermine the first principles of a conservative order. To express these several radicalisms in terms of a common denominator probably is presumptuous, foreign to the philosophical tenets of conservatism. All the same, in a hastily generalizing fashion one may say that radicalism since 1790 has tended to attack the prescriptive arrangement of society on the following grounds –

(1) The perfectibility of man and the illimitable progress of

society: meliorism. Radicals believe that education, positive legislation, and alteration of environment can produce men like gods; they deny that humanity has a natural proclivity toward violence and sin.

(2) Contempt for tradition. Reason, impulse, and materialistic determinism are severally preferred as guides to social welfare, trustier than the wisdom of our ancestors. Formal religion is rejected and various ideologies are presented as substitutes.

(3) Political levelling. Order and privilege are condemned; total democracy, as direct as practicable, is the professed radical ideal. Allied with this spirit, generally, is a dislike of old parliamentary arrangements and an eagerness for centralization and consolidation.

(4) Economic levelling. The ancient rights of property, especially property in land, are suspect to almost all radicals; and collectivistic reformers hack at the institution of private property root and branch.

As a fifth point, one might try to define a common radical view of the state's function; but here the chasm of opinion between the chief schools of innovation is too deep for any satisfactory generalization. One can only remark that radicals unite in detesting Burke's description of the state as ordained of God, and his concept of society as joined in perpetuity by a moral bond among the dead, the living, and those yet to be born – the community of souls. . . .

In a revolutionary epoch, sometimes men taste every novelty, sicken of them all, and return to ancient principles so long disused that they seem refreshingly hearty when they are rediscovered. History often appears to resemble a roulette wheel; there is truth in the old Greek idea of cycles, and round again may come the number which signifies a conservative order. One of those flaming clouds which we deny to the Deity but arrogate to our own employment may erase our present elaborate constructions so abruptly as the tocsin in the Faubourg St. Germain terminated an age equally tired of itself. Yet this roulette-wheel simile would be repugnant to Burke (or to John Adams), who knew history to be the unfolding of a Design. The true conservative thinks of this process, which looks like chance or fate, as, rather, the providential operation of a moral law of polarity. And Burke, could he see our century, never would concede that a consumption-society, so near to suicide, is the end for which Providence has prepared man. If a conservative order is indeed to return, we ought to know the tradition which is attached to it, so that we may rebuild society; if it is not to be restored, still we ought to understand conservative ideas so that we may rake from the ashes what scorched fragments of civilization escape the conflagration of unchecked will and appetite.

12
Joseph de Maistre

Joseph Marie, Comte de Maistre (1753–1821), was the son of a recently ennobled legal official in Savoy. Brought up in a deeply pious family, he was throughout his life a committed Roman Catholic. He followed his father as a public lawyer, and – after a brief spell of enthusiasm for the Revolution – settled into the counter-revolutionary attitude for which he was subsequently known. Fleeing from Savoy he moved to Lausanne, as ambassador to the Sardinian Crown, and then, after a brief return to Italy, travelled again as Sardinian ambassador, this time to St Petersburg, where he remained until 1817.

De Maistre's most important works are On the Pope *(1819),* Evenings in St Petersburgh *(1821), and* Essay on The Generative Principle of Constitutions *(1821); it is from the latter that the following extracts are taken. His argument that constitutions are not created but found, has been one of the cornerstones of conservative political thinking. The rage for constitution-making which characterized the governments of his day was, according to de Maistre, founded on a misconception of the American constitution, which is in fact no more than an explicit summary of a spirit already present in the common law from which it grew. All constitutions and all states are inseparable from the spirit of the society that is governed by them; the attempt to separate the legal form from the social matter spells the death of the body politic. De Maistre combined this argument with an attack on the liberal theory of the social contract as the source of political obligation, and with a defence of a revealed order, divine in origin, which is the true source of all legitimacy. In the end it is God and not man who is the maker of constitutions and the ultimate legislator – and it is characteristic of de Maistre thus to take one step further than is necessary to defend the conservative viewpoint, in order to anchor his vision in the transcendental.*

I

One of the gravest errors of a century which embraced them all was to believe that a political constitution could be written and created a priori, whereas reason and experience agree that a constitution is a divine work and that it is precisely the most fundamental and essentially constitutional elements in a nation's laws that cannot be written.

II

Frenchmen have often been asked as a joke *in what book the Salic Law was written*; but Jérôme Bignon replied exactly to the point, very probably without understanding how aptly, *that it was written in the hearts of Frenchmen*. Indeed, supposing that a law of this importance exists only because it is written, it is certain that whatever authority has written it will have the right to annul it; the law would not therefore have that aura of sanctity and immutability that distinguishes truly constitutional laws. The essence of a fundamental law is that no one has the right to abolish it: but how is it beyond human power if it has been made by someone? The agreement of a people is impossible, and, even if it were, an agreement is not a law and obliges no one unless there is a superior authority guaranteeing it. . . .

. . . Consequently, primordial good sense, happily anterior to sophisms, has everywhere sought the sanction for laws in a power above men, either by recognizing that sovereignty derives from God, or by revering certain unwritten laws as God's word.

III

The editors of the Roman laws have included in the first chapter of their collection a very remarkable fragment of Greek jurisprudence. *Among the laws which govern us*, says this passage, *some are written and others are not*. Nothing could be simpler and nothing more profound. Is there any Turkish law expressly permitting the sovereign to send a man to his death immediately without the intermediate decision of a court? Is there any *written* law, even a religious one, which forbids this to the sovereign of Christian

Europe? Yet the Turk is no more surprised to see his ruler order an immediate execution than to see him go to the mosque. Like all of Asia and even all of antiquity, he believes that the immediate power of life and death is a legitimate appendage of sovereignty. But our kings shudder at the very idea of condemning a man to death; for, in our eyes, such a condemnation would be a vile murder, and yet I doubt if it would be possible to forbid them this power through a written fundamental law without it leading to greater evils than those which one wished to prevent. . . .

V

The English constitution is an example nearer to us and consequently more striking. If it is examined closely, it can be seen that *it works only by not working* (if this play on words is excused). It maintains itself only by exceptions. *Habeas corpus,* for example, has been suspended so often and for such long periods that it could be argued that the exception has become the rule. Suppose for a moment that the authors of this famous Act had attempted to lay down the cases when it could be suspended, they would by that deed have destroyed it. . . .

VI

In spite of this, we are still told of written constitutions and constitutional laws made a priori. It is impossible to conceive how a rational man can believe in such chimeras. If any scheme was carried through in England to give the cabinet a formal constitutional status by law and thus to regulate and circumscribe rigorously its privileges and powers, together with the precautions necessary to limit its influence and prevent it from abusing it, the state would be undermined.

The real English constitution is the public spirit, admirable, unique, infallible, and above praise, which leads, conserves, and protects all – what is written is nothing.

VII

At the end of the last century, loud complaints were made about a statesman who conceived the idea of introducing this same English constitution (or what went under the name) into a convulsed kingdom that was demanding any constitution whatever with a kind of madness. If you like, he was wrong, so far at least as one can be wrong when acting in good faith, which it is reasonable to suppose he was and as I believe wholeheartedly. But who then has the right to condemn him? *Vel duo, vel nemo.* He did not assert a wish to destroy anything of his own authority: he wanted only, he said, to substitute something which seemed to him to be reasonable for something that was no longer wanted and that, even by that fact, no longer existed. Moreover, if the principle is accepted (as in fact it was) *that a man can create a constitution*, this minister (who was certainly a man) had the right to create his as much as anyone else and more than some. Was opinion at all divided on this point? Was it not everywhere believed that a constitution is as much a work of the imagination as an ode or a tragedy? Had not *Paine* asserted, with a profundity which enraptured the universities, *that a constitution does not exist if one cannot put it in one's pocket*? The eighteenth century, which questioned nothing, had no doubts of itself: that is the rule; and I do not believe that it produced a single youth of any talent whatever who had not made three things by the time he left school – a new system of education, a constitution, and a society. If therefore a mature and talented man, deeply versed in economics and contemporary philosophy, had undertaken only the second of these projects, this in itself would have convinced me of his extreme moderation: but I must admit that he seems to me to be a veritable prodigy of wisdom and modesty when, putting experience (at least as he saw it) in place of foolish theories, he humbly demanded a constitution on the English model instead of drawing one up himself. It will be said that *even this was not possible*. I agree, but he did not know this; and how could he have known? Who was there who could have told him?

IX

The more you examine the part human action plays in the formation of political constitutions, the clearer it becomes that it is

effective only in an extremely subordinate role or as a simple instrument; and I do not believe that any doubt at all remains of the incontrovertible truth of the following propositions:
1. That the fundamentals of political constitutions exist before all written laws.
2. That a constitutional law is and can be only the development or the sanction of a preexistent and unwritten right.
3. That the most essential, the most intrinsically constitutional, and the really fundamental is not written and even should not be if the state is not to be imperiled.
4. That the weakness and fragility of a constitution is in direct relationship to the number of written constitutional articles.

X

We are misled on this point by a fallacy so natural that it entirely escapes our attention. Because a man acts, he believes he acts by himself; and because he is conscious of his liberty, he forgets his dependence. As far as the physical order is concerned, he listens to reason; and although he can, for example, plant an acorn, water it, and so on, yet he is capable of admitting that he does not make oaks, since he sees that the tree grows and perfects itself without human interference and that, moreover, he has not made the acorn; but, in the social order in which he is a participant and actor, he begins to believe that he is really the direct author of everything that happens through him: in a sense, the trowel believes himself to be the architect. Doubtless, man is intelligent, free, and sublime, but he is nonetheless an *implement of God*. . . .

XII

Consider, now, any political constitution whatever, that of England, for example. Certainly it has not been made a priori. Never have statesmen gathered together and said: *Let us create three powers, balance them in such and such a manner*, and so on: no one has thought this. The constitution is the work of circumstances, and the number of these circumstances is infinite. Roman, ecclesiastic, and feudal law, Saxon, Norman and Danish customs, every kind of class privilege, prejudice and ambition, wars, revolts, revolutions, conquests and crusades, all the virtues, vices, sciences, errors and passions; all these elements, acting together and forming by their intermixture and interaction endlessly multiplying combinations, have finally produced after many centuries the most complex unity and the most delicate equilibrium of political forces the world has ever known.

XIII

However, since these elements, so cast into space, have fallen into such meaningful order without a single man among the multitude who have acted on this huge stage knowing what relation his actions had with the whole scheme of things or what the future was to be, it follows that these elements were guided in their fall by an unerring hand, superior to man. Perhaps the greatest folly of a century of follies was to believe that fundamental laws could be written a priori, whereas they are obviously the work of a power above men, and the very act of writing them down, later on, is the surest sign that their real force has gone. . . .

XIX

These ideas, taken in their general aspects, are not foreign to the philosophers of antiquity: they well understood the weakness, I almost said the nullity, of writing in great institutions; but no one has better seen or expressed this truth than Plato, who is always the first on the path to all the great truths. According to him, first of all, 'the man who owes all his education to written discourses *has always just the appearance of wisdom.*' 'The spoken word,' he adds, 'is to writing what a man is to his portrait. The creations of the painter strike us as being lifelike, yet *if you question them, they preserve a solemn silence*. It is the same with a book, *which does not know what to say to one man or to hide from another*. If it is attacked or insulted needlessly, it cannot defend itself, *for its father is never there to protect it*. So that whoever imagines himself able to establish a clear and durable doctrine by the written word alone is a great fool. If he did possess the real seeds of truth, he would take great care not to believe that, *with a little black liquid and a pen*, he could make them take root among men, protect them against inclement weather, and induce in them strong growth. As for the man who undertakes to write *laws or civil constitutions*, imagining that, because he has written them down, he has been able to give them the proper clarity and stability, he disgraces himself, whatever he is, whether private citizen or legislator, and whatever men say; for he has thereby shown that he is equally ignorant of inspiration and madness, justice and injustice, good and evil. Such ignorance is disgraceful even if he has the applause of the whole of the vulgar masses.'[1]

XX

Having heard the *wisdom of nations*, it will be useful, I think, to listen again to Christian philosophy.

'Doubtless it would have been most desirable, the most eloquent of Greek Fathers has said, for us to have had no need of writing and for the divine precepts to have been written only in our hearts by grace, as they are written by ink in our books; but, as we have lost this grace through our own fault, let us then, of necessity, seize a *plank in place of a ship*, without forgetting however the superiority of the first state. God never revealed anything to the Elect of the Old Testament; he always talked to them directly, for he saw the purity of their hearts; but once the Hebrew people were thrown into the abyss of vice, books and laws became necessary. This course was resumed under the influence of the new revelation; for Christ did not leave a single writing to his Apostles. In place of books, he promised them the Holy Spirit. *It is it*, he said to them, *that will inspire what you will have to say*.[2] But, because in the course of time, guilty men revolted against dogmas and morality, it was necessary to resort to books.'

XXI

The whole truth is to be found in these two authorities. They show the profound stupidity (it is permissible to talk like Plato, who never lost his temper), the profound stupidity, as I say, of those poor people who imagine that legislators are men, that laws are pieces of paper and that nations can be created *by ink*. They show, to the contrary, that writing is always a sign of weakness, ignorance, or danger; that the more perfect an institution, the less it writes; so that the institution which is certainly divine has no written document as its basis, showing us that every written law is only a necessary evil produced by human infirmity or malice, and that it is nothing at all if it has not received a previous and unwritten sanction.

XXIV

... If the wishes of a common mortal were worthy of obtaining from Providence one of those memorable decrees which shape the great crises of history, I would ask it to inspire in some powerful nation that had offended it gravely the arrogant intention of constituting itself politically, starting at the very foundations. If, in spite of my unworthiness, I was allowed the ancient intimacy of the patriarchs, I would say: 'Grant it everything! Give it spirit, knowledge, wealth, courage, above all an unlimited confidence in itself and that adaptable and enterprising genius which is not checked or intimidated by anything. Wipe out its ancient government; take away its memory; slay its affections; spread terror around it; blind or freeze its enemies; arrange for it to be victorious on all its frontiers at once, so that none of its neighbors can meddle in its affairs or trouble it in its plans. Let this nation be distinguished in science, rich in philosophy, sated with human power, free from all prejudices, all ties, every superior influence, lest one day it might be able to say, *I lacked this or I was hampered by that*; finally let it act freely with this plenitude of means so that it becomes, under your unfailing protection, an eternal lesson for humanity.'

XXV

Doubtless one cannot expect a conjunction of circumstances which would literally be a miracle; but events of a similar order, if less remarkable, have shown themselves here and there in history, even in the history of our own day; and although they have not, to serve as an example, that ideal force that I just now asked for, nonetheless they point some important lessons.

Less than twenty-five years ago, we witnessed a serious attempt to regenerate a great but mortally sick nation. This was the first draft of a great work, and the *preface*, so to speak, of the frightening book that we have since had to read. Every precaution had been taken. . . . Alas, all human wisdom was at fault, and everything ended in death.

XXVI

It has been said: *But we know the causes of the failure of the undertaking.* How so? Do you want God to send angels in human form, charged with destroying a constitution? It will always be very necessary for secondary agents to be employed; this or that, what does it matter? Every tool is useful in the hands of the great craftsman; but so blind are men that if tomorrow some constitution-mongers came again to organize a people and to constitute it with *a little black liquid*, the crowd would again lose no time in believing in the promised miracle. Once more, it would be said, *Nothing is lacking; all is foreseen; all is written*; whereas, the very fact that all had been foreseen, discussed, and written would demonstrate the worthlessness and insubstantiality of the constitution.

XXVII

I think I have read somewhere *that there are very few sovereignties able to justify the legitimacy of their origins*. Admitting the justice of this claim, it does not imply the least blemish on the successors of a ruler against whose actions many objections might be raised: the shadows which to a greater or lesser degree fall across the origins of his authority should be regarded only as an inconvenience, a necessary consequence of a law of the moral world. If it was otherwise, it would follow that a sovereign could reign legitimately only by virtue of a deliberation of the whole people, that is to say, *by grace of the people*; which will never happen, for nothing is more true than what has been said by the author of *Considerations on France: that the people will always accept masters and will never choose them.* It is always necessary for the origin of sovereignty to appear as being outside the sphere of human control; so that the very men who appear to be directly involved are nevertheless only circumstances. As for legitimacy, if it seemed ambiguous in its beginning,

God has explained himself through his prime minister in the affairs of this world, *time*. . . .

XXVIII

Everything therefore brings us back to the general rule: *Man cannot make a constitution, and no legitimate constitution can be written.* The corpus of fundamental laws that must constitute a civil or religious society have never been and never will be written. This can be done only when the society is already constituted, yet it is impossible to spell out or explain in writing certain individual articles; but almost always these declarations are the effect or the cause of very great evils, and they always cost the people more than they are worth.

XXX

But, since every constitution is divine in its origin, it follows that man cannot do anything unless he relies on God, in which case he becomes an instrument. This is a truth to which the whole of humanity has constantly rendered the most striking witness. If we refer to history, which is experimental politics, we shall see there continually the cradle of nations surrounded by priests and hear a constant call to God for help in human weakness. Myth, much truer than ancient history for trained eyes, adds to this proof. It is always an oracle who founds communities; it is always an oracle who announces divine protection and the successes of the founding heroes. Above all, kings, leaders of nascent empires, are continually designated and almost stamped by Heaven in some extraordinary way. How many frivolous men have laughed at the Holy Ampulla, without thinking that it is a hieroglyphic which only needs interpreting.

XXXI

The coronation of kings springs from the same roots. There has never been a ceremony or, more properly, a profession of faith more significant and worthy of respect. The finger of the Pontiff has always touched the brow of the new sovereign. The many writers who have seen in these august rites nothing but ambitious designs, and even the open alliance of superstition and tyranny, have spoken against truth, almost all even against their conscience. This subject merits examination. Sometimes sovereigns have sought coronation, and sometimes coronation has sought sovereigns. Others have been seen to reject coronation as a sign of dependence. We know enough of the facts to be able to judge sufficiently soundly; but it would be necessary to distinguish carefully between different men, periods, nations, and religions. Here it is sufficient to insist on the general and universal opinion which invokes the divine power in the establishment of empires.

XXXII

The most famous nations of antiquity, above all the most serious and wisest, such as the Egyptians, the Etruscans, the Spartans, and the Romans, were precisely those with the most religious constitutions; and the length of empires has always been proportionate to the influence that the religious principle has acquired in the political system. 'The towns and nations most devoted to a cult of divinity have always been the most durable and the wisest, just as the most religious ages have always been the most distinguished by genius.'[3]

XXXIII

Nations have never been civilized except by religion. No other force known has a hold on primitive man. Without recourse to antiquity, which is very decisive on this point, we see a striking proof of it in America. We have been there for three centuries with our laws, arts, sciences, culture, commerce, and wealth; how have we helped the indigenous population? In no way. We are destroying these unfortunate people with the sword and spirits; we are gradually pushing them back into the deserted interior, until in the end they will be wiped out completely, the victims of our vices as much as of our cruel superiority.

XXXIV

Has any philosopher ever dreamed of leaving his native land and his pleasures to go to the American forests in chase of savages, to prise them from vice and to give them a moral code?[4] They have done much better; they have written splendid books to prove that the savage is the *natural* man and that we can wish for nothing happier than to resemble him. Condorcet has said that *the missionaries have carried into Asia and America only shameful superstitions.*[5] Rousseau has said, with a truly inconceivable compounding of folly, that *the missionaries seemed to him scarcely wiser than the conquerors.*[6] Finally, their leader has had the impudence (but what had he to lose?) to throw the most vulgar ridicule on these pacific conquerors of whom antiquity would have made gods.[7]

XL

Not only is creation not one of man's proper functions; it does not seem as if our *unassisted* power extends to the reform of established institutions. Nothing is plainer to man than the existence of two opposed forces which ceaselessly battle in the universe. There is no good that evil does not defile and debase; there is no evil that good does not restrain and attack, in impelling all things toward a more perfect state. These two forces are everywhere present. They can be seen equally in the growth of plants, in the generation of animals, in the formation of languages and of empires (two inseparable things), and so on. Human power extends perhaps only to removing or combating evil to free the good from it and to restore to the good the power to grow according to its nature. The celebrated Zanotti has said, *It is difficult to change things for the better.*[8] This thought hides a profound meaning under the appearance of extreme simplicity. It accords completely with another saying of Origen, which is alone worth a whole volume. *Nothing,* he said, *can be changed for the better in social matters without divine help.*[9] All men feel the truth of this, without being able themselves to express it. It is from this that follows the unconscious aversion of all right-thinking men to innovations. The word *reform,* in itself and before any scrutiny, will always be suspect to the wise, and the experience of every age justifies this kind of instinct. It is too well known what has been the fruit of the finest speculations in this line.

XLI

To apply these generalizations to a particular case, it is from the sole consideration of the grave danger of innovations based on simplified human theories that, without believing that I am in a position to hold a reasoned opinion on the great question of parliamentary reform which has so deeply and for such a long time stirred English minds, I nevertheless feel led to believe that this idea is dangerous and that, if the English surrender to it too readily, they will repent of it. *But*, say the partisans of reform (for this is the great argument), *the abuses are striking and incontestable: can a formal abuse, a vice, be constitutional*? Yes, indisputably it can be; for every political constitution has its essential faults which spring from its nature and which cannot be separated from it; and what should make every reformer hesitate is that these faults can change with circumstances; so that by showing that they are new, one has not thus shown that they are not necessary. What sensible man will not therefore be scared to undertake such work? Social harmony is subject to the law of *temperament*, as is harmony properly speaking *in the musical scale*. Get the *fifths* carefully in tune and the *octaves* will clash, and *vice versa*. Discord being therefore inevitable, rather than removing it, which is impossible, it is necessary to *temper* it, by distributing it. Thus in both cases, *fault is an element in possible perfection*. This proposition is only apparently paradoxical. *But*, it will perhaps still be said, *what is the rule to distinguish an accidental fault from that which belongs to the nature of things and which is impossible to eliminate*? Men to whom nature has given only ears put this kind of question, and those with an ear for music shrug their shoulders.

XLII

It is still more necessary to take care, when it is a question of abuses, to judge political institutions only by their constant effects and never by any of their causes, which are not important, still less by certain collateral disadvantages (if it can be so expressed) which can easily engross shortsighted views and prevent them from seeing things as a whole. In fact, cause, according to the hypothesis that seems to be proved, not having any necessary logical relation to effect, and the drawbacks of a good institution in itself being, as I have just said, only *the necessary discord in the musical scale*, how can institutions be judged on the basis of their causes and disadvantages? Voltaire, who talked of everything for a whole age without once piercing below the surface, reasoned curiously on the sale of judicial offices which took place in France; and perhaps no example could show more accurately the truth of the theory I am expounding. *The proof*, he said, *that this sale is an abuse is that it has been produced only by another abuse.*[10] Voltaire is not merely mistaken here, since all men are liable to error. He is shamefully mistaken. This is a complete reversal of common sense. *Everything that springs from an abuse is an abuse*! On the contrary, it is one of the most general and most evident of the laws of the hidden yet apparent power which operates and makes itself felt on all sides that the remedy for an abuse springs from the abuse itself and that an evil, carried to a certain point, is necessarily its own destroyer; for evil, which is no more than a negative, has the same dimension and duration as the being to which it is attached and which it devours. It is like a cancer which can fulfill itself only by destroying itself. But then a new reality necessarily rushes into the place of that which has just disappeared; *since nature abhors a vacuum*, and good – But I am wandering too far from Voltaire.

XLIII

The error of this man comes from the fact that this great writer, *divided between twenty sciences*, as he has somewhere said himself, and moreover continually occupied with instructing the world, had only very rarely the time to think. 'A voluptuous and spendthrift court, reduced to extremities by its wastefulness, conceived the idea of selling judicial offices, and thus created (what it would never have done freely and with full knowledge of the case) it created, I say, a rich, immovable and independent judiciary; in this way the infinite power *playing over the world*[11] makes use of corruption to create incorruptible courts (as much as it allows to human weakness).' In truth, nothing is more plausible than this to a true philosopher, nothing conforms more to human experience and to that indisputable law which lays down that the most important institutions are never the result of deliberation but of circumstances. The problem is now almost resolved when it is posed, as happens to every problem. *Could a country such as France be served better than by hereditary judges*? If this is agreed, as I assume, it immediately becomes necessary to propose a second problem like this: *The judiciary being necessarily hereditary, is there a more advantageous method of constituting it in the first place and subsequently of recruiting to it than that which adds millions at the very least to the state funds, and which guarantees at the same time the wealth, the independence and even the nobility* (of every kind) *of the higher judiciary?* If the sale of offices is considered only as a means of making them hereditary, every impartial mind is struck by the truth of this view. This is not the place to develop the point; but enough has been said to show that Voltaire did not even see it.

XLIV

Let us now suppose at the head of affairs a man such as he, combining in perfect harmony superficiality, incapacity, and temerity. He will not fail to act according to his foolish theories of laws and abuses. He will borrow to the last halfpenny to reimburse officeholders, to the last shilling to reimburse creditors: he will prepare the public mind by paying for a host of writings insulting the judiciary and sapping public confidence in it. Soon patronage, a thousand times more foolish than chance, will begin its endless career of folly; the man of distinction, no longer seeing in heredity a counterweight to overwhelming labors, will stand down for ever; and the high courts will be open to adventurers without name, wealth, or reputation, in place of that respected judiciary, in which virtue and knowledge had become, like rank, hereditary, a true priesthood envied by foreign nations up to the time when the cult of philosophy, having excluded wisdom from all the places it used to visit, ended its splendid exploits by expelling it from its true home.

XLV

This is a true reflection of the majority of reforms: because not only does creation not belong to man, but even reformation belongs to him in only a secondary manner and with a host of severe restrictions. . . . Man in harmony with his Creator is sublime and his action creative; equally, once he separates himself from God and acts alone, he does not cease to be powerful, since that is a privilege of his nature, but his acts are negative and lead only to destruction.

XLIX

For myself, I *believe*, and indeed I *know*, that no human institution can last if it has not a religious base; *and moreover* (I beg that particular attention be paid to this), *if it has not a name taken from the national language and self-generated, without any previous or known deliberation.*

LII

Names therefore being far from arbitrary and being derived in their origin, like all things, more or less immediately from God, it should not be thought that man has the right to name without restriction even those things of which he has some right to regard himself as the author, and to impose names on them according to the idea he has formed of them. God has reserved for himself in this respect a kind of original jurisdiction impossible to ignore. *My dear Hermogenes, the imposition of names is an important matter, and cannot belong to the evil or even the common man. . . . This right belongs only to the maker of names, that is to say, as it seems, to the legislator alone; but a legislator is the rarest of all human beings.*[12]

LIII

However, man likes nothing so much as to give names. That is what he does, for example, when he applies conventional epithets to things, a talent which distinguishes the great writer and above all the great poet. The happy imposition of an adjective renders a noun illustrious, makes it celebrated in this new combination. . . . Man will never lost the memory of his original powers; it can even be said that, in a certain sense, he will always exercise them; but how much has his degradation restricted them. Here is a law true as God who made it:
It is forbidden to man to give great names to the things of which he is the

author and which he believes to be great; but if he has acted legitimately, the great thing will ennoble the vulgar name and it will become great....

LV

Another reason, which, if less important, still has its value, must oblige us to mistrust all pretentious names imposed a priori. It is that, man's conscience almost always warning him against the imperfection of the work he has just produced, rebellious pride, while it cannot mislead itself, seeks at least to mislead others by inventing an honorable name that assumes precisely the opposite merit; so that this name, instead of giving a true witness to the excellence of the work, is really confession of the blemish that characterizes it....

LVI

But, as I have said, all this is only secondary: let us return to the general principle that *man has not, or has no longer, the right to name things* (at least in the sense I have given). What is especially significant is that the names most worthy of respect have in every language an origin in common speech. The name is never adapted to the thing itself: in every case the thing adds luster to the name. The name must *grow*, so to speak; otherwise it is inappropriate. What does the word *throne* mean originally? a *seat*, or even a *stool*. What does *scepter* mean? a walking stick. But the *stick* of kings was soon distinguished from all the others, and this name, in its *new* meaning, has lasted for three thousand years. Is there anything nobler in literature and yet humbler in its origins than the word *tragedy*? And the now almost stinking word *flag*, raised and ennobled by warriors' lances, what a varied fate has it had in our own language. Many other words come in varying degrees to the support of the same principle, such as, for example, *senate, dictator, consul, emperor, church, cardinal, marshal*. Let us end by considering the names *constable* and *chancellor*, given to two high offices of modern times; the first meant originally only the *keeper of the stables*, and the second, *the man who stood behind a grille* (so as not to be overwhelmed by a crowd of supplicants).

LVII

There are therefore two infallible rules for judging all human creations, whatever they may be, *origin* and *name;* and properly understood these two rules are easily applied. If the origin is purely human, the structure must be unsound; the more the human interference and the greater the role of deliberation, science, and *above all writing*, in a word of human means of every kind, the more fragile will be the institution. It is primarily by this rule that the work of kings or assemblies in civilizing, establishing, or regenerating nations must be judged.

LVIII

For the opposite reason, the more divine an institution in its origin, the more durable it is. It is as well to point out, for the sake of clarity, that the religious principle is in essence creative and conservative, in two ways. In the first place, as it is the most effective influence on the human mind, it can stimulate prodigious efforts. So, for example, a man persuaded by his religious beliefs that it is very advantageous to him that after his death his body should be preserved as far as possible as it was in life, without any prying or profane hand being able to touch it, such a man, having brought the art of embalment to perfection, will end by constructing the pyramids of Egypt. In the second place, the religious principle, already so strong because of what it effects, is still stronger because of what it prevents, through the respect with which it surrounds everything it takes under its wings. If a pebble is consecrated, that immediately becomes a reason for keeping it from those who might mislay or misuse it. The world is full of proofs of this truth. For example, Etruscan vases, preserved by the sanctity of the tomb, have in spite of their fragility come down to us in greater numbers than marble or bronze statues of the same period. If therefore you wish to *conserve* all, *consecrate* all.

LIX

The second rule, that of names, is to my mind neither less clear nor less decisive than the first. If a name is imposed by an assembly; if it is established by a previous deliberation, so that it precedes the thing to which it applies; if the name is pompous; if it is as portentous as the object it should represent; finally, if it is taken from a foreign language, and especially an ancient language, it is completely useless and both the name and the thing it stands for will certainly disappear in a short time. The opposite conditions are a mark of the legitimacy and consequently the durability of the institution. It is very necessary to guard against dealing with this subject superficially. The true philosopher must never lose sight of language, a barometer that registers faithfully *good and bad weather*. To keep to my present subject, the unlimited introduction of foreign words, above all when applied to national institutions of every kind, is certainly one of the surest signs of a people's degradation.

LX

If the formation of empires, the progress of civilization, and the unanimous agreement of all history and tradition is still not sufficient to convince us, the death of empires will complete the proof begun by their birth. Just as it is the religious principle that has created all things, so it is the absence of this same principle that has destroyed all things. The Epicureans, who could be called the *ancient unbelievers*, first degraded and soon destroyed every government which had the misfortune to tolerate them. Everywhere *Lucretius* heralded *Caesar*.

But all past experience dwindles to nothing beside the astonishing example furnished by the last century. Still drunk with its heady fumes, men in general are far from having sufficient composure to look at this example in its true light and especially to draw from it the necessary conclusions; it is therefore essential to scrutinize this terrible epoch with every care.

LXI

There have always been religions in this world, and there have always been the ungodly to fight them; also, blasphemy has always been a sin; for, since every false religion must contain some element of truth, every blasphemous doctrine must attack some divine truth more or less distorted; *but true blasphemy can exist only in the bosom of a true religion*; and inevitably blasphemy has never been able to produce in the past the evils it has produced in our own day, for its culpability is always relative to the general standard of enlightenment. It is by this rule that the eighteenth century must be judged, for it is from this point of view that it differs from every other. It is often said *that every age is alike and that all men have always been the same*; but it is very necessary to guard against believing these generalizations invented by laziness or superficiality to escape from real thought. On the contrary, every age and every nation has a particular and distinctive character which must be carefully considered. No doubt there have always been vices in the world, but these vices can differ in quantity, in nature, in dominant quality, and in intensity. Although there has always been impiety, there had never been, before the eighteenth century and in the heart of the Christian world, *an insurrection against God*; above all there had never been seen before a sacrilegious conspiracy of all the talents against their author. Now, this is what we have seen in our own day. Comedy has vied with tragedy in blasphemy, and the novel with history and natural philosophy. The men of this age have prostituted their talents to irreligion, and, to use the admirable phrase of the dying St. Louis, THEY HAVE WAGED WAR AGAINST GOD WITH HIS GIFTS. The impiety of the ancient world is never angry; sometimes it is reasonable, ordinarily it is lighthearted, but it is never bitter. Even Lucretius scarcely ever descends to an insult; and although his somber and melancholy temperament leads him to see things in their darkest colors, yet, even when he attacks religion for having produced great evils, he remains composed. The ancient religions were not sufficiently worthwhile to merit the anger of contemporary skeptics.

LXIV

Then for the first time the unique character of eighteenth century atheism revealed itself. It no longer speaks in the cold tone of indifference, still less with the biting irony of skepticism; there is a deadly hatred, a tone of anger and often of fury. The writers of this age, at least the most outstanding, no longer treat Christianity as an inconsequential human error, but hunt it like a mortal enemy: it becomes a fight to the end, a war to the death; and what would seem unbelievable, if we did not have sad proofs of it before our eyes, is that many of these self-styled philosophers raised their hatred of Christianity to a personal hatred of its divine Author. They really detest him as a living enemy is detested. Two men above all, who will be for ever cursed by posterity, have distinguished themselves by a kind of wickedness which might seem beyond the powers of even the most depraved human nature.

LXV

However, the whole of Europe having been civilized by Christianity, and its ministers having gained an important place in the politics of every country, civil and religious institutions had been intermingled and even amalgamated to a surprising degree; so that it could be said with more or less truth of every European state what Gibbon said of France, *that this Kingdom had been made by bishops*. It was therefore inevitable that the philosophy of the age did not hesitate to vilify the social institutions identified with the religious principle. This is what happened; every government and institution in Europe displeased it, precisely *because* they were Christian; and *in proportion to* the influence of Christianity, a malaise of opinion, a general discontent seized men's minds. In France especially, this philosophic fury no longer recognized any limits; and soon many voices were joined in one chorus which was heard at the heart of sinful Europe:

LXVI

'Depart from us, God![13] Must we for ever tremble before priests, and receive from them whatever instruction they care to give us? Throughout Europe, truth is hidden by the smoke of incense; it is time that it emerged from this fatal cloud. We shall no longer speak of you to our children; it is for them, when they become men, to decide if you are and what you are and what you ask of them. All things displease us, because your name is written on all things. We wish to destroy everything and to re-create it without your help. Depart from our councils of state, our schools, our homes; we shall be better off alone, reason will be a sufficient guide. Depart from us, God!'

How has God punished this abominable delirium? He has punished it as he created the world, by a single phrase. He has said: LET IT BE – and the political world collapsed.

This is how the two proofs join to convince even the least farseeing minds. On the one side, the religious principle presides over every political creation; and on the other everything crumbles once it withdraws.

LXVII

Europe's sin is to have closed men's eyes to these great truths, and it is because it has sinned that it suffers. Yet it still rejects the true light and ignores the hand that punishes it. Very few men in this materialist generation are capable of knowing the *time*, the *nature*, and the *enormity* of certain crimes committed by individuals, nations, and sovereigns, still less of understanding the kind of expiation these crimes necessitate and the wonderful miracle that forces evil to clean with its own hands the place that the eternal architect has already surveyed for his awesome works. The men of this age have made up their minds. *They have sworn to bow their eyes to the earth.*[14] But it would be useless, perhaps even dangerous, to go into greater detail. We are enjoined *to speak the truth in love.*[15] It is more necessary on certain occasions not to speak it except with respect; and, in spite of every imaginable precaution, the way would be difficult for even the calmest and best intentioned of writers. The world, moreover, always holds an innumerable host of men so perverse, so profoundly corrupted, that, if they have been allowed to doubt certain things, they will also take the opportunity to redouble their wickedness and make themselves, so to speak, as guilty as the rebel angels. Rather let them grow more like brutes, if this is possible, so that, as less than men, their guilt will be the less. Blindness is no doubt a terrible punishment; yet sometimes it still allows the perception of love: this is all that can usefully be said at this time.

Notes

1. Plato, *Phaedrus*, 275–277.
2. Matthew 10:19.
3. Xenophon: *Memorabilia*, Book i, Chap. iv.
4. As a matter of fact, Condorcet promised us that the philosophers would undertake tirelessly the civilization and welfare of the barbarian nations (*Esquisse d'un tableau historique de l'esprit humain*, p. 335). We shall wait till they really intend to start.
5. Ibid., p. 335.
6. *Lettre à l'archevêque de Paris*.
7. Voltaire, *Essai sur les moeurs et l'esprit*.
8. Quoted in *Transunto delle R. Academia di Torino*, 1788–89, p. 6.
9. Origen, *Against Celsus*, Book i, Chap. xxvi.
10. *Précis du siécle de Louis XV*, Chap. xlii.
11. Proverbs 8:31.
12. Plato, *Cratylus* 388e.
13. Job 21:14.
14. Psalms 17:11.
15. Ephesians 4:15.

13
F. W. Maitland

Frederic William Maitland (1850–1906) was a legal historian, and, from 1888 until his death, Downing Professor of Law at Cambridge. In his posthumously published lectures, The Constitutional History of England *(1908), he gave the classic statement of the theory that the constitution of the United Kingdom is tacit and procedural, to be deduced from custom rather than from any written document. Maitland also attempted to establish that limited government had been the rule rather than the exception in England, and to show that legal history reveals far more continuities than radical breaks. He thereby provided the foundations for a conservative vision of social history, and also a refutation of the Marxist theory of history, as determined by changes in the forces and relations of production.*

Maitland's essays on corporate personality – profoundly influenced by the German conservative historian Otto Gierke – occur in Volume 3 of his Collected Papers *(1911), edited by H.A.L. Fisher. 'Moral Personality and Legal Personality', from which the following extracts are taken, provides a powerful summary of arguments which should never be neglected by conservatives, however much they may seem to tend in a 'collectivist' direction.*

. . . Lately in the House of Commons the Prime Minister spoke of trade unions as corporations. Perhaps, for he is an accomplished debater, he anticipated an interruption. At any rate, a distinguished lawyer on the Opposition benches interrupted him with 'The trade unions are not corporations.' 'I know that,' retorted Mr Balfour, 'I am talking English, not law.' A long story was packed into that admirable reply.[1]

And my second text is taken from Mr Dicey, who delivered the Sidgwick lecture last year [1902]. 'When,' he said, 'a body of twenty, or two thousand, or two hundred thousand men bind themselves together to act in a particular way for some common purpose, they create a body, which by no fiction of law, but by the very nature of things, differs from the individuals of whom it is constituted.'[2] I have been waiting a long while for an English lawyer of Professor Dicey's eminence to say what he said – to talk so much 'English.' Let me repeat a few of his words with the stress where I should like it to lie: 'they create a body, which *by no fiction of law, but by the very nature of things*, differs from the individuals of whom it is constituted.' So says Blackstone's successor. Blackstone himself would, I think, have inverted that phrase, and would have ascribed to a fiction of law that phenomenon – or whatever we are to call it – which Mr Dicey ascribes to the very nature of things.

Now for a long time past the existence of this phenomenon has been recognised by lawyers, and the orthodox manner of describing it has been somewhat of this kind. Besides men or 'natural persons,' law knows persons of another kind. In particular it knows the corporation, and for a multitude of purposes it treats the corporation very much as it treats the man. Like the man, the corporation is (forgive this compound adjective) a right-and-duty-bearing unit. Not all the legal propositions that are true of a man will be true of a corporation. For example, it can neither marry nor be given in marriage; but in a vast number of cases you can make a legal statement about x and y which will hold good whether these symbols stand for two men or for two corporations, or for a corporation and a man. The University can buy land from Downing, or hire the gildhall from the Town, or borrow money from the London Assurance; and we may say that *exceptis excipiendis* a court of law can treat these transactions, these acts in the law, as if they took place between two men, between Styles and Nokes. But further, we have to allow that the corporation is in some sense composed of men, and yet between the corporation and one of its members there may exist many, perhaps most, of those legal relationships which can exist between two human beings. I can contract with the University: the University can contract with me. You can contract with the Great Northern Company as you can with the Great Eastern, though you happen to be a shareholder in the one and not in the other. In either case there stands opposite to you another right-and-duty-bearing unit – might I not say another individual? – a single 'not-yourself' that can pay damages or exact them. You expect results of this character, and, if you did not get them, you would think ill of law and lawyers. Indeed, I should say that, the less we know of law, the more confidently we Englishmen expect that the organised group, whether called a corporation or not, will be treated as person: that is, as right-and-duty-bearing unit.

LEGAL ORTHODOXY AND THE FICTITIOUS PERSON

Perhaps I can make the point clearer by referring to an old case. We are told that in Edward IV's day the mayor and commonalty – or, as we might be tempted to say, the municipal corporation – of Newcastle gave a bond to the man who happened to be mayor, he being named by his personal name, and that the bond was held to be void because a man cannot be bound to himself.[3] The argument that is implicit in those few words seems to us quaint, if not sophistical. But the case does not stand alone; far from it. If our business is with medieval history and our aim is to re-think it before we re-present it, here lies one of our most serious difficulties. Can we allow the group – gild, town, village, nation – to stand over against each and all of its members as a distinct person? To be concrete, look at Midsummer Common. It belongs, and, so far as we know, has always in some sense belonged, to the burgesses of Cambridge. But in what sense? Were they co-proprietors? were they corporators? Neither – both? . . .

To steer a clear or any course is hard, for controversial rocks abound. Still, with some security we may say that at the end of the Middle Age a great change in men's thoughts about groups of men was taking place, and that the main agent in the transmutation was Roman Law. Now just how the classical jurists of Rome conceived their *corpora* and *universitates* became in the nineteenth century a much debated question. The profane outsider says of the Digest what some one said of another book:

> Hic liber est in quo quaerit sua dogmata quisque
> Invenit et pariter dogmata quisque sua.

Where people have tried to make antique texts do modern work, the natural result is what Mr Buckland has happily called 'Wardour Street Roman Law.'[4] Still, of this I suppose there can be no doubt, that there could, without undue pressure, be obtained from the Corpus Juris a doctrine of corporations, which, so far as some main outlines are concerned, is the doctrine which has ruled the modern world. Nor would it be disputed that this work was done by the legists and canonists of the Middle Age, the canonists leading the way. The group can be a person: co-ordinated, equiparated, with the man, with the natural person.

With the 'natural' person – for the personality of the *universitas*, of the corporation, is not natural – it is fictitious. This is a very important part of the canonical doctrine, first clearly proclaimed, so we are told, by the greatest lawyer that ever sat upon the chair of St Peter, Pope Innocent IV. You will recall Mr Dicey's words: 'not by fiction of law, but by the very nature of things.' Invert those words, and you will have a dogma that works like leaven in the transformation of medieval society.

If the personality of the corporation is a legal fiction, it is the gift of the prince. It is not for you and me to feign and to force our fictions upon our neighbours. 'Solus princeps fingit quod in rei veritate non est.'[5] An argument drawn from the very nature of fictions thus came to the aid of less questionably Roman doctrines about the illicitness of all associations, the existence of which the prince has not authorised. I would not exaggerate the importance of a dogma, theological or legal. A dogma is of no importance unless and until there is some great desire within it. But what was understood to be the Roman doctrine of corporations was an apt lever for those forces which were transforming the medieval nation into the modern State. The federalistic structure of medieval society is threatened. No longer can we see the body politic as *communitas communitatum*, a system of groups, each of which in its turn is a system of groups. All that stands between the State and the individual has but a derivative and precarious existence.

Do not let us at once think of England. English history can never be an elementary subject: we are not logical enough to be elementary. If we must think of England, then let us remember that we are in the presence of a doctrine which in Charles II's day condemns all – yes, all – of the citizens of London to prison for 'presuming to act as a corporation.' We may remember also how corporations appear to our absolutist Hobbes as troublesome entozoa. But it is always best to begin with France, and there, I take it, we may see the pulverising, macadamising tendency in all its glory, working from century to century, reducing to impotence, and then to nullity, all that intervenes between Man and State.

THE STATE AND THE CORPORATION

In this, as in some other instances, the work of the monarchy issues in the work of the revolutionary assemblies. It issues in the famous declaration of August 18, 1792: 'A State that is truly free ought not to suffer within its bosom any corporation, not even such as, being dedicated to public instruction, have merited well of the country.'[6] That was one of the mottoes of modern absolutism: the absolute State faced the absolute individual. An appreciable part of the interest of the French Revolution seems to me to be open only to those who will be at pains to give a little thought to the theory of corporations. Take, for example, those memorable debates touching ecclesiastical property. To whom belong these broad lands when you have pushed fictions aside, when you have become a truly philosophical jurist with a craving for the natural? To the nation, which has stepped into the shoes of the prince. That is at least a plausible answer, though an uncomfortable suspicion that the State itself is but a questionably real person may not be easily dispelled. And as with the churches, the universities, the trade-gilds, and the like, so also with the communes, the towns and villages. Village property – there was a great deal of village property in France – was exposed to the dilemma: it belongs to the State, or else it belongs to the now existing villagers. I doubt we Englishmen, who never clean our slates, generally know how clean the French slate was to be.

ASSOCIATIONS IN FRANCE

Was to be, I say. Looking back now, French lawyers can regard the nineteenth century as the century of association, and, if there is to be association, if there is to be group-formation, the problem of personality cannot be evaded, at any rate if we are a logical people. Not to mislead, I must in one sentence say, that even the revolutionary legislators spared what we call partnership, and that for a long time past French law has afforded comfortable quarters for various kinds of groups, provided (but notice this) that the group's one and only object was the making of pecuniary gain. Recent writers have noticed it as a paradox that the State saw no harm in the selfish people who wanted dividends, while it had an intense dread of the comparatively unselfish people who would combine with some religious, charitable, literary, scientific, artistic purpose in view. I cannot within my few minutes be precise, but at the beginning of this twentieth century it was still a misdemeanour to belong to any unauthorised *association* having more than twenty members. A licence from the prefect, which might be obtained with some ease, made the *association* non-criminal, made it licit; but personality – 'civil personality,' as they say in France – was only to be acquired with difficulty as the gift of the central government.

Now I suppose it to be notorious that during the last years of the nineteenth century law so unfavourable to liberty of association was still being maintained, chiefly, if not solely, because prominent, typically prominent, among the *associations* known to Frenchmen stood the *congrégations* – religious houses, religious orders. The question how these were to be treated divided the nation, and at last, in 1901, when a new and very important law was made about 'the contract of association,' a firm line was drawn between the non-religious sheep and the religious goats. With the step then taken and the subsequent woes of the congregations I have here no concern; but the manner in which religious and other groups had previously been treated by French jurisprudence seems to me exceedingly instructive. It seems to me to prove so clearly that in a country where people take their legal theories seriously, a country where a Prime Minister will often talk law without ceasing to talk agreeable French, the question whether the group is to be, as we say, 'a person in the eye of the law' is the question whether the group as group can enjoy more than an uncomfortable and precarious existence. I am not thinking of attacks directed against it by the State. I am thinking of collisions between it and private persons. It lives at the mercy of its neighbours, for a law-suit will dissolve it into its constituent atoms. Nor is that all. Sometimes its neighbours will have cause to complain of its legal impersonality. They will have been thinking of it as a responsible right-and-duty-bearing unit, while at the touch of law it becomes a mere many, and a practically, if not theoretically, irresponsible many.

GROUP-PERSONALITY

During the nineteenth century (so I understand the case) a vast mass of experience, French, German, Belgian, Italian, and Spanish (and I might add, though the atmosphere is hazier, English and

American), has been making for a result which might be stated in more than one way. (1) If the law allows men to form permanently organised groups, those groups will be for common opinion right-and-duty-bearing units; and if the law-giver will not openly treat them as such, he will misrepresent, or, as the French say, he will 'denature' the facts: in other words, he will make a mess and call it law. (2) Group-personality is no purely legal phenomenon. The law-giver may say that it does not exist, where, as a matter of moral sentiment, it does exist. When that happens, he incurs the penalty ordained for those who ignorantly or wilfully say the thing that is not. If he wishes to smash a group, let him smash it, send the policeman, raid the rooms, impound the minute-book, fine, and imprison; but if he is going to tolerate the group, he must recognise its personality, for otherwise he will be dealing wild blows which may fall on those who stand outside the group as well as those who stand within it. (3) For the morality of common sense the group is a person, is a right-and-duty-bearing unit. Let the moral philosopher explain this, let him explain it as illusion, let him explain it away; but he ought not to leave it unexplained, nor, I think, will he be able to say that it is an illusion which is losing power, for, on the contrary, it seems to me to be persistently and progressively triumphing over certain philosophical and theological prejudices.

You know that classical distribution of Private Law under three grand rubrics – Persons, Things, Actions. Half a century ago the first of these three titles seemed to be almost vanishing from civilised jurisprudence. No longer was there much, if anything, to be said of exceptional classes, of nobles, clerics, monks, serfs, slaves, excommunicates or outlaws. Children there might always be, and lunatics; but women had been freed from tutelage. The march of the progressive societies was, as we all know, from status to contract. And now? And now that forlorn old title is wont to introduce us to ever new species and new genera of persons, to vivacious controversy, to teeming life; and there are many to tell us that the line of advance is no longer from status to contract, but through contract to something that contract cannot explain, and for which our best, if an inadequate, name is the personality of the organised group.

FACT OR FICTION?

Theorising, of course, there has been. I need not say so, nor that until lately it was almost exclusively German. Our neighbours' conception of the province of jurisprudence has its advantages as well as its disadvantages. On the one hand, ethical speculation (as we might call it) of a very interesting kind was until these last days too often presented in the unattractive guise of Wardour Street Roman Law, or else, raising the Germanistic cry of 'Loose from Rome!' it plunged into an exposition of medieval charters. On the other hand, the theorising is often done by men who have that close grasp of concrete modern fact which comes of a minute and practical study of legal systems. Happily it is no longer necessary to go straight to Germany. That struggle over 'the contract of association' to which I have alluded, those woes of the 'congregations' of which all have heard, invoked foreign learning across the border, and now we may read in lucid French of the various German theories. Good reading I think it; and what interests me especially is that the French lawyer, with all his orthodoxy (legal orthodoxy) and conservatism, with all his love of clarity and abhorrence of mysticism, is often compelled to admit that the traditional dogmas of the law-school have broken down. Much disinclined though he may be to allow the group a real will of its own, just as really real as the will of a man, still he has to admit that if n men unite themselves in an organised body, jurisprudence, unless it wishes to pulverise the group, must see $n + 1$ persons. And that for the mere lawyer should I think be enough. 'Of heaven and hell he has no power to sing,' and he might content himself with a phenomenal reality – such reality, for example, as the lamp-post has for the idealistic ontologist. Still, we do not like to be told that we are dealing in fiction, even if it be added that we needs must feign, and the thought will occur to us that a fiction that we needs must feign is somehow or another very like the simple truth.

Why we English people are not interested in a problem that is being seriously discussed in many other lands, that is a question to which I have tried to provide some sort of answer elsewhere.[7] It is a long, and you would think it a very dreary, story about the most specifically English of all our legal institutes; I mean the trust. All that I can say here is that the device of building a wall of trustees enabled us to construct bodies which were not technically corporations and which yet would be sufficiently protected from the assaults of individualistic theory. The personality of such bodies – so I should put it – though explicitly denied by lawyers, was on the whole pretty well recognised in practice. That something of this sort happened you might learn from one simple fact. For some time past we have had upon our statute book the term 'unincorporate body.' Suppose that a Frenchman saw it, what would he say? 'Unincorporate body: inanimate soul! No wonder your Prime Minister, who is a philosopher, finds it hard to talk English and talk law at the same time.'

One result of this was, so I fancy, that the speculative Englishman could not readily believe that in this quarter there was anything to be explored except some legal trickery unworthy of exploration. The lawyer assured him that it was so, and he saw around him great and ancient, flourishing and wealthy groups – the Inns of Court at their head – which, so the lawyer said, were not persons. To have cross-examined the lawyer over the bodiliness of his 'unincorporate body' might have brought out some curious results; but such a course was hardly open to those who shared our wholesome English contempt for legal technique.

THE ULTIMATE MORAL UNIT

Well, I must finish; and yet perhaps I have not succeeded in raising just the question that I wanted to ask. Can I do that in two or three last sentences? It is a moral question, and therefore I will choose my hypothetical case from a region in which our moral sentiments are not likely to be perplexed by legal technique. My organised group shall be a sovereign state. Let us call it Nusquamia. Like many other sovereign states, it owes money, and I will suppose that you are one of its creditors. You are not receiving the expected interest and there is talk of repudiation. That being so, I believe that you will be, and indeed I think that you ought to be, indignant, morally, righteously indignant. Now the question that I want to raise is this: Who is it that really owes you money? Nusquamia. Granted, but can you convert the proposition that Nusquamia owes you money into a series of propositions imposing duties on certain human beings that are now in existence? The task will not be easy. Clearly you do not think that every Nusquamian owes you some aliquot share of the debt. No one thinks in that way. The debt of Venezuela is not owed by Fulano y Zutano and the rest of them. Nor, I think, shall we get much good out of the word 'collectively,' which is the smudgiest word in the English language, for the largest 'collection' of zeros is only zero. I do not wish to say that I have suggested an impossible task, and that the right-and-duty-bearing group must be for the philosopher an ultimate and unanalysable moral unit: as ultimate and unanalysable, I mean, as is the man. Only if that task can be performed, I think that in the interests of jurisprudence and of moral philosophy it is eminently worthy of circumspect performance. As to our national law, it has sound instincts, and muddles along with semi-personality and demi-semi-personality towards convenient conclusions. Still, I cannot think that Parliament's timid treatment of the trade unions has been other than a warning, or that it was a brilliant day in our legal annals when the affairs of the Free Church of Scotland were brought before the House of Lords, and the dead hand fell with a resounding slap upon the living body. As to philosophy, that is no affair of mine. I speak with conscious ignorance and unfeigned humility; only of this I feel moderately sure, that those who are to tell us of the very nature of things and the very nature of persons will not be discharging their duties to the full unless they come to close terms with that triumphant fiction, if fiction it be, of which I have said in your view more than too much, and in my own view less than too little.

Notes

1. The *Standard*, April 23, 1904. *Mr Balfour*: 'The mere fact that funds can be used, or are principally used, for benefit purposes, is surely not of itself a sufficient reason for saying that trade unions, and trade unions alone, out of all the corporations in the country, commercial—' *Sir R. Reid*: 'The trade unions are not corporations.' *Mr Balfour*: 'I know; I am talking English, not law' (*cheers and laughter*).
2. Professor Dicey's lecture on the Combination Laws is printed in *Harvard Law Review*, xvii. 511. See p. 513.
3. Year Book, 21 Edw. IV, f. 68: 'Come fuit ajugdé en le cas del Maior de Newcastle ou le Maior et le Cominalty fist un obligation a mesme le person que fuit Maior par son propre nosme, et pur ceo que il mesme fuit Maior, et ne puti faire obligation a luy mesme, il [= l'obligation] fuit tenus voide.'

4. Buckland, 'Wardour Street Roman Law,' *Law Quarterly Review*, xvii, 179.
5. Lucas de Penna, cited in Gierke, *Das deutsche Genossenschaftsrecht*, iii, 371.
6. 'Considérant qu'un État vraiment libre ne doit souffrir dans son sein aucune corporation, pas même celles qui, vouées à l'enseignement public, ont bien mérité de la patrie.'
7. Maitland, 'Trust und Korporation,' Wien, 1904 (from *Grünhut's Zeitschrift für das Privat- und Öffentliche-Recht*, vol. xxxii).

14
W.H. Mallock

William Hurrell Mallock (1849–1923), one of the rare conservatives to emerge from an education at Balliol College, Oxford, is best known as the author of The New Republic *(1877) – a beautifully-written satire on English society and on the ideas which circulated in it. A man of letters, with a refined and poetic sensibility, Mallock turned his attention to politics only later in life, fired by a passionate conviction that socialism is not only nonsense as economics, but also a source of moral and spiritual confusion. His classic* A Critical Examination of Socialism *(1907) is a model of lucidity, and presents arguments which – perhaps because of their simplicity – no socialist has bothered to answer. Mallock also wrote* The Reconstruction of Belief *(1892), in which he endeavoured to provide the spiritual alternative to the socialist gospel of his day, and a trenchant criticism of secular democratic thinking,* Limits of Pure Democracy *(1919), from which the following extracts are taken.*

Our general argument thus far may be briefly restated thus. It starts with insisting on the fact that, in communities small and primitive and isolated, pure democracy, or government determined by the spontaneous wills of all, is not only a possible system, but is practically the system which exists; and, further, that it continues to exist with regard to those fundamental questions which, in all communities, simple or complex, are the same. In its relation, therefore, to questions such as these, we have a working example of what pure democracy is, by which we can measure how far, with regard to others, its only effective action diverges from the pure type. The extent and nature of its divergence may be indicated once again by a series of simple illustrations such as those which have been used already.

Let us suppose that all the voters of England are assembled in some vast hall, and that the executive government is represented in the person of a single minister, who asks for their corporate will as to the three following questions which he puts before them thus.

(1) 'Of late, as you all know, there have been constant attempts at incendiarism by the use of matches and kerosene. Is it your will that the government shall still maintain the police-force which, as you all know, has proved itself able to frustrate them?

(2) 'Of late, as you all know, a number of conflagrations have been caused, and might any day be caused again, by incendiary bombs dropped from German airships. Is it your will that the government shall produce an anti-aircraft gun which will shoot down airships as easily as a sportsman shoots a pheasant?

(3) 'What is the precise construction, or what are the vital peculiarities, of the gun which, for that purpose, you will that the government shall produce?'

The first question would at once be answered by acclamation, and this would tell the minister everything he asked to be told. All the citizens would know what is meant by the word 'policeman,' and in expressing by a unanimous shout their will that the police-force should be maintained, they would be giving a definite order which could at once be carried into execution.

The second question would probably be answered by acclamation likewise, and this would tell the minister something of what he asked to be told. It would mean that the people spontaneously willed or ordered the production of a gun of some sort.

But a gun of some sort is practically a gun of no sort. If the minister wanted an order which could definitely guide his actions, he would have to go on to the third question; and if he put this to his audience – if he asked for any working instructions as to what sort of gun this particular gun should be – his question would elicit a response of a very different kind. Most of the assembled voters would stare at him in awkward silence. Some of them would giggle, and think that the minister was laughing at them. Then from a miscellaneous minority would come a volley of answers, most of them worthless, whilst those which were not worthless were so conflicting and various that no ingenuity could invest them with any corporate meaning. The unhappy minister would be driven to shout out to his instructors the very familiar adjuration, 'Don't all speak at once.'

But that everybody should speak at once is the very thing which the theory of pure democracy demands, and the fact that this demand elicits in some cases the precise result desired illustrates by contrast the absurdity of supposing that it would, or ever could, do so in others. Of the three typical questions which we have just now been imagining, the first elicits a will which is spontaneous, which is unanimous, which is complete. The will elicited by the second is spontaneous, it is unanimous, but it is incomplete, stopping far short of the point at which definite orders must begin. It is, therefore, for purposes of practical guidance, a nullity. The third question, which demands that this incomplete will shall complete itself, fails to elicit any general will at all. Between will and action there must be a further will which is still missing. This must be the will of the minister or oligarchy on whose behalf he speaks, and if the construction of the desired weapon is ever to be accomplished at all, the only will which can render its accomplishment possible is not any will which the many dictate to the few. It is essentially one which the few dictate to the many, and which the many must somehow or other be induced to make their own. Or to put the matter in more general terms, in proportion as political questions recede from fundamental simplicity, the power of unalloyed democracy to deal with such questions evaporates, and, unless it is quasi-chemically changed by combination with oligarchy, ceases practically to exist.

Now the general truth of this argument, as we have seen in the preceding chapter, has come to be admitted even by the prophets of extreme revolution. In what sense, then, can it be contended by persons of more moderate principles that the people as a homogeneous whole, or the units of the average mass, have, in spite of all appearances to the contrary, some definite will of their own, complete in itself, and independent of any minority whose talents may happen to be necessary for the transaction of detailed business? The idea which such persons have at the back of their minds is well expressed by a writer who has here been quoted already as able to state bluntly what many other persons mean. This writer maintains that, with regard to political questions, no matter how complex, a will is naturally immanent in the units of the average mass, which, due to the likeness of one unsophisticated man to another, deserves to be called the specific will of the people, in the only important sense which that phrase is intended to suggest. That is to say, in complex cases no less than in simple, the mass of the people, as distinct from special minorities, have a definite will with regard to 'the general objective of government,' though they may not in complex cases be able to prescribe the means.

There is enough of truth in this argument, and also of very common error, to render it worth attention.

Both the truth and the error are connected with a confusion of thought which, at once fostered and hidden by an inaccurate use of language, makes the term 'will' interchangeable with the term 'wish.' The most careless thinker, if he only gives his mind to the matter, is bound to recognise that, although he constantly confuses them, they stand for two different things, and that though a will must always include a wish, and the two in practice may thus often coincide, a wish in itself is very far from constituting a will. Thus a man may wish, what is probably wished by most men, that he had not perpetrated in his youth a number of foolish actions; but nobody can will, and nobody would say that he wills, not to have done something which twenty years ago he did. He may wish that he could get to Mars, and have a look at the supposed canals. He may wish to get from London to York, and have a look at the Minster. But his wish that he could get to Mars must remain a wish, or an idle emotion only. Why? Because no means exist which he can possibly employ for getting there. His wish to get from London to York may be any day matured into a will. Why? Because means of getting there exist, such as trains or his own legs, by choosing and employing which his wish any day may be accomplished. In other words, a wish is no more than a feeling of desire for a mentally imaged something which, whether possible or absolutely impossible, the imagination presents to the consciousness of the wisher as desirable. A will is a feeling of desire for a mentally imaged something which the person so desiring it knows or believes to be possible by the use of specific means; and only becomes a will when it causes him to adopt, or do his best to adopt them.

These observations as to the difference between wish and will have a special bearing on the question of a general will in politics. When the writer to whom we are here referring claims that in the sphere of political government there is always a general will with regard to the governmental objective, though except in very simple cases there is no such will as to means, what he obviously intends to say – and the nature of his argument shows this – is that, with regard to the objective, there is not a general will, but only some general wish. In the statement, as thus amended, there is doubtless a certain truth. Let us consider how much it comes to.

Governments and their actions are not ends in themselves. Free

Trade is not an end in itself. Even the legal administration of justice is not an end in itself. Each is valued only as conducing to some end or objective ulterior to it. The objective in the former case is some kind of prosperity. In the latter it is justice itself, not the means of administering it. Every voluntary action which man is capable of performing is performed, says Aristotle, for the sake of some immediate end; but all such ends, except one, are one after another subsidiary to some end which is beyond themselves; and the ultimate end or objective which alone is desired for its own sake, and which has often been identified with pleasure, is best described, says Aristotle, as 'eudaimonia,' or happiness. What Aristotle says of human action in general is, with one qualification, true of the actions performed by governments. The objective of governmental action is not happiness itself, but it is the next thing to it. It is best described as Welfare, or the conditions out of which Happiness is most likely to arise, in so far as regulation by an external power can produce them.

The statement must, therefore, in a certain sense be true, that, with regard to the governmental objective, all the units of the average mass, and those indeed of exceptional classes also, do spontaneously wish for one and the same thing; for any one man may be trusted, 'in virtue of his manhood alone,' to wish for his own welfare just as devoutly as any other man. But a wish of this kind, in so far as it has any relation to the detailed possibilities of life or the possible action of any government whatsoever, is general and unanimous so long only as it is vague. Thus if each citizen, as one out of so many millions, were asked to describe in detail his own conception of the conditions which would constitute welfare for himself, the first condition which they all would agree in naming would no doubt be an income of at least some hundreds a year. Most people, while they were about it, would probably say some thousands.[1] Here, in one sense, would be a very happy unanimity, and it is quite possible that a government might so act (whether by granting monopolies, by creating new posts, or otherwise) as to realise this wish in the case of a citizen here and there. But since there is no country under the sun whose resources could provide even half of such an income for everybody, it is obvious that so many millions of individual wishes, of which only a few thousands or a few hundreds could be gratified, would not, if considered as a guide to governmental actions, be a general wish at all. It would, on the contrary, be a general conflict of wishes, like the wishes of persons pushing for the best seats in a theatre; for every man would be wishing for himself a something which, if obtained by him, would render the fulfilment of other men's wishes impossible.

Let us suppose, however, that the citizens perceive this, and that their wishes for welfare are sobered down to wishes for such conditions only as governmental action of any kind is competent to secure for all; and let us consider how far in detail their wishes are likely to coincide, and thus coalesce into any general will which, to a government waiting for orders, would be clear or even approximately intelligible.

In a simple society, or one relatively simple, which has just emerged from the hunting stage into the agricultural, welfare is spontaneously identified in the minds of most of the citizens with the tenure by each of a sufficient quantity of land, which tenure shall be so secured to him by law that his sole means of earning a livelihood shall never be taken away from him. All such men, therefore, in wishing for their own welfare, wish for the enactment or maintenance of some particular land-law, the essential content of which can be grasped and expressed by everybody; and the expression of it, as addressed to the government, transforms a general wish into a true general will. It must, however, be observed that, simple though this case is, there is one element in it which is not at first sight apparent. If a government in obedience to such a will is to render each man's right to a given plot of land inalienable, it can do so only by depriving him of the right to quit it; and so long as a society consists mainly of cultivators this deprivation will be hardly so much as noticed, for no one would wish to run away from his sole means of subsistence. But if trade and manufactures begin, as they did in mediæval England, to offer the cultivator chances of greater gain than any which he can hope for whilst he is tethered to the clods of a few acres, his idea of welfare (as happened in mediæval England) begins to be complicated by the intrusion of a new element. To the wish for security is added a wish for freedom. Hence a further wish arises in a growing number of minds that a law, which can only secure the means of subsistence for a man by chaining the man to one means of subsistence, shall be superseded by a law which will render this connection dissoluble, and allow him to choose, if he can find it, a means of subsistence for himself. At the same time, the new law, although it would have its advantages, would obviously deprive him of those secured by the old; and every interested person, before his wish could mature itself into a will that the new law should be enacted, would have to balance against its promised advantages the advantages it would take away – to calculate which alternative would yield him a net gain: and different minds would be certain to work out such a sum differently.

This case is typical. In any complex society, out of all the many wishes which, in the mind of every average man, vaguely make up the general idea of welfare, there are few which, if fulfilled completely, would not be found inconsistent with the complete fulfilment of others.[2] The wished-for objective is not a single condition, but a plexus of many, each of which must be limited by the co-existence of others, in order that all together may produce the result, welfare. If the people, then, in respect of their several complete objectives are to have any common will which they are able to impose on the government, this will must be a highly complex thing; and if it is to be expressed in a manner which any government can understand, the expression of it must be equivalent to a picture representing welfare divided into its component parts, the position, dimensions and configuration of each being indicated with such precision that the government may be able to shape its conduct accordingly. Further, if a picture of this kind, with all its complex details, is really to represent the will of the average mass, all the units of the mass must, spontaneously and without prompting, draw it – each for himself – in precisely the same way. But there are two reasons why such a result is impossible. In the first place, a picture of this elaborate kind would have to be drawn from a conception no less elaborate, which the person drawing it had already thought out and matured; and the train of thought required for this purpose would be not only so intricate, but would also deal with quantities so incapable of exact measurement, that the conception thus formed of welfare by any one mind would rarely coincide, even in its main details, with that formed by any other. In the second place, whatever the conception of welfare in a man's own mind may be, it would in most cases bear very little resemblance to the only definite picture by means of which he would be able to communicate it to a government or to anybody else. Such a picture, as drawn by most men, would be like a drawing of its mother by a child, who, being lost in a crowd, should hand it to a policeman in order that he might be able to find her. If the policeman appeared at the door of the child's nursery afterwards with a creature whose features and proportions were like those of the child's drawing – a creature with legs like sticks, with one eye in its forehead, and another eye in its cheek – the child would certainly exclaim that this was not its mother, but the devil. The truth of the matter is that for any man to analyse accurately his own conception of the welfare for which he himself wishes, and express it in terms intelligible to any other human being, is a task requiring talents of an exceedingly rare order. The task of inducing millions of men to unify, for governmental purposes, their various conceptions of what they wish for, by adopting a single conception which is not identical with any of these, is a task requiring talent of a rarer order still; and it is only when this latter task has been accomplished with something like substantial success that a multitude of wishes, previously vague, unlike in their content, and ineffectual, can be converted into a demand for a single set of conditions, all of them absolutely specific, and thus be made to constitute a cumulative and effective will.

Those, then, who claim that the units of the average mass, though they cannot dictate means to the government or the executive oligarchy, have nevertheless, with regard to the governmental objective, some corporate will of their own which a government could be ordered to execute, absolutely ignore the essential point at issue. It is true, and has been said already, that just as will must always precede voluntary action, so must wish always precede will. The very idea of government, the very idea of a people to be governed, presupposes on the part of the people one common wish at all events – that is to say, the wish to live; and the wish to live, owing to the constitution of the human body, is primarily identified with, and is indistinguishable from, the wish for food. Now if all men were congregated on an absolutely barren rock, the wish for food would be a wish and a wish only. No action could follow it, and the human race would die. Nature, however, has taught men for countless thousands of years that this wish can be satisfied by the immemorial practice of agriculture; but the wish for food is not agriculture itself, although there would be no agriculture without the wish for food. Agriculture is a wish for food-stuffs which has translated itself into a will to produce them by certain means, such as ploughing, sowing, draining, selection of seeds, rotation of crops, and so forth. Similarly, the wish for welfare in a highly civilised State is not political government, though there would be no political government if nobody wished for welfare.

Welfare, in so far as political action can secure it, is in any complex society a plexus of intricate and interconnected means, each of which must represent some will as definite as itself; and if each of these means is to represent a will of the people generally, each must represent an indefinite number of wills, all so exactly unified that they practically amount to one. For, just as the same pig can be killed in one way only, so this plexus of means which, so far as government can affect the matter, constitutes welfare in its only possible form, cannot in any one country and at any given moment be, even in the smallest detail, other than the thing it is.

If, then, in order that any particular plexus may be definitely willed by the people to the exclusion of all others, it is necessary (as most serious democrats are now coming to admit) that the means comprised in this plexus, or at all events the larger part of them, shall be first devised by the few, and the people in some way or other induced to will the adoption of them, we are brought by a new route back to the old conclusion. The people, except with regard to simple and fundamental questions, have, apart from an oligarchy, no place in the arena of political life whatever. The contention, in short, that the people, without any oligarchy to guide them, have a definite will of their own as to a highly complex objective, though they have, apart from an oligarchy, no such will as to the means, is a contradiction in terms. It is a contradiction which is disguised by, and due to, a confusion of wish with will; for in the world of political government, as in the world of action generally, the bald truth is this – that a wish which is not identified with a will as to definite means is not a will at all.

Nobody in his senses can deny that such is the case with regard to certain governmental means or objectives when these are taken individually – such, for example, as safety and an anti-aircraft gun. Welfare as a general objective is not only no exception to this rule, but it is, on the contrary, the crowning and the all-comprehensive illustration of it.

The theory, however, of a phantom objective, the realisation of which can be definitely willed by the people though they cannot dictate the means by which such a result may be accomplished, is not the less interesting because it is altogether illusory. On the contrary, it is more so; for it is simply the condensed expression of a vague idea or feeling which the theory of pure democracy tends to develop in the consciousness of the average man. That theory means for each average man who accepts it that there is no individual in the world whose wishes are more important than his own, and no individual who, if all men had their rights, would have greater power than he to impose his own wishes on the government. It thus engenders in him the feeling (which is far more intimate and less open to regulation than the thought) that welfare, as wished for by himself, he being secretly the hero of it, is the special kind of welfare which the government ought to realise.

A homely illustration of this general fact may be found in a letter which was addressed to an American journal by a workman – an immigrant from Austria – after some prolonged experience of affairs in the great Republic. 'I was brought up,' he said, 'in the most aristocratic country in the world, and I have come here to the most democratic. But what good has all this democracy done me? I am no more up to the top of the tree than I ever was.' This man's ingenuous complaint was an expression of what millions of other men more or less vaguely feel. Each of these others, animated by the democratic idea that he has no superior either in rights or power, wishes to be at or near the top of the tree somehow. He expects the government somehow or other to put him there; and since the top of the tree, from the nature of things, can be occupied by a few men only, each member of the majority, let the government do what it may, will feel that he is defrauded by it of his own democratic due. The more democratic a government may be in semblance, and the more profuse, as a consequence, it is in its popular promises, the greater is the discrepancy between its promises and the utmost it is able to perform. The more widely amongst the governed does a sense of grievance diffuse itself – a mood of unrest and suspicion – which makes it increasingly difficult for any executive oligarchy to secure a democratic assent to such limited measures as alone can, when the time for action comes, be put before the people by any statesmen as practicable. In a word, the broad result of the theory of pure governmental democracy, especially with reference to the general governmental objective, is to render the people restive by popularising impossible expectations.

That such is the case is shown clearly enough by the course of modern and comparatively modern history. If we take it roughly that the ideas at the root of modern political democracy first became widely effective towards the close of the eighteenth century, we may say that such a mood of restiveness has from the very first, in one country or another, accompanied all attempts at translating the conception of pure democracy into practice. The true content of such moods, however, has been not precisely what it may seem to have been. It has not amounted, and it does not amount, to a mere uneasy protest that this or that particular government (such as those which formed and dissolved themselves during the course of the French Revolution) was not governmental democracy in its pure and proper form. It comprised from the first the germs of a wider judgment, to the effect that no democracy, the scope of which is purely political, can do anything to secure the conditions which the idea of democracy suggests. The Austrian immigrant in America who attacked political democracy at the beginning of the twentieth century because it had not enabled him to reach the 'top of the tree,' did but express a feeling which had developed itself, as we shall see hereafter, when the French Revolution was merely a maturing dream. Before the more immediate effects of that movement had spent themselves Babeuf had boldly declared that no purely political revolutions could have for the masses of the people any meaning whatever, and lost his head in consequence for conspiring against the French Republic. During the earlier years of the nineteenth century, to mention a few names only, (George Rapp, a German; St. Simon and Fourier, Frenchmen; and Robert Owen, an Englishman,) whilst political democracy was by a large majority still regarded as the key to a near millennium, each in their several ways, and supported by numerous followers, denounced it as wholly incapable of fulfilling its own promises. What these men and others said in effect was this: 'The great thing the people want, and the only thing about which they really care, is not to vote equally, but to live equally; and equal living is a thing which political democracy by itself does not give, and does not even tend to give them.'

From the middle of the nineteenth century onwards this kind of criticism has continued to increase in volume, and to seek for justification in an increasing number of illustrations. Thus, in France, those who had hoped most from democracy in political government, complain to-day that it has, as a working system, replaced a noblesse by a bourgeoisie far more oppressive; whilst in America, where political democracy has been attempted on the largest scale, conditions are more unequal than in any other country in the world.

But the judgments and the mood of mind which such criticism expresses have been far from taking the turn which at first sight might have seemed likely. Though directed against democracy as a principle which vainly attempts to realise itself so long as it is applied to problems of mere political government, they have not been directed against the principle of pure democracy as such. Their actual meaning has gradually developed into one, which is merely the meaning foreshadowed by men like Babeuf and Owen – that the democratic principle has failed to accomplish its promises hitherto, because it has sought to display itself in too narrow a field. It has followed men to their doorsteps, but has left them when they went inside. Its action has stopped short just where it ought to begin. If democracy is ever to result in a scheme of equal living, it must mainly be realised in connection with the affairs of private life, such as industrial production, the distribution of industrial products, and the social interests and intercourse to which such distribution ministers.

The word 'Democracy,' when used in this extended sense, is, as has been said already, commonly distinguished by the epithet 'industrial' or 'social,' or by both, these being taken to indicate two substantially different, though closely associated things. Each of these will here be considered in its proper order. Meanwhile, as to democracy in the sphere of political government, the results of our analysis may be recapitulated thus.

Pure political democracy, or government in which every citizen plays really an equal part, is not in itself, or under all circumstances, impossible. On the contrary, it is the type of government which in certain communities actually tends to exist. These are communities which are minute, primitively simple in their conditions, and isolated. In such communities pure democracy is possible, and indeed inevitable, because all the questions are simple which the government has to settle, and everybody tends to think about them in virtually the same way. Thus, according to Cæsar, the Gallic tribes of his day were democracies in times of peace, and oligarchies in times of war; for in times of war alone was there any scope or need for the leadership of men more sagacious and more courageous than the rest. Further, since in all communities, no matter what their character, certain simple questions persist as the basis of associated life, there is an element of pure democracy in all governments alike. In proportion, however, as communities increase in size, advance in civilisation, and come to have chronic dealings with communities other than themselves, the problems of government multiply, and most of them become more complex.

With regard to most of them there is room for endless differences of opinion. The mere task of considering them carefully is congenial only to men whose mental energy is somewhat above the average, whilst the task of solving them successfully calls for talents and knowledge of special and unusual kinds. For these reasons, two results are inevitable. In the first place, the business of dealing actively with political problems at all tends, from the mere fact of its being laborious, to pass into the hands of the more energetic minority, this body being thus a sort of oligarchic nebula. In the second place, since the solution of these complex problems is not only laborious but difficult, out of this large and nebular oligarchy smaller oligarchies nucleate themselves, which represent, not energy only, but energy combined with various unusual talents, until at last some group is reached (or on critical occasions some one individual) under whose will the wills of the nebular oligarchy range themselves, and are transmitted by oratory or by other means to the mass.

Such is the process which, in every highly civilised country possessing a popular constitution, is taking place under our very eyes. This persistence of oligarchic action is not, as some thinkers contend, due to any defect in the details of mere constitutional mechanism. On the contrary, it becomes more and more pervasive in proportion as such details conform in outer semblance to the democratic ideal. It reveals itself, as we have seen, in the internal organisation of even those sectional parties whose avowed aim is to raise popular power to a maximum. It is due to the permanent facts of human nature on the one hand, and the inevitably complex character of all civilised societies on the other. The case, indeed, may be summed up thus. Nobody would contend, in dealing with the affairs of any great country or empire, whether in times of peace or war, that all exceptional intellect, all exceptional knowledge, all exceptional sagacity and strength of character were superfluous. If talents like these, then, are not absolutely superfluous, it follows that oligarchy of some kind is a necessity; for talent as applied to government can exert itself in one way only – namely that of an influence exercised by a few men over many. The most talented man in the world might be a Cæsar, a Napoleon or a Lincoln within the limits of his own bedroom; but, if he could influence nobody besides himself, his talents would be paralysed if he sat as the chairman of a parish council.

The paralysis of oligarchy would be, therefore, the paralysis of talent. It must, however, be clearly recognised – for here we have a complementary fact which is no less important – that the activity of oligarchy is not the paralysis of democracy. It leaves democracy, in relation to simple and fundamental questions, untouched; whilst with regard to the composite questions which civilisation adds to these, it provides the only means by which, in any definite form, it is practically possible for the principle of democracy to express itself.

Notes

1. Amongst the early incidents of the Russian revolution, the strike was announced by a mass of workmen at Rostoff, who demanded wages at the rate of £90 a month, or more than £1000 a year. The total income of Russia did not come to as much as £13 per head of the population.
2. Here, again, is a fact which has been strikingly illustrated by incidents of the Russian revolution. The dockers at Archangel refused to work for more than six hours a day or for more than three days a week. The docks were blocked with cargoes of coal and other necessaries, which could not be unloaded. By the strikers themselves fuel was hardly obtainable. The workmen in one great factory insisted on an increase of wages in the ratio of 1 to 5. The value of the total product, out of which alone their wages could come, had presently sunk in the ratio of 200 to 15. Unskilled girls demanded and managed to secure £3 10s. a week. They presently found that their boots cost them £10 a pair. Peasants, who demanded communism in land, were aghast when grain was demanded of them for certain other workers and the army.

15
J.C. Murray

John Courtney Murray (1904–67) was a Jesuit priest and Professor of Theology at Woodstock College. Murray represented a vital current of opinion within American conservatism, and his political essays, collected in 1961 as We Hold These Truths, *offer a powerful warning to conservatives everywhere, that political freedom stands in need of moral virtue if it is to be serious, durable or a genuine good. Murray published two other books:* The Problem of God, Yesterday and Today, *1963, and* The Problem of Religious Freedom, *1965. In his political and theological articles he endeavoured to express an authoritarian conception of a society founded upon moral order, in which the habit of obedience takes precedence over the gratification of individual desires.*

As it arose in America, the problem of pluralism was unique in the modern world, chiefly because pluralism was the native condition of American society. It was not, as in Europe and in England, the result of a disruption or decay of a previously existent religious unity. This fact created the possibility of a new solution; indeed, it created a demand for a new solution. The possibility was exploited and the demand was met by the American Constitution. . . .

THE NATION UNDER GOD

The first truth to which the American Proposition makes appeal is stated in that landmark of Western political theory, the Declaration of Independence. It is a truth that lies beyond politics; it imparts to politics a fundamental human meaning. I mean the sovereignty of God over nations as well as over individual men. This is the principle that radically distinguishes the conservative Christian tradition of America from the Jacobin laicist tradition of Continental Europe. The Jacobin tradition proclaimed the autonomous reason of man to be the first and the sole principle of political organization. In contrast, the first article of the American political faith is that the political community, as a form of free and ordered human life, looks to the sovereignty of God as to the first principle of its organization. In the Jacobin tradition religion is at best a purely private concern, a matter of personal devotion, quite irrelevant to public affairs. Society as such, and the state which gives it legal form, and the government which is its organ of action are by definition agnostic or atheist. The statesman as such cannot be a believer, and his actions as a statesman are immune from any imperative of judgment higher than the will of the people, in whom resides ultimate and total sovereignty (one must remember that in the Jacobin tradition 'the people' means 'the party'). This whole manner of thought is altogether alien to the authentic American tradition.

From the point of view of the problem of pluralism this radical distinction between the American and the Jacobin traditions is of cardinal importance. The United States has had, and still has, its share of agnostics and unbelievers. But it has never known organized militant atheism on the Jacobin, doctrinaire Socialist, or Communist model; it has rejected parties and theories which erect atheism into a political principle. In 1799, the year of the Napoleonic *coup d'état* which overthrew the Directory and established a dictatorship in France, President John Adams stated the first of all American first principles in his remarkable proclamation of March 6:

> . . . it is also most reasonable in itself that men who are capable of social arts and relations, who owe their improvements to the social state, and who derive their enjoyments from it, should, as a society make acknowledgements of dependence and obligation to Him who hath endowed them with these capacities and elevated them in the scale of existence by these distinctions. . . .

President Lincoln on May 30, 1863, echoed the tradition in another proclamation:

> Whereas the Senate of the United States, devoutly recognizing the supreme authority and just government of Almighty God in all the affairs of men and nations, has by a resolution requested the President to designate and set apart a day for national prayer

and humiliation; And whereas it is the duty of nations as well as of men to own their dependence upon the overruling power of God, to confess their sins and trespasses in humble sorrow, yet with the assured hope that genuine repentance will lead to mercy and pardon. . . .

The authentic voice of America speaks in these words. And it is a testimony to the enduring vitality of this first principle – the sovereignty of God over society as well as over individual men – that President Eisenhower in June, 1952, quoted these words of Lincoln in a proclamation of similar intent. There is, of course, dissent from this principle, uttered by American secularism (which, at that, is a force far different in content and purpose from Continental laicism). But the secularist dissent is clearly a dissent; it illustrates the existence of the American affirmation. And it is continually challenged. For instance, as late as 1952 an opinion of the United States Supreme Court challenged it by asserting: 'We are a religious people whose institutions presuppose a Supreme Being.' Three times before in its history – in 1815, 1892, and 1931 – the Court had formally espoused this same principle.

THE TRADITION OF NATURAL LAW

The affirmation in Lincoln's famous phrase, 'this nation under God,' sets the American proposition in fundamental continuity with the central political tradition of the West. But this continuity is more broadly and importantly visible in another, and related, respect. In 1884 the Third Plenary Council of Baltimore made this statement: 'We consider the establishment of our country's independence, the shaping of its liberties and laws, as a work of special Providence, its framers "building better than they knew," the Almighty's hand guiding them.' The providential aspect of the matter, and the reason for the better building can be found in the fact that the American political community was organized in an era when the tradition of natural law and natural rights was still vigorous. Claiming no sanction other than its appeal to free minds, it still commanded universal acceptance. And it furnished the basic materials for the American consensus.

The evidence for this fact has been convincingly presented by Clinton Rossiter in his book, *Seedtime of the Republic*,[1] a scholarly account of the 'noble aggregate of "self-evident truths" that vindicated the campaign of resistance (1765–1775), the resolution for independence (1776), and the establishment of the new state governments (1776–1780).' These truths, he adds, 'had been no less self-evident to the preachers, merchants, planters, and lawyers who were the mind of colonial America.' It might be further added that these truths firmly presided over the great time of study, discussion, and decision which produced the Federal Constitution. 'The great political philosophy of the Western world,' Rossiter says, 'enjoyed one of its proudest seasons in this time of resistance and revolution.' By reason of this fact the American Revolution, quite unlike its French counterpart, was less a revolution than a conservation. It conserved, by giving newly vital form to, the liberal tradition of politics, whose ruin in Continental Europe was about to be consummated by the first great modern essay in totalitarianism.

The force for unity inherent in this tradition was of decisive importance in what concerns the problem of pluralism. Because it was conceived in the tradition of natural law the American Republic was rescued from the fate, still not overcome, that fell upon the European nations in which Continental Liberalism, a deformation of the liberal tradition, lodged itself, not least by the aid of the Lodges. There have never been 'two Americas,' in the sense in which there have been, and still are, 'two Frances,' 'two Italys,' 'two Spains.' Politically speaking, America has always been one. The reason is that a consensus was once established, and it still substantially endures, even in the quarters where its origins have been forgotten.

Formally and in the first instance this consensus was political, that is, it embraced a whole constellation of principles bearing upon the origin and nature of society, the function of the state as the legal order of society, and the scope and limitations of government. 'Free government' – perhaps this typically American shorthand phrase sums up the consensus. 'A free people under a limited government' puts the matter more exactly. It is a phrase that would have satisfied the first Whig, St. Thomas Aquinas.

To the early Americans government was not a phenomenon of force, as the later legal positivists would have it. Nor was it a 'historical category,' as Marx and his followers were to assert. Government did not mean simply the power to coerce, though this power was taken as integral to government. Government, properly speaking, was the right to command. It was authority. And its authority derived from law. By the same token its authority was limited by law. In his own way Tom Paine put the matter when he said, 'In America Law is the King.' But the matter had been better put by Henry of Bracton (d. 1268) when he said, 'The king ought not to be under a man, but under God and under the law, because the law makes the king.' This was the message of Magna Carta; this became the first structural rib of American constitutionalism.

Constitutionalism, the rule of law, the notion of sovereignty as purely political and therefore limited by law, the concept of government as an empire of laws and not of men – these were ancient ideas, deeply implanted in the British tradition at its origin in medieval times. The major American contribution to the tradition – a contribution that imposed itself on all subsequent political history in the Western world – was the written constitution. However, the American document was not the *constitution octroyée* of the nineteenth-century Restorations – a constitution graciously granted by the King or Prince-President. Through the American techniques of the constitutional convention and of popular ratification, the American Constitution is explicitly the act of the people. It embodies their consensus as to the purposes of government, its structure, the extent of its powers and the limitations on them, etc. By the Constitution the people define the areas where authority is legitimate and the areas where liberty is lawful. The Constitution is therefore at once a charter of freedom and a plan for political order.

THE PRINCIPLE OF CONSENT

Here is the second aspect of the continuity between the American consensus and the ancient liberal tradition; I mean the affirmation of the principle of the consent of the governed. Sir John Fortescue (d. 1476), Chief Justice of the Court of King's Bench under Henry VI, had thus stated the tradition, in distinguishing between the absolute and the constitutional monarch: 'The secounde king [the constitutional monarch] may not rule his people by other laws than such as thai assenten to. And therefore he may set uppon thaim non imposicions without their consent.' The principle of consent was inherent in the medieval idea of kingship; the king was bound to seek the consent of his people to his legislation. The American consensus reaffirmed this principle, at the same time that it carried the principle to newly logical lengths. Americans agreed that they would consent to none other than their own legislation, as framed by their representatives, who would be responsible to them. In other words, the principle of consent was wed to the equally ancient principle of popular participation in rule. But, since this latter principle was given an amplitude of meaning never before known in history, the result was a new synthesis, whose formula is the phrase of Lincoln, 'government by the people.'

Americans agreed to make government constitutional and therefore limited in a new sense, because it is representative, republican, responsible government. It is limited not only by law but by the will of the people it represents. Not only do the people adopt the Constitution; through the techniques of representation, free elections, and frequent rotation of administrations they also have a share in the enactment of all subsequent statutory legislation. The people are really governed; American political theorists did not pursue the Rousseauist will-o'-the-wisp: how shall the individual in society come to obey only himself? Nevertheless, the people are governed because they consent to be governed; and they consent to be governed because in a true sense they govern themselves.

The American consensus therefore includes a great act of faith in the capacity of the people to govern themselves. The faith was not unrealistic. It was not supposed that everybody could master the technical aspects of government, even in a day when these aspects were far less complex than they now are. The supposition was that the people could understand the general objectives of governmental policy, the broad issues put to the decision of government, especially as these issues raised moral problems. The American consensus accepted the premise of medieval society, that there is a sense of justice inherent in the people, in virtue of which they are empowered, as the medieval phrase had it, to 'judge, direct, and correct' the processes of government.

It was this political faith that compelled early American agreement to the institutions of a free speech and a free press. In the American concept of them, these institutions do not rest on the thin theory proper to eighteenth-century individualistic rationalism, that a man has a right to say what he thinks merely because he thinks it. The American agreement was to reject political censorship of opinion as unrightful, because unwise, imprudent, not to say impossible. However, the proper premise of these freedoms lay in the fact that they were social necessities. 'Colonial thinking about each of these rights had a strong social rather than individualistic bias,' Rossiter says. They were regarded as conditions essential to the conduct of free, representative, and responsible government. People who are called upon to obey have the right first to be heard. People who are to bear burdens and make sacrifices have the right first to pronounce on the purposes which their sacrifices serve. People who are summoned to contribute to the common good have the right first to pass their own judgment on the question, whether the good proposed be truly a good, the people's good, the common good. Through the technique of majority opinion this popular judgment becomes binding on government.

A second principle underlay these free institutions – the principle that the state is distinct from society and limited in its offices toward society. This principle too was inherent in the Great Tradition. Before it was cancelled out by the rise of the modern omnicompetent society-state, it had found expression in the distinction between the order of politics and the order of culture, or, in the language of the time, the distinction between *studium* and *imperium*. The whole order of ideas in general was autonomous in the face of government; it was immune from political discipline, which could only fall upon actions, not ideas. Even the medieval Inquisition respected this distinction of orders; it never recognized a crime of opinion, *crimen opinionis*; its competence extended only to the repression of organized conspiracy against public order and the common good. It was, if you will, a Committee on un-Christian Activities; it regarded activities, not ideas, as justiciable.

The American Proposition, in reviving the distinction between society and state, which had perished under the advance of absolutism, likewise renewed the principle of the incompetence of government in the field of opinion. Government submits itself to judgment by the truth of society; it is not itself a judge of the truth in society. Freedom of the means of communication whereby ideas are circulated and criticized, and the freedom of the academy (understanding by the term the range of institutions organized for the pursuit of truth and the perpetuation of the intellectual heritage of society) are immune from legal inhibition or government control. This immunity is a civil right of the first order, essential to the American concept of a free people under a limited government.

A VIRTUOUS PEOPLE

'A free people': this term too has a special sense in the American Proposition. America has passionately pursued the ideal of freedom, expressed in a whole system of political and civil rights, to new lengths; but it has not pursued this ideal so madly as to rush over the edge of the abyss, into sheer libertarianism, into the chaos created by the nineteenth-century theory of the 'outlaw conscience,' *conscientia exlex*, the conscience that knows no law higher than its own subjective imperatives. Part of the inner architecture of the American ideal of freedom has been the profound conviction that only a virtuous people can be free. It is not an American belief that free government is inevitable, only that it is possible, and that its possibility can be realized only when the people as a whole are inwardly governed by the recognized imperatives of the universal moral law.

The American experiment reposes on Acton's postulate, that freedom is the highest phase of civil society. But it also reposes on Acton's further postulate, that the elevation of a people to this highest phase of social life supposes, as its condition, that they understand the ethical nature of political freedom. They must understand, in Acton's phrase, that freedom is 'not the power of doing what we like, but the right of being able to do what we ought.' The people claim this right, in all its articulated forms, in the face of government; in the name of this right, multiple limitations are put upon the power of government. But the claim can be made with the full resonance of moral authority only to the extent that it issues from an inner sense of responsibility to a higher law. In any phase civil society demands order. In its highest phase of freedom it demands that order should not be imposed from the top down, as it were, but should spontaneously flower outward from the free obedience to the restraints and imperatives that stem from inwardly possessed moral principle. In this sense democracy is more than a political experiment; it is a spiritual and moral enterprise. And its success depends upon the virtue of the people who undertake it. Men who would be politically free must discipline themselves. Likewise institutions which would pretend to be free with a human freedom must in their workings be governed from within and made to serve the ends of virtue. Political freedom is endangered in its foundations as soon as the universal moral values, upon whose shared possession the self-discipline of a free society depends, are no longer vigorous enough to restrain the passions and shatter the selfish inertia of men. The American ideal of freedom as ordered freedom, and therefore an ethical ideal, has traditionally reckoned with these truths, these truisms.

Note

1. New York: Harcourt, Brace and Co., 1953.

16
Robert Nozick

Robert Nozick (1938–) is an American philosopher who, in Anarchy, State, and Utopia *(1974), led the reaction against received ideas of social justice, and against the egalitarian view of human society which had been defended in John Rawls's* Theory of Justice *(1971). Nozick's defence of private property and its unequal distribution owes much to Hayek; but it is a defence conducted from the liberal individualist premises of John Locke. The argument is therefore more agreeable to a conservative on account of its anti-socialist conclusions, than on account of the vision of man and society which inspires it. Nozick's defence of the 'minimal state' has, nevertheless, met with considerable approval among recent conservative writers, many of whom share his assumption that political order can be justified only if it can be shown to reinforce individual rights, and many of whom have been, like Nozick, indifferent to the fact of corporate personality, and unaware that there are rights which are not the rights of individuals (cf. Maitland, in this volume). Whatever the relation of Nozick to the conservative tradition, however, it is undeniable that his 'entitlement theory' of justice, sketched in the following extract, captures one of the central strands of conservative opposition to the socialist ideas of ownership. The extract is from* Anarchy, State, and Utopia.

. . . A distribution is just if it arises from another just distribution by legitimate means. The legitimate means of moving from one distribution to another are specified by the principle of justice in transfer. The legitimate first 'moves' are specified by the principle of justice in acquisition.* Whatever arises from a just situation by just steps is itself just. The means of change specified by the principle of justice in transfer preserve justice. As correct rules of

---

* Applications of the principle of justice in acquisition may also occur as part of the move from one distribution to another. You may find an unheld thing now and appropriate it. Acquisitions also are to be understood as included when, to simplify, I speak only of transitions by transfers.

inference are truth-preserving, and any conclusion deduced via repeated application of such rules from only true premises is itself true, so the means of transition from one situation to another specified by the principle of justice in transfer are justice-preserving, and any situation actually arising from repeated transitions in accordance with the principle from a just situation is itself just. The parallel between justice-preserving transformations and truth-preserving transformations illuminates where it fails as well as where it holds. That a conclusion could have been deduced by truth-preserving means from premises that are true suffices to show its truth. That from a just situation a situation *could* have arisen via justice-preserving means does *not* suffice to show its justice. The fact that a thief's victims voluntarily *could* have presented him with gifts does not entitle the thief to his ill-gotten gains. Justice in holdings is historical; it depends upon what actually has happened. We shall return to this point later.

Not all actual situations are generated in accordance with the two principles of justice in holdings: the principle of justice in acquisition and the principle of justice in transfer. Some people steal from others, or defraud them, or enslave them, seizing their product and preventing them from living as they choose, or forcibly exclude others from competing in exchanges. None of these are permissible modes of transition from one situation to another. And some persons acquire holdings by means not sanctioned by the principle of justice in acquisition. The existence of past injustice (previous violations of the first two principles of justice in holdings) raises the third major topic under justice in holdings: the rectification of injustice in holdings. If past injustice has shaped present holdings in various ways, some identifiable and some not, what now, if anything, ought to be done to rectify these injustices? What obligations do the performers of injustice have toward those whose position is worse than it would have been had the injustice not been done? Or, than it would have been had compensation been paid promptly? How, if at all, do things change if the beneficiaries and those made worse off are not the direct parties in the act of injustice, but, for example, their descendants? Is an injustice done to someone whose holding was itself based upon an unrectified injustice? How far back must one go in wiping clean the historical slate of injustices? What may victims of injustice permissibly do in order to rectify the injustices being done to them, including the many injustices done by persons acting through their government? I do not know of a thorough or theoretically sophisticated treatment of such issues.[1] Idealizing greatly, let us suppose theoretical investigation will produce a principle of rectification. This principle uses historical information about previous situations and injustices done in them (as defined by the first two principles of justice and rights against interference), and information about the actual course of events that flowed from these injustices, until the present, and it yields a description (or descriptions) of holdings in the society. The principle of rectification presumably will make use of its best estimate of subjunctive information about what would have occurred (or a probability distribution over what might have occurred, using the expected value) if the injustice had not taken place. If the actual description of holdings turns out not to be one of the descriptions yielded by the principle, then one of the descriptions yielded must be realized.*

The general outlines of the theory of justice in holdings are that the holdings of a person are just if he is entitled to them by the principles of justice in acquisition and transfer, or by the principle of rectification of injustice (as specified by the first two principles). If each person's holdings are just, then the total set (distribution) of holdings is just. To turn these general outlines into a specific theory we would have to specify the details of each of the three principles of justice in holdings: the principle of acquisition of holdings, the principle of transfer of holdings, and the principle of rectification of violations of the first two principles. I shall not attempt that task here. (Locke's principle of justice in acquisition is discussed below.)

HISTORICAL PRINCIPLES AND END-RESULT PRINCIPLES

The general outlines of the entitlement theory illuminate the nature and defects of other conceptions of distributive justice. The entitlement theory of justice in distribution is *historical*; whether a

---

* If the principle of rectification of violations of the first two principles yields more than one description of holdings, then some choice must be made as to which of these is to be realized. Perhaps the sort of considerations about distributive justice and equality that I argue against play a legitimate role in *this* subsidiary choice. Similarly, there may be room for such considerations in deciding which otherwise arbitrary features a statute will embody, when such features are unavoidable because other considerations do not specify a precise line; yet a line must be drawn.

distribution is just depends upon how it came about. In contrast, *current time-slice principles* of justice hold that the justice of a distribution is determined by how things are distributed (who has what) as judged by some *structural* principle(s) of just distribution. A utilitarian who judges between any two distributions by seeing which has the greater sum of utility and, if the sums tie, applies some fixed equality criterion to choose the more equal distribution, would hold a current time-slice principle of justice. As would someone who had a fixed schedule of trade-offs between the sum of happiness and equality. According to a current time-slice principle, all that needs to be looked at, in judging the justice of a distribution, is who ends up with what; in comparing any two distributions one need look only at the matrix presenting the distributions. No further information needs to be fed into a principle of justice. It is a consequence of such principles of justice that any two structurally identical distributions are equally just. (Two distributions are structurally identical if they present the same profile, but perhaps have different persons occupying the particular slots. My having ten and your having five, and my having five and your having ten are structurally identical distributions.) Welfare economics is the theory of current time-slice principles of justice. The subject is conceived as operating on matrices representing only current information about distribution. This, as well as some of the usual conditions (for example, the choice of distribution is invariant under relabeling of columns), guarantees that welfare economics will be a current time-slice theory, with all of its inadequacies.

Most persons do not accept current time-slice principles as constituting the whole story about distributive shares. They think it relevant in assessing the justice of a situation to consider not only the distribution it embodies, but also how that distribution came about. If some persons are in prison for murder or war crimes, we do not say that to assess the justice of the distribution in the society we must look only at what this person has, and that person has, and that person has, . . . at the current time. We think it relevant to ask whether someone did something so that he *deserved* to be punished, deserved to have a lower share. Most will agree to the relevance of further information with regard to punishments and penalties. Consider also desired things. One traditional socialist view is that workers are entitled to the product and full fruits of their labor; they have earned it; a distribution is unjust if it does not give the workers what they are entitled to. Such entitlements are based upon some past history. No socialist holding this view would find it comforting to be told that because the actual distribution A happens to coincide structurally with the one he desires D, A therefore is no less just than D; it differs only in that the 'parasitic' owners of capital receive under A what the workers are entitled to under D, and the workers receive under A what the owners are entitled to under D, namely very little. This socialist rightly, in my view, holds onto the notions of earning, producing, entitlement, desert, and so forth, and he rejects current time-slice principles that look only to the structure of the resulting set of holdings. (The set of holdings resulting from what? Isn't it implausible that how holdings are produced and come to exist has no effect at all on who should hold what?) His mistake lies in his view of what entitlements arise out of what sorts of productive processes.

We construe the position we discuss too narrowly by speaking of *current* time-slice principles. Nothing is changed if structural principles operate upon a time sequence of current time-slice profiles and, for example, give someone more now to counterbalance the less he has had earlier. A utilitarian or an egalitarian or any mixture of the two over time will inherit the difficulties of his more myopic comrades. He is not helped by the fact that *some* of the information others consider relevant in assessing a distribution is reflected, unrecoverably, in past matrices. Henceforth, we shall refer to such unhistorical principles of distributive justice, including the current time-slice principles, as *end-result principles* or *end-state principles*.

In contrast to end-result principles of justice, *historical principles* of justice hold that past circumstances or actions of people can create differential entitlements or differential deserts to things. An injustice can be worked by moving from one distribution to another structurally identical one, for the second, in profile the same, may violate people's entitlements or deserts; it may not fit the actual history.

PATTERNING

The entitlement principles of justice in holdings that we have sketched are historical principles of justice. To better understand their precise character, we shall distinguish them from another subclass of the historical principles. Consider, as an example, the principle of distribution according to moral merit. This principle requires that total distributive shares vary directly with moral merit; no person should have a greater share than anyone whose moral merit is greater. (If moral merit could be not merely ordered but measured on an interval or ratio scale, stronger principles could be formulated.) Or consider the principle that results by substituting 'usefulness to society' for 'moral merit' in the previous principle. Or instead of 'distribute according to moral merit,' or 'distribute according to usefulness to society,' we might consider 'distribute according to the weighted sum of moral merit, usefulness to society, and need,' with the weights of the different dimensions equal. Let us call a principle of distribution *patterned* if it specifies that a distribution is to vary along with some natural dimension, weighted sum of natural dimensions, or lexicographic ordering of natural dimensions. And let us say a distribution is patterned if it accords with some patterned principle. (I speak of natural dimensions, admittedly without a general criterion for them, because for any set of holdings some artificial dimensions can be gimmicked up to vary along with the distribution of the set.) The principle of distribution in accordance with moral merit is a patterned historical principle, which specifies a patterned distribution. 'Distribute according to I.Q.' is a patterned principle that looks to information not contained in distributional matrices. It is not historical, however, in that it does not look to any past actions creating differential entitlements to evaluate a distribution; it requires only distributional matrices whose columns are labeled by I.Q. scores. The distribution in a society, however, may be composed of such simple patterned distributions, without itself being simply patterned. Different sectors may operate different patterns, or some combination of patterns may operate in different proportions across a society. A distribution composed in this manner, from a small number of patterned distributions, we also shall term 'patterned.' And we extend the use of 'pattern' to include the overall designs put forth by combinations of end-state principles.

Almost every suggested principle of distributive justice is patterned: to each according to his moral merit, or needs, or marginal product, or how hard he tries, or the weighted sum of the foregoing, and so on. The principle of entitlement we have sketched is *not* patterned.* There is no one natural dimension or weighted sum

---

* One might try to squeeze a patterned conception of distributive justice into the framework of the entitlement conception, by formulating a gimmicky obligatory

or combination of a small number of natural dimensions that yields the distributions generated in accordance with the principle of entitlement. The set of holdings that results when some persons receive their marginal products, others win at gambling, others receive a share of their mate's income, others receive gifts from foundations, others receive interest on loans, others receive gifts from admirers, others receive returns on investment, others make for themselves much of what they have, others find things, and so on, will not be patterned. Heavy strands of patterns will run through it; significant portions of the variance in holdings will be accounted for by pattern-variables. If most people most of the time choose to transfer some of their entitlements to others only in exchange for something from them, then a large part of what many people hold will vary with what they held that others wanted. More details are provided by the theory of marginal productivity. But gifts to relatives, charitable donations, bequests to children, and the like, are not best conceived, in the first instance, in this manner. Ignoring the strands of pattern, let us suppose for the moment that a distribution actually arrived at by the operation of the principle of entitlement is random with respect to any pattern. Though the resulting set of holdings will be unpatterned, it will not be incomprehensible, for it can be seen as arising from the operation of a small number of principles. These principles specify how an initial distribution may arise (the principle of acquisition of holdings) and how distributions may be transformed into others (the principle of transfer of holdings). The process whereby the set of holdings is generated will be intelligible, though the set of holdings itself that results from this process will be unpatterned.

The writings of F. A. Hayek focus less than is usually done upon what patterning distributive justice requires. Hayek argues that we cannot know enough about each person's situation to distribute to

---

'principle of transfer' that would lead to the pattern. For example, the principle that if one has more than the mean income one must transfer everything one holds above the mean to persons below the mean so as to bring them up to (but not over) the mean. We can formulate a criterion for a 'principle of transfer' to rule out such obligatory transfers, or we can say that no correct principle of transfer, no principle of transfer in free society will be like this. The former is probably the better course, though the latter also is true.

Alternatively, one might think to make the entitlement conception instantiate a pattern, by using matrix entries that express the relative strength of a person's entitlements as measured by some real-valued function. But even if the limitation to natural dimensions failed to exclude this function, the resulting edifice would *not* capture our system of entitlements to *particular* things.

each according to his moral merit (but would justice demand we do so if we did have this knowledge?); and he goes on to say, 'our objection is against all attempts to impress upon society a deliberately chosen pattern of distribution, whether it be an order of equality or of inequality.'[2] However, Hayek concludes that in a free society there will be distribution in accordance with value rather than moral merit; that is, in accordance with the perceived value of a person's actions and services to others. Despite his rejection of a patterned conception of distributive justice, Hayek himself suggests a pattern he thinks justifiable: distribution in accordance with the perceived benefits given to others, leaving room for the complaint that a free society does not realize exactly this pattern. Stating this patterned strand of a free capitalist society more precisely, we get 'To each according to how much he benefits others who have the resources for benefiting those who benefit them.' This will seem arbitrary unless some acceptable initial set of holdings is specified, or unless it is held that the operation of the system over time washes out any significant effects from the initial set of holdings. As an example of the latter, if almost anyone would have bought a car from Henry Ford, the supposition that it was an arbitrary matter who held the money then (and so bought) would not place Henry Ford's earnings under a cloud. In any event, *his* coming to hold it is not arbitrary. Distribution according to benefits to others *is* a major patterned strand in a free capitalist society, as Hayek correctly points out, but it is only a strand and does not constitute the whole pattern of a system of entitlements (namely, inheritance, gifts for arbitrary reasons, charity, and so on) or a standard that one should insist a society fit. Will people tolerate for long a system yielding distributions that they believe are unpatterned?[3] No doubt people will not long accept a distribution they believe is *unjust*. People want their society to be and to look just. But must the look of justice reside in a resulting pattern rather than in the underlying generating principles? We are in no position to conclude that the inhabitants of a society embodying an entitlement conception of justice in holdings will find it unacceptable. Still, it must be granted that were people's reasons for transferring some of their holdings to others always irrational or arbitrary, we could find this disturbing. (Suppose people always determined what holdings they would transfer, and to whom, by using a random device.) We feel more comfortable upholding the justice of an entitlement system if most of the transfers under it are done for reasons. This does not mean necessarily that all deserve what holdings they receive. It means only that there is a purpose or point to someone's transferring a holding to one person rather than to another; that usually we can see what the transferrer thinks he's gaining, what cause he thinks he's serving, what goals he thinks he's helping to achieve, and so forth. Since in a capitalist society people often transfer holdings to others in accordance with how much they perceive these others benefiting them, the fabric constituted by the individual transactions and transfers is largely reasonable and intelligible.* (Gifts to loved ones, bequests to children, charity to the needy also are nonarbitrary components of the fabric.) In stressing the large strand of distribution in accordance with benefit to others, Hayek shows the point of many transfers, and so shows that the system of transfer of entitlements is not just spinning its gears aimlessly. The system of entitlements is defensible when constituted by the individual aims of individual transactions. No overarching aim is needed, no distributional pattern is required.

To think that the task of a theory of distributive justice is to fill in the blank in 'to each according to his ———' is to be predisposed to search for a pattern; and the separate treatment of 'from each according to his ———' treats production and distribution as two separate and independent issues. On an entitlement view these are *not* two separate questions. Whoever makes something, having bought or contracted for all other held resources used in the process (transferring some of his holdings for these cooperating factors), is entitled to it. The situation is *not* one of something's getting made, and there being an open question of who is to get it. Things come into the world already attached to people having entitlements over them. From the point of view of the historical entitlement conception of justice in holdings, those who start afresh to complete 'to each according to his ———' treat objects as

---

* We certainly benefit because great economic incentives operate to get others to spend much time and energy to figure out how to serve us by providing things we will want to pay for. It is not mere paradox mongering to wonder whether capitalism should be criticised for most rewarding and hence encouraging, not individualists like Thoreau who go about their own lives, but people who are occupied with serving others and winning them as customers. But to defend capitalism one need not think businessmen are the finest human types. (I do not mean to join here the general maligning of businessmen, either.) Those who think the finest should acquire the most can try to convince their fellows to transfer resources in accordance with *that* principle.

if they appeared from nowhere, out of nothing. A complete theory of justice might cover this limit case as well; perhaps here is a use for the usual conceptions of distributive justice.[4]

So entrenched are maxims of the usual form that perhaps we should present the entitlement conception as a competitor. Ignoring acquisition and rectification, we might say:

> From each according to what he chooses to do, to each according to what he makes for himself (perhaps with the contracted aid of others) and what others choose to do for him and choose to give him of what they've been given previously (under this maxim) and haven't yet expended or transferred.

This, the discerning reader will have noticed, has its defects as a slogan. So as a summary and great simplification (and not as a maxim with any independent meaning) we have:

> *From each as they choose, to each as they are chosen.*

HOW LIBERTY UPSETS PATTERNS

It is not clear how those holding alternative conceptions of distributive justice can reject the entitlement conception of justice in holdings. For suppose a distribution favored by one of these non-entitlement conceptions is realized. Let us suppose it is your favorite one and let us call this distribution D_1; perhaps everyone has an equal share, perhaps shares vary in accordance with some dimension you treasure. Now suppose that Wilt Chamberlain is greatly in demand by basketball teams, being a great gate attraction. (Also suppose contracts run only for a year, with players being free agents.) He signs the following sort of contract with a team: In each home game, twenty-five cents from the price of each ticket of admission goes to him. (We ignore the question of whether he is 'gouging' the owners, letting them look out for themselves.) The season starts, and people cheerfully attend his team's games; they buy their tickets, each time dropping a separate twenty-five cents of their admission price into a special box with Chamberlain's name on it. They are excited about seeing him play; it is worth the total admission price to them. Let us suppose that in one season one million persons attend his home games, and Wilt Chamberlain winds up with $250,000, a much larger sum than the average income and larger even than anyone else has. Is he entitled to this income? Is this new distribution D_2, unjust? If so, why? There is *no* question about whether each of the people was entitled to the control over the resources they held in D_1; because that was the distribution (your favorite) that (for the purposes of argument) we assumed was acceptable. Each of these persons *chose* to give twenty-five cents of their money to Chamberlain. They could have spent it on going to the movies, or on candy bars, or on copies of *Dissent* magazine, or on *Monthly Review*. But they all, at least one million of them, converged on giving it to Wilt Chamberlain in exchange for watching him play basketball. If D_1 was a just distribution, and people voluntarily moved from it to D_2, transferring parts of their shares they were given under D_1 (what was it for if not to do something with?), isn't D_2 also just? If the people were entitled to dispose of the resources to which they were entitled (under D_1), didn't this include their being entitled to give it to, or exchange it with, Wilt Chamberlain? Can anyone else complain on grounds of justice? Each other person already has his legitimate share under D_1. Under D_1, there is nothing that anyone has that anyone else has a claim of justice against. After someone transfers something to Wilt Chamberlain, third parties *still* have their legitimate shares; *their* shares are not changed. By what process could such a transfer among two persons give rise to a legitimate claim of distributive justice on a portion of what was transferred, by a third party who had no claim of justice on any holding of the others *before* the transfer?* To cut off objections irrelevant here, we might

---

* Might not a transfer have instrumental effects on a third party, changing his feasible options? (But what if the two parties to the transfer independently had used their holdings in this fashion?) I discuss this question below, but note here that this question concedes the point for distributions of ultimate intrinsic noninstrumental goods (pure utility experiences, so to speak) that are transferrable. It also might be objected that the transfer might make a third party more envious because it worsens his position relative to someone else. I find it incomprehensible how this can be thought to involve a claim of justice. . . .

Here and elsewhere in this chapter, a theory which incorporates elements of pure procedural justice might find what I say acceptable, *if* kept in its proper place; that is, if background institutions exist to ensure the satisfaction of certain conditions on distributive shares. But if these institutions are not themselves the sum or invisible-hand result of people's voluntary (nonaggressive) actions, the constraints they impose require justification. At no point does *our* argument assume any background institutions more extensive than those of the minimal night-watchman state, a state limited to protecting persons against murder, assault, theft, fraud, and so forth.

imagine the exchanges occurring in a socialist society, after hours. After playing whatever basketball he does in his daily work, or doing whatever other daily work he does, Wilt Chamberlain decides to put in *overtime* to earn additional money. (First his work quota is set; he works time over that.) Or imagine it is a skilled juggler people like to see, who puts on shows after hours.

Why might someone work overtime in a society in which it is assumed their needs are satisfied? Perhaps because they care about things other than needs. I like to write in books that I read, and to have easy access to books for browsing at odd hours. It would be very pleasant and convenient to have the resources of Widener Library in my back yard. No society, I assume, will provide such resources close to each person who would like them as part of his regular allotment (under D_1). Thus, persons either must do without some extra things that they want, or be allowed to do something extra to get some of these things. On what basis could the inequalities that would eventuate be forbidden? Notice also that small factories would spring up in a socialist society, unless forbidden. I melt down some of my personal possessions (under D_1) and build a machine out of the material. I offer you, and others, a philosophy lecture once a week in exchange for your cranking the handle on my machine, whose products I exchange for yet other things, and so on. (The raw materials used by the machine are given to me by others who possess them under D_1, in exchange for hearing lectures.) Each person might participate to gain things over and above their allotment under D_1. Some persons even might want to leave their job in socialist industry and work full time in this private sector. I shall say something more about these issues in the next chapter. Here I wish merely to note how private property even in means of production would occur in a socialist society that did not forbid people to use as they wished some of the resources they are given under the socialist distribution D_1.[5] The socialist society would have to forbid capitalist acts between consenting adults.

The general point illustrated by the Wilt Chamberlain example and the example of the entrepreneur in a socialist society is that no end-state principle or distributional patterned principle of justice can be continuously realized without continuous interference with people's lives. Any favored pattern would be transformed into one unfavored by the principle, by people choosing to act in various ways; for example, by people exchanging goods and services with other people, or giving things to other people, things the transferrers are entitled to under the favored distributional pattern. To maintain a pattern one must either continually interfere to stop people from transferring resources as they wish to, or continually (or periodically) interfere to take from some persons resources that others for some reason chose to transfer to them. (But if some time limit is to be set on how long people may keep resources others voluntarily transfer to them, why let them keep these resources for *any* period of time? Why not have immediate confiscation?) It might be objected that all persons voluntarily will choose to refrain from actions which would upset the pattern. This presupposes unrealistically (1) that all will most want to maintain the pattern (are those who don't, to be 'reeducated' or forced to undergo 'self-criticism'?), (2) that each can gather enough information about his own actions and the ongoing activities of others to discover which of his actions will upset the pattern, and (3) that diverse and far-flung persons can coordinate their actions to dovetail into the pattern. Compare the manner in which the market is neutral among persons' desires, as it reflects and transmits widely scattered information via prices, and coordinates persons' activities.

It puts things perhaps a bit too strongly to say that every patterned (or end-state) principle is liable to be thwarted by the voluntary actions of the individual parties transferring some of their shares they receive under the principle. For perhaps some *very* weak patterns are not so thwarted.* Any distributional pattern with any egalitarian component is overturnable by the voluntary actions of individual persons over time; as is every patterned

---

* Is the patterned principle stable that requires merely that a distribution be Pareto-optimal? One person might give another a gift or bequest that the second could exchange with a third to their mutual benefit. Before the second makes this exchange, there is not Pareto-optimality. Is a stable pattern presented by a principle choosing that among the Pareto-optimal positions that satisfies some further condition C? It may seem that there cannot be a counterexample, for won't any voluntary exchange made away from a situation show that the first situation wasn't Pareto-optimal? (Ignore the implausibility of this last claim for the case of bequests.) But principles are to be satisfied over time, during which new possibilities arise. A distribution that at one time satisfies the criterion of Pareto-optimality might not do so when some new possibilities arise (Wilt Chamberlain grows up and starts playing basketball); and though people's activities will tend to move then to a new Pareto-optimal position, *this* new one need not satisfy the contentful condition C. Continual interference will be needed to ensure the continual satisfaction of C. (The theoretical possibility of a pattern's being maintained by some invisible-hand process that brings it back to an equilibrium that fits the pattern when deviations occur should be investigated.)

condition with sufficient content so as actually to have been proposed as presenting the central core of distributive justice. Still, given the possibility that some weak conditions or patterns may not be unstable in this way, it would be better to formulate an explicit description of the kind of interesting and contentful patterns under discussion, and to prove a theorem about their instability. Since the weaker the patterning, the more likely it is that the entitlement system itself satisfies it, a plausible conjecture is that any patterning either is unstable or is satisfied by the entitlement system.

Notes

1. See, however, the useful book by Boris Bittket, *The Case for Black Reparations* (New York: Random House, 1973).
2. F. A. Hayek, *The Constitution of Liberty* (Chicago: University of Chicago Press, 1960), p. 87.
3. This question does not imply that they will tolerate any and every patterned distribution. In discussing Hayek's views Irving Kristol has recently speculated that people will not long tolerate a system that yields distributions patterned in accordance with value rather than merit. ('"When Virtue Loses All Her Loveliness – Some Reflections on Capitalism and The Free Society."' *The Public Interest*, Fall 1970, pp. 3–15.) Kristol, following some remarks of Hayek's, equates the merit system with justice. Since some case can be made for the external standard of distribution in accordance with benefit to others. We ask about a weaker (and therefore more plausible) hypothesis.
4. Varying situations continuously from that limit situation to our own would force us to make explicit the underlying rationale of entitlements and to consider whether entitlement considerations lexicographically precede the considerations of the usual theories of distributive justice, so that the *slightest* strand of entitlement outweighs the considerations of the usual theories of distributive justice.
5. See the selection from John Henry MacKay's novel, *The Anarchists*, reprinted in Leonard Krimmerman and Lewis Perry, eds, *Patterns of Anarchy* (New York: Doubleday Anchor Books, 1966), in which an individualist anarchist presses upon a communist anarchist the following question 'Would you, in the system of society which you call "free Communism" prevent individuals from exchanging their labor among themselves by means of their own medium of exchange? And further: Would you prevent them from occupying land for the purpose of personal use?' The novel continues: '[the] question was not to be escaped. If he answered "Yes!" he admitted that society had the right

of control over the individual and threw overboard the autonomy of the individual which he had always zealously defended; if on the other hand, he answered "No!" he admitted the right of private property which he had just denied so emphatically. . . . Then he answered, "In Anarchy any number of men must have the right of forming a voluntary association, and so realizing their ideas in practice. Nor can I understand how any one could justly be driven from the land and house which he uses and occupies . . . every serious man must declare himself: for Socialism, and thereby for force and against liberty, or for Anarchism, and thereby for liberty and against force."' In contrast, we find Noam Chomsky writing, 'Any consistent anarchist must oppose private ownership of the means of production,' 'the consistent anarchist then . . . will be a socialist . . . of a particular sort.' Introduction to Daniel Guerin, *Anarchism: From Theory to Practice* (New York: Monthly Review Press, 1970), pages xiii, xv.

17
Michael Oakeshott

Michael Joseph Oakeshott (1901–90), was an historian by training, who graduated at Cambridge in 1923, and became a fellow of Gonville and Caius College, Cambridge two years later. In 1951 he was appointed to the University Chair in political science at the LSE, from which he retired in 1968. From the point of view of conservative thinking, his most important works are Rationalism in Politics and other essays *(1962), from which one of the extracts below is taken,* On Human Conduct *(1975), and* On History and other essays *(1983).*

Oakeshott's central concern was to defend a vision of 'civil association', as he called it, in which the conservative respect for custom, prejudice and tradition is reconciled with liberal values, and with an idea of the state as standing aloof from the affairs of society. His attack on rationalism and ideology strikes at the heart of socialist politics, which he criticizes for its attempt to find a single goal behind which the whole of political life can be conscripted. By contrast to socialism, Oakeshott presents a picture of politics as a 'conversation', in which no voice prevails, and whose purpose is to engage the participants, but not to reach a goal. As with Aristotle, it is friendship, rather than contract, which is the root of political order: an idea which Oakeshott sets within the context of a subtle, if elusive, theory of human nature.

From 'On Being Conservative'

To be conservative is to be disposed to think and behave in certain manners; it is to prefer certain kinds of conduct and certain conditions of human circumstances to others; it is to be disposed to make certain kinds of choices. And my design here is to construe this disposition as it appears in contemporary character, rather than to transpose it into the idiom of general principles.

The general characteristics of this disposition are not difficult to discern, although they have often been mistaken. They centre upon a propensity to use and to enjoy what is available rather than to wish for or to look for something else; to delight in what is present rather than what was or what may be. Reflection may bring to light an appropriate gratefulness for what is available, and consequently the acknowledgment of a gift or an inheritance from the past; but there is no mere idolizing of what is past and gone. What is esteemed is the present; and it is esteemed not on account of its connections with a remote antiquity, nor because it is recognized to be more admirable than any possible alternative, but on account of its familiarity: not, *Verweile doch, du bist so schön* ['Stay awhile, you are so beautiful': Goethe, *Faust*, II, V], but, *Stay with me because I am attached to you*. . . .

To be conservative, then, is to prefer the familiar to the unknown, to prefer the tried to the untried, fact to mystery, the actual to the possible, the limited to the unbounded, the near to the distant, the sufficient to the superabundant, the convenient to the perfect, present laughter to utopian bliss. Familiar relationships and loyalties will be preferred to the allure of more profitable attachments; to acquire and to enlarge will be less important than to keep, to cultivate and to enjoy; the grief of loss will be more acute than the excitement of novelty or promise. It is to be equal to one's own fortune, to live at the level of one's own means, to be content with the want of greater perfection which belongs alike to oneself and one's circumstances. With some people this is itself a choice; in others it is a disposition which appears, frequently or less frequently, in their preferences and aversions, and is not itself chosen or specifically cultivated. . . .

Changes are without effect only upon those who notice nothing, who are ignorant of what they possess and apathetic to their circumstances; and they can be welcomed indiscriminately only by those who esteem nothing, whose attachments are fleeting and who are strangers to love and affection. The conservative disposition provokes neither of these conditions: the inclination to enjoy what is present and available is the opposite of ignorance and apathy and it breeds attachment and affection. Consequently, it is averse from change, which appears always, in the first place, as deprivation. A storm which sweeps away a copse and transforms a favourite view, the death of friends, the sleep of friendship, the desuetude of customs of behaviour, the retirement of a favourite clown, involuntary exile, reversals of fortune, the loss of abilities enjoyed and their replacement by others – these are changes, none perhaps without its compensations, which the man of conservative temperament unavoidably regrets. But he has difficulty in reconciling himself to them, not because what he has lost in them was intrinsically better than any alternative might have been or was incapable of improvement, nor because what takes its place is inherently incapable of being enjoyed, but because what he has lost was something he actually enjoyed and had learned how to enjoy and what takes its place is something to which he has acquired no attachment. Consequently, he will find small and slow changes more tolerable than large and sudden; and he will value highly every appearance of continuity. Some changes, indeed, will present no difficulty; but, again, this is not because they are manifest improvements but merely because they are easily assimilated: the changes of the seasons are mediated by their recurrence and the growing up of children by its continuousness. And, in general, he will accommodate himself more readily to changes which do not offend expectation than to the destruction of what seems to have no ground of dissolution within itself.

Moreover, to be conservative is not merely to be averse from change (which may be an idiosyncrasy); it is also a manner of accommodating ourselves to changes, an activity imposed upon all men. For, change is a threat to identity, and every change is an emblem of extinction. But a man's identity (or that of a community) is nothing more than an unbroken rehearsal of contingencies, each at the mercy of circumstance and each significant in proportion to its familiarity. It is not a fortress into which we may retire, and the only means we have of defending it (that is, ourselves) against the hostile forces of change is in the open field of our experience; by throwing our weight upon the foot which for the time being is most firmly placed, by cleaving to whatever familiarities are not immediately threatened and thus assimilating what is new without becoming unrecognizable to ourselves. The Masai, when they were moved from their old country to the present Masai reserve in Kenya, took with them the names of their hills and plains and rivers and gave them to the hills and plains and rivers of the new country. And it is by some such subterfuge of conservatism that every man or people compelled to suffer a notable change avoids the shame of extinction.

Changes, then, have to be suffered; and a man of conservative temperament (that is, one strongly disposed to preserve his identity) cannot be indifferent to them. In the main, he judges them by the disturbance they entail and, like everyone else, deploys his resources to meet them. The idea of innovation, on the other hand, is improvement. Nevertheless, a man of this temperament will not himself be an ardent innovator. In the first place, he is not inclined to think that nothing is happening unless great changes are afoot and therefore he is not worried by the absence of innovation: the use and enjoyment of things as they are occupies most of his attention. Further, he is aware that not all innovation is, in fact, improvement; and he will think that to innovate without improving is either designed or inadvertent folly. Moreover, even when an innovation commends itself as a convincing improvement, he will look twice at its claims before accepting them. From his point of view, because every improvement involves change, the disruption entailed has always to be set against the benefit anticipated. But when he has satisfied himself about this, there will be other considerations to be taken into the account. Innovating is always an equivocal enterprise, in which gain and loss (even excluding the loss of familiarity) are so closely interwoven that it is exceedingly difficult to forecast the final upshot: there is no such thing as an unqualified improvement. For, innovating is an activity which generates not only the 'improvement' sought, but a new and complex situation of which this is only one of the components. The total change is always more extensive than the change designed; and the whole of what is entailed can neither be foreseen nor circumscribed. Thus, whenever there is innovation there is the certainty that the change will be greater than was intended, that there will be loss as well as gain and that the loss and the gain will not be equally distributed among the people affected; there is the chance that the benefits derived will be greater than those which were designed; and there is the risk that they will be off-set by changes for the worse.

From all this the man of conservative temperament draws some appropriate conclusions. First, innovation entails certain loss and possible gain, therefore, the onus of proof, to show that the proposed change may be expected to be on the whole beneficial, rests with the would-be innovator. Secondly, he believes that the more closely an innovation resembles growth (that is, the more clearly it is intimated in and not merely imposed upon the situation) the less likely it is to result in a preponderance of loss. Thirdly, he thinks that an innovation which is a response to some specific defect, one designed to redress some specific disequilibrium, is more desirable than one which springs from a notion of a generally improved condition of human circumstances, and is far more desirable than one generated by a vision of perfection. Consequently, he prefers small and limited innovations to large and indefinite. Fourthly, he favours a slow rather than a rapid pace, and pauses to observe current consequences and make appropriate adjustments. And lastly, he believes the occasion to be important; and, other things being equal, he considers the most favourable occasion for innovation to be when the projected change is most likely to be limited to what is intended and least likely to be corrupted by undesired and unmanageable consequences.

The disposition to be conservative is, then, warm and positive in respect of enjoyment, and correspondingly cool and critical in respect of change and innovation: these two inclinations support and elucidate one another. The man of conservative temperament believes that a known good is not lightly to be surrendered for an unknown better. He is not in love with what is dangerous and difficult; he is unadventurous; he has no impulse to sail uncharted seas; for him there is no magic in being lost, bewildered or shipwrecked. If he is forced to navigate the unknown, he sees virtue in heaving the lead every inch of the way. What others plausibly identify as timidity, he recognizes in himself as rational prudence; what others interpret as inactivity, he recognizes as a disposition to enjoy rather than to exploit. He is cautious, and he is disposed to indicate his assent or dissent, not in absolute, but in graduated terms. He eyes the situation in terms of its propensity to disrupt the familiarity of the features of his world. . . .

How, then, are we to construe the disposition to be conservative in respect of politics? And in making this inquiry what I am interested in is not merely the intelligibility of this disposition in any set of circumstances, but its intelligibility in our own contemporary circumstances. . . .

Let us begin at what I believe to be the proper starting-place; not in the empyrean, but with ourselves as we have come to be. I and my neighbours, my associates, my compatriots, my friends, my enemies and those who I am indifferent about, are people engaged in a great variety of activities. We are apt to entertain a multiplicity of opinions on every conceivable subject and are disposed to change these beliefs as we grow tired of them or as they prove unserviceable. Each of us is pursuing a course of his own; and there is no project so unlikely that somebody will not be found to engage in it, no enterprise so foolish that somebody will not undertake it. There are those who spend their lives trying to sell copies of the Anglican Catechism to the Jews. And one half of the world is engaged in trying to make the other half want what it has hitherto never felt the lack of. We are all inclined to be passionate about our own concerns, whether it is making things or selling them, whether it is business or sport, religion or learning, poetry, drink or drugs. Each of us has preferences of his own. For some, the opportunities of making choices (which are numerous) are invitations readily accepted; others welcome them less eagerly or even find them burdensome. Some dream dreams of new and better worlds: others are more inclined to move in familiar paths or even to be idle. Some are apt to deplore the rapidity of change, others delight in it; all recognize it. At times we grow tired and fall asleep: it is a blessed relief to gaze in a shop window and see nothing we want; we are grateful for ugliness merely because it repels attention. But, for the most part, we pursue happiness by seeking the satisfaction of desires which spring from one another inexhaustably. We enter into relationships of interest and of emotion, of competition, partnership, guardianship, love, friendship, jealousy and hatred, some of which are more durable than others. We make agreements with one another; we have expectations about one another's conduct; we approve, we are indifferent and we disapprove. This multiplicity of activity and variety of opinion is apt to produce collisions: we pursue courses which cut across those of others, and we do not all approve the same sort of conduct. But, in the main, we get along with one another, sometimes by giving way, sometimes by standing fast, sometimes in a compromise. Our conduct consists of activity assimilated to that of others in small, and for the most part unconsidered and unobtrusive, adjustments.

Why all this should be so, does not matter. It is not necessarily so. A different condition of human circumstance can easily be imagined, and we know that elsewhere and at other times activity is, or has been, far less multifarious and changeful and opinion far less diverse and far less likely to provoke collision; but, by and large, we recognize this to be our condition. It is an acquired condition, though nobody designed or specifically chose it in preference to all others. It is the product, not of 'human nature' let loose, but of human beings impelled by an acquired love of making choices for themselves. And we know as little and as much about where it is leading us as we know about the fashion in hats of twenty years' time or the design of motor-cars.

Surveying the scene, some people are provoked by the absence of order and coherence which appears to them to be its dominant feature; its wastefulness, its frustration, its dissipation of human energy, its lack not merely of a premeditated destination but even of any discernible direction of movement. It provides an excitement similar to that of a stock-car race; but it has none of the satisfaction of a well-conducted business enterprise. Such people are apt to exaggerate the current disorder; the absence of plan is so conspicuous that the small adjustments, and even the more massive arrangements, which restrain the chaos seem to them nugatory; they have no feeling for the warmth of untidiness but only for its inconvenience. But what is significant is not the limitations of their powers of observation, but the turn of their thoughts. They feel that there ought to be something that ought to be done to convert this so-called chaos into order, for this is no way for rational human beings to be spending their lives. Like Apollo when he saw Daphne with her hair hung carelessly about her neck, they sigh and say to themselves: 'What if it were properly arranged.' Moreover, they tell us that they have seen in a dream the glorious, collisionless manner of living proper to all mankind, and this dream they understand as their warrant for seeking to remove the diversities and occasions of conflict which distinguish our current manner of living. Of course, their dreams are not all exactly alike; but they have this in common: each is a vision of a condition of human circumstance from which the occasion of conflict has been removed, a vision of human activity co-ordinated and set going in a single direction and of every resource being used to the full. And such people appropriately understand the office of government to be the imposition upon its subjects of the condition of human circumstances of their dream. To govern is to turn a private dream into a public and compulsory manner of living. Thus, politics becomes an encounter of dreams and the activity in which government is held to this understanding of its office and provided with the appropriate instruments. . . .

. . . I do not propose to criticize this jump to glory style of politics in which governing is understood as a perpetual take-over bid for the purchase of the resources of human energy in order to concentrate them in a single direction; it is not at all unintelligible, and there is much in our circumstances to provoke it. My purpose is merely to point out that there is another quite different understanding of government, and that it is no less intelligible and in some respects perhaps more appropriate to our circumstances.

The spring of this other disposition in respect of governing and the instruments of government – a conservative disposition – is to be found in the acceptance of the current condition of human circumstances as I have described it: the propensity to make our own choices and to find happiness in doing so, the variety of enterprises each pursued with passion, the diversity of beliefs each held with the conviction of its exclusive truth; the inventiveness, the changefulness and the absence of any large design; the excess, the over-activity and the informal compromise. And the office of government is not to impose other beliefs and activities upon its subjects, not to tutor or to educate them, not to make them better or happier in another way, not to direct them, to galvanize them into action, to lead them or to coordinate their activities so that no occasion of conflict shall occur; the office of government is merely to rule. This is a specific and limited activity, easily corrupted when it is combined with any other, and, in the circumstances, indispensable. The image of the ruler is the umpire whose business is to administer the rules of the game, or the chairman who governs the debate according to known rules but does not himself participate in it.

Now people of this disposition commonly defend their belief that the proper attitude of government towards the current condition of human circumstance is one of acceptance by appealing to certain general ideas. They contend that there is absolute value in the free play of human choice, that private property (the emblem of choice) is a natural right, that it is only in the enjoyment of diversity of opinion and activity that true belief and good conduct can be expected to disclose themselves. But I do not think that this disposition requires these or any similar beliefs in order to make it intelligible. Something much smaller and less pretentious will do: the observation that this condition of human circumstance is, in fact, current, and that we have learned to enjoy it and how to manage it; that we are not children *in statu pupillari* but adults who do not consider themselves under any obligation to justify their preference for making their own choices; and that it is beyond human experience to suppose that those who rule are endowed with a superior wisdom which discloses to them a better range of beliefs and activities and which gives them authority to impose upon their subjects a quite different manner of life. In short, if the man of this disposition is asked: Why ought governments to accept the current diversity of opinion and activity in preference to imposing upon their subjects a dream of their own? it is enough for him to reply: Why not? Their dreams are no different from those of anyone else; and if it is boring to have to listen to dreams of others being recounted, it is insufferable to be forced to re-enact them. We tolerate monomaniacs, it is our habit to do so; but why should we be *ruled* by them? Is it not (the man of conservative disposition asks) an intelligible task for a government to protect its subjects against the nuisance of those who spend their energy and their wealth in the service of some pet indignation, endeavouring to impose it upon everybody, not by suppressing their activities in favour of others of a similar kind, but by setting a limit to the amount of noise anyone may emit?

Nevertheless, if this acceptance is the spring of the conservative's disposition in respect of government, he does not suppose that the office of government is to do nothing. As he understands it, there is work to be done which can be done only in virtue of a genuine acceptance of current beliefs simply because they are current and current activities simply because they are afoot. And, briefly, the office he attributes to government is to resolve some of the collisions which this variety of beliefs and activities generates; to preserve peace, not by placing an interdict upon choice and upon the diversity that springs from the exercise of preference, not by imposing substantive uniformity, but by enforcing general rules of procedure upon all subjects alike. . . .

To some people, 'government' appears as a vast reservoir of power which inspires them to dream of what use might be made of it. They have favourite projects, of various dimensions, which they sincerely believe are for the benefit of mankind, and to capture this source of power, if necessary to increase it, and to use it for imposing their favourite projects upon their fellows is what they understand as the adventure of governing men. They are, thus, disposed to recognize government as an instrument of passion; the art of politics is to inflame and direct desire. In short, governing is understood to be just like any other activity – making and selling a brand of soap, exploiting the resources of a locality, or developing a housing estate – only the power here is (for the most part) already mobilized, and the enterprise is remarkable only because it aims at monopoly and because of its promise of success once the source of power has been captured. Of course a private enterprise politician of this sort would get nowhere in these days unless there were people with wants so vague that they can be prompted to ask for what he has to offer, or with wants so servile that they prefer the promise of a provided abundance to the opportunity of choice and activity on their own account. And it is not all as plain sailing as it might appear: often a politician of this sort misjudges the situation; and then, briefly, even in democratic politics, we become aware of what the camel thinks of the camel driver. . . .

It is not, then, mere stupid prejudice which disposes a conservative to take this view of the activity of governing; nor are any highfalutin metaphysical beliefs necessary to provoke it or make it intelligible. It is connected merely with the observation that where activity is bent upon enterprise the indispensable counterpart is another order of activity, bent upon restraint, which is unavoidably corrupted (indeed, altogether abrogated) when the power assigned to it is used for advancing favourite projects. An 'umpire' who at the same time is one of the players is no umpire; 'rules' about which we are not disposed to be conservative are not rules but incitements to disorder; the conjunction of dreaming and ruling generates tyranny.

Political conservatism is, then, not at all unintelligible in a people disposed to be adventurous and enterprising, a people in love with change and apt to rationalize their affections in terms of 'progress'. And one does not need to think that the belief in 'progress' is the most cruel and unprofitable of all beliefs, arousing cupidity without satisfying it, in order to think it inappropriate for a government to be conspicuously 'progressive'. Indeed, a disposition to be conservative in respect of government would seen to be pre-eminently appropriate to men who have something to do and something to think about on their own account, who have a skill to practise or an intellectual fortune to make, to people whose passions do not need to be inflamed, whose desires do not need to be provoked and whose dreams of a better world need no prompting. Such people know the value of a rule which imposes orderliness without directing enterprise, a rule which concentrates duty so that room is left for delight. They might even be prepared to suffer a legally established ecclesiastical order; but it would not be because they believed it to represent some unassailable religious truth, but merely because it restrained the indecent competition of sects and (as Hume said) moderated 'the plague of a too diligent clergy'.

Now, whether or not these beliefs recommend themselves as reasonable and appropriate to our circumstances and to the abilities we are likely to find in those who rule us, they and their like are in my view what make intelligible a conservative disposition in respect of politics. What would be the appropriateness of this disposition in circumstances other than our own, whether to be conservative in respect of government would have the same relevance in the circumstances of an unadventurous, a slothful or a spiritless people, is a question we need not try to answer: we are concerned with ourselves as we are. I myself think that it would occupy an important place in any set of circumstances. But what I hope I have made clear is that it is not at all inconsistent to be conservative in respect of government and radical in respect of almost every other activity. And, in my opinion, there is more to be learnt about this disposition from Montaigne, Pascal, Hobbes and Hume than from Burke or Bentham.

Of the many entailments of this view of things that might be pointed to, I will notice one, namely, that politics is an activity unsuited to the young, not on account of their vices but on account of what I at least consider to be their virtues.

Nobody pretends that it is easy to acquire or to sustain the mood of indifference which this manner of politics calls for. To rein-in one's own beliefs and desires, to acknowledge the current shape of things, to feel the balance of things in one's hand, to tolerate what is abominable, to distinguish between crime and sin, to respect formality even when it appears to be leading to error, these are difficult achievements; and they are achievements not to be looked for in the young.

Everybody's young days are a dream, a delightful insanity, a sweet solipsism. Nothing in them has a fixed shape, nothing a fixed price; everything is a possibility, and we live happily on credit. There are no obligations to be observed; there are no accounts to be kept. Nothing is specified in advance; everything is what can be made of it. The world is a mirror in which we seek the reflection of our own desires. The allure of violent emotions is irresistible. When we are young we are not disposed to make concessions to the world; we never feel the balance of a thing in our hands – unless it be a cricket bat. We are not apt to distinguish between our liking and our esteem; urgency is our criterion of importance; and we do not easily understand that what is humdrum need not be despicable. We are impatient of restraint; and we readily believe, like Shelley, that to have contracted a habit is to have failed. These, in my opinion, are among our virtues when we are young; but how remote they are from the disposition appropriate for participating in the style of government I have been describing. Since life is a dream, we argue (with plausible but erroneous logic) that politics must be an encounter of dreams, in which we hope to impose our own. Some unfortunate people, like Pitt (laughably called 'the Younger'), are born old, and are eligible to engage in politics almost in their cradles; others, perhaps more fortunate, belie the saying that one is young only once, they never grow up. But these are exceptions. For most there is what Conrad called the 'shadow line' which, when we pass it, discloses a solid world of things each with its fixed shape, each with its own point of balance, each with its price; a world of fact, not poetic image, in which what we have spent on one thing we cannot spend on another; a world inhabited by others besides ourselves who cannot be reduced to mere reflections of our own emotions. And coming to be at home in this commonplace world qualifies us (as no knowledge of 'political science' can ever qualify us), if we are so inclined and have nothing better to think about, to engage in what the man of conservative disposition understands to be political activity.

From 'Rationalism in Politics'

. . . By one road or another, by conviction, by its supposed inevitability, by its alleged success, or even quite unreflectively, almost all politics today have become Rationalist or near-Rationalist.

The general character and disposition of the Rationalist are, I think, not difficult to identify. At bottom he stands (he always *stands*) for independence of mind on all occasions, for thought free from obligation to any authority save the authority of 'reason'. His circumstances in the modern world have made him contentious: he is the *enemy* of authority, or prejudice, of the merely traditional, customary or habitual. His mental attitude is at once sceptical and optimistic: sceptical, because there is no opinion, no habit, no belief, nothing so firmly rooted or so widely held that he hesitates to question it and to judge it by what he calls his 'reason'; optimistic, because the Rationalist never doubts the power of his 'reason' (when properly applied) to determine the worth of a thing, the truth of an opinion or the propriety of an action. Moreover, he is fortified by a belief in a 'reason' common to all mankind, a common power of rational consideration, which is the ground inspiration of argument: set up on his door is the precept of Parmenides – judge by rational argument. But besides this, which gives the Rationalist a touch of intellectual equalitarianism, he is something also of an individualist, finding it difficult to believe that anyone who can think honestly and clearly will think differently from himself. . . .

Now, of all worlds, the world of politics might seem the least amenable to rationalist treatment – politics, always so deeply veined with both the traditional, the circumstantial and the transitory. And, indeed, some convinced Rationalists have admitted defeat here: Clemenceau, intellectually a child of the modern Rationalist tradition (in his treatment of morals and religion, for example), was anything but a Rationalist in politics. But not all have admitted defeat. If we except religion, the greatest apparent victories of Rationalism have been in politics: it is not to be expected that whoever is prepared to carry his rationalism into the conduct of life will hesitate to carry it into the conduct of public affairs. . . .

The conduct of affairs, for the Rationalist, is a matter of solving problems, and in this no man can hope to be successful whose reason has become inflexible by surrender to habit or is clouded by the fumes of tradition. In this activity the character which the Rationalist claims for himself is the character of the engineer, whose mind (it is supposed) is controlled throughout by the appropriate technique and whose first step is to dismiss from his attention everything not directly related to his specific intentions. This assimilation of politics to engineering is, indeed, what may be called the myth of rationalist politics. And it is, of course, a recurring theme in the literature of Rationalism. The politics it inspires may be called the politics of the felt need; for the Rationalist, politics are always charged with the feeling of the moment. He waits upon circumstance to provide him with his problems, but rejects its aid in their solution. That anything should be allowed to stand between a society and the satisfaction of the felt needs of each moment in its history must appear to the Rationalist a piece of mysticism and nonsense. And his politics are, in fact, the rational solution of those practical conundrums which the recognition of the sovereignty of the felt need perpetually creates in the life of a society. Thus, political life is resolved into a succession of crises, each to be surmounted by the application of 'reason'. Each generation, indeed, each administration, should see unrolled before it the blank sheet of infinite possibility. And if by chance this *tabula rasa* has been defaced by the irrational scribblings of tradition-ridden ancestors, then the first task of the Rationalist must be to scrub it clean; as Voltaire remarked, the only way to have good laws is to burn all existing laws and to start afresh.[1]

Two other general characteristics of rationalist politics may be observed. They are the politics of perfection, and they are the politics of uniformity; either of these characteristics without the other denotes a different style of politics, the essence of rationalism is their combination. The evanescence of imperfection may be said to be the first item of the creed of the Rationalist. He is not devoid of humility; he can imagine a problem which would remain impervious to the onslaught of his own reason. But what he cannot imagine is politics which do not consist in solving problems, or a political problem of which there is no 'rational' solution at all. Such a problem must be counterfeit. And the 'rational' solution of any problem is, in its nature, the perfect solution. There is no place in his scheme for a 'best in the circumstances', only a place for 'the best'; because the function of reason is precisely to surmount circumstances. Of course, the Rationalist is not always a perfectionist in general, his mind governed in each occasion by a comprehensive Utopia; but invariably he is a perfectionist in detail. And from this politics of perfection springs the politics of uniformity; a scheme which does not recognize circumstance can have no place for variety. 'There must in the nature of things be one best form of government which all intellects, sufficiently roused from the slumber of savage ignorance, will be irresistibly incited to approve,' writes Godwin. This intrepid Rationalist states in general what a more modest believer might prefer to assert only in detail; but the principle holds – there may not be one universal remedy for all political ills, but the remedy for any particular ill is as universal in its application as it is rational in its conception. If the rational solution for one of the problems of a society has been determined, to permit any relevant part of the society to escape from the solution is, *ex hypothesi*, to countenance irrationality. There can be no place for preference that is not rational preference, and all rational preferences necessarily coincide. Political activity is recognized as the imposition of a uniform condition of perfection upon human conduct. . . .

Note

1. Cf. Plato, *Republic*, 501A. The idea that you can get rid of a law by burning it is characteristic of the Rationalist, who can think of a law only as something written down.

18
Vilfredo Pareto

Vilfredo, Marchese Pareto (1848–1923), an Italian philosopher and economist, was also one of the founders of modern sociology, and a vigorous political pamphleteer, who argued in the cause of free trade on the one hand, and authoritarian politics on the other, and against socialism as enemy of the first, and liberalism as enemy of the second. Pareto prided himself on being a hard-headed realist, whose social and political principles reflected an ideal of rational and calculating conduct – an ideal which led him to an admiration for Machiavelli. Recognising that most people do not conform to his paradigms of rationality, he put forward ambitious (and often satirical) sociological theories of irrational conduct.

Pareto's arguments against socialism, presented in Les Systèmes Socialistes *(1902), from which the following extract is taken, contain his well-known theory of elites as inevitable and necessary components of social order, and of socialism as the ideology of a new elite, striving to seize power behind the mask of egalitarian principles. The extract conveys some of the flavour of this influential and impetuous work.*

It is, as a general rule, necessary always to distinguish between the concrete *objective* phenomenon and the form in which our mind perceives it: a form constituting another phenomenon which we may call *subjective*. To cite an everyday example: a straight stick immersed in water is the objective phenomenon. As we see it, this stick seems to be bent; and we would in fact say it was bent if we did not know it to be otherwise. This represents the subjective phenomenon.

Livy is taking for bent a stick which in reality is straight when he relates an anecdote to explain certain facts signalising the rise of plebeian families to power in Rome. A trifling event occurred, he says, which, as is often the case, had far-reaching consequences. One daughter of M. Fabius Ambustus married a patrician; his other daughter married a plebeian. The animosity between the two sisters was such that in the end it led to the plebeians' being granted privileges hitherto denied them. But modern historians have straightened this particular bent stick. Niebuhr was one of the first to understand clearly the upwards movement of the plebeian nobility, the new elite, in Rome. He was guided mainly by the analogy of the struggles in our own societies between the bourgeoisie and the mass of the people. This is a realistic analogy for it relates to particular cases of a single and consistent general phenomenon.

The notion that great historical occurrences are attributable to small personal causes is now almost wholly discarded, but it is frequently replaced by another error, that of denying the individual any influence at all on circumstances. Unquestionably, the battle of Austerlitz could have been won by some general other than Napoleon if this other had been a great battle commander. But if the French had been led by an incompetent general, they would have lost the battle well and truly. The way to avoid one error is not to embrace the opposite error. Because straight sticks on occasion appear bent, it must not be assumed that bent sticks do not in fact exist. The subjective phenomenon partly coincides with the objective phenomenon and partly differs from it. Our ignorance of the facts, our passions and prejudices, the ideas in vogue in the societies in which we live, the events which powerfully affect us – all these with a thousand other circumstances conceal the truth from us and prevent us from getting an exact impression of the objective phenomenon giving rise to them. We are like a man who sees objects in a curved mirror; their outlines and proportions are to some degree altered. We must realise that most often we are aware only of this subjective phenomenon – i.e., the objective phenomenon is distorted form – knowing it either directly through investigation or the state of mind of the men witnessing a given event, or indirectly through the testimony of a historian who has conducted such an investigation. The problem which historical criticism has to resolve is therefore quite other than that involved in textual criticism. It amounts first and foremost to reconstituting the object itself, the image of which has been distorted.

This is a difficult and delicate operation, and is made even more formidable by a particular circumstance: very frequently, individuals and groups are unaware of the forces prompting their behaviour. They ascribe to their actions imaginary causes which differ considerably from the real causes. It is mistaken to believe that those who thus deceive others are always acting in bad faith. Most often such people start off with self-deception, believing with all the sincerity in the world in the existence of these imaginary causes which they claim to be determining their actions. The testimony of men who have witnessed, and even of those who have taken part in, a particular social movement, is not to be accepted without reservation when considering this movement's real cause. Unwittingly they may be induced to disregard the real causes and to assign imaginary causes to it.

. . . The circulatory movement which carries to the summit elites born in the lower strata, and leads to the decline and disappearance of the elites in power, is very often concealed by several factors. As it is in general a fairly slow movement, it is only by studying history over a long period of time – for several centuries, for example – that one can perceive the general direction and the main lines of this movement. The contemporary observer who brings his gaze to bear only on a short period of time perceives only the secondary circumstances. He sees the rivalry of castes, the oppression of tyrants, popular uprisings, liberal protests, aristocracies, theocracies and ochlocracies [i.e. mob-rule]; but the general phenomenon, of which these are but particular aspects, often wholly escapes him. Amongst the illusions thus produced are some which, because very common, deserve to be singled out for attention.

It is very difficult to avoid the influence of sentiment in dealing with a concrete example; to prevent our discussion from being clouded by this influence, let us deal with the matter in an abstract way. Let A be the elite in power, B the social element seeking to drive it from power and to replace it, and C the rest of the population, comprising the incompetent, those lacking energy, character and intelligence: in short, that section of society which remains when the elites are subtracted. A and B are the leaders, counting on C to provide them with partisans, with instruments. The C on their own would be impotent: an army without commanders. They become important only if guided by the A or B. Very often – in fact almost always – it is the B who put themselves at the head of the C, the A reposing in a false security or despising the C. Moreover, it is the B who are best able to lure the C for the simple reason that, not having power, their inducements are long-dated. It sometimes happens, however, that the A endeavour to get the better of the B, seeking to content the C with apparent concessions without going too far in the direction of real concessions. If the B gradually take the place of the A by slow infiltration, if the movement of social circulation is not interrupted, the C become deprived of the leaders capable of spurring them to revolt, and there ensues a period of prosperity. The A usually strive to resist this infiltration, but their resistance may be ineffective and amount in the end only to an inconsequent resentment. But if the resistance of the A is effective, the B can wrest the position from them only by open conflict, with the help of the C. If they succeed and get into power, a new challenging elite, D, will be formed and will play the same role vis-à-vis the B as the B played vis-à-vis the A, and so on.

Most historians do not perceive this movement. They describe the phenomenon as if it were the struggle of an aristocracy or an oligarchy, always the same, against a people, likewise always the same. But in fact:

1. What is involved is the struggle between one aristocracy and another;
2. The aristocracy in power changes constantly, that of today being replaced, after a certain lapse of time, by its adversary.

When the B attain power, replacing the A elite in full decadence, it is generally observed that a period of great prosperity follows. Certain historians ascribe all the merit of this to the 'people', that is, to the C. Such truth as there is in this observation subsists only in the fact that the lower classes produce new elites. So far as these lower classes themselves are concerned, they are incapable of ruling; ochlocracy has never resulted in anything save disaster.

But more significant than the illusion of those who see things from afar is that of those who are involved in the movement and take an active part in it. Many of the B genuinely believe that they are pursuing, not a personal advantage for themselves and their class, but an advantage for the C, and that they are simply struggling for what they call justice, liberty, humanity. This illusion operates also on the A; many among them betray the interests of their class, believing they are fighting for the realisation of these fine principles all to help the unfortunate C, whereas in reality the sole effect of their action is to help the B to attain power only to fasten on the C a yoke which may often be more severe than that of the A. Those who finally understand that this is the outcome sometimes make accusations of hypocrisy against the B or the A – as the case may be – who claimed they were guided solely by the desire of helping the C. But on the whole, this accusation of hypocrisy is ill-founded, for many of the B as well as the A are irreproachable in point of sincerity.

A sign which almost invariably presages the decadence of an aristocracy is the intrusion of humanitarian feelings and of affected sentimentalising which render the aristocracy incapable of defending its position. Violence, we should note, is not to be confused with force. Often enough one observes cases in which individuals and classes which have lost the force to maintain themselves in power make themselves more and more hated because of their outbursts of random violence. The strong man strikes only when it is absolutely necessary, and then nothing stops him. Trajan was strong, not violent: Caligula was violent, not strong.

When a living creature loses the sentiments which, in given circumstances, are necessary to it in order to maintain the struggle for life, this is a sign certain of degeneration, for the absence of these sentiments will, sooner or later, entail the extinction of the species. The living creature which shrinks from giving blow for blow and from shedding its adversary's blood thereby puts itself at the mercy of this adversary. The sheep has always found a wolf to devour it; if it now escapes this peril, it is only because man reserves it for his own prey. Any people which has horror of blood to the point of not knowing how to defend itself will sooner or later become the prey of some bellicose people or other. There is not perhaps on this globe a single foot of ground which has not been conquered by the sword at some time or other, and where the people occupying it have not maintained themselves on it by force. If the Negroes were stronger than the Europeans, Europe would be partitioned by the Negroes and not Africa by the Europeans. The 'right', claimed by people who bestow on themselves the title of 'civilised' to conquer other peoples, whom it pleases them to call 'uncivilised', is altogether ridiculous, or rather, this right is nothing other than force. For as long as the Europeans are stronger than the Chinese, they will impose their will on them; but if the Chinese should become stronger than the Europeans, then the roles would be reversed, and it is highly probable that humanitarian sentiments could never be opposed with any effectiveness to an army.

In the same way, for right or law to have reality in a society, force is necessary. Whether developed spontaneously or whether the work of a minority, law and order cannot be imposed on dissidents save by force. The utility of certain institutions, the sentiments they inspire, prepare the ground for their establishment, but for them to become established fact it is quite obvious that those desiring these institutions must have the power to impose them on those who do not desire them. Anton Menger fancies he proves that our present law needs to be changed because it 'rests almost exclusively on traditional relationships based on force'; but such is the characteristic of all laws that have ever existed, and if the law desired by Menger ever becomes reality, this will only be because he, in his turn, will have at his disposal the force to make it so; if he hasn't, then it will always remain a dream. 'Right' and 'law' originated in the force of isolated individuals; they are now maintained by the force of the community; but it is still force.

In considering successful changes of institutions, persuasion should not, as is so often the case, be contrasted with force. Persuasion is but a means for procuring force. No one has ever persuaded all the members of a society without exception; to ensure success only a section of the individuals in a society need to be persuaded: the section which has the force, either because it is the most numerous or for some quite different reason. It is by force that social institutions are established, and it is by force that they are maintained.

Any elite which is not prepared to join in battle to defend its positions is in full decadence, and all that is left to it is to give way to another elite having the virile qualities it lacks. It is pure day-dreaming to imagine that the humanitarian principles it may have proclaimed will be applied to it: its vanquishers will stun it with the implacable cry, *Vae Victis*. The knife of the guillotine was being sharpened in the shadows when, at the end of the eighteenth century, the ruling classes in France were engrossed in developing their 'sensibility'. This idle and frivolous society, living like a parasite off the country, discoursed at its elegant supper parties of delivering the world from superstition and of crushing *l'Infâme*, all unsuspecting that it was itself going to be crushed.

Parallel with the phenomenon of the succession of elites, another of great importance is observable among civilised peoples. The production of economic goods goes on increasing, thanks mainly to the growth of personal capital, the average amount of which per head is one of the surest indices of civilisation and progress. Material well-being is thus expanding more and more. On the other hand, foreign and civil wars, becoming less and less lucrative as an industry, are diminishing in number and intensity. In consequence, habits are growing softer and morals becoming purer. Outside the vain agitations of politicians, there is being accomplished what G. de Molinari has called 'the silent revolution' – the slow transformation and improvement of social conditions. This movement is impeded, sometimes halted, by the squanderings of state socialism and by protectionist legislation of all kinds, but it is not the less real for that, and all the statistics of the most civilised peoples bear traces of it.

Having noted the importance in history of the succession of elites, we must not fall into the kind of error which is only too common, and claim that all is explained by this single cause. Social evolution is extremely complex; we can identify in it several main currents, but to seek to reduce them to one is a rash enterprise, at least for the present. For the time being, what is necessary is to study these great classes of phenomena and endeavour to discover their relationships.

SPOLIATION

We must again stress the point . . . that historians often see these events only through the veil of their passions and prejudices, depicting to us as a battle for liberty what is a straightforward struggle between two competing elites. They believe – and wish us to share the belief – that the elite which in reality is seeking to get hold of power to use it and misuse it in just the same way as the elite it is opposing, is moved only by pure love of its fellow men; or, if we prefer the phraseology of our day, by desire for the well-being of the 'small and humble'. It is only when they seek to join issue with certain adversaries of theirs in historical and political debate that such historians alight on the truth, at least so far as these adversaries are concerned. Thus Taine produces the declamations of the Jacobins and shows us the greedy interests lurking beneath them. Likewise Jan Jensen shows us theological dissensions which are no more than very transparent veils cloaking exclusively worldly interests. His work is a remarkable description of how new elites, when they achieve power, deal with their allies of the day before, the 'small and humble', who discover that they have merely exchanged yokes. The socialists of our own day have clearly perceived that the revolution at the end of the eighteenth century led merely to the bourgeoisie's taking the place of the old elite. They exaggerate a good deal the burden of oppression imposed by the new masters, but they do sincerely believe that a new elite of politicians will stand by their promises better than those which have come and gone up to the present day. All revolutionaries proclaim, in turn, that previous revolutions have ultimately ended up by deceiving the people; it is their revolution alone which is the *true* revolution. 'All previous historical movements,' declared the *Communist Manifesto* of 1848, 'were movements of minorities or in the interest of minorities. The proletarian movement is the self-conscious, independent movement of the immense majority, in the interest of the immense majority.' Unfortunately this *true* revolution, which is to bring men an unmixed happiness, is only a deceptive mirage that never becomes a reality. It is akin to the golden age of the millenarians: for ever awaited, it is for ever lost in the mists of the future, for ever eluding its devotees just when they think they have it.

Socialism is motivated by certain factors, some of which are present in almost all classes of society, while others differ according to the classes.

Among the first we should reckon the sentiments which move men to sympathise with the troubles and misfortunes of others, and to seek a remedy for them. This sentiment is one of the worthiest and most useful to society; indeed, it is the very cement of society.

Today almost everyone pays court to the socialists because they have become powerful. But it is not very long ago that many people were reckoning them to be scarcely better than criminals. Such an attitude could not be more false. So far, the socialists have certainly not been morally inferior to the members of the 'bourgeois' parties, especially of those parties which have used legislation to exact tribute from other citizens and which constitute what one may term 'bourgeois socialism'. If the 'bourgeois' were being animated by the same spirit of abnegation and sacrifice for their class as the socialists are for theirs, socialism would be far from being as menacing as it actually is. The presence in its ranks of the new elite is attested precisely by the moral qualities displayed by its adepts and which have enabled them to emerge victorious from the bitter test of numerous persecutions.

The sentiment of benevolence men have for their fellows, and without which society probably could not exist, is in no way incompatible with the principle of the class struggle. Even the most energetic defence of one's own rights may perfectly well be allied to a respect for the rights of others. Each class, if it wishes to avoid being oppressed, must have the force to defend its interests, but this does not at all imply that it must aim at oppressing other classes. On the contrary, it should be able to learn from experience that one of the best ways of defending these interests is in fact to take account, with justice, equity and even benevolence, of the interests of others.

Unfortunately, this sentiment of benevolence is not always very enlightened. Those who have it at times resemble the good women who crowd round a sick friend, each recommending a remedy. Their desire to be useful to the unfortunate is beyond question; it is only the efficacy of the remedies which is doubtful. How ever great their devoted concern for him, this cannot supply them with the medical knowledge they lack. When they find themselves in like-minded company, all of them advocating their own special nostrums, they usually end up by choosing a remedy almost at random, because really 'one must do *something*', and the ailing victim is lucky if his malady does not grow worse.

19
Roger Scruton

I include the following extract from my Meaning of Conservatism *(1981), since it touches on questions and ideas that are not elsewhere mentioned in this volume.*

The conservative attitude demands the persistence of a civil order. What is this order? And why should it be conserved? . . .

. . . any organization in which there is genuine government possesses two aspects, of civil society and state. Neither aspect can exist independently, and the reader must accept therefore that the conservative vision of society – which it is the purpose of this chapter to explore – will already contain strong intimations of the conservative vision of the state.

Nevertheless, conservatism originates in an attitude to civil society, and it is from a conception of civil society that its political doctrine is derived. But a political doctrine must contain a motive to action, and a source of appeal. The conservative, unable as he is to appeal to a utopian future, or to any future that is not, as it were, already contained in the present and past, must avail himself of conceptions which are both directly applicable to things as they are and at the same time indicative of a motivating force in men. And this force must be as great as the desire for the 'freedom' and 'social justice' offered by his rivals. There are three concepts which immediately present themselves, and whose contemporary application we must examine: the concepts of authority, allegiance and tradition.

AUTHORITY AND POWER

. . . 'Authority' can mean many things. In particular, it can mean either established or legitimate power. In either sense it can be granted, delegated, removed, respected, ignored, opposed. A person who has authority has it from a certain source – although it is well if he has authority in another sense, according to which it means not the legitimate or established principle of rule, but the natural gift to command allegiance. For the Marxist, 'authority', and the concept of 'legitimacy' through which it dignifies itself, are simply parts of the ideology of class rule, concepts belonging to and inculcated by a ruling 'hegemony'. They belong to that immense unconscious conspiracy whereby power has sought to entrench itself in accepted institutions, and whereby the historical nature (which is to say, the impermanence) of those institutions is masked. What is historical is presented as natural; power is represented as unchangeable power. But make no mistake, says the Marxist – the only *reality* here is power.

It is important to see that such doctrines, whether true or false, may be irrelevant to the practice of politics. What distinguishes political activity from the biological grouping of the herd is that the structure of the first is determined by the concepts of those who engage in it, whereas that of the second obeys only the inexorable laws of unconscious nature. And you can try as hard as you like to undermine the 'ruling ideology' which first placed legitimacy in the centre of common consciousness, but you will not succeed in making people remove from their minds a concept which – in their actual dealings with the world – is indispensable to them. People have the *idea* of legitimacy, and see the world as coloured in its terms; and it is how they *see* the world which determines how they act on it. Now the belief in legitimacy exists and will always exist as part of common political consciousness, and a society is not happy in which men cannot see that legitimacy enacted, in which they see *only* establishment, and only established power. The strength of this belief in legitimacy needs no comment. From the Norman Conquest to the contemporary reactions to trade-union power, the concept of legitimacy has governed political practice, and whether or not there is any reality which corresponds to this concept is a question that may be put aside as of no political (although of great philosophical) significance.

THE SOCIAL CONTRACT

In order to understand the conservative attitude to authority, we must examine a recent and now seemingly irrepressible political idea, the idea that there can be 'no obligation on any man which ariseth not from some act of his own' as Thomas Hobbes once put it. The most popular version of this idea sees the transition from power to legitimacy as residing in an unspoken, unknown and unknowable 'social contract'. Now no one, least of all a conservative, is likely to believe that government is possible without the propagation of myths. But this particular fiction – which at one time proved convenient in persuading men that the legitimacy of government lay elsewhere than in the divine right of kings – bears about as little relation to the facts as the view that my parents and I once surreptitiously contracted that they would nourish and educate me in return for my later care. Naturally, not every contract has to be explicit: there are implied contracts in law, brought about, for example, by an act of part performance. But even in implied contracts (except for those peculiar cases where a contract is implied by statute) there must be, somewhere, a choice, and a deliberation; a knowledge of consequences and a belief in, if not a mutual recognition of, an exchange of promises. The idea that there *must* be, at the heart of all political, and indeed all social organization, something in the nature of a contract (but a contract which, as it were, arises from social intercourse and does not – because clearly it could not – precede it), that idea stems from a singular pattern of thought which . . . bears directly on our theme.

The pattern of thought is this: Human beings, as free, autonomous agents, fall under the rule of Justice. Which is to say, to put it very roughly and . . . in the abstract terminology of Kant, that they must be treated as ends and not as means. To treat them as means only is to disrespect their freedom, and hence to sacrifice one's right to any similar respect from them. The fulfilment of a contract is, not the highest point, but the clearest case of just relations. A promise is made, another given, knowingly and in full cognizance of consequences. To promise in such a situation, and to rely on the other's fulfilment, while withholding any intention to return, is to treat the other as a means, to abuse his trust, and hence to act unjustly towards him. Here we can see that one man has assumed a right over another to which he is not entitled; for although the other granted him that right, he did so only conditionally, only on the understanding that he acquired a similar right in return. So now we can distinguish between legitimate and illegitimate claims; the 'rights' so vociferously claimed by Mr Boffin in *Our Mutual Friend* are evidently of the latter kind. The interest of contract is that it consists entirely of rights freely granted, and in that freedom (so both common sense and common law have always suggested) lies their legitimacy. To transfer the language of contract to the social sphere provides us at once, then, with a means to distinguish legitimate from illegitimate power. The criterion may be complex in its application, taking in many subtleties and qualifications as society develops in response to it; but its essence is simple. Does power arise out of and express the contractual basis, or does it claim some right which transcends it? The power of the police might be seen in this light as legitimate, that of the Mafia as not.

It is difficult to be persuaded by such a view. For the very possibility of free and open contract presupposes a sufficient social order, not because it would otherwise be impossible to enforce contracts (although that too is true), but because without social order the very notion of an individual *committing* himself, through a promise, would not arise. Already we have supposed shared institutions and a conception of human freedom, which could hardly have their origin in the very practice of contract which they serve to make possible. This is not to say that one cannot *see* society in this contractual way, in the way of contemporary American liberalism, and so construe all forms of social organization as assemblages of their members, with choice or consent as the ultimate binding principle. But for this vision to capture even the smallest part of what is recognized as the 'authority' of state, the social arrangement must be given plausible historical antecedents (such as those of New England) with which to mystify the inquiring mind. Perhaps the most remarkable thing that has happened in American politics during this century is the recognition that the powers of state in fact transcend their supposed contractual basis, and must therefore look for their authority elsewhere.

AUTHORITY AND FAMILY

But let us again step down from the political to the private realm. Consider the family. I have already suggested that it would be absurd to think of family ties as contractual, or family obligations as in any way arising from a free relinquishing of autonomy, or even from some unspoken bargain which rises into consciousness, so to speak, at some later stage. Even as a metaphor, the language of contract here fails to make contact with the facts. . . .

The family . . ., is a small social unit which shares with civil-society the singular quality of being non-contractual, of arising (both for the children and for the parents) not out of choice but out of natural necessity. And (to turn the analogy round) it is obvious that the bond which ties the citizen to society is likewise not a voluntary but a kind of natural bond. Locke, and the other great individualists, who thought otherwise, were also constrained to think that the world contained many 'vacant places' which could be filled by those who chose to withdraw from their inherited arrangement. As we now know, every country sports the sign 'engaged'. And besides, is it not psychological naïvety to think that I, now, at thirty-five, rooted in my language, culture and history, could suddenly do a volte-face and see myself as English only by *accident*, free at every moment to change? If I go elsewhere I take my Englishness with me, as much as I take my attachment to family, language, life and self. I go as a colonial or as an exile, and either sink like the Tibetans or swim like the Jews.

The analogy with the family is useful if we are to understand the role of authority in politics. It is clear from the start that a child must be acted upon by its parents' power: its very love for them will accord to them that power, and parents no more escape from its exercise by being permissive than does an officer cease to command his troops by leaving them constantly at ease. A child is what it is by virtue of its parents' will, and consequently the parent has an indefeasible obligation to form and influence the child's development. In this very process is power, and it is of necessity an established power, since it resides already with the parent at the child's first coming into the world. Now there is a sense in which every child does not only need its parents to exercise that power, but will also demand that they do so, to the extent that it cherishes their protection. There can be no ministering to the love of a child, and no granting of love, that is not also, in the first instance, an exercise of established power. For how is the child to recognize, from all those beings that surround it, the object which is its parent, that is, its principle of protection and its source of love? Surely, it must feel the influence of a will in its life, of a desire *for* its life, besides its own. It must feel the constraint of another's love for it. And it is only in recognizing the existence of an objective power over what it will do that the child is pulled out of its self-immersion into the recognition of its parent as an autonomous being, a being who not only gives love but gives it freely, and towards whom it owes love in return. The kind of personal love that we envisage as the end of family union requires, as its precondition, the sense of established power – the child's unformed recognition that, in respect of at least one other being, he is helpless – combined with the growing awareness that the power of that being is also an exercise of freedom. And it is a similar recognition of constraint, helplessness, and subjection to external will that heralds the citizen's realization of his membership of society; in this recognition love of one's country is born.

Consider the other side of family loyalties. We are apt to think of children as having a responsibility towards their parents, a responsibility that in no way reflects any merely contractual right, but which is simply *due* to the parents as a recognition of the filial tie. This sense of obligation is not founded in justice – which is the sphere of free actions between beings who *create* their moral ties – but rather in respect, honour, or (as the Romans called it) piety. To neglect my parents in old age is not an act of injustice but an act of impiety. Impiety is the refusal to recognize as legitimate a demand that does not arise from consent or choice. And we see that the behaviour of children towards their parents cannot be understood unless we admit this ability to recognize a bond that is 'transcendent', that exists, as it were 'objectively', outside the sphere of individual choice. It is this ability that is transferred by the citizen from hearth and home to place, people and country. The bond of society – as the conservative sees it – is just such a 'transcendent' bond, and it is inevitable that the citizen will be disposed to recognize its legitimacy, will be disposed, in other words, to bestow authority upon the existing order. He will be deterred from doing so largely by acts of arbitrary power, or by a general 'unfriendliness' in the public order, of the kind experienced by the deprived and unfostered child.

Authority, in the sense that we have considered, is an enormous artifact. By which I mean, not that authority is intentionally constructed, but rather that it exists only in so far as men exercise, understand and submit to it. The condition of society presupposes this general connivance, and a conservative will seek to uphold all those practices and institutions – among which, of course, the family is pre-eminent – through which the habits of allegiance are acquired. As we shall see, this necessary corollary of conservative thinking is incompatible with any suggestions that the conservative is an advocate either of liberal ideals, or of the so-called 'minimal state'. . . . No serious person *can* believe that there ought to be a power greater than that of the state, a power that can, if it chooses, put itself beyond the reach of law. The conservative believes in the power of state as necessary to the state's authority, and will seek to establish and enforce that power in the face of every influence that opposes it. However, his desire is to see power standing not naked in the forum of politics, but clothed in constitution, operating always through an adequate system of law, so that its movement seems never barbarous or oppressive, but always controlled and inevitable, an expression of the civilized vitality through which allegiance is inspired. The constitution, therefore, and the institutions which sustain it, will always lie at the heart of conservative thinking. The conservative places his faith in arrangements that are known and tried, and wishes to imbue them with all the authority necessary to constitute an accepted and objective public realm. It is from this that his respect for tradition and custom arises, and not from any end – such as freedom – towards which these practices are seen as a means. This point is of the essence, and I shall elaborate it further.

ALLEGIANCE

Consider, then, the concept of allegiance. It is allegiance which defines the condition of society, and which constitutes society as something greater than the 'aggregate of individuals' that the liberal mind perceives. It is proper for a conservative to be sceptical of claims made on behalf of the value of the individual, if these claims should conflict with the allegiance necessary to society, even though he may wish the *state* (in the sense of the apparatus of government) to stand in a fairly loose relation to the activities of individual citizens. Individuality too is an artifact, an achievement which depends upon the social life of man. And indeed, as many historians have pointed out, it is a recent venture of the human spirit for men and women to define themselves as individuals, as creatures whose nature and value is summed up in their unique individual being. The condition of man requires that the individual, while he exists and acts as an autonomous being, does so only because he can first identify himself as something greater – as a member of a society, group, class, state or nation, of some arrangement to which he may not attach a name, but which he recognizes instinctively as home. Politically speaking, this bond of allegiance – which, seen from the heights of intellectual speculation as 'my station and its duties', is experienced as a peculiar certainty in the activity of day to day – is of a value which transcends the value of individuality. For the majority of men, the bond of allegiance has immediate authority, while the call to individuality is unheard. It is therefore wrong to consider that a stateman has some kind of duty to minister to the second of these, and ignore the first. If the two impulses are not in conflict, as they perhaps were not, for example, in the society described by Fielding (and defended by Burke), then well and good. But if the second threatens the first – as it must do in a society where individuality seeks to realize itself independently of the institutions and traditions that have nurtured it – then the civil order is threatened too. And the business of politics is to maintain the civil order, and to prevent the 'dust and powder of individuality' that was once described as its ruin.

I have sketched the formation of allegiance in the family bond, and the residue of respect or piety which grows from that, ripe for transference to whatever might present itself as a fitting social object. The primary object of allegiance is, as I argued, authority, which is to say power conceived as legitimate, and so bound by responsibility. In the family this authority and responsibility have their foundation and end in love, but from the beginning they transcend the personal love of individuals. (There is, surely, a great mystification involved in the Freudian idea of the 'family romance'. Freud was getting at something of immense importance, which is the connection – perceived also by Hegel and Wagner – between the prohibition of incest and the existence of the family as 'home'. But this surely need not persuade us that the natural bond is always and inevitably erotic. In this area the distinctions, and not the similarities, have the greatest meaning.) Authority and responsibility arise from and sustain the sense of the family as something greater than the aggregate of its members, an entity in which the members participate, so that its being and their being are intermingled. Man is increased and not diminished through his participation in such arrangements. Mere individuality, relinquished first to the family, and then to the whole social organism, is finally replaced by the mature allegiance which is the only politically desirable form of 'freedom'. It is obvious that such allegiance is a matter of degree, being fervent at some times, passive or failing at others. The possibility of conservatism supposes only that it exists to some degree, and in most active people.

It would seem, then, that the healthy state or nation must command the allegiance of its subjects. Patriotism of some kind – the individual's sense of his identity with a social order – is politically indispensable. . . .

. . ., it has to be recognized that patriotism is not simply a stance towards the international world. It is in the first instance a condition of private life, and occupies a unique place in the deliberations of the citizen. To understand it we must refer again to two axioms of conservative thought. I call them axioms, although, naturally, they are implicit and unspoken in the instincts of *homo conservans*.

THE NATIONAL FOCUS

The first axiom is the simple principle that, lacking an overmastering ideal . . . conservatism must necessarily take many forms. Solon, asked what is the best form of government, replied 'For whom? And at what time?' It is a *particular* country, a *particular* history, a *particular* form of life that commands the conservative's respect and energy, and while he may have an imaginative grasp of other real or ideal arrangements, he is not immersed in them as he is immersed in the society that is his own. No utopian vision will have force for him compared to the force of present practice, for while the former is abstract and incomplete, the latter is concrete, qualified by familiar complexities that may be understood without describing them. To the extent that there are arrangements that have been proved in social life, and which have power to command the loyalty of their participants, to that extent is there variety among the forms of conservative politics. Moral scruples may turn the conservative from condoning the practices of others of his kind; but his preferred form of political life will not be a deduction from abstract principles sufficient in themselves to forbid what he finds distasteful. . . .

THE PRIORITY OF APPEARANCE

The second axiom is more difficult, although equally fundamental to the conservative creed. This is that the political activity of the citizen is determined by his own conception of his social nature. The *reality* of politics is not to be found outside the motives of those who engage in it, and whatever Marxists may say about the relation between base and superstructure, or about the economic causation of social behaviour, its truth does not bear on the *political* understanding of humanity. . . .

The argument may be illustrated by an analogy from the science of linguistics. Suppose that a linguist presented a law of English speech, which told us when a man will say 'The house is white', and when he will say 'Something is white'. Given sufficient theory, this law would provide a complete account of the relation between those sentences, since it would tell us all the facts about their utterance: when, where and why. But in another sense it would be incomplete. For there is a connection between those sentences that may have nothing to do with causality, and yet which is of the first importance, a connection of meaning. It is this connection which is grasped by the man who understands them, and he may have a *complete* understanding of them while being ignorant of the linguist's laws. And conversely, the linguist may have a full knowledge of causal laws, and yet lack the native speaker's understanding of what is said. For his laws may not issue in a dictionary.

Similarly, whatever the economic, social and biological determinants of a man's behaviour, that behaviour is *understood* by him and his fellows in another way: in terms of its *meaning*. To describe this meaning one would have to use the concepts available to the agent, and not the specialized classifications of a predictive science. Moreover, a man's intentions and acts derive from his own conception of the world; there can be no 'impartial observer' of human behaviour, if that means an observer who has no imaginative understanding of the concepts which determine agency. To engage in political activity is to understand, and in varying degrees to share, the common way of seeing things. This may require an act of imaginative identification; but it does not involve (and indeed is largely incompatible with) the application of any neutral 'science of man'.

What is this 'surface' of social affairs, this thing that is understood in participation but which may resist translation into words? In the first instance, to put the matter very simply, one may refer to the 'culture' of a society, race or nation. By 'culture' I mean all those activities which endow the world with meaning, so that it bears the mark of appropriate action and appropriate response. It is this which constitutes the individual's understanding of his social nature. Such understanding is given not through choice, but rather through concepts and perceptions embodied in the social organism, practices (such as that of marriage) which it does not make sense to think of as the products of individual will, or the outcome of some 'social contract' the terms of which no one can state or remember. A practice belongs to culture whenever it leads its participants to perceive the *value* of what they do. This perception may not be fully available to an outsider, but it may be essential to the intention which underlies a social act.

There is, to put it bluntly, something deeply self-deceived in the idea of a fulfilled human being whose style of life is entirely of his own devising. The cult of 'authenticity' – emphasizing the truth that the individual self is in some sense an artifact – espouses the self-contradictory position that it is by himself that he is made. This myth of self as *causa sui* is one to which few people now subscribe. Clearly the artifact of self is not of *my* making; it was cast first in the mould of a social arrangement and lives with that shape stamped permanently upon it, more or less distorted or embellished by later acts of choice.

I shall argue that, once we have rejected the cult of 'authenticity', we shall be forced to reject along with it the entire apparatus of dissent. In particular, we shall have to abandon the attempt to erode whatever is 'established', whatever has a vested power to overcome opposition, which is the first principle of liberal as of socialist thought. Which is not to say that we must *accept* all that is established; but we will be forced to acknowledge that, whatever we postulate by way of an ideal, the ideal itself may have little life outside the social arrangement which provided the concepts and the perceptions of those who pursue it. And once it is clear that a major and perhaps central part of those concepts and perceptions is inherited, then custom, tradition and common culture become ruling conceptions in politics. If these provide the common man with a sense of the value of his acts, then his self-identity and his allegiance to public forms are ultimately one and the same.

PATRIOTISM

We now begin to see the relevance of our second conservative axiom – the axiom that politics deals with the surface of social consciousness. A full understanding of the idea of allegiance will require in its turn an understanding of tradition, custom and ceremony – of the totality of practices through which the citizen is able to perceive his allegiance as an *end*. For the liberal, allegiance to society is a means: 'stick to this arrangement and on the whole you'll be left to yourself'. But the conservative cannot see it as a means to an end, since there is no description of the end in question that does not refer back to the values – and hence to the customs, institutions and allegiances – of those who pursue it. It follows that while the forms of allegiance will be many and varied, they will seek always to translate themselves into *symbolic* acts, acts which resist translation as 'means to an end'.

Consider the Englishman's allegiance to the Crown, as he envisages and enacts it. Monarchy is an institution, with a complex constitutional background, that elevates the person of the monarch above the realm of individual character and endows him or her with the dignity and, so to speak, the objectivity of office. It is not the personal qualities of the Queen that draw the Englishman to her nor is it any considered knowledge of the function and history of the Crown. It is rather a sense of the monarch as a symbol of nationhood, as an incarnation of the historical entity of which he is a part. His loyalty to the monarch requires ceremonial enactment, customary usage, an established code of deference: for this is the style of all symbolic gestures in which society and individual are merged.

Now a conservative is likely to value the institution of monarchy, and the kind of patriotism that it engenders. For the legitimacy of monarchical rule arises 'transcendentally', in the manner of the duties and obligations of family life. The monarch is not chosen for his personal attributes, nor does he have obligations and expectations which are the subject-matter of any 'social contract'. He is simply the representation of sovereignty, and its ceremonial presence. His will as monarch is not his individual will, but the will of state. The monarch forms part of that surface of concepts and symbols whereby the citizen can perceive his social identity, and perceive society not as a means to an end, but as an end in itself. Attachment to the monarch is therefore patriotism in a pure form, a form that could not be translated into attachment to a policy, or to a choice of means.

As a matter of fact, even when the titular head of state is 'chosen' – where there is an elected president, say, who offers 'promises' to the people – the choice is not in fact a choice of policy. The aims of politics, as they arise from day to day, are beyond the voter's competence, the ideals of social policy largely beyond his care. Usually, therefore, the president is chosen not as a means to an end, but as a peculiar kind of end in himself – as a 'figure of state'. Once again, he is a symbol. In a world of mass communication this means that a president will be chosen for his 'style', where style carries an implication of inward identity between president and nation, an identity that derives from no common end to which they might both be moving. This attachment to style represents an attempt to escape from the burden of democratic election, to escape from the 'contractual' element of the choice, to escape most of all from the sense of the state as constantly remade at each election, like a machine that has become outclassed. It is an expression of the conservative instinct, the instinct to make a future in the image of the past.

But just as the past constrains the future, so does the future commandeer the past. The past enacted by the citizen is the past *directed* to the future. Continuity is a selective aim; it looks both backwards and forwards with a measure of distrust. But we must remember the distinctive place of the past in our practical understanding: unlike the future, the past is *known*. How then should it enter our political calculations?

TRADITION

That question brings us to the final concept that will be necessary in giving articulate voice to the conservative instinct towards society, the concept of tradition. Under this concept I include all manner of custom, ceremony, and participation in institutional life, where what is done is done, not mechanically, but for a reason, and where the reason lies, not in what will be, but in what *has* been. It does not matter if the reason cannot be voiced by the man who obeys it: traditions are enacted and not designed, and none the less conscious for the lack of speech.

The power of tradition is twofold. First, it makes history into reason, and therefore the past into a present aim (as the whole history of the nation is enacted in the ceremony of coronation). Secondly, tradition arises from every organization in society, and is no mere trapping of the exercise of power. Traditions arise and command respect wherever the individual seeks to relate himself to something transcendent. They arise in clubs and societies, in local life, in religion and family custom, in education, and in every institution where man is brought into contact with his kind. Later, in considering questions of politics, we must show how the state can bring authority, allegiance, and tradition together, in order to define the citizen as *subject*.

I am aware that any reference to tradition will cause scepticism among those who believe themselves free from its charm. And there is no doubt that, while the concept may be essential to conservative dogma, it will also (like the 'equality', 'freedom' and 'social justice' which rival it) have to bear more weight of political argument than any single conception can sustain. But we must do our best for it. Whatever difficulties may attend the enterprise of defending tradition, the fight concerns no fiction but a genuine reality. Now it is salutary at this juncture to compare the realms of politics and art. Both activities are imbued with significance and purposefulness, and yet neither (on the conservative view) has any real external purpose. Art shows in microcosm the great architectural problem of politics as we are beginning to envisage it. And the comparison enables us to see why we should consider again the complaint that conservatism holds no prospect for the 'modern man': that it is far from being the impulse of life in death, but rather the will for death in life. For in art too we have felt the cravings, the disorientation, the overwhelming estrangement of 'modern' man, and in art too it has seemed necessary to present as self-conscious what was previously felt as nature, instinct and life.

But in the very sphere where the embattled consciousness of 'modern man' has most displayed itself, so too has the conservative principle been repeatedly affirmed. By this I do not mean that the artists who brought about the major aesthetic achievements of our century were, politically, of a conservative cast. If this is true, then it is only an instance of a more general truth – swallowed with some difficulty by critics of the New Left – that significant artists can be, and very often are, that way. (It is interesting to note the frequency with which it has been assumed, since the Romantic movement, that art must necessarily be a revolutionary force, simply because it has revolutionized *itself*. The assumption looks very odd when set beside the varieties of social conservatism expressed and advocated by James, Conrad, Yeats, Pound, Eliot, Joyce, Waugh and Lawrence – to name only the greatest of those who created our modern literature.)

What does it mean, then, to say that the conservative principle has been repeatedly reaffirmed in contemporary art? Partly this: that for most significant artists – for Eliot, Pound and Joyce, for Schoenberg and Stravinsky, for Braque and Moore – the problem of giving articulate voice to the modern consciousness was conceived as the problem of making that consciousness part of a *tradition* of artistic expression, and so bringing it back, by whatever complicated route, to the point where it might be understood. For Schoenberg the tradition of German music was what principally mattered: the problem was to re-create it, through self-conscious understanding of its inner life. The 'live tradition' that Pound hoped to 'gather from the air' was conceived in equally self-conscious terms. Eliot went so far as to represent tradition as an individual artifact: to belong to a tradition is also to make that tradition; to be part of history is to have created history. However, this process, which begins in loss and in conscious exploration, ends too in genuine discovery, the discovery that 'History is now and England'. In that discovery is a restoration of the whole of things.

It would be interesting to digress further into the transformation of the idea of tradition in the mind of alienated man. But let us simply draw the obvious conclusion from our parallel. Just as tradition circumscribes the possibilities of artistic expression, and so must be constantly re-created in artistic change, so too does it lay down the forms of political life, and must be re-created in every conscious political act. Now it is both difficult and yet (it seems) at the same time necessary for the modern consciousness to create tradition, setting itself in the centre of tradition as it sets tradition in the centre of itself. It may require an act of imagination, insight and will for a politician, in the midst of confusion, to reassert the identity of the society that he seeks to govern, even when, in their most secret innervations, it is just such an adventure that the people require from him. His route back to that place he started from will not find the place unchanged, and the way will be hard and uncertain. He will need exceptional qualities – the qualities of a De Gaulle or a Disraeli – if he is to reaffirm as a statesman the reality which he knows as a man. Yet, if he has the will to live, and the will to govern, nothing short of that can satisfy him.

As one writer has suggested, there is no general explanation of *how* men re-create and accept traditions. Nor is it easy to draw the line between genuine re-creation and the establishment of new and divergent social forms. But in all attempts to restore, re-create and assimilate tradition, the feature of continuity remains. When a man acts from tradition he sees what he *now* does as belonging to a pattern that transcends the focus of his present interest, binding it to what has previously been done, and done successfully. (This is obvious from the case of artistic creation.) Naturally there are rival traditions, and it would be vain to pretend that there is reason to belong to *all* of them. There are traditions of torture, crime and revolution. The traditions which the conservative fosters and upholds must therefore satisfy independent criteria. First, they must have the weight of a *successful* history – which is to say that they must be the palpable remainder of something that has flourished, and not the latest in a series of abortive starts. Secondly, they must engage the loyalty of their participants, in the deep sense of moulding their idea of what they are and should be. (Contrast the traditions of family life with those of torture.) Finally, they must point to something durable, something which survives and gives meaning to the acts that emerge from it.

But what does this tradition concretely amount to? No simple answer to this question can prove satisfactory: the task of dogma is to bridge the gap between philosophy and practice, and it is only in practice that the sum of our traditions can be understood. Nevertheless, it still belongs to dogma to delineate the *kind* of thing that is intended, and to present some partial exposition of its instances. Tradition, then, must include all those practices which serve to define the individual's 'being in society'. It constitutes his image of himself as a fragment of the greater social organism, and at the same time as the whole of that organism implicit in this individual part. The institution of the family, as it has variously developed, provides a clear example. No man who participates in that institution can remain unaffected in his conception of himself. He can no longer regard the fact of fatherhood, for example, as a biological accident. In seeing himself as father he finds himself entangled in a social bond, a bond of responsibility. And the reason for this bond and for the actions which express it, lies in the fact that this is how things are. Moreover, they are like this because they have been like this. The idea of 'family', through which his responsibilities, aims and preoccupations are from day to day defined, is one inherited without thought from his own participation in the arrangement which it designates. This is what is 'given'. Had he not conceived his activities as exemplifying the historical pattern contained in that concept, then he would nevertheless have needed some adequate replacement, some rival conception in terms of which to define his ends. And if this conception does not belong to tradition it will make way for the dangerous thought: 'Perhaps I do this, not for its own sake, not for what it *is*, but as a means to an end. Where then is the end? Where is the profit?' This thought signifies the emergence of the individual from social life, and the first glimpse of the empty solipsism that waits outside. Tradition restores the individual to the present act: it shows the reason *in* the act, and stills the desire for a justifying aim.

The family is of course an obvious example. But there are others, such as the customs which surround the momentous occasions of birth, coupling and death, the customs of hospitality, rivalry and class allegiance, of manners, dress and common courtesy. There are also the institutions of religion, in which man's desire for an identity greater than his nature provides reaches out of history altogether, to what is outside time and change. Only some of these institutions, it might be thought, are truly political. But to take such a view is to take too narrow a view of politics. Every tradition of any importance in the life of the citizen will tend to become part of the establishment of a state. This principle – which we might call the law of establishment . . . – is part of the natural history of politics, and shows the continuing necessity for political action to extend beyond the bounds of economic management. It is illustrated not only by the explicit establishment of the Church and, through the operation of law, of the family and private property, but by the implicit establishment of class rule in parliamentary institutions, by the more recent establishment of the traditions of organized labour in the trade-union movement, and by the extension of law (less automatic in America than in England, but manifest even there) to protect every aspect of social life, just so soon as it seems to be of more than individual concern.

A NOTE OF SCEPTICISM

What of the conservative attitude to social transformation? What 'tradition' has force, in comparison with the violence of industrial expansion and of over-population, with the spread of irreligion, and the growth of the urban working-class? Is there not an element of make-believe in the view that allegiance, authority and custom might have survived these historical convulsions, so as still to provide the bond from which politics derives its inspiration and appeal?

If this scepticism is the prelude to a rival politics, then it calls for only one reply: what other bond are you imagining? And how will you bring it about? But usually it takes a more unsettling form, the form, as one might put it, of the 'broad historical perspective'. It makes no recommendations, espouses no policies, and stands above the particular beliefs of the communities which it seeks to observe. The historical perspective looks down on the world of men from a height where their activity is seen only as the movement of impersonal forces, which propel the politician precisely when he most believes that he is guiding them. Withdrawing to this height, it may for the moment seem as though the task of discovering and asserting continuity is a hopeless one, that all things have changed utterly, and that in nothing is there a lasting principle of government.

I shall try to answer certain common forms of this historian's doubt. But two things should be said at once in reply to it. First, some of the items of dogma that I have considered have a philosophical basis which places them beyond the reach of historical criticism. The view of society as requiring forms of allegiance, and a recognition of authority, both of which transcend the operation of any contractual bond, is a view not of this or that community, but of the essence of civil life. It is this transcendent bond that constitutes society, and which is misrepresented by the liberal theories of contract and consent. Moreover, one particular tradition, which both embodies a transcendent bond, and also reinforces social allegiance, has survived all the upheavals of recent history. This is the tradition of family life. Even a 'revolutionary state' will find itself dependent upon it, and placed under the necessity to create (usually through the old expedient of belligerent foreign policy) the corresponding bond of social unity.

Secondly, it may be true that particular bonds of allegiance have decayed or fallen apart. But if some people *think* (in their vociferous part) that the bond of English citizenship has been loosened or undone, this does not show that their thought corresponds either to reality or to the true political sentiments which guide them. Much is disturbed; old allegiances have gone under and new ones risen in their place. But through all this, I shall argue, the conservative can find and uphold a genuine continuity. And his reason for doing so will be apparent in the attempt.

CONCLUDING REMARKS

I have surveyed the great 'datum' of civil society. What, then, are the dogmas to which that survey gives support? There are two principles so basic as to constitute axioms of conservative thinking. First, the principle that there is no general politics of conservatism. The forms of conservatism will be as varied as the forms of social order. Second, the principle that conservatism engages with the surface of things, with the motives, reasons, traditions and values of the society from which it draws its life. There are further dogmas, abstract in their origin, but specific in their implications. Society exists through authority, and the recognition of this authority requires the allegiance to a bond that is not contractual but transcendent, in the manner of the family tie. Such allegiance requires tradition and custom through which to find enactment. But tradition is no static thing. It is the active achievement of continuity; it can be restored, rescued and amended as grace and opportunity allow.

20
Sir James Fitzjames Stephen

Sir James Fitzjames Stephen (1829–94) was the brother of Sir Leslie Stephen (father of Virginia Woolf), a member of the Governor-General's Council in India (1869–72) and a High Court Judge (1879–91). An author of diverse talents, he produced books on legal theory, history and literature, as well as writing satirical stories. His Liberty, Equality, Fraternity *(1873), from which the following extracts are taken, was the most important of his political works, and contains a challenging response to the liberal theory of law, as this had been defended by John Stuart Mill in* On Liberty. *Stephen was a kind of utilitarian – hard-headed, sceptical and rationalistic. His value to the conservative lies not so much in his positive vision of human society, as in his trenchant diagnosis of the contradictions involved in liberal and socialist ways of thinking. Like Burke he defended prejudice and custom – but very much from the external point of view, as the prejudice and custom of others: a view conditioned in part by his experience of India.*

So far I have considered the theoretical grounds of Mr Mill's principle and its practical application to liberty of thought and discussion. I now proceed to consider its application to morals. It may be well to restate it for fear that I may appear to be arguing with an imaginary opponent. 'The object of this essay is to assert one very simple principle as entitled to govern absolutely all the dealings of society with the individual in the way of compulsion and control, whether the means used be physical force or the moral coercion of public opinion. That principle is, that the sole end for which mankind are warranted, individually or collectively, in interfering with the liberty of action of any of their number is self-protection.' A little further on we are told that 'from the liberty of each individual follows the liberty within the same limits of combination among individuals – freedom to unite for any purpose not involving harm to others.'

The following consequences would flow legitimately from this principle. A number of persons form themselves into an association for the purpose of countenancing each other in the practice of seducing women, and giving the widest possible extension to the theory that adultery is a good thing. They carry out these objects by organizing a system for the publication and circulation of lascivious novels and pamphlets calculated to inflame the passions of the young and inexperienced. The law of England would treat this as a crime. It would call such books obscene libels, and a combination for such a purpose a conspiracy. Mr Mill, apparently, would not only regard this as wrong, but he would regard it as an act of persecution if the newspapers were to excite public indignation against the parties concerned by language going one step beyond the calmest discussion of the expediency of such an 'experiment in living.' Such an association would be impossible in this country, because if the law of the land did not deal with it, lynch law infallibly would. This Mr Mill ought in consistency to regard as a lamentable proof of our bigotry and want of acquaintance with the true principles of liberty.

The manner in which he discusses an illustration closely analogous to this, and in which he attempts to answer an objection which must suggest itself to every one, throws the strongest possible light on the value of his own theory. His illustration is as follows: 'Fornication must be tolerated and so must gambling; but should a person be free to be a pimp or to keep a gambling house?' He puts the arguments on each side without drawing any conclusion, and the strongest of them are as follows:

> On the side of toleration it may be said that if the principles which we have hitherto defended are true, society has no business *as* society to decide anything to be wrong which concerns only the individual; that it cannot go beyond persuasion, and that one person should be as free to persuade as another to dissuade. In opposition to this it may be contended that, although the public or the State are not warranted in authoritatively deciding for purposes of repression or punishment that such or such conduct affecting only the interests of the individual is good or bad, they are fully justified in assuming, if they regard it

as bad, that its being so or not is at least a disputable question; that this being supposed they cannot be acting wrongly in endeavouring to exclude the influence of solicitations which are not disinterested, of instigators who cannot possibly be impartial, who have a direct personal interest on one side, and that the side which the State believes to be wrong and who confessedly promote it for personal objects only.[1]

There is a kind of ingenuity which carries its own refutation on its face. How can the State or the public be competent to determine any question whatever if it is not competent to decide that gross vice is a bad thing? I do not think the State ought to stand bandying compliments with pimps. 'Without offence to your better judgment, dear sir, and without presuming to set up my opinion against yours, I beg to observe that I am entitled for certain purposes to treat the question whether your views of life are right as one which admits of two opinions. I am far from expressing absolute condemnation of an experiment in living from which I dissent (I am sure that mere dissent will not offend a person of your liberality of sentiment), but still I am compelled to observe that you are not altogether unbiassed by personal considerations in the choice of the course of life which you have adopted (no doubt for reasons which appear to you satisfactory, though they do not convince me). I venture, accordingly, though with the greatest deference, to call upon you not to exercise your profession; at least I am not indisposed to think that I may, upon full consideration, feel myself compelled to do so.' My feeling is that if society gets its grip on the collar of such a fellow it should say to him, 'You dirty rascal, it may be a question whether you should be suffered to remain in your native filth untouched, or whether my opinion about you should be printed by the lash on your bare back. That question will be determined without the smallest reference to your wishes or feelings; but as to the nature of my opinion about you, there can be no question at all.'

Most people, I think, would feel that the latter form of address is at all events the more natural. Which is the more proper I shall try to show further on, but by way of preface it will be as well to quote the other passage from Mr Mill to which I have referred. After setting forth his theory as to personal vices being left to take their own course, he proceeds as follows:

The distinction here pointed out between the part of a person's life which concerns only himself and that which concerns others many persons will refuse to admit. How (it may be asked) can any part of the conduct of a member of society be a matter of indifference to the other members? No person is an entirely isolated being; it is impossible for a person to do anything seriously or permanently hurtful to himself without mischief reaching at least to his near connections, and often far beyond them.[2]

He proceeds to enforce this by highly appropriate illustrations, which I need not quote. Further on he quotes a passage from an advocate of the suppression of intemperance, of which the following is a sample: 'If anything invades my social rights, certainly the traffic in strong drink does. It invades my primary right of security by constantly creating and stimulating social disorder.' Upon this Mr Mill observes:

A theory of 'social rights', the like of which probably never before found its way into distinct language, being nothing short of this, that it is the absolute social right of every individual that every other individual should act in every respect precisely as he ought, that whosoever fails thereof in the smallest violates my social right and entitles me to demand from the Legislature the removal of the grievance. So monstrous a principle is far more dangerous than any single violation of liberty . . . The doctrine ascribes to all mankind a vested interest in each other's moral, intellectual, and even physical perfection, to be defined by each according to his own standard.[3]

At the risk of appearing paradoxical, I own that the theory which appears to Mr Mill so monstrous appears to me defective only in its language about rights and legislation, upon which I shall have more to say hereafter. It is surely a simple matter of fact that every human creature is deeply interested not only in the conduct, but in the thoughts, feelings, and opinions of millions of persons who stand in no other assignable relation to him than that of being his fellow-creatures. A great writer who makes a mistake in his speculations may mislead multitudes whom he has never seen. The strong metaphor that we are all members one of another is little more than the expression of a fact. A man would no more be a man if he was alone in the world than a hand would be a hand without the rest of the body. . . .

. . . Complete moral tolerance is possible only when men have become completely indifferent to each other – that is to say, when society is at an end. If, on the other hand, every struggle is treated as a war of extermination, society will come to an end in a shorter and more exciting manner, but not more decisively. . . .

The real problem of liberty and tolerance is simply this: What is the object of contention worth? Is the case one – and no doubt such cases do occur – in which all must be done, dared, and endured that men can do, dare, or endure; or is it one in which we can honourably submit to defeat for the present subject to the chance of trying again? According to the answer given to this question the form of the struggle will range between internecine war and friendly argument.

These explanations enable me to restate without fear of misapprehension the object of morally intolerant legislation. It is to establish, to maintain, and to give power to that which the legislator regards as a good moral system or standard. For the reasons already assigned I think that this object is good if and in so far as the system so established and maintained is good. How far any particular system is good or not is a question which probably does not admit of any peremptory final decision; but I may observe that there are a considerable number of things which appear good and bad, though no doubt in different degrees, to all mankind. For the practical purpose of legislation refinements are of little importance. In any given age and nation virtue and vice have meanings which for that purpose are quite definite enough. In England at the present day many theories about morality are current, and speculative men differ about them widely, but they relate not so much to the question whether particular acts are right or wrong, as to the question of the precise meaning of the distinction, the manner in which the moral character of particular actions is to be decided, and the reasons for preferring right to wrong conduct. The result is that the object of promoting virtue and preventing vice must be admitted to be both a good one and one sufficiently intelligible for legislative purposes.

If this is so, the only remaining questions will be as to the efficiency of the means at the disposal of society for this purpose, and the cost of their application. Society has at its disposal two great instruments by which vice may be prevented and virtue promoted – namely, law and public opinion; and law is either criminal or civil. The use of each of these instruments is subject to certain limits and conditions, and the wisdom of attempting to make men good either by Act of Parliament or by the action of public opinion depends entirely upon the degree in which those limits and conditions are recognized and acted upon.

First, I will take the case of criminal law. What are the conditions under which and the limitations within which it can be applied with success to the object of making men better? In considering this question it must be borne in mind that criminal law is at once by far the most powerful and by far the roughest engine which society can use for any purpose. Its power is shown by the fact that it can and does render crime exceedingly difficult and dangerous. Indeed, in civilized society it absolutely prevents avowed open crime committed with the strong hand, except in cases where crime rises to the magnitude of civil war. Its roughness hardly needs illustration. It strikes so hard that it can be enforced only on the gravest occasions, and with every sort of precaution against abuse or mistake. Before an act can be treated as a crime, it ought to be capable of distinct definition and of specific proof, and it ought also to be of such a nature that it is worth while to prevent it at the risk of inflicting great damage, direct and indirect, upon those who commit it. These conditions are seldom, if ever, fulfilled by mere vices. It would obviously be impossible to indict a man for ingratitude or perfidy. Such charges are too vague for specific discussion and distinct proof on the one side, and disproof on the other. Moreover, the expense of the investigations necessary for the legal punishment of such conduct would be enormous. It would be necessary to go into an infinite number of delicate and subtle inquiries which would tear off all privacy from the lives of a large number of persons. These considerations are, I think, conclusive reasons against treating vice in general as a crime.

The excessive harshness of criminal law is also a circumstance which very greatly narrows the range of its application. It is the *ratio ultima* of the majority against persons whom its application assumes to have renounced the common bonds which connect men together. When a man is subjected to legal punishment, society appeals directly and exclusively to his fears. It renounces the attempt to work upon his affections or feelings. In other words, it puts itself into distinct, harsh, and undisguised opposition to his wishes; and the effect of this will be to make him rebel against the law. The violence of the rebellion will be measured partly by the violence of the passion the indulgence of which is forbidden, and partly by the degree to which the law can count upon an ally in the man's own conscience. A law which enters into a direct contest with a fierce imperious passion, which the person who feels it does not admit to be bad, and which is not directly injurious to others, will generally do more harm than good; and this is perhaps the principal reason why it is impossible to legislate directly against unchastity, unless it takes forms which every one regards as monstrous and horrible. The subject is not one for detailed discussion, but any one who will follow out the reflections which this hint suggests will find that they supply a striking illustration of the limits which the harshness of criminal law imposes upon its range.

If we now look at the different acts which satisfy the conditions specified, it will, I think, be found that criminal law in this country actually is applied to the suppression of vice and so to the promotion of virtue to a very considerable extent; and this I say is right.

The punishment of common crimes, the gross forms of force and fraud, is no doubt ambiguous. It may be justified on the principle of self-protection, and apart from any question as to their moral character. It is not, however, difficult to show that these acts have in fact been forbidden and subjected to punishment not only because they are dangerous to society, and so ought to be prevented, but also for the sake of gratifying the feeling of hatred – call it revenge, resentment, or what you will – which the contemplation of such conduct excites in healthily constituted minds. If this can be shown, it will follow that criminal law is in the nature of a persecution of the grosser forms of vice, and an emphatic assertion of the principle that the feeling of hatred and the desire of vengeance above-mentioned are important elements of human nature which ought in such cases to be satisfied in a regular public and legal manner.

The strongest of all proofs of this is to be found in the principles universally admitted and acted upon as regulating the amount of punishment. If vengeance affects, and ought to affect, the amount of punishment, every circumstance which aggravates or extenuates the wickedness of an act will operate in aggravation or diminution of punishment. If the object of legal punishment is simply the prevention of specific acts, this will not be the case. Circumstances which extenuate the wickedness of the crime will often operate in aggravation of punishment. If, as I maintain, both objects must be kept in view, such circumstances will operate in different ways according to the nature of the case.

A judge has before him two criminals, one of whom appears, from the circumstances of the case, to be ignorant and depraved, and to have given way to very strong temptation, under the influence of the other, who is a man of rank and education, and who committed the offence of which both are convicted under comparatively slight temptation. I will venture to say that if he made any difference between them at all every judge on the English bench would give the first man a lighter sentence than the second.

What should we think of such an address to the prisoners as this? You, A, are a most dangerous man. You are ignorant, you are depraved, and you are accordingly peculiarly liable to be led into crime by the solicitations or influence of people like your accomplice B. Such influences constitute to men like you a temptation practically all but irresistible. The class to which you belong is a large one, and is accessible only to the coarsest possible motives. For these reasons I must put into the opposite scale as heavy a weight as I can, and the sentence of the court upon you is that you be taken to the place from whence you came and from thence to a place of execution, and that there you be hanged by the neck till you are dead. As to you, B, you are undoubtedly an infamous wretch. Between you and your tool A there can, morally speaking, be no comparison at all. But I have nothing to do with that. You belong to a small and not a dangerous class. The temptation to which you gave way was slight, and the impression made upon me by your conduct is that you really did not care very much whether you committed this crime or not. From a moral point of view, this may perhaps increase your guilt; but it shows that the motive to be overcome is less powerful in your case than in A's. You belong, moreover, to a class, and occupy a position in society, in which exposure and loss of character are much dreaded. This you will have to undergo. Your case is a very odd one, and it is not likely that you will wish to commit such a crime again, or that others will follow your example. Upon the whole, I think that what has passed will deter others from such conduct as much as actual punishment. It is, however, necessary to keep a hold over you. You will therefore be discharged on your own recognizance to come up and receive judgment when called upon, and unless you conduct yourself better for the future, you will assuredly be so called upon, and if you do not appear, your recognizance will be inexorably forfeited.

Caricature apart, the logic of such a view is surely unimpeachable. If all that you want of criminal law is the prevention of crime by the direct fear of punishment, the fact that a temptation is strong is a reason why punishment should be severe. In some instances this actually is the case. It shows the reason why political crimes and offences against military discipline are punished so severely. But in most cases the strength of the temptation operates in mitigation of punishment, and the reason of this is that criminal law operates not merely by producing fear, but also indirectly, but very powerfully, by giving distinct shape to the feeling of anger, and a distinct satisfaction to the desire of vengeance which crime excites in a healthy mind.

Other illustrations of the fact that English criminal law does recognize morality are to be found in the fact that a considerable number of acts which need not be specified[4] are treated as crimes merely because they are regarded as grossly immoral.

I have already shown in what manner Mr Mill deals with these topics. It is, I venture to think, utterly unsatisfactory. The impression it makes upon me is that he feels that such acts ought to be punished, and that he is able to reconcile this with his fundamental principles only by subtleties quite unworthy of him. Admit the relation for which I am contending between law and morals, and all becomes perfectly clear. All the acts referred to are unquestionably wicked. Those who do them are ashamed of them. They are all capable of being clearly defined and specifically proved or disproved, and there can be no question at all that legal punishment reduces them to small dimensions, and forces the criminals to carry on their practices with secrecy and precaution. In other words, the object of their suppression is good, and the means adequate. In practice this is subject to highly important qualifications, of which I will only say here that those who have due regard to the incurable weaknesses of human nature will be very careful how they inflict penalties upon mere vice, or even upon those who make a trade of promoting it, unless special circumstances call for their infliction. It is one thing however to tolerate vice so long as it is inoffensive, and quite another to give it a legal right not only to exist, but to assert itself in the face of the world as an 'experiment in living' as good as another, and entitled to the same protection from law. . . .

It would, of course, be idle to suppose that you can measure the real importance of the meaning of a popular cry by weighing it in logical scales. To understand the popular enthusiasm about liberty, something more is wanted than the bare analysis of the word. In poetry and popular and pathetic language of every kind liberty means both more and less than the mere absence of restraint. It means the absence of those restraints which the person using the words regards as injurious, and it generally includes more or less distinctly a positive element as well – namely, the presence of some distinct original power acting unconstrainedly in a direction which the person using the word regards as good. When used quite generally, and with reference to the present state of the political and moral world, liberty means something of this sort – The forward impulses, the energies of human nature are good; they were regarded until lately as bad, and they are now in the course of shaking off trammels of an injurious kind which had in former ages been imposed upon them.[5] The cry for liberty, in short, is a general condemnation of the past and an act of homage to the present in so far as it differs from the past, and to the future in so far as its character can be inferred from the character of the present.

If it be asked, What is to be thought of liberty in this sense of the word, the answer would obviously involve a complete discussion of all the changes in the direction of the diminution of authority which have taken place in modern times, and which may be expected hereafter as their consequence. Such an inquiry, of course, would be idle, to say nothing of its being impossible. A few remarks may, however, be made on points of the controversy which are continually left out of sight.

The main point is that enthusiasm for liberty in this sense is hardly compatible with anything like a proper sense of the importance of the virtue of obedience, discipline in its widest sense. The attitude of mind engendered by continual glorification of the present time, and of successful resistance to an authority assumed to be usurped and foolish, is almost of necessity fatal to the recognition of the fact that to obey a real superior, to submit to a real necessity and make the best of it in good part, is one of the most important of all virtues – a virtue absolutely essential to the attainment of anything great and lasting. Every one would admit this when stated in general terms, but the gift of recognizing the necessity for acting upon the principle when the case actually arises is one of the rarest in the world. To be able to recognize your superior, to know whom you ought to honour and obey, to see at what point resistance ceases to be honourable, and submission in good faith and without mental reservation becomes the part of courage and wisdom, is supremely difficult. All that can be said about these topics on the speculative side goes a very little way. It is like the difficulty which every one who has had any experience of the administration of justice will recognize as its crowning difficulty, the difficulty of knowing when to believe and when to disbelieve a direct assertion on a matter of importance made by a person who has the opportunity of telling a lie if he is so minded.

In nearly every department of life we are brought at last by long and laborious processes, which due care will usually enable us to perform correctly, face to face with some ultimate problem where logic, analogy, experiment, all the apparatus of thought, fail to help us, but on the value of our answer to which their value depends. The questions, Shall I or shall I not obey this man? accept this principle? submit to this pressure? and the like, are of the number. No rule can help towards their decision; but when they are decided, the answer determines the whole course and value of the life of the man who gave it. Practically, the effect of the popularity of the commonplaces about liberty has been to raise in the minds of ordinary people a strong presumption against obeying anybody, and by a natural rebound to induce minds of another class to obey the first person who claims their obedience with sufficient emphasis and self-confidence. It has shattered to pieces most of the old forms in which discipline was a recognized and admitted good, and certainly it has not produced many new ones.

The practical inference from this is that people who have the gift of using pathetic language ought not to glorify the word 'liberty' as they do, but ought, as far as possible, to ask themselves before going into ecstasies over any particular case of it, Who is left at liberty to do what, and what is the restraint from which he is liberated? By forcing themselves to answer this question distinctly, they will give their poetry upon the subject a much more definite and useful turn than it has at present.

Of course these remarks apply, as all such remarks must, in opposite directions. When liberty is exalted as such, we may be sure that there will always be those who are opposed to liberty as such, and who take pleasure in dwelling upon the weak side of everything which passes by the name. These persons should ask themselves the converse questions before they glorify acts of power: Who is empowered to do what, and by what means? or, if the words chosen for eulogy are 'order' and 'society,' it would be well for them to ask themselves, What order and what sort of society it is to which their praises refer?

Notes

1. The passage quoted is from ch. V of *On Liberty* (p. 154, Everyman edition).
2. See Mill *On Liberty*, ch. IV (p. 136, Everyman edition).
3. See Mill *On Liberty*, ch. IV (p. 146, Everyman edition).
4. [Stephen here refers to what the Victorians generally called 'unnatural vice'. Sodomy was a capital crime until 1861.]
5. On this passage . . ., Mr Morley observes that you do not condemn the past by recognizing the fact that its institutions are unsuited for the present, and that I write as if 'the old forms had not been disorganised by internal decrepitude' previously to the growth of those commonplaces about liberty, which, as I say, have 'shattered to pieces' the old forms of discipline. He says Mr Stephen 'is one of those absolute thinkers who bring to the problems of society the methods of geometry.'

   This is rather an inversion of parts. The very thing of which I complain in this passage is the accent of triumph and passion with which the word 'liberty' is generally used, so as to suggest that every restraint is oppressive. A calm statement of the advantages and disadvantages of particular institutions, and of the degree in which they are adapted to the present state of the world, is always good; but, as far as my experience goes, I should say that for one such utterance before the public in which the word 'liberty' is used, fifty or more are coloured by rhetorical exaggeration, condemnation of all restraints as restraints, and of the past as the past. The gist of this passage is to show that such language is hollow bombast, and that what Mr Morley calls the historical method, that is, the unimpassioned discussion of the special effects and objects of each particular restrains, is the only true one.

21

Gustave Thibon

Gustave Thibon (1903–) exemplifies a reactionary Catholic school of French thought whose other representatives include Charles Maurras (1868–1952) and the philosopher Jacques Maritain. Thibon is of peasant stock, and a peasant by inclination, who at the same time defends landed and aristocratic values. His eloquent invocation of what Maurras was to call the pays réel *(which lies concealed beneath the* pays légal *of the French republic) presents the emotional roots of twentieth-century conservatism in France as well as any other text. In a series of writings –* Diagnostics *(1940),* L'Échelle de Jacob *(1942),* Le Pain de chaque jour *(1946), and* Nietzsche ou le declin de l'esprit *(1948) – Thibon expounded his moral and spiritual repudiation of the fashions of modernity. The following extracts are from the selection entitled* Back to Reality, *published in London in 1952.*

The prodigious shrinkage of the world due to technical progress and, above all else, democratic exhibitionism have led the mass of men to hold opinions, and experience feelings, about matters far beyond their very moderate intellectual and affective capacity. That, I think, is one of the principal causes of modern unrealism. And what is more serious still, the sham ideas and feelings thus produced establish themselves like parasites on genuine ideas and affections. Every mirage deprives us of a fragment of oasis.

Artificially aroused and maintained, these states of mind are true to their origin: they continue to be necessarily factitious and unreal. Nothing comes from them in the way of active virtue; they take no hold on the individual, they bind him to nothing; not being made to measure, all they clothe in him is emptiness. For instance, we all know people who are loud in their enthusiasm for some politician or political programme; yet, so far from offering their lives in such a cause, they show themselves daily incapable of the slightest sacrifice for it, even of a fraction of their personal goods or peace of mind.

True ideas and true desires – even, for that matter, true *words* – are to be recognised as such by their motive power; they naturally tend to become incarnate in action. The problem we have to solve to-day – and it is a matter of life and death to us – is primarily a problem of *incarnation*. Leave alone whatever you don't understand, what you can do nothing about: it is not for you to rule and organise the country – or the world. But, whoever you are, you have within you, you carry in your hands, a portion of the country's life and the world's. You have a family, a calling, social surroundings: there lies the particular field entrusted to you; there none can take your place and it is there if anywhere that your ideal must flower. No abstract conversion can count for anything: there must be a change, not only of ideas but of life; not to-morrow but to-day; not by way of others but by way of yourself. Has it ever happened to you, at the end of the day, to strike a balance between what you have thought and dreamed and what you have actually *done*? The humiliation produced by such an exercise is the best possible reviver of a feeling and respect for reality. What I propose is that we should have recourse to a general examination of conscience; it is not enough alone, but it has this advantage: it is incompatible with any excessive internal anarchy and contradiction. There are certain enormities of speech and feeling that it is impossible to explain on any other grounds than a complete refusal to indulge in introspection. Monstrosities have a horror of mirrors – which make them even more monstrous than they are.

Such an incarnation of duty in the immediate affairs of everyday life is the only way to the country's salvation. There must be a strengthening of the vital bonds between the individual and all that directly touches him, and a general social regrouping from the bottom upwards. Life is impossible for any organism unless the cells that compose it preserve their own life and their mutual relationship. For every person his country should mean first: this particular child to bring up, this neighbour to help, this field to cultivate, this task to accomplish; otherwise the country, however eloquently extolled, remains no more than a corpse.

And realism exacts not only action but discipline. When you talk of the conduct of a war, of international relations or the future status of Europe, you know very well that what is involved is your own personal destiny and that of everything dear to you. But you are also aware that you lack the information, you lack the necessary competence to deal with such questions and that in any case they are not your *direct* concern. So there is only one thing to do: to acknowledge the nation's true leaders and trust them unreservedly. Your discipline strengthens their hands: your dreams and criticisms – and especially your differences – are a source of weakness to them. Doubtless your leaders are far from perfect; like all men, they have their frailties and errors; but humility and good sense must assure you that you are far more likely to be saved by remaining loyal to your imperfect leaders than by creating anarchy through seeking perfection. The following line of Victor Hugo's is one that can never be repeated too often to the impatient and revolutionary, to all intransigents: '*Le mal qu'on fait est lourd plus que le bien qu'on rêve. . . .*'[1]

The same realism also counsels silence. When you take it on you to judge, to decide and criticise political events, and when you are shown how useless it is to talk, you are the first to say: 'There is nothing I can *do* about it!' In that case, say nothing. When it is impossible to do anything there is no need to talk. The present is full of darkness and difficulties; of the future we know nothing. There is one duty that is immediately obvious: we must reclimb the slope and *live* once again. Our one task is to recreate, to regroup our forces, and even now, in the grip of winter, to prepare for new birth. This is the time for germination and incubation: a time, that is, for waiting in silence. It is in secret only that living things evolve. 'They never ripen', wrote a saint, 'by being talked about.' Verbal anticipations kill the future in the womb: words are the greatest of all abortionists. When the grain is germinating it makes no sound; a brooding bird never sings.

. . . I have denounced individualism as the chief moral factor making for the decline of the population. But in a being so dependent, so social as man, such individualism is never unalloyed; it is bound to lead to a compromise between the self and the non-self. It is the compromise called idolatry. Idolatry is merely a projection of individualism: it wears the mask of love, but in fact knows nothing of it. For it is not enough to love (everyone in this life loves someone or something), it is a matter of knowing whether the people and things we love serve us as *doors* that open on the world and on God, or merely as *mirrors* sending us back to ourselves. False love, I mean the love which separates the being loved from the rest of the world and makes it an absolute centre, conflicts as much as selfishness with the duty of having children.

First there is the false love of the partner in marriage. Without leaving that microcosm, my own hamlet, I note how the so-called love-matches have perceptibly increased in the last fifty years. In the old days people married without waiting for 'the call of the heart'; they married under the pressure of an obscure social imperative, and the choice of a partner was primarily governed by similarities of rank and fortune, of political and religious traditions, and so on. All that was left to individual inclination – and it was quite enough – was that the future bride or bridegroom should not be completely repulsive. Love would come later. There were cases, from time to time, when the social veto was defied and passionate love-affairs occurred between young people of different social backgrounds; but even so, such passions generally led to premature pregnancy which procured, as by magic, the consent of the two families! All this has greatly changed to-day. Before marrying, people wait till they are in love, or think they are, and each is more or less free to wed the person of his choice. Truth, unhappily, compels me to state that these love-matches provide not only most of the divorces and unhappy homes ('meet in love, part in hate', runs the old popular saying), but also the majority of homes without children. The paradox is only apparent. The same social imperative which in the old days led our ancestors to embark on marriage without being too particular in their choice of a partner ('one has got to settle down . . . it's the way of the world', etc.), induced them also to have children. And to-day it is the same individualism, the same impoverishment of an ego unable to transcend itself, which leads us to choose our mate – and reject the children we do not choose. What is called love (sentimental intoxication and carnal appetite based on a vast deal of selfishness, with the petty well-being and petty security *à deux* that result) is too recent and shallow, too deprived of roots to culminate in the flower which is a child. When you have found a shoe for your foot and can at last walk in comfort (your foot is so tender), the arrival of a child is more like a nail in the sole than a gift from heaven. This is the state of things that justifies the moralist's bitterness when he says: The child's worst enemy is still – love!

I am not attacking the true love that is due to choice. There is nothing greater in this world. The love I am discussing is simply a transposed egoism. Unhappily it is more common than the other. It is only in a few exceptional beings that personal passion can rise superior to social background and take its place. When Tristan and Yseult, instead of wandering in the inhospitable forest with nothing to sustain them but their love, repose comfortably side by side in a bedroom without a cradle, they are no longer really of interest to anyone. . . .

. . . there is an aristocratic atheism, hostile alike to Christianity and democracy, which merges its two aversions by trying to show that both the religious ideal and the ideology of the Left have really one and the same root.

Superficially there is much to confirm this idea. The democratic movement seems to continue and crown with success the reversal of human values effected by Jesus Christ. 'You have but one master, and you are all brethren alike. . . . The last shall be first. . . .' Is not the democratic ideal, like the Gospel, founded on the abolition of an old order of society, both oppressive and isolating; is not the basis of both a universal appeal and universal love? And surely it is in a democratic society that the divine words, *I am moved with pity for the multitude*, find their truest and most faithful application? It is certainly a fact that many great minds have seen in the ideal which the French Revolution introduced into the world the sequel, or even the actual completion, of the Gospel message of deliverance and brotherhood. Democracy, at its birth, appeared not so much a vulgar change of political régime as the creation of a new humanity.

> But Europe at that time was thrilled with joy,
> France standing on the top of golden hours,
> And human nature seeming born again.

So sang Wordsworth. The opening words of the Sermon on the Mount announce blessings for men. Saint-Just echoed the Beatitudes when he proclaimed: 'Happiness is a new idea in Europe!' Christ regenerated the individual, democracy regenerates society; a new world, in both cases, emerges out of the ruin and decay of the old.

It has now become a commonplace that the democratic impulse has produced results diametrically opposed to the 'spirit' of democracy. The September Massacres and the days of the Terror are not so very remote from the night of August 4th.[2] The purity and incorruptibility of those 'great ancestors' gave place to something different: the nineteenth-century's thirst for material riches and the twentieth's appetite for immediate pleasure. Fraternity has turned to a separation of class from class and an atomising of individuals such as had never been encountered before in history. Liberty has produced a particularly inhuman form of tyranny, and it must not be forgotten that the most draconian of political régimes, from Napoleon to the present day, have in fact, whether they laid claim to democracy or repudiated it, all sprung from a democratic soil. Finally the development of the great revolutionary principles, saluted by some as the echo and complement of the preaching of Jesus, has led multitudes to practical and theoretical atheism.

It will be answered that the history of individuals and peoples is all shot through with contradictions like this; it is the very rhythm of life that causes contraries to attract and succeed one another. I confess I am unconvinced by these Hegelian fantasies. In nature, it is not contraries but opposite poles that tend to attract and succeed one another. These two things should never be confused. Poles are *complementary*, they are mutually sustaining; contraries are *antagonistic*, they devour one another. Night is not in opposition to day, nor autumn to spring, in the sense that being is opposed to non-existence, yes to no, evil to good. When contraries attract one another, it is because they have some fundamental similarity; in other words, because they are not true contraries. There are certainly some authentic conversions, but they are rare. Human conduct, generally speaking, however full of apparent contradictions, is much more homogeneous, deep down, than might be thought. The kind of chastity that breaks out into sudden debauchery is already fed by debauchery below the surface; a love that turns to hate is already impregnated with a latent hatred. It is just the same with the case we are considering here: if the democratic idea, which apparently conforms to certain Christian principles, has in fact contributed to destroy throughout the world all the true evangelical values, it is because it had no more than a Christian mask, and because from the very beginning, under an outer coating of Christianity, it concealed an essence that was really anti-Christian. What we have to do here is to define the precise nature of this parody of Christianity.

. . . It is impossible not to feel a certain misgiving when very Catholic writers use expressions like the 'fourth estate', the 'emancipated people' who have now arrived at 'historical existence', the 'social majority of the masses' and so forth; and all the more so in that they talk of such things as though they were unheard-of marvels, totally new and fresh, prodigies (as it were) of the coming dawn. If only we could have some exact definitions. . . . If all these sonorous phrases simply mean that the so-called lower strata of society are composed of human persons whose freedom and dignity should be recognised and respected, we are wholly in agreement. But what is there new in this? The humblest Christian was well aware of it a thousand years before the declaration of the Rights of Man. On the other hand, if these formulas are meant to insinuate that the education of the 'masses' is complete, that they have no more need of tutelage and are capable by themselves of governing their destiny, then this is something truly new; only it is one of those novelties impossible to take seriously. . . .

It is not a question of writing an apology for the ideas of the 'right'. These labels are stupid. But when the social apple-cart is in process of overturning into the left-hand ditch, anyone who draws attention to the middle of the road can hardly do other than veer to the right. Authority, as I understand it, has no other mission but to save freedom from itself. My reactionary spirit merely demands for the people the form of tutelage that assures to the freedom, to the idiosyncrasies (if you will), of persons and groups the utmost possible harmony and scope. We too perceive the imperfections of the old social systems: we are touched as much as anyone by the material and moral misery of humanity; it may even happen that our programme of 'reforms' coincides, at certain points, with that of the revolutionaries. But the essential difference between them and us lies in the fact that we, before setting out to promote a 'just and liberal' reform, insist that the three following conditions be fulfilled:

1. The reform must be *possible*. There are certain transformations (complete communism, for instance) which are not compatible with the natural exigencies – and therefore the eternal exigencies –

of human society. We know where St Thomas More located the nation in which perfect socialism flourished. . . .

2. It must be opportune: adapted, that is, to the spirit of time and place; and there must be moral preparation for it, especially when the reforms are of the emancipating type. It was thus that, in the course of ages, the Church was able to make an end of slavery, to temper the rigours of war, of serfdom and so on; and these results, slow and moderate though they appear, were at any rate *achieved*. Whereas the seeds of liberty and material well-being, broadcast over lands inadequately prepared, have produced by way of harvest corruption and slavery in new refined forms.

3. Lastly, there must be a pure intention in the mode of demanding it. There is an envious and vindictive manner of claiming justice which itself amounts to injustice and if it succeeds must necessarily aggravate injustice. 'An evil tree cannot bring forth good fruit. . . .'

For instance, let us consider for a moment the democratic myth of the 'sovereign people'. For a long time now, everyone of any intelligence has detected here an outrageous piece of trickery: with one hand the people are given a power for which they are not fitted, and which therefore always remains something spectral and Platonic; with the other they are deprived of the rights which do belong to their proper rôle in the body politic. The polling-booth flourishes over the tomb of communal and corporative liberties. And what does the abstract right to vote amount to, against the slavery of a people given over to the horrors of economic liberalism, as in nineteenth-century Europe, or to the horrors of state-tyranny, as in so many countries of the twentieth century? In law and in theory the people drive the chariot of state with a sovereign hand; in practice they can no longer control or organise even the things that touch them most nearly, the things they should rightly control and organise: all that concerns their daily bread, the dignity and independence of their various callings.

It is healthy and necessary that the 'masses' should exercise a certain power in the body politic. But in the first place there should be no 'masses', in the sense in which the word is understood to-day. My idea of a healthy people is a collection of local and professional organisms, highly differentiated and mutually adjusted, but each functioning at its own level. This amorphous *mass*, brandishing, bear-like, the *massive* club of its *massive* claims, is characteristic of a society in the last stages of decadence.

But to return to my point. In a normal society, no class, no individual, is completely excluded from power. An element of 'democracy' is indispensable to the life of the State: the central government, however independent in its own order, needs to rest on the solid foundations of freedom – individual, regional and corporative freedom. But this government by the people should remain something relative and subordinate. What I complain of, in the modern democratic ideal, is not the power of all,[3] it is the absence of any hierarchy of powers, it is the *confusion of powers*; it is not 'the power of the people' but the granting to the people of a sovereign yet fictitious and sterile power, *to the detriment* of that limited but authentic and profitable power which belongs to them naturally. In fact it is simply an application of one of the great laws ('Hell itself has its laws', said Goethe) which seem to govern our modern folly: the sacrifice of the relative, not to the true absolute which is God (who saves and crowns what is relative), but *to the shadow of the absolute*.

THE PROBLEM OF CLASSES

The spirit of liberalism and democracy has left the forming of social classes to the unhealthy workings of politics and finance: thus a hierarchy has been created which corresponds to no real vital necessity, and merely feeds, and goes on feeding, the spirit of division and revolt. The great problem at the present day is to remake a social organism, to remake a whole world, in which social differences rest on real foundations and so contribute to the cause of unity.

To achieve this end, I should be glad to be told of a system any better than the hereditary organisation of society. I am keenly aware of its shortcomings; but I know of no other. A general return to the laws of family and environment I believe to be absolutely necessary. No society can be healthily and soundly organised on the sole basis of individual contingencies (what a chaos of unruly 'vocations' would the world be then!); what is needed is that weight of necessity which goes with hereditary differentiation and continuity. A promiscuous opening of all the doors to everyone at large is an invitation, at every grade of the hierarchy, to that frenzied ambition which is the worst social evil. There again we have an unhealthy projection of the Gospel truth into the field of politics. None is excluded from the divine banquet: all men are called to the celestial heights, to sanctity. It is a parody of this divine universal appeal to desire that all members of society should be called to the *terrestrial* heights (fortune, power and the rest); instead of the harmonious progress of every soul towards a divine privilege that by its very essence is *indefinitely extensible,* we have an anarchical stampede after temporal privileges which of their very nature are reserved for the few.

It is only too obvious that there is no room for everyone on the topmost rung of the social ladder. The eliminating factor of birth is attacked as unjust. But in the first place it is not absolute: in the kind of society we are thinking of, the function of birth would be to prove and select vocations to rise, not kill them in the egg. And what of democracy as an eliminating factor, the result of fortune's caprice, or the clash of unleashed ambitions? Is this any less hazardous and less unjust? For answer you have only to look at the hideous upside-down selection effected here with us by the outcome of financial or electoral battles!

If there were any automatic means of assigning the highest functions to the worthiest representatives of all social classes, I should be much less inclined to urge the benefits of heredity. But meanwhile, until such a means has been discovered, I shall continue to believe that the division of society into distinct organisms, preserving stability as the generations go by, still offers the fewest drawbacks of any; it serves to restrict that anarchy and conflict which the total abolition of hereditary cadres merely helps to envenom and make universal. Human ambitions, all jumbled together, are like a basket of crabs: it is better for the basket to be divided into compartments. . . .

PERSONALISM IN POLITICS

A people is hardened by purely collective treatment; it grows soft and flabby when deferred to without consideration for authority, without consideration for the keeping of distance. The two errors cancel out if there is a ruling *élite* that knows how to *love* the people *with severity*. For this to be possible there must be social grades that are both *living* and *rigid*. What I believe to be necessary is the restoring of a patriarchal type of society. For where, more than in a father, will there be found combined the two things that a people so essentially needs: love and authority? A state-organisation can result, if it is slack, only in a watery caricature of love; if it is rigid, in a deadening caricature of authority. To my mind the ideal type of personalist institution would be a monarchical form of government, superimposed on a variety of social formations, far more private than to-day, more local and more human: a type of society in which the immediate contact of superior with inferior would be purified of every taint of promiscuity by a deep hierarchical reserve.

SOCIAL GRADES AND INDIVIDUAL FULFILMENT

I still know a few old countrymen who have never emerged from their environment, from their family, social and professional milieu. They have never left their native village, never opened a newspaper; the idea of 'escaping', or 'living their own life', has never crossed their minds. Now nearly all these old people have vigorous and original personalities; but their more emancipated children – who travel about, go to the cinema, listen to the wireless, abandon the land and break with all their ancestral traditions – have, generally speaking, no ideas of their own, no emotions that can be said to be really personal: their dim souls are all much alike.

It is far too often forgotten that the social cadres are a kind of bark that protects the sap. The depth of the river is due not only to what it derives from its source; it is also deep because its bed is narrow.

These social cadres are often attacked in the name of the rights of the individual. But in practice they were the best supports for healthy individualism. They prevented from emerging only those unworthy of doing so. They were the tests and the purifiers of true personalities and true vocations. They helped the strong – those capable of escaping upwards – to be all the more themselves. The weak, all those who aimed at escaping downwards, they defended against themselves. They contributed, in both cases, to raise up the level of *individual* dignity and *individual* worth.

THE DUTY OF THE ÉLITE

It will never be sufficiently realised how easily and how directly the masses are corruptible. The people can stand up to centuries of tyranny without losing their basic equilibrium: a few years of demagogy and they become rotten through and through. They are hard to crush but easy to corrupt; they are like those insects, protected by their armour from external shocks, but very easily poisoned: a drop is enough to kill them. To escape from our present chaos, what is needed is not a rectified democracy, it is a new aristocracy; one that can impose on itself and impose on others the pure rigorous climate that makes an end of corruption.

Let there be no mistake: the more a people is lulled with illusions and steeped in an easy life, the more the *élite*, whose mission it is to save it, must lead a life of austerity and self-sacrifice: only in this way can it disarm envy and win confidence; only thus can it serve as a priming to any new discipline, any raising of the moral tone. It is by the head that societies grow diseased, and it is by the head that they are cured.

A life of austerity is necessary for all men, in every walk of life. The only difference is this: austerity must be imposed on the masses by necessity (by natural forces or the working of institutions) and on a responsible *élite* by choice and freedom.

ONTOLOGY AND POLITICS

'I believe in democracy because I have faith in man, in his value and in his immortal soul.' These words of Masaryk's shed a flood of light on the confusion at the bottom of Christian democracy. God preserve us from making our politics an *exact* replica of the data of ontology and the Christian faith. Personality, spirit, immortal soul, child of God – all these things represent for man an *end* rather than a *fact*: man is on his way to realising his essence, to attaining his goal; and how heavy-going that journey is, how beset with obstacles, how threatened at every step by the sinister snares of materiality and evil! Paradox as it may seem, the essence and goal of man are present with us not as a good already acquired, but as a promise and a hope – a forlorn hope. . . .

The politician who sets too much store by this hope runs the danger of smothering it. To treat a child as a grown-up person is to weaken and possibly destroy his power of ever becoming a normal adult. In the same way, to treat the mass of men as a collection of developed personalities is to run a grave risk of slaying, before ever it grows to maturity, the fragile germ of the spirit.

Out of respect for the human person itself we should beware of excessive personalism in politics. Political wisdom has to deal with man in process of formation, not with man already achieved; it must take account of the sub-human necessities which weigh on this embryo of man. Its mission is to aid the embryo to grow. This is impossible without respecting the stages of the slow and difficult process of maturing. The crime of one sort of democracy is precisely that of having forced man's growth. It has invested human beings, still unripe, with the powers and liberties of a matured personality: thus it has inevitably barred the way to maturity. Less harm may well have been done by the men and the theories that aimed quite frankly at keeping the people in ignorance and servitude: of all the ways of killing the *man* in a man, the most fatal of all is to force the human fruit to ripen before its time.

Notes

1. 'Ill done weighs more than good but dreamed.'
2. The session of the National Assembly (1789) when feudal privileges were relinquished. (Tr.)
3. To clear up an ambiguity here. The power of all is healthy in so far as 'all' means all the organic members of the social, labouring body, each in his place and for the good of all. It is unhealthy if 'all' is understood as the anonymous and disorganised multitude. Then Demos can cry, with Victor Hugo: 'I am *all men*, the mysterious enemy of *the whole.*'

22

Alexis de Tocqueville

Alexis, Comte de Tocqueville (1805–59), French politician, political theorist and historian, is one of the many great political thinkers upon whom liberals and conservatives lay equal claim. In his brilliant work Democracy in America *(1835) written at the astonishing age of 29, de Tocqueville summed up his observations of American democracy, as providing the model and the motive for the politics of the future, and as embodying a 'principle of equality' which would henceforth be the ruling idea in the life of nations. The major problem of modern society, as he saw it, was that of reconciling equality with liberty, in the increasing absence of the diversity and dispersal of power that are the marks of aristocratic regimes. In his analysis of democratic despotism, here reproduced, de Tocqueville goes a long way towards foretelling what J. L. Talmon has called 'totalitarian democracy' – the kind of directed mass-politics which has arisen in the twentieth century.*

De Tocqueville expressed, in his earlier work, a qualified admiration for American democracy; in his The Old Régime and the Revolution *(1856) however, he expounds a much more sceptical and conservative critique of the new principles of egalitarian politics, and – in pages heavily indebted to Burke – offers a penetrating analysis of the social catastrophe brought about by the French Revolutionaries. In both works, however, de Tocqueville's attitude is dispassionate, subtle, and untainted by dogma – so much so that the controversy will persist to the end of time, as to whether he was a liberal with conservative sympathies, or a conservative with liberal ideals. The following extract is from* Democracy in America, *translated by Henry Reeve (1840).*

The notion of secondary powers, placed between the sovereign and his subjects, occurred naturally to the imagination of aristocratic nations, because those communities contained individuals or families raised above the common level, and apparently destined to command by their birth, their education, and their wealth. This same notion is naturally wanting in the minds of men in democratic ages, for converse reasons; it can only be introduced artificially, it can only be kept there with difficulty; whereas they conceive, as it were without thinking upon the subject, the notion of a sole and central power which governs the whole community by its direct influence. Moreover in politics, as well as in philosophy and in religion, the intellect of democratic nations is peculiarly open to simple and general notions. Complicated systems are repugnant to it, and its favourite conception is that of a great nation composed of citizens all resembling the same pattern, and all governed by a single power.

The very next notion to that of a sole and central power, which presents itself to the minds of men in the ages of equality, is the notion of uniformity of legislation. As every man sees that he differs but little from those about him, he cannot understand why a rule which is applicable to one man should not be equally applicable to all others. Hence the slightest privileges are repugnant to his reason; the faintest dissimilarities in the political institutions of the same people offend him, and uniformity of legislation appears to him to be the first condition of good government.

I find, on the contrary, that this same notion of a uniform rule, equally binding on all the members of the community, was almost unknown to the human mind in aristocratic ages; it was either never entertained, or it was rejected.

These contrary tendencies of opinion ultimately turn on either side to such blind instincts and such ungovernable habits, that they still direct the actions of men, in spite of particular exceptions. Notwithstanding the immense variety of conditions in the middle ages, a certain number of persons existed at that period in precisely similar circumstances; but this did not prevent the laws then in force from assigning to each of them distinct duties and different rights. On the contrary, at the present time all the powers of government are exerted to impose the same customs and the same laws on populations which have as yet but few points of resemblance.

As the conditions of men become equal amongst a people, individuals seem of less importance, and society of greater dimensions; or rather, every citizen, being assimilated to all the rest, is lost in the crowd, and nothing stands conspicuous but the great and imposing image of the people at large. This naturally gives the men of democratic periods a lofty opinion of the privileges of society, and a very humble notion of the rights of individuals; they are ready to admit that the interests of the former are everything, and those of the latter nothing. They are willing to acknowledge that the power which represents the community has far more information and wisdom than any of the members of that community; and that it is the duty, as well as the right, of that power to guide as well as govern each private citizen. . . .

As in ages of equality no man is compelled to lend his assistance to his fellow-men, and none has any right to expect much support from them, every one is at once independent and powerless. These two conditions, which must never be either separately considered or confounded together, inspire the citizen of a democratic country with very contrary propensities. His independence fills him with self-reliance and pride amongst his equals; his debility makes him feel from time to time the want of some outward assistance, which he cannot expect from any of them, because they are all impotent and unsympathizing. In this predicament he naturally turns his eyes to that imposing power which alone rises above the level of universal depression. Of that power his wants and especially his desires continually remind him, until he ultimately views it as the sole and necessary support of his own weakness.

This may more completely explain what frequently takes place in democratic countries, where the very men who are so impatient of superiors patiently submit to a master, exhibiting at once their pride and their servility.

The hatred which men bear to privilege increases in proportion as privileges become more scarce and less considerable, so that democratic passions would seem to burn most fiercely at the very time when they have least fuel. I have already given the reason of this phenomenon. When all conditions are unequal, no inequality is so great as to offend the eye; whereas the slightest dissimilarity is odious in the midst of general uniformity: the more complete is this uniformity, the more insupportable does the sight of such a difference become. Hence it is natural that the love of equality should constantly increase together with equality itself, and that it should grow by what it feeds upon.

This never-dying ever-kindling hatred, which sets a democratic people against the smallest privileges, is peculiarly favourable to the gradual concentration of all political rights in the hands of the representative of the state alone. The sovereign, being necessarily and incontestably above all the citizens, excites not their envy, and each of them thinks that he strips his equals of the prerogative which he concedes to the crown.

The man of a democratic age is extremely reluctant to obey his neighbour who is his equal; he refuses to acknowledge in such a person ability superior to his own; he mistrusts his justice, and is jealous of his power; he fears and he contemns him; and he loves continually to remind him of the common dependence in which both of them stand to the same master.

Every central power which follows its natural tendencies courts and encourages the principle of equality; for equality singularly facilitates, extends, and secures the influence of a central power.

In like manner it may be said that every central government worships uniformity: uniformity relieves it from inquiry into an infinite number of small details which must be attended to if rules were to be adapted to men, instead of indiscriminately subjecting men to rules: thus the government likes what the citizens like, and naturally hates what they hate. These common sentiments, which, in democratic nations, constantly unite the sovereign and every member of the community in one and the same conviction, establish a secret and lasting sympathy between them. The faults of the government are pardoned for the sake of its tastes; public confidence is only reluctantly withdrawn in the midst even of its excesses and its errors, and it is restored at the first call. Democratic nations often hate those in whose hands the central power is vested; but they always love that power itself.

Thus, by two separate paths, I have reached the same conclusion. I have shown that the principle of equality suggests to men the notion of a sole, uniform, and strong government: I have now shown that the principle of equality imparts to them a taste for it. To governments of this kind the nations of our age are therefore tending. They are drawn thither by the natural inclination of mind and heart; and in order to reach that result, it is enough that they do not check themselves in their course.

I am of opinion, that, in the democratic ages which are opening upon us, individual independence and local liberties will ever be the produce of artificial contrivance; that centralization will be the natural form of government.

... I think then that the species of oppression by which democratic nations are menaced is unlike anything which ever before existed in the world: our contemporaries will find no prototype of it in their memories. I am trying myself to choose an expression which will accurately convey the whole of the idea I have formed of it, but in vain; the old words despotism and tyranny are inappropriate: the thing itself is new; and since I cannot name it, I must attempt to define it.

I seek to trace the novel features under which despotism may appear in the world. The first thing that strikes the observation is an innumerable multitude of men all equal and alike, incessantly endeavouring to procure the petty and paltry pleasures with which they glut their lives. Each of them, living apart, is as a stranger to the fate of all the rest – his children and his private friends constitute to him the whole of mankind; as for the rest of his fellow-citizens, he is close to them, but he sees them not; – he touches them, but he feels them not; he exists but in himself and for himself alone; and if his kindred still remain to him, he may be said at any rate to have lost his country.

Above this race of men stands an immense and tutelary power, which takes upon itself alone to secure their gratifications, and to watch over their fate. That power is absolute, minute, regular, provident, and mild. It would be like the authority of a parent, if, like that authority, its object was to prepare men for manhood; but it seeks on the contrary to keep them in perpetual childhood: it is well content that the people should rejoice, provided they think of nothing but rejoicing. For their happiness such a government willingly labours, but it chooses to be the sole agent and the only arbiter of that happiness: it provides for their security, foresees and supplies their necessities, facilitates their pleasures, manages their principal concerns, directs their industry, regulates the descent of property, and subdivides their inheritances – what remains, but to spare them all the care of thinking and all the trouble of living?

Thus it every day renders the exercise of the free agency of man less useful and less frequent; it circumscribes the will within a narrower range, and gradually robs a man of all the uses of himself. The principle of equality has prepared men for these things: it has predisposed men to endure them, and oftentimes to look on them as benefits.

After having thus successively taken each member of the community in its powerful grasp, and fashioned them at will, the supreme power then extends its arm over the whole community. It covers the surface of society with a net-work of small complicated rules, minute and uniform, through which the most original minds and the most energetic characters cannot penetrate, to rise above the crowd. The will of man is not shattered, but softened, bent, and guided: men are seldom forced by it to act, but they are constantly restrained from acting: such a power does not destroy, but it prevents existence; it does not tyrannize, but it compresses, enervates, extinguishes, and stupefies a people, till each nation is reduced to be nothing better than a flock of timid and industrious animals, of which the government is the shepherd.

I have always thought that servitude of the regular, quiet, and gentle kind which I have just described, might be combined more easily than is commonly believed with some of the outward forms of freedom; and that it might even establish itself under the wing of the sovereignty of the people.

Our contemporaries are constantly excited by two conflicting passions; they want to be led, and they wish to remain free: as they cannot destroy either one or the other of these contrary propensities, they strive to satisfy them both at once. They devise a sole, tutelary, and all-powerful form of government, but elected by the people. They combine the principle of centralization and that of popular sovereignty; this gives them a respite: they console themselves for being in tutelage by the reflection that they have chosen their own guardians. Every man allows himself to be put in leading-strings, because he sees that it is not a person or a class of persons, but the people at large that holds the end of his chain.

By this system the people shake off their state of dependence just long enough to select their master, and then relapse into it again. A great many persons at the present day are quite contented with this sort of compromise between administrative despotism and the sovereignty of the people; and they think they have done enough for the protection of individual freedom when they have surrendered it to the power of the nation at large. This does not satisfy me: the nature of him I am to obey signifies less to me than the fact of extorted obedience. . . .

Another tendency, which is extremely natural to democratic nations and extremely dangerous, is that which leads them to despise and undervalue the rights of private persons. The attachment which men feel to a right, and the respect which they display for it, is generally proportioned to its importance, or to the length of time during which they have enjoyed it. The rights of private persons amongst democratic nations are commonly of small importance, of recent growth, and extremely precarious, – the consequence is that they are often sacrificed without regret, and almost always violated without remorse.

But it happens that at the same period and amongst the same nations in which men conceive a natural contempt for the rights of private persons, the rights of society at large are naturally extended and consolidated: in other words, men become less attached to private rights at the very time at which it would be most necessary to retain and to defend what little remains of them. It is therefore most especially in the present democratic ages, that the true friends of the liberty and the greatness of man ought constantly to be on the alert to prevent the power of government from lightly sacrificing the private rights of individuals to the general execution of its designs. At such times no citizen is so obscure that it is not very dangerous to allow him to be oppressed – no private rights are so unimportant that they can be surrendered with impunity to the caprices of a government. The reason is plain: – if the private right of an individual is violated at a time when the human mind is fully impressed with the importance and the sanctity of such rights, the injury done is confined to the individual whose right is infringed; but to violate such a right, at the present day, is deeply to corrupt the manners of the nation and to put the whole community in jeopardy, because the very notion of this kind of right constantly tends amongst us to be impaired and lost. . . .

23

Eric Voegelin

Eric Voegelin (1901–85) was born in Cologne, and educated in Vienna. After Hitler's Anschluss in 1938, he made his home in the United States, returning briefly to Munich as Professor of Political Science between 1958 and 1966. A single meditative thread, inspired alike by Christian theology and Greek philosophy, runs through his writings, which constitute a profound and troubled reaction to the fate of Central Europe, enslaved by successive totalitarian powers.

The most important of Voegelin's works are The New Science of Politics (1952), Anamnesis (1966) and Order and History (1956–87). Voegelin's philosophy consists in a somewhat disorderly search for order, an anxious longing for serenity, and a disenchanted invocation of enchantment. Through the veil of scholarly prose can be discerned the spiritual quest of modern conservatism, its hopes, its fears, and its final reconciliation to an imperfect world. The following extract, from the pair of short essays entitled Science, Politics and Gnosticism (1968), discusses one of the leading themes of Voegelin's writings: the theme of gnosticism, as a recurrent disorder, the origin of man's defiance of the transcendental, and the spiritual force behind the totalitarian doctrines of our time.

Political science, *politike episteme*, was founded by Plato and Aristotle.

At stake in the spiritual confusion of the time was whether there could be fashioned an image of the right order of the soul and society – a paradigm, a model, an ideal – that could function for the citizens of the polis as had paraenetic myth for the Homeric heroes. To be sure, fourth-century Athens afforded plenty of opinions about the right manner of living and the right order of society. But was it possible to show that one of the multitude of sceptic, hedonist, utilitarian, power oriented, and partisan *doxai* was the true one? Or, if none of them could stand up to critical examination, could a new image of order be formed that would not also bear the marks of a non-binding, subjective opinion (*doxa*)?

The science of political philosophy resulted from the efforts to find an answer to this question.

In its essentials the classical foundation of political science is still valid today.... A scientific analysis ... makes it possible to judge of the truth of the premises implied by an opinion. It can do this, however, only on the assumption that truth about the order of being – to which, of course, opinions also refer – is objectively ascertainable. And Platonic–Aristotelian analysis does in fact operate on the assumption that there is an order of being accessible to a science beyond opinion. Its aim is knowledge of the order of being, of the levels of the hierarchy of being and their interrelationships, of the essential structure of the realms of being, and especially of human nature and its place in the totality of being. Analysis, therefore, is scientific and leads to a science of order through the fact that, and insofar as, it is ontologically oriented. . . .

Only when the order of being as a whole, unto its origin in transcendent being, comes into view, can the analysis be undertaken with any hope of success; for only then can current opinions about right order be examined as to their agreement with the order of being. When the strong and successful are highly rated, they can then be contrasted with those who possess the virtue of *phronesis*, wisdom, who live *sub specie mortis* and act with the Last Judgment in mind. When statesmen are praised for having made their people great and powerful, as Themistocles and Pericles had made Athens, Plato can confront them with the moral decline that was the result of their policies. (One thinks here not only of classical examples, but perhaps also of what Gladstone said of Bismarck: He made Germany great and the Germans small.) Again: when impetuous young men are repelled by the vulgarity of democracy, Plato can point out to them that energy, pride, and will to rule can indeed establish the despotism of a spiritually corrupt elite, but not a just government; and when democrats rave about freedom and equality and forget that government requires spiritual training and intellectual discipline, he can warn them that they are on the way to tyranny.

These examples will suffice to indicate that political science goes beyond the validity of propositions to the truth of existence. The opinions for the clarification of which the analysis is undertaken are not merely false: they are symptoms of spiritual disorder in the men who hold them. And the purpose of the analysis is to persuade – to have its own insights, if possible, supplant the opinions in social reality. Analysis is concerned with the therapy of order.[1]

Society resists the therapeutic activity of science. Because not only the validity of the opinions is called into question but also the truth of the human attitudes expressed in the opinions, because the effort in behalf of truth is directed at the untruth of existence in particular men, the intellectual debate is intensified beyond the point of analysis and argument to that of existential struggle for and against truth – a struggle that can be waged on every level of human existence, from spiritual persuasion, *peitho* in the Platonic sense, to psychological propaganda, to even physical attack and destruction. Today, under the pressure of totalitarian terror, we are perhaps inclined to think primarily of the physical forms of opposition. But they are not the most successful. The opposition becomes truly radical and dangerous only when philosophical questioning is itself called into question, when *doxa* takes on the appearance of philosophy, when it arrogates to itself the name of science and prohibits science as non-science. Only if this prohibition can be made socially effective will the point have been reached where *ratio* can no longer operate as a remedy for spiritual disorder. Hellenic civilization never came to this: philosophizing could be mortally dangerous, but philosophy, especially political science, flourished. Never did it occur to a Greek to prohibit analytical inquiry as such.

The frame of reference of political science has changed considerably in the more than two thousand years since its founding. The broadening of temporal and spatial horizons has yielded to comparative analysis enormous amounts of material that were unknown in antiquity. And the appearance of Christianity in history, with the resulting tension between reason and revelation, has profoundly affected the difficulties of philosophizing. The Platonic–Aristotelian paradigm of the best polis cannot provide an answer for the great questions of our time – either for the organizational problems of industrial society or for the spiritual problems of the struggle between Christianity and ideology. But the basic situation of political science, which I have briefly outlined here, has, except in one respect, not changed at all. Today, just as two thousand years ago, *politike episteme* deals with questions that concern everyone and that everyone asks. Though different opinions are current in society today, its subject matter has not changed. Its method is still scientific analysis. And the prerequisite of analysis is still the perception of the order of being unto its origin in transcendent being, in particular, the loving openness of the soul to its transcendent ground of order.

Only in one respect has the situation of political science changed. As indicated, there has emerged a phenomenon unknown to antiquity that permeates our modern societies so completely that its ubiquity scarcely leaves us any room to see it at all: the prohibition of questioning. This is not a matter of resistance to analysis – that existed in antiquity as well. It does not involve those who cling to opinions by reason of tradition or emotion, or those who engage in debate in a naive confidence in the rightness of their opinions and who take the offensive only when analysis unnerves them. Rather, we are confronted here with persons who know that, and why, their opinions cannot stand up under critical analysis and who therefore make the prohibition of the examination of their premises part of their dogma. This position of a conscious, deliberate, and painstakingly elaborated obstruction of *ratio* constitutes the new phenomenon. . . .

1

The prohibition of questions as it appears in some of the early writings of Karl Marx – the 'Economic and Philosophical Manuscripts' of 1844 – can serve as the point of departure.

Marx is a speculative gnostic. He construes the order of being as a process of nature complete in itself. Nature is in a state of becoming, and in the course of its development it has brought forth man: '*Man* is directly a *being of nature.*'[2] Now, in the development of nature a special role has devolved upon man. This being, which is itself nature, also stands over against nature and assists it in its development by human labor – which in its highest form is technology and industry based on the natural sciences: 'Nature as it develops in human history . . . as it develops through industry . . . is true *anthropological* nature.'[3] In the process of creating nature, however, man at the same time also creates himself to the fullness of his being; therefore, '*all of so-called world history* is nothing but the production of man by human labor.'[4] The purpose of this speculation is to shut off the process of being from transcendent being and have man create himself. This is accomplished by playing with equivocations in which 'nature' is now all-inclusive being, now nature as opposed to man, and now the nature of man in the sense of *essentia*. This equivocal wordplay reaches its climax in a sentence that can easily be overlooked: 'A being that does not have its nature outside of itself is not a *natural* being; it does not participate in the being of nature.'[5]

In connection with this speculation Marx himself now brings up the question of what objection the 'particular individual' would probably have to the idea of the spontaneous generation ('*generatio aequivoca*') of nature and man: 'The being-of-itself (*Durchsichselbstsein*) of nature and man is *inconceivable* to him, because it contradicts all the *tangible aspects* of practical life.' The individual man will, going back from generation to generation in search of his origin, raise the question of the creation of the first man. He will introduce the argument of infinite regress, which in Ionian philosophy led to the problem of the *arche* (origin). To such questions, prompted by the 'tangible' experience that man does not exist of himself, Marx chooses to reply that they are 'a product of abstraction.' 'When you inquire about the creation of nature and man, you abstract from nature and man.' Nature and man are real only as Marx construes them in his speculation. Should his questioner pose the possibility of their non-existence, then Marx could not prove that they exist.[6]

In reality, his construct would collapse with this question. And how does Marx get out of the predicament? He instructs his questioner, 'Give up your abstraction and you will give up your question along with it.' If the questioner were consistent, says Marx, he would have to think of himself as not existing – even while, in the very act of questioning, he *is*. Hence, again the instruction: 'Do not think, do not question me.'[7] The 'individual man,' however, is not obliged to be taken in by Marx's syllogism and think of himself as not existing because he is aware of the fact that he does not exist of himself. Indeed, Marx concedes this very point – without, however, choosing to go into it. Instead, he breaks off the debate by declaring that 'for socialist man' – that is, for the man who has accepted Marx's construct of the process of being and history – such a question 'becomes a practical impossibility.' The questions of the 'individual man' are cut off by the ukase of the speculator who will not permit his construct to be disturbed. When 'socialist man' speaks, man has to be silent. . . .[8]

And now for the Marxian suppression of questions. It represents, as we shall see, a very complicated psychological phenomenon, and we must isolate each of its components in turn. First, the most 'tangible': here is a thinker who knows that his construct will collapse as soon as the basic philosophical question is asked. Does this knowledge induce him to abandon his untenable construct? Not in the least: it merely induces him to prohibit such questions. But his prohibition now induces us to ask, Was Marx an intellectual swindler? Such a question will perhaps give rise to objections. Can one seriously entertain the idea that the lifework of a thinker of considerable rank is based on an intellectual swindle? Could it have attracted a mass following and become a political world power if it rested on a swindle? But we today are inured to such scruples: we have seen too many improbable and incredible things that were nonetheless real. Therefore, we hesitate neither to ask the question that the evidence presses upon us, nor to answer, Yes, Marx *was* an intellectual swindler. This is certainly not the last word on Marx. We have already referred to the complexity of the psychological phenomenon behind the passages quoted. But it must unrelentingly be the first word if we do not want to obstruct our understanding of the prohibition of questions.

When we establish that Marx was an intellectual swindler, the further question of why immediately arises. What can prompt a man to commit such a swindle? Is there not something pathological about this act? For an answer to this question let us turn to Nietzsche, who was also a speculative gnostic, but a more sensitive psychologist than Marx.

2

Nietzsche introduces the will to power, the will to dominion, the *libido dominandi*, as the passion that accounts for the will to intellectual deception. Let us examine the *via dolorosa* along which this passion drives the gnostic thinker from one station to the next.

In *Jenseits von Gut und Böse*, Aphorism 230, Nietzsche speaks of a 'fundamental will of the spirit' which wants to feel itself master. The spirit's will to mastery is served in the first place by 'a suddenly erupting resolve for ignorance, for arbitrary occlusion . . . a kind of defensive stand against much that is knowable.' Moreover, the spirit *wills* to let itself be deceived on occasion, 'perhaps with a mischievous suspicion that things are *not* thus and so, but rather only allowed to pass as such . . . a satisfaction in the arbitrariness of all these manifestations of power.' Finally, there belongs here 'that not unscrupulous readiness of the spirit to deceive other spirits and to dissemble before them,' the enjoyment of 'cunning and a variety of masks.'[9]

The *libido dominandi*, however, has a violence and cruelty that go beyond the delight in masquerade and in the deception of others. It turns on the thinker himself and unmasks his thought as a cunning will to power. 'A kind of cruelty of the intellectual conscience,' 'an extravagant honesty,' clears up the deception; however – and this is the decisive point – not in order to advance to the truth beyond the deception, but only to set up a new one in place of the old. The game of masks continues; and those who allow themselves to be deceived remain deceived. In this 'cruelty of the intellectual conscience' can be seen the movement of the spirit that in Nietzsche's gnosis corresponds functionally to the Platonic *periagoge*, the turning-around and opening of the soul. But in the gnostic movement man remains shut off from transcendent being. The will to power strikes against the wall of being, which has become a prison. It forces the spirit into the rhythm of deception and self-laceration.[10]

. . . The gnostic thinker really does commit an intellectual swindle, and he knows it. One can distinguish three stages in the action of his spirit. On the surface lies the deception itself. It could be self-deception; and very often it is, when the speculation of a creative thinker has culturally degenerated and become the dogma of a mass movement. But when the phenomenon is apprehended at its point of origin, as in Marx or Nietzsche, deeper than the deception itself will be found the awareness of it. The thinker does not lose control of himself: the *libido dominandi* turns on its own work and wishes to master the deception as well. This gnostic turning back on itself corresponds spiritually, as we have said, to the philosophic conversion, the *periagoge* in the Platonic sense. However, the gnostic movement of the spirit does not lead to the erotic opening of the soul, but rather to the deepest reach of persistence in the deception, where revolt against God is revealed to be its motive and purpose.

With the three stages in the spirit's action it is now possible also to differentiate more precisely the corresponding levels of deception:

1) For the surface act it will be convenient to retain the term

Nietzsche used, 'deception.' But in content this action does not necessarily differ from a wrong judgment arising from another motive than the gnostic. It could also be an 'error.' It becomes a deception only because of the psychological context.

2) In the second stage the thinker becomes aware of the untruth of his assertion or speculation, but persists in it in spite of this knowledge. Only because of his awareness of the untruth does the action become a deception. And because of the persistence in the communication of what are recognized to be false arguments, it also becomes an 'intellectual swindle.'

3) In the third stage the revolt against God is revealed and recognized to be the motive of the swindle. With the continuation of the intellectual swindle in full knowledge of the motive of revolt the deception further becomes 'demonic mendacity.'

3

The first and second of the three stages Nietzsche described can be seen in the texts that we have quoted from Marx. How does Marx stand with respect to the third stage in this movement of the spirit, where rebellion against God is revealed to be the motive for the deception? This is exactly what is revealed in the context of the quoted passages:

> A *being* regards itself as independent only when it stands on its own feet; and it stands on its feet only when it owes its *existence* to itself alone. A man who lives by the grace of another considers himself a dependent being. But I live by the grace of another completely if I owe him not only the maintenance of my life but also *its creation*: if he is the *source* of my life; and my life necessarily has such a cause outside itself if it is not my own creation.[11]

Marx does not deny that 'tangible experience' argues for the dependence of man. But reality must be destroyed – this is the great concern of gnosis. In its place steps the gnostic who produces the independence of his existence by speculation. It would indeed be difficult to find another passage in gnostic literature that so clearly exposes this speculation as an attempt to replace the reality of being with a 'second reality' (as Robert Musil called this undertaking).

A passage from Marx's doctoral dissertation of 1840–41 takes us still further into the problem of revolt:

Philosophy makes no secret of it. The confession of Prometheus, 'In a word, I hate all the gods,' is its own confession, its own verdict against all gods heavenly and earthly who do not acknowledge human self-consciousness as the supreme deity. There shall be none beside it.[12]

In this confession, in which the young Marx presents his own attitude under the symbol of Prometheus, the vast history of the revolt against God is illuminated as far back as the Hellenic creation of the symbol.

Let us first clarify the relationship between Marx's comments and the verse he quotes from Aeschylus.

Prometheus is riveted to a rock by the sea. Below on the strip of beach stands Hermes looking up at him. The fettered Prometheus gives his bitterness free reign. Hermes tries to calm him and urges moderation. Then, Prometheus crams his impotence and rebellion into the line quoted by Marx: 'In a word, I hate all the gods.'[13] But the line is not part of a monologue. At this outbreak of hatred the messenger of the gods replies admonishingly: 'It appears you have been stricken with no small madness.'[14] The word translated here as 'madness' is the Greek *nosos* which Aeschylus employed as a synonym for *nosema*.[15] It means bodily or mental sickness. In the sense of a disease of the spirit it can mean hatred of the gods or simply being dominated by one's passions. For example, Plato speaks of the *nosema tes adikias*, the sickness of injustice.[16] Here we touch on the diseased – the pneumopathological – nature of the revolt that was pointed out earlier. And what does Marx say to this observation of the messenger of the gods? He says nothing. Anyone who does not know *Prometheus Bound* must conclude that the quoted 'confession' sums up the meaning of the tragedy, not that Aeschylus wished to represent hatred of the gods as madness. In the distortion of the intended meaning into its opposite the suppression of questions can be seen again on all its levels: the deception of the reader by isolating the text (the confession appears in the preface to a doctoral dissertation), the awareness of the swindle (for we assume that Marx had read the tragedy), and the demonic persistence in the revolt against better judgment.

The soul's rebellion against the order of the cosmos, hatred of the gods, and the revolt of the Titans are not, to be sure, unheard of in Hellenic myth. But the Titanomachia ends with the victory of Jovian justice (*dike*), and Prometheus is fettered. The revolutionary reversal of the symbol – the dethronement of the gods, the victory of Prometheus – lies beyond classical culture; it is the work of gnosticism. Not until the gnostic revolt of the Roman era do Prometheus, Cain, Eve, and the serpent become symbols of man's deliverance from the power of the tyrannical god of this world.

4

... Now just what is (the) new 'philosophy'? What is its connection with the Promethian revolt and with the suppression of questions? Marx modelled his idea of science and philosophy on Hegel. Let us turn, therefore, to the greatest of speculative gnostics for the answer to these questions.

It is to be found in a fundamental statement in the Preface to the *Phänomenologie* of 1807:

> The true form in which truth exists can only be the scientific system of it. To contribute to bringing philosophy closer to the form of science – the goal of being able to cast off the name *love of knowledge* (*Liebe zum Wissen*) and become *actual knowledge* (*wirkliches Wissen*) – is the task I have set for myself.[17]

The expressions 'love of knowledge' and 'actual knowledge' are italicized by Hegel himself. If we translate them back into the Greek, into *philosophia* and *gnosis*, we then have before us the program of advancing from philosophy to gnosis. Thus, Hegel's programmatic formula implies the perversion of the symbols science and philosophy.

By philosophy Hegel means an undertaking of thought that approaches and can finally attain actual knowledge. Philosophy is subsumed under the idea of progress in the eighteenth-century sense of the term. As opposed to this progressivist idea of philosophy let us recall Plato's efforts to clarify its nature. In the *Phaedrus* Plato has Socrates describe the characteristics of the true thinker. When Phaedrus asks what one should call such a man, Socrates, following Heraclitus, replies that the term *sophos*, one who knows, would be excessive: this attribute may be applied to God alone; but one might well call him *philosophos*.[18] Thus, 'actual knowledge' is reserved to God; finite man can only be the 'lover of knowledge,' not himself the one who knows. In the meaning of the passage, the lover of the knowledge that belongs only to the knowing God, the *philosophos*, becomes the *theophilos*, the lover of God. If we now place Hegel's idea of philosophizing alongside Plato's, we shall have to conclude that while there is indeed a progress in clarity and precision of knowledge of the order of being, the leap over the bounds of the finite into the perfection of actual knowledge is impossible. If a thinker attempts it, he is not advancing philosophy, but abandoning it to become a gnostic. Hegel conceals the leap by translating *philosophia* and *gnosis* into German so that he can shift from one to the other by playing on the word 'knowledge.' This wordplay is structurally analogous to Plato's in the *Phaedrus*. But the philosophic wordplay serves to illuminate the thought, while the gnostic wordplay is designed to conceal the non-thought. This point is worth noting because the German gnostics, especially, like to play with language and hide their non-thought in wordplay.

The result of such transitions – which are in fact leaps – is that the meanings of words are changed. The gnostic program that Hegel successfully carries out retains for itself the name 'philosophy,' and the speculative system in which the gnostic unfolds his will to make himself master of being insists on calling itself 'science.'

Philosophy springs from the love of being; it is man's loving endeavor to perceive the order of being and attune himself to it. Gnosis desires dominion over being; in order to seize control of being the gnostic constructs his system. The building of systems is a gnostic form of reasoning, not a philosophical one.

But the thinker can seize control of being with his system only if being really lies within his grasp. As long as the origin of being lies beyond the being of this world; as long as eternal being cannot be completely penetrated with the instrument of world-immanent, finite cognition; as long as divine being can be conceived of only in the form of the *analogia entis*, the construction of a system will be impossible. If this venture is to be seriously launched at all, the thinker must first eliminate these inconveniences: he must so interpret being that on principle it lies within the grasp of his construct. Here is Hegel addressing himself to this problem:

> According to my view, which will have to be justified only through the presentation of the system itself, everything depends on comprehending and expressing the true as *subject* no less than as *substance*.[19]

The conditions required for the solution are formulated just as for a mathematical problem: if being is at one and the same time substance and subject, then, of course, truth lies within the grasp of the apprehending subject. But, we must ask, are substance and subject really identical? Hegel dispenses with this question by declaring that the truth of his 'view' is proven if he can justify it 'through the presentation of the system.' If, therefore, I can build a system, the truth of its premise is thereby established; that I can build a system on a false premise is not even considered. The system is justified by the fact of its construction; the possibility of calling into question the construction of systems, as such, is not acknowledged. That the form of science is the system must be assumed as beyond all question. We are confronted here with the same phenomenon of the suppression of questions that we met in Marx. But we now see more clearly that an essential connection exists between the suppression of questions and the construction of a system. Whoever reduces being to a system cannot permit questions that invalidate systems as a form of reasoning.[20]

5

The essential connection between the *libido dominandi*, the system, and the prohibition of questions, although by no means completely worked out, has been made clear by the testimony of the gnostics themselves. Let us return now for the last time to Marx's prohibition against questions.

We recall that Marx un-Socratically breaks off the dialogue with his philosophical interrogator with a ukase. But though he refuses to go any further into the arguments, he is still very careful to base his refusal on the logic of his system. He does not simply dismiss the questioner; he directs him to the path of reason. When the man brings up the problem of the *arche*, Marx admonishes: 'Ask yourself whether that progression exists as such for rational thought.'[21] Let this person become reasonable; then he will stop his questioning. For Marx, however, reason is not the reason of man but, in the perversion of symbols, the standpoint of his system. His questioner is supposed to cease to be man: he is to become socialist man. Marx thus posits that his construct of the process of being (which comprises the historical process) represents reality. He takes the historical evolution of man into socialist man – which is part of his conceptual construct – and inserts it into his encounters with others; he calls upon the man who questions the assumptions of his system to enter into the system and undergo the evolution it prescribes. In the clash between system and reality, reality must give way. The intellectual swindle is justified by referring to the demands of the historical future, which the gnostic thinker has speculatively projected in his system. . . .

6

This completes the analysis. There remains only the task of defining the results conceptually and terminologically.

For this purpose we shall take over from Heidegger's interpretation of being the term 'parousia,' and speak of parousiasm as the mentality that expects deliverance from the evils of the time through the advent, the coming in all its fullness, of being construed as immanent. We can then speak of the men who express their parousiasm in speculative systems as parousiastic thinkers, of their structures of thought as parousiastic speculations, of the movements connected with some of these thinkers as parousiastic mass movements, and of the age in which these movements are socially and politically dominant as the age of parousiasm. We thus acquire a concept and a terminology for designating a phase of Western gnosticism that have hitherto been lacking. Moreover, by conceiving of it as parousiastic we can distinguish this phase more adequately than heretofore from the preceding chiliastic phase of the Middle Ages and the Renaissance, when the gnostic movements expressed themselves in terms of the Judaeo-Christian apocalypse.[22] The long history of post-classical Western gnosticism thus appears in its continuity as the history of Western sectarianism.

In the Middle Ages this movement could still be kept below the threshold of revolution. Today it has become, not, to be sure, the power of being, but world power. To break the spell of this world and its power – each of us in himself – is the great task at which we all must work. Political science can assist in exorcising the demons – in the modest measure of effectiveness that our society grants to *episteme* and its therapy.

Notes

1. On the problem of rational debate in a heavily idelogized society, see Eric Voegelin, 'On Debate and Existence,' *The Intercollegiate Review*, III (1967), 143–52.
2. Karl Marx, '*Nationalökonomie und Philosophie*,' in Karl Marx, *Der Historische Materialismus: Die Frühschriften*, ed. Landshut and Meyer (Leipzig, 1932), p. 333 ['Economic and Philosophical Manuscripts,' in *Early Writings*, ed. and trans. T. B. Bottomore (New York, 1964), p. 206].
3. Ibid., p. 304 [Bottomore, p. 164].
4. Ibid., p. 307 [Bottomore, p. 166].
5. Ibid., p. 333 [Bottomore, p. 207].
6. Ibid., pp. 306–7 [Bottomore, pp. 165–66].
7. Ibid., p. 307 [Bottomore, p. 166].
8. Ibid., [Bottomore, pp. 166–67].
9. Nietzsche, No. 230, *Jenseits von Gut und Böse*, in *Werke*, VII (Leipzig, 1903), pp. 187–88 [*Beyond Good and Evil*, trans. Marianne Cowan (Chicago, 1955), pp. 158–59].
10. Ibid., p. 189 [Cowan, p. 160].
11. Marx, '*Nationalökonomie und Philosophie*,' pp. 305–6 [Bottomore, p. 165].
12. Marx, *Differenz der demokritischen und epikurischen Naturphilosophie nebst einem Anhang*, in Karl Marx and Friedrich Engels, *Historisch-Kritische Gesamtausgabe*, Part I, I/1 (Frankfurt, 1927), 10. The dissertation was written in 1839–41; the preface was dated: Berlin, March 1841. ['Foreword to Thesis: *The Difference Between the Natural Philosophy of Democritus and the Natural Philosophy of Epicurus*,' in Karl Marx and Friedrich Engels, *On Religion* (New York, 1964), p. 15].
13. Aeschylus, *Prometheus Bound*, 975.
14. Ibid., 977.
15. Ibid., 978.
16. Plato, *Gorgias*, 480b.
17. Hegel, *Phänomenologie des Geistes*, ed. Johannes Hoffmeister (Hamburg, 1952), p. 12 [*The Phenomenology of Mind*, trans. J. B. Baillie, 2nd ed., revised (London, 1949), p. 70].
18. Plato, *Phaedrus*, 278d.

19. Hegel, *Phänomenologie*, p. 19 [Baillie, p. 80].
20. An analysis of Hegel's 'philosophy of history' will reveal the same gnostic program that we have seen in the *Phänomenologie*. See the Note on Hegel's 'Philosophy of World History,' infra, pp. 77–80.
21. Marx, *'Nationalökonomie und Philosophie,'* p. 306 [Bottomore, p. 166].
22. For the history of the chiliastic phase, see Norman Cohn, *The Pursuit of the Millennium*, 2nd ed. (New York, 1961).

24

Simone Weil

A Christian of Jewish extraction, Simone Weil (1910–43) died in a Sanatorium in Ashford, Kent, impatient to return to the France which she loved and for which she would willingly – and certainly – have given her life. All her publications were posthumous, and include Gravity and Grace *(1948) (presented to the reading public by Gustave Thibon) and* The Need for Roots *(1949) from which the following short extract is taken. She was, in T.S. Eliot's words, 'a stern critic of both Right and Left; at the same time more truly a lover of order than most of those who call themselves Conservative, and more truly a lover of the people than most of those who call themselves Socialist.'*

Her lapidary thoughts – expressed in a dogmatic idiom, with little argument, and an assumption of agreement which is reminiscent of the prophetic mode – have caused irritation in some, and been an inspiration to others. In expounding the duties and the needs of mankind, however, she writes with an authority that commands respect, if not agreement, and her thinking adds an important element to the modern conservative vision of society. In her list of 'needs of the soul' she includes, in addition to those discussed below: equality (in the sense of equal respect); hierarchism; honour; punishment; freedom of opinion; security; risk; private property; collective property and truth.

THE NEEDS OF THE SOUL

The notion of obligations comes before that of rights, which is subordinate and relative to the former. A right is not effectual by itself, but only in relation to the obligation to which it corresponds, the effective exercise of a right springing not from the individual who possesses it, but from other men who consider themselves as being under a certain obligation towards him. Recognition of an obligation makes it effectual. An obligation which goes unrecognized by anybody loses none of the full force of its existence. A right which goes unrecognized by anybody is not worth very much.

It makes nonsense to say that men have, on the one hand, rights, and on the other hand, obligations. Such words only express differences in point of view. The actual relationship between the two is as between object and subject. A man, considered in isolation, only has duties, amongst which are certain duties towards himself. Other men, seen from his point of view, only have rights. He, in his turn, has rights, when seen from the point of view of other men, who recognize that they have obligations towards him. A man left alone in the universe would have no rights whatever, but he would have obligations.

The notion of rights, being of an objective order, is inseparable from the notions of existence and reality. This becomes apparent when the obligation descends to the realm of fact; consequently, it always involves to a certain extent the taking into account of actual given states and particular situations. Rights are always found to be related to certain conditions. Obligations alone remain independent of conditions. They belong to a realm situated above all conditions, because it is situated above this world.

The men of 1789 did not recognize the existence of such a realm. All they recognized was the one on the human plane. That is why they started off with the idea of rights. But at the same time they wanted to postulate absolute principles. This contradiction caused them to tumble into a confusion of language and ideas which is largely responsible for the present political and social confusion. The realm of what is eternal, universal, unconditioned is other than the one conditioned by facts, and different ideas hold sway there, ones which are related to the most secret recesses of the human soul.

Obligations are only binding on human beings. There are no obligations for collectivities, as such. But they exist for all human beings who constitute, serve, command or represent a collectivity, in that part of their existence which is related to the collectivity as in that part which is independent of it.

All human beings are bound by identical obligations, although these are performed in different ways according to particular circumstances. No human being, whoever he may be, under whatever circumstances, can escape them without being guilty of crime; save where there are two genuine obligations which are in fact incompatible, and a man is forced to sacrifice one of them.

The imperfections of a social order can be measured by the number of situations of this kind it harbours within itself.

But even in such a case, a crime is committed if the obligation so sacrificed is not merely sacrificed in fact, but its existence denied into the bargain.

The object of any obligation, in the realm of human affairs, is always the human being as such. There exists an obligation towards every human being for the sole reason that he or she *is* a human being, without any other condition requiring to be fulfilled, and even without any recognition of such obligation on the part of the individual concerned.

This obligation is not based upon any *de facto* situation, nor upon jurisprudence, customs, social structure, relative state of forces, historical heritage, or presumed historical orientation; for no *de facto* situation is able to create an obligation.

This obligation is not based upon any convention; for all conventions are liable to be modified according to the wishes of the contracting parties, whereas in this case no change in the mind and will of Man can modify anything whatsoever.

This obligation is an eternal one. It is coextensive with the eternal destiny of human beings. Only human beings have an eternal destiny. Human collectivities have not got one. Nor are there, in regard to the latter, any direct obligations of an eternal nature. Duty towards the human being as such – that alone is eternal.

This obligation is an unconditional one. If it is founded on something, that something, whatever it is, does not form part of our world. In our world, it is not founded on anything at all. It is the one and only obligation in connexion with human affairs that is not subject to any condition.

This obligation has no foundation, but only a verification in the common consent accorded by the universal conscience. It finds expression in some of the oldest written texts which have come down to us. It is recognized by everybody without exception in every single case where it is not attacked as a result of interest or passion. And it is in relation to it that we measure our progress.

The recognition of this obligation is expressed in a confused and imperfect form, that is, more or less imperfect according to the particular case, by what are called positive rights. To the extent to which positive rights are in contradiction with it, to that precise extent is their origin an illegitimate one.

Although this eternal obligation is coextensive with the eternal destiny of the human being, this destiny is not its direct motive. A human being's eternal destiny cannot be the motive of any obligation, for it is not subordinate to external actions.

The fact that a human being possesses an eternal destiny imposes only one obligation: respect. The obligation is only performed if the respect is effectively expressed in a real, not a fictitious, way; and this can only be done through the medium of Man's earthly needs. . . .

ORDER

The first of the soul's needs, the one which touches most nearly its eternal destiny, is order; that is to say, a texture of social relationships such that no one is compelled to violate imperative obligations in order to carry out other ones. It is only where this, in fact, occurs that external circumstances have any power to inflict spiritual violence on the soul. For he for whom the threat of death or suffering is the one thing standing in the way of the performance of an obligation, can overcome this disability, and will only suffer in his body. But he who finds that circumstances, in fact, render the various acts necessitated by a series of strict obligations incompatible with one another is, without being able to offer any resistance thereto, made to suffer in his love of good.

At the present time, a very considerable amount of confusion and incompatibility exists between obligations.

Whoever acts in such a way as to increase this incompatibility is a trouble-maker. Whoever acts in such a way as to diminish it is an agent of order. Whoever, so as to simplify problems, denies the existence of certain obligations has, in his heart, made a compact with crime.

Unfortunately, we possess no method for diminishing this incompatibility. We cannot even be sure that the idea of an order in which all obligations would be compatible with one another isn't itself a fiction. When duty descends to the level of facts, so many independent relationships are brought into play that incompatibility seems far more likely than compatibility.

Nevertheless, we have every day before us the example of a universe in which an infinite number of independent mechanical actions concur so as to produce an order that, in the midst of variations, remains fixed. Furthermore, we love the beauty of the world, because we sense behind it the presence of something akin to that wisdom we should like to possess to slake our thirst for good.

In a minor degree, really beautiful works of art are examples of *ensembles* in which independent factors concur, in a manner impossible to understand, so as to form a unique thing of beauty.

Finally, a consciousness of the various obligations always proceeds from a desire for good which is unique, unchanging and identical with itself for every man, from the cradle to the grave. This desire, perpetually stirring in the depths of our being, makes it impossible for us ever to resign ourselves to situations in which obligations are incompatible with one another. Either we have recourse to lying in order to forget their existence, or we struggle blindly to extricate ourselves from them.

The contemplation of veritable works of art, and much more still that of the beauty of the world, and again much more that of the unrealized good to which we aspire, can sustain us in our efforts to think continually about that human order which should be the subject uppermost in our minds.

The great instigators of violence have encouraged themselves with the thought of how blind, mechanical force is sovereign throughout the whole universe.

By looking at the world with keener senses than theirs, we shall find a more powerful encouragement in the thought of how these innumerable blind forces are limited, made to balance one against the other, brought to form a united whole by something which we do not understand, but which we call beauty.

If we keep ever-present in our minds the idea of a veritable human order, if we think of it as of something to which a total sacrifice is due should the need arise, we shall be in a similar position to that of a man travelling, without a guide, through the night, but continually thinking of the direction he wishes to follow. Such a traveller's way is lit by a great hope.

Order is the first need of all; it even stands above all needs properly so-called. To be able to conceive it, we must know what the other needs are.

The first characteristic which distinguishes needs from desires, fancies or vices, and foods from gluttonous repasts or poisons, is that needs are limited, in exactly the same way as are the foods corresponding to them. A miser never has enough gold, but the time comes when any man provided with an unlimited supply of bread finds he has had enough. Food brings satiety. The same applies to the soul's foods.

The second characteristic, closely connected with the first, is that needs are arranged in antithetical pairs and have to combine together to form a balance. Man requires food, but also an interval between his meals; he requires warmth and coolness, rest and exercise. Likewise in the case of the soul's needs.

What is called the golden mean actually consists in satisfying neither the one nor the other of two contrary needs. It is a caricature of the genuinely balanced state in which contrary needs are each fully satisfied in turn.

LIBERTY

One of the indispensable foods of the human soul is liberty. Liberty, taking the word in its concrete sense, consists in the ability to choose. We must understand by that, of course, a real ability. Wherever men are living in community, rules imposed in the common interest must necessarily limit the possibilities of choice.

But a greater or lesser degrees of liberty does not depend on whether the limits set are wider or narrower. Liberty attains its plenitude under conditions which are less easily gauged.

Rules should be sufficiently sensible and sufficiently straightforward so that any one who so desires and is blessed with average powers of application may be able to understand, on the one hand the useful ends they serve, and on the other hand the actual necessities which have brought about their institution. They should emanate from a source of authority which is not looked upon as strange or hostile, but loved as something belonging to those placed under its direction. They should be sufficiently stable, general and limited in number for the mind to be able to grasp them once and for all, and not find itself brought up against them every time a decision has to be made.

Under these conditions, the liberty of men of goodwill, though limited in the sphere of action, is complete in that of conscience. For, having incorporated the rules into their own being, the prohibited possibilites no longer present themselves to the mind, and have not to be rejected. Just as the habit, formed by education, of not eating disgusting or dangerous things is not felt by the normal man to be any limitation of his liberty in the domain of food. Only a child feels such a limitation.

Those who are lacking in goodwill or who remain adolescent are never free under any form of society.

When the possibilities of choice are so wide as to injure the commonweal, men cease to enjoy liberty. For they must either seek refuge in irresponsibility, puerility and indifference – a refuge where the most they can find is boredom – or feel themselves weighed down by responsibility at all times for fear of causing harm to others. Under such circumstances, men, believing, wrongly, that they are in possession of liberty, and feeling that they get no enjoyment out of it, end up by thinking that liberty is not a good thing.

OBEDIENCE

Obedience is a vital need of the human soul. It is of two kinds: obedience to established rules and obedience to human beings looked upon as leaders. It presupposes consent, not in regard to every single order received, but the kind of consent that is given once and for all, with the sole reservation, in case of need, that the demands of conscience be satisfied.

It requires to be generally recognized, and above all by leaders themselves, that consent and not fear of punishment or hope of reward constitutes, in fact, the mainspring of obedience, so that submission may never be mistaken for servility. It should also be realized that those who command, obey in their turn, and the whole hierarchy should have its face set in the direction of a goal whose importance and even grandeur can be felt by all, from the highest to the lowest.

Obedience being a necessary food of the soul, whoever is definitely deprived of it is ill. Thus, any body politic governed by a sovereign ruler accountable to nobody is in the hands of a sick man.

That is why wherever a man is placed for life at the head of the social organism, he ought to be a symbol and not a ruler, as is the case with the king of England; etiquette ought also to restrict his freedom more narrowly than that of any single man of the people. In this way, the effective rulers, rulers though they be, have somebody over them; on the other hand, they are able to replace each other in unbroken continuity, and consequently to receive, each in his turn, that indispensable amount of obedience due to him.

Those who keep masses of men in subjection by exercising force and cruelty deprive them at once of two vital foods, liberty and obedience; for it is no longer within the power of such masses to accord their inner consent to the authority to which they are subjected. Those who encourage a state of things in which the hope of gain is the principal motive take away from men their obedience, for consent which is its essence is not something which can be sold.

There are any number of signs showing that the men of our age have now for a long time been starved of obedience. But advantage has been taken of the fact to give them slavery.

RESPONSIBILITY

Initiative and responsibility, to feel one is useful and even indispensable, are vital needs of the human soul.

Complete privation from this point of view is the case of the unemployed person, even if he receives assistance to the extent of being able to feed, clothe and house himself. For he represents nothing at all in the economic life of his country, and the voting paper which represents his share in its political life doesn't hold any meaning for him.

The manual labourer is in a scarcely better position.

For this need to be satisfied it is necessary that a man should often have to take decisions in matters great or small affecting interests that are distinct from his own, but in regard to which he feels a personal concern. He also requires to be continually called upon to supply fresh efforts. Finally, he requires to be able to encompass in thought the entire range of activity of the social organism to which he belongs, including branches in connexion with which he has never to take a decision or offer any advice. For that, he must be made acquainted with it, be asked to interest himself in it, be brought to feel its value, its utility and, where necessary, its greatness, and be made fully aware of the part he plays in it.

Every social organism, of whatever kind it may be, which does not provide its members with these satisfactions, is diseased and must be restored to health.

In the case of every person of fairly strong character, the need to show initiative goes so far as the need to take command. A flourishing local and regional life, a host of educational activities and youth movements, ought to furnish whoever is able to take advantage of it with the opportunity to command at certain periods of his life.

Bibliography

The following is a representative, but by no means exhaustive, bibliography of modern conservatism, as exemplified in the extracts contained in the present volume.

Acton, J.E.E.D., Lord Acton, *The History of Freedom and Other Essays*, edited by J.N. Figgis and R.V. Laurence, London, 1907.
Adams, Brooks, *The Law of Civilization and Decay*, New York, 1943.
Adams, John, *Works*, edited by Charles Francis Adams, 10 vols, Boston, 1851.
Ames, Fisher, *Works*, Boston, 1809; Ames's writings have been reissued, edited by W.B. Allen, Liberty Classics, Indianapolis, 1983.
Arnold, Matthew, *Culture and Anarchy*, Cambridge, 1960.
———, *Essays in Criticism*, 3rd Edition, London, 1875.
Babbitt, Irving, *Democracy and Leadership*, Boston, 1924.
———, *Rousseau and Romanticism*, Boston, 1919. (Babbitt was T.S. Eliot's mentor at Harvard, and a writer whom many would place higher than Eliot as an exponent of cultural conservatism.)
Barker, Sir Ernest, *Reflections of Government*, Oxford, 1942.
———, *Political Thought in England 1848–1914*, London, 1980.
Belloc, Hilaire, *The Servile State*, New York, 1946.
Bonald, Louis Gabriel de, *Théorie du Pouvoir*, Constance, 1796.
Bosanquet, Bernard, *The Philosophical Theory of the State*, London, 1965.
Boutany, Pierre, *La Politique*, Paris, 1948.
Bradley, F.H., *Ethical Studies*, 2nd Edition, Oxford, 1988.
Buckley, William F. and Kesler, Charles R. (eds) *Keeping the Tablets: American Conservative Thought in the Twentieth Century*, New York, Harper & Row, 1988 (the latest edition of an anthology, the contents of which have evolved over the eighteen years of its publication, in a decidedly 'neo-conservative' direction).
Burke, Edmund, *Works*, 9 vols, Bohn Edition, London, 1854–7.
Calhoun, John C., *Works*, ed. by R.K. Crallé, 6 vols, New York, 1851–56. (Calhoun was one of the most outspoken critics of the continuing centralisation of American society under the impact of the Federal constitution, and his reflections are of continuing relevance to the dilemmas of modern American politics.)
Carlyle, Thomas, *Miscellaneous Essays*, Chapman & Hall, London, 1872 (especially 'Signs of The Times' and 'Characteristics').
———, *Carlyle Reader*: Selections, ed. Tennyson, Cambridge, 1984.
Cecil, Lord Hugh, *Conservatism*, London, 1912. (The last unselfconscious English defence of the aristocratic principle.)
Chateaubriand, François-René de, *La génie du Christianisme*, extraits, Paris, 1962.

Chesterton, G.K., *Orthodoxy*, London, 1909.
——, *The Thing*, London, 1939.
Coleridge, Samuel Taylor, *The Constitution of Church and State, According to the Idea of Each*, ed. H.N. Coleridge, London, 1852.
——, *Lay Sermons*, ed. Derwent Coleridge, 3rd edn, London, 1852.
Cuddihy, John Murray, *The Ordeal of Civility*, Beacon Press, US, 1987.
Dicey, Albert V., *Introduction to the Study of the law of the Constitution*, 10th edn, London, 1959.
Disraeli, Benjamin, *Lord George Bentinck*, London, 1852.
——, *Selected Speeches*, ed. T.E. Kebbel, 2 vols, London 1882.
——, *Vindication of the English Constitution*, London, 1855.
Donoso-Cortes, *Essays on Catholicism, Liberalism & Socialism considered in their Fundamental Principles*, tr. Madeline Vinton Goddard, Philadelphia, 1862.
Durkheim, Émile, *Division of Labour in Society*, London, 1985.
——, *On Politics and the State*, ed. Anthony Giddens, Oxford, 1986.
——, *Suicide: A Study in Sociology*, ed. George Simpson, London, 1970.
Eastman, Max, *Reflections on the Failure of Socialism*, n.e. London, 1982.
——, *Marxism, Is it Science?*, London, 1941.
Eliot, T.S., *After Strange Gods*, London, 1934.
——, *The Idea of a Christian Society*, London, 1939.
——, *Notes Towards the Definition of Culture*, London, 1948.
——, *The Sacred Wood*, London, 1950.
Gehlen, M.P., *Man: His Nature and Place in the World*, New York, 1987.
——, *Man in the Age of Technology*, New York, 1980.
Gierke, Otto, *Das deutsche Genossenschaftsrecht*, Berlin, 1868. Fragments of this great work, by the leading German conservative of the late nineteenth century, have been translated by F.W. Maitland and Sir Ernest Barker as follows:
Gierke, Otto, *Political Theories of the Middle Age*, tr: F.W. Maitland, n.e. Cambridge, 1988; *Natural Law and the Theory of Society 1500–1800*, tr. Sir Ernest Barker, Cambridge, 1934.
Grant, George Parkin, *English-Speaking Justice*, 1978. (The leading Canadian conservative of our time.)
Green, T.H., *Lectures on Political Obligation*, Cambridge, 1986.
——, *The Philosophy of T.H. Green*, ed. Vincent, London, 1986.
Hamilton, Alexander, *The Papers of Alexander Hamilton*, ed. H.C. Syrett, 10 vols, New York, 1961–6. (Together with John Adams and Thomas Jefferson, Hamilton formulated the conservative principles behind the US Constitution.)
——, *Selected Writings and Speeches*, ed. Frisch, M.I., USA, 1987.
——, *Works*, ed. Lodge, Henry Cabot, n.e. of 1904 edition, USA, 1982.
Hauriou, Maurice, *Précis de droit administratif*, Paris, 1914 (especially introduction).
Hayek, F.A., *The Road to Serfdom*, London, 1944.
——, *The Constitution of Liberty*, n.e. London, 1976.
——, *The Fatal Conceit: Errors of Socialism*, ed. William, Bartley, Warren, London, 1988.
——, *Law, Legislation and Liberty: A new Statement of the Liberal Principles of*

Justice and Political Economy, 3 vols, London, 1976–9.
Hegel, G.W.F., *The Philosophy of Right*, tr. T.M. Knox, Oxford, 1952.
——, *The Phenomenology of Spirit*, tr. A.V. Miller, Oxford, 1977.
Hogg, Quintin (Lord Hailsham), *The Case for Conservatism*, London, 1947.
Inge, W.R. (Dean Inge), *Outspoken Essays*, First and Second Series, London, 1919 and 1923.
Jewkes, John, *Ordeal by Planning*, London, 1949.
Jouvenel, Bertand de, *On Sovereignty: an inquiry into the Political Good*; tr. Huntington, Chicago, 1958.
——, *De la Politique Pure*, Paris, 1977; Cambridge, 1963.
Kirk, Russell, *The Conservative Mind*, 7th edn, Washington, 1986.
——, *Enemies of the Permanent Things*, La Sale, Illinois, 1985.
——, *A program for Conservatives*, Chicago, 1962.
Lamennais, Félicité Robert de, *Oeuvres Complètes*, Paris, 1836–7.
——, *De L'absolutisme et de la liberté et autres essais*, Paris, 1978.
Leavis, F.R., *The Common Pursuit*, n.e. of 1952 edition, London, 1984.
——, *Nor Shall my Sword*, London, 1972.
Levy, David J., *Political Order: Philosophical Anthropology, Modernity and the Challenge of Ideology*, Louisiana, 1988.
Lewis, C.S., *The Abolition of Man*, n.e., Count, 1978.
Maine, Sir Henry Sumner, *The Early History of Institutions*, London, 1890.
——, *Popular Government*, London, 1886.
Maistre, Joseph de, *The Works of J. de Maistre*, ed. J. Lively, London, 1965.
Maitland, F.W., *The Constitutional History of England*: a course of lectures delivered by Maitland, edited by H.A.L. Fisher, Cambridge, 1961.
——, *Collected Papers*, edited by H.A.L. Fisher, Cambridge, 1911.
Mallock, W.H., *A Critical Examination of Socialism*, London, 1908.
——, *The Limits of Pure Democracy*, London, 1919.
——, *The Reconstruction of Belief*, London, 1892.
Mandeville, Bernard de, *The Fable of the Bees, or, Private Vices, Public Benefits*: with an essay on charity and charity-schools; and a search into the nature of society, London, 1725.
Maurras, Charles, *Oeuvres Capitales, vol. 11: Essais Politiques*, Paris, 1954.
——, *Mes Idées Politiques*, Paris, 1937.
Mises, Ludwig von, *Human Action*, London, 1949.
——, *National, State and Economy*: contributions to the politics and history of our time; tr. Leland B. Yeager, New York, 1983.
Molnar, Thomas, *The Decline of the Intellectual*, New York, 1961.
——, *The Counter-Revolution*, New York, 1969.
——, *Utopias; the Perennial Heresy*, New York, 1971.
More, Paul, Elmer, *Shelburne Essays*, 11 vols, Boston, 1904–21. (More was associated with Irvin Babbitt, an articulate cultural conservative, and also a spokesman for the Bostonian civilisation.)
Moser, Justin, *Sämtliche Werke*, 1853–91.
Müller, Adam, *Kritische, ästhetische und philosophische Schriften*, Luchterhand, 1967.

Murray, J.C., *We Hold These Things*, New York, 1960.
Newman, John Henry, *Essays Critical and Historical*, London, 1871.
——, *The Idea of a University Defined and Illustrated*, London, 1853.
——, *Essays and Sketches*, ed. Harrold, Charles Frederick, n.e. of 1948 edition, London.
Nisbet, Robert, *The Quest for Community*, New York, 1953.
——, *The Sociological Tradition*, New York, 1966.
——, *Conservatism*, Open University Press, 1986.
——, *History of the Idea of Progress*, London, 1980.
——, *Twilight of Authority*, Oxford University Press, New York, 1977.
Nozick, Robert, *Anarchy, State and Utopia*, Oxford, 1974.
Oakeshott, Michael, *Rationalism in Politics and other Essays*, London, 1972.
——, *On Human Conduct*, Oxford, 1975.
——, *On History and Other Essays*, Oxford, 1983.
Ortega y Gasset, José, *The Revolt of the Masses*, London, 1964.
——, *An Interpretation of Universal History*, tr. M. Adams, London, 1973. (A series of lectures on A.J. Toynbee's *A Study of History*.
Paley, William, *The Principles of Moral and Political Philosophy*, London, 1794.
Pareto, Vilfredo, *Manuel of Political Economy*, ed. Schweir, A.S., and Page, A.N., Kelsey, USA, 1980.
——, *Compendium of General Sociology*, ed. and collated by Elizabeth Abbott, Minneapolis: University of Minnesota Press, 1980.
——, *The Other Pareto*, ed. Placido Bucolo; tr. Ronald Fletcher, London, 1980.
Polanyi, Michael, *Science, Faith and Society*, Chicago, 1964.
——, *Study of Man*, Chicago, 1959.
——, *Personal Knowledge; towards a post-critical philosophy*, London, 1973.
——, *Knowing and Being; Essays*, Chicago, 1969.
Pound, Roscoe, *Interpretations of Legal History*, Cambridge, Mass., 1923.
Reiss, Hans (ed.), *The Political Thought of the German Romantics, 1793–1815*, Oxford, 1955.
Röpke, Wilhelm, *Civitas Humana*, London, 1948.
——, *A Humane Economy*, London and Chicago, 1958.
Santayana, George, *Dominations and Powers*, New York, 1951.
——, *The Life of Reason*, 5 vols, London, 1972.
Schmitt, Carl, *Political Theology*, Cambridge, Mass. and London, 1985.
——, *The Concept of the Political*, New Brunswick, NJ, 1976.
——, *Cases of Parliamentary Democracy*, MITI, 1986.
Schucttinger, Robert, *The Conservative tradition in European Thought*, Capricorn Books, New York, 1971.
Schumpeter, Joseph A., *Capitalism, Socialism and Democracy*, London, 1965.
Scruton, R., *The Meaning of Conservatism*, London, 1980.
—— (ed.), *Conservative Thinkers*, London, 1988.
—— (ed.), *Conservative Thoughts*, London, 1988. (The last two volumes, of articles from *The Salisbury Review*, give an impression of the state of conservative thinking in Britain at the present time.)

Bibliography

Shestov, Lev, *Speculation and Revelation*, tr. from Russian, B. Martin, Ohio, 1982.
Shils, Edward A., *Constitution of Sociology*, Chicago, 1982.
——, *Centre and Periphery: Essays in Macrosociology*, Chicago, 1975.
——, *Intellectuals and the Powers and other Essays*, Chicago, 1972.
——, *Tradition*, London, 1981.
Stephen, Sir James F., *A History of the Criminal Law in England*, 3 vols, London, 1883.
——, *Liberty, Equality, Fraternity*, London, 1973.
Strauss, Leo, *Liberalism, Ancient & Modern*, New York, 1968. (Strauss, a defender of Natural Law, and an exponent of Greek political philosophy, has had enormous influence in America, where he is regarded as a conservative, despite his commitment to an abstract and universal idea of political order.)
Talmon, J.L., *The Origins of Totalitarian Democracy*, London, 1952.
Tate, Allen, *Reactionary Essays on Poetry and Ideas*, New York, 1936. (Leader of the 'Southern Agrarian' school of writers, the poet Allen Tate also tried to express, in his essays, the deeply conservative feelings of the old South in America, and to defend them against the trashiness of modernity.)
Thibon, Gustav, *Back to Reality*, London, 1955.
Tocqueville, Alexis de, *Democracy in America*, ed. Phillip Bradley, New York, 1948.
——, *The Old Régime and the French Revolution*, tr. Stuart Gilbert, New York, 1955.
Trilling, Lionel, *The Liberal Imagination*, New York, 1950.
——, *Sincerity and Authenticity*, Oxford & Camb. Mass., 1972.
——, *Beyond Culture*, Oxford, 1980.
Utley, T.E., *Essays in Conservatism*, London, 1949.
——, *Terrorism & Tolerance, Flaws in the Liberal Tradition*, London, 1981.
Valéry, Paul, *Les Principes d'anarchie pure et appliqué*, Paris, 1984.
——, *Reflections on the World Today*, tr. Francis Sarfe, USA, 1951.
Voegelin, Eric, *The New Science of Politics*, Chicago, 1952.
——, *Order and History*, 5 vols, Baton Rouge, 1954–87.
——, *Science, Politics and Gnosticism*, Chicago, 1968.
Weaver, Richard, *The Southern Tradition at Bay*, New Rochester, NY, 1968.
——, *Visions of Order*, Baton Rouge, 1964.
Weil, Simone, *The Need for Roots*, tr. A.F. Wills, Preface by T.S. Eliot, London, 1978.
Wilson, Francis Graham, *The Case for Conservatism*, Seattle, 1951.

Index of Names

Acton, Lord 225
Adams, John, President 165, 168, 219
Aeschylus 325
Aquinas, St Thomas viii, 221
Aristotle viii, 24, 93, 113, 114, 208, 317, 318, 319
Arnold, Matthew 63
Aron, Raymond viii
Augustine, St viii, 65
Austin, John 122
Avilov, L. 79

Babeuf, François 215
Bacon, Sir Francis, Viscount Verulam 115, 122
Bagehot, Walter 166
Balfour, Arthur 193, 202
Beccaria, C. 125, 134–5
Bentham, Jeremy 187, 252
Bignon, Jérôme 171
Bismarck, Otto, Prince 318
Bittket, Boris 240
Blackstone, Sir William 16, 194
Böhm-Bawerk, Eugen von 4, 94
Bolingbroke, Henry St John, Viscount 165
Bonald, Vicomte de viii, 14
Bracton, Henry de 222
Bradley, A.C. 40, 85
Bradley, F.H. vii, 3, 8, 40–57
Braque, Georges 280
Buckland, W.W. 195, 203
Burke, Edmund vii, 2, 3, 6, 11, 16, 27, 29–39, 63, 71, 164, 165f, 167, 168, 252, 273

Caesar (Julius Caesar) 215, 216
Caligula 261
Canning, Viscount 165
Carlyle, Thomas viii
Chesterton, G.K. 59–62
Chomsky, Noam 241
Clarendon, Edward Hyde, Earl of 165
Clemenceau, Georges 254
Coke, Sir Edward 115
Coleridge, Samuel Taylor 63–70, 85, 165, 166
Comte, Auguste 167
Condorcet, Marie Jean, Marquis de 192
Conrad, Joseph 253, 280
Croker, J. Wilson 165
Crombie, A. 65

Dante Alighieri 90f
Darwin, Charles 42, 167
De Gaulle, Charles 280
Dicey, A.V. 193–4, 196, 202
Disraeli, Benjamin, Earl of Beaconsfield 71–7, 280
D'Israeli, Isaac 71
Donoso Cortes viii

Eastman, Crystal 78
Eastman, Max 78–84
Edwards, Jonathan 65

Index

Eisenshower, Dwight, President 220
Eliot, T.S. 3, 6, 63, 85–93, 164, 280, 332
Engels, Friedrich 5, 264

Falkland, Viscount 165
Feiling, Keith 166
Feuerbach, P.J.A. 133
Fichte, J.G. 129, 147
Fielding, Henry 273
Filmer, Sir Robert 165
Fortescue, Sir John 222
Fourier, F.M.C. 214

Gadamer, Hans Georg viii
Gehlen, Arnold viii
Genêt, J.M. 164
Gibbon, Edward 190
Gierke, Otto viii, 13, 193, 203
Gladstone, William 318
Glyn, Elinor 40
Godwin, William 255
Goethe, J.W. von 243
Görres, Johann Joseph von 165
Graves, Robert 166
Grotius, Hugo viii

Hale, Matthew 115
Halifax, Lord 165
Hamilton, Alexander 165
Hamilton, W.G. 29
Hayek, F.A. von viii, 4f, 7, 16, 21, 80, 94–128, 227, 233–5, 240
Hearnshaw, F.J.C. 166
Hegel, G.W.F. viii, 8, 9, 40, 81, 107, 129–163, 165f, 273, 302, 326–7, 328
Heidegger, Martin 329

Helvetius 37
Hobbes, Thomas viii, 115, 122, 165, 196, 252, 268
Homer 88
Hooker, Robert 165, 166
Hugo, Victor 299, 309
Hume, David viii, 2, 63, 123, 165, 252

Ibn Khaldun viii

James, Henry 280
Jensen, Jan 264
Johnson, Samuel viii, 29, 165
Jouvenel, Bertrand de viii
Joyce, James 280
Justinian, Emperor 113f

Kant, Immanuel 63, 268
Keats, John 91
Kern, Fritz 114
Kirk, Russell 63, 164–9
Klein, E.F. 163
Knox, T.M. (Sir Malcolm) 130
Koestler, Arthur 83
Kristol, Irving 240

Lammenais, F.R. de 14
Lawrence, D.H. 280
Lawrence, Sir Thomas 65
Leavis, F.R. viii, 63
Lenin, V.I. 78
Lincoln, Abraham, President 166, 216, 219–20, 223
Livy, Titus 257
Locke, John 15, 126, 227, 229, 270
Louis, St 189
Lucretius 188
Lysenko, Vladil 79

Macaulay, Lord   165
Machiavelli, Niccolò   8, 257
Mackay, J.H.   240
Maistre, Joseph, comte de   14, 16, 170–92
Maitland, F.W.   3, 13, 26, 121, 193–203, 227
Mallock, W.H.   14, 25, 204–15
Mansfield, Lord   116
Maritain, Jacques   297
Marx, Karl, 5, 6, 25, 79–83, 166, 167, 221, 264, 320–2, 323, 324–6, 328–9
Masaryk, T.G.   308
Maurras, Charles   297
Menger, Anton   262
Mill, J.S.   27, 285–96
Mises, Ludwig von   21, 78
Molinari, G. de   263
Montaigne, Michel de   252
Montesquieu, Charles Louis, baron de   viii, 15, 115–16, 149
Moore, Henry   280
More, St Thomas   304
Morley, John   296
Murray, John Courtney   218–26

Napoleon Bonaparte   216, 258, 302
Niebuhr, R.   258
Nietzsche, F.W.   25, 322–4
Newman, J.H., Cardinal   viii
Nozick, Robert   21, 227–41

Oakeshott, Michael   6, 11, 242–56
Origen   181, 192
Ortega y Gasset, José   viii
Owen, Robert   214, 215

Paine, Thomas   66, 164, 173, 222
Pareto, Vilfredo, Marchese   25, 239, 257–65
Parmenides   254
Pascal, Blaise   252
Peel, Sir Robert   66, 165
Penna, Lucas de   203
Pericles   318
Pitt, William, the younger   165, 253
Plato,   167, 175–6, 192, 256, 317, 318, 319, 323, 326f
Plutarch   89
Polanyi, Michael   4
Portland, Duke of   165
Pound, Ezra   280
Price, Richard   30

Randolph, Thomas   165
Rapp, George   214
Rawls, John   227
Rockingham, Marquis of   29
Röpke, Wilhelm   viii, 80, 81–2
Rossiter, Clinton   220f, 223–4
Rousseau, Jean-Jacques, 37, 63, 79, 147, 167, 181, 223
Ruskin, John   viii, 63

Saint-Simon, Claude Henri de Rouvroy, comte de   214
Saint-Just, L. de   301
Santayana, George   viii
Schelling, F.W.J.   62
Schlegel, Friedrich   165
Schoenberg, Arnold   280
Scott, Sir Walter   165
Shakespeare, William   88, 89, 91
Shaw, G.B.   59, 82

Shelley, P.B. 253
Sieyès, Emmanuel, Abbé 30
Smith, Adam 4, 5, 29, 94, 95, 97
Solon 274
Southey, Robert 5, 165
Spinoza, Benedict de 14
Stalin, Joseph 78, 79, 94
Stephen, Sir James Fitzjames 27, 285–96
Stephen, Sir Leslie 285
Stolberg, Friedrich Leopold 165
Strafford, Earl of 165, 166
Strauss, Leo viii, 17
Stravinsky, Igor 280

Taine, H.A. 165, 263–4
Talmon, T.J. 310
Themistocles 318
Thibon, Gustave 14, 25, 297–309
Tocqueville, Alexis, comte de 3, 5f, 165, 310–16

Trajan, Emperor 261
Trotsky, Leon 78

Voegelin, Eric 28, 317–31
Voltaire (F.-M. Arouet) 37, 183–4, 255

Wagner, Richard 7, 273
Waugh, Evelyn 280
Webb, Beatrice and Sidney 82
Weber, Max 25
Webster, John 91
Weil, Simone 3, 332–40
Wilberforce, William 29
Wittgenstein, Ludwig 3
Woolf, Virginia 285
Wordsworth, William 63, 92, 165, 301

Xenophon 180

Zanotti, L.J. 181

Subject Index

allegiance 9–10, 121–3, 272–4
American Revolution 164, 220f
art, 86–92, 279f
authenticity 276
authority 2, 8, 11f, 18, 254, 266–7, 269–72, 305
autonomy 8–9
autonomous institutions 27, 197f

'capitalism' 2, 5, 24
Christianity 51, 61f, 189f, 218–26, 300–5, 319, 329f
Church 69f, 72, 74–5, 85, 151–6, 202
civil society 9–10, 11, 34, 139, 144–5, 162, 266
class 12, 25–7, 73–4, 119, 167, 305f
common law 16, 113–28
communism 83, 219, 264
community 8f, 40–57
conscience 55
consent 10, 222–4
constitution 14, 66–7, 156–8, 170–92, 193, 218–26, 272
corporations 144–5, 147, 162, 193–203
crime and punishment 130–8, 290–6
culture 276

democracy 5f, 13f, 59–61, 82–3, 204–15, 301, 308–9, 310–16

dialectic 129–30
due process 16
duty 40–57, 149f, 298f, 333–5

economics 2, 4, 78–83
education 61f
élites 257–65, 307–8
Enlightenment 29
enterprise 2
equality 24f, 81f, 167, 214f, 310–16
establishment 2, 27f
executive power 257–65, 307–8

Fabianism 59, 82
family 9, 24f, 139–44, 269–72, 281f
freedom 2, 8, 16, 80, 167, 266, 273f, 285–96, 310–16, 337–8
free market 3, 4–5, 6, 7, 80f, 101, 104
French Revolution 1, 14, 27, 29, 164, 197, 221f, 301, 310

game theory 4
gnosticism 317–31

heredity 30f, 67, 161
hierarchy 24f

idealism, metaphysical 8, 40, 129–63
idealism, political 57
ideology 267

350

individualism 8f, 40–57, 227ff, 270, 299f, 307, 321
inheritance 30f, 161
institutions 9, 31f, 281f

judicial independence 15, 115ff, 123–8
justice 20–4, 227–41

language 3, 112, 275
law 7–8, 12, 16f, 111–28, 129–38, 171ff, 193–203, 262, 286–96
legislation 111–28, 157f
legitimacy 1, 16, 178, 181, 267
Leninism 20
liberalism 1f, 8, 15f, 27, 72f, 83, 221, 257, 272, 277
Liberal Party 70–7
libertarianism 5, 227–41
liberty, *see* freedom
limited government 15, 193
literature 85–93
love 300–1

marriage 7, 139, 140–4, 300
Marxism 5, 7, 12, 79–83, 129, 193, 267, 275
monarchy 12, 19, 71f, 158–160, 277
morality 27f, 44–57, 201–3, 225–6, 285–96

nation 41, 274
natural law 17, 34, 115, 220–2

obedience 338–9
opposition 19

pantisocracy 63
Pareto-optimality 239

partnership 10–11, 28, 39
patriotism 150f, 274, 277–8
personality 12f, 18f, 23, 26, 47f, 159, 193–205, 306–7, 309
personal government 18f, 20f
philistinism 57
piety 8, 10, 141, 143–4, 146, 271
political science 317ff
power 266–7
prejudice 2, 3, 37–9, 52, 254
property 20–4, 31f, 67f, 167
punishment 132–3, 136–8

rationalism 253–6
religion 1, 27f, 61f, 69f, 151–6, 185–91, 218–26
representation 13, 223
responsibility 339–40
revolution 5, 18, 19, 20, 83
rights 16, 17–18, 22, 30f, 33–6, 149f, 269
rule of law 16, 20
rules 108f

separation of powers 15, 174
social contract 10f, 39, 63f, 268–9
socialism 1f, 4f, 11, 20f, 25f, 78–83, 204, 219, 230–31, 238, 242f, 257, 264–5, 304f, 321f
'social justice', 21f, 266
sovereignty 13, 121–3, 159f, 172, 178
spontaneous order 7, 95–110, 335–7
state 9–10, 13–18, 53f, 66, 67–9, 107, 139, 145–8, 151–6, 196, 266

tacit knowledge/
    understanding 4, 6, 94, 111
toleration 285–96
totalitarianism 26, 27, 94, 304, 310f, 319
Tory Party 71–7

tradition 5, 60–2, 85–93, 168, 278–82
trusts 200–1

utilitarianism 230

welfare state 21, 76f